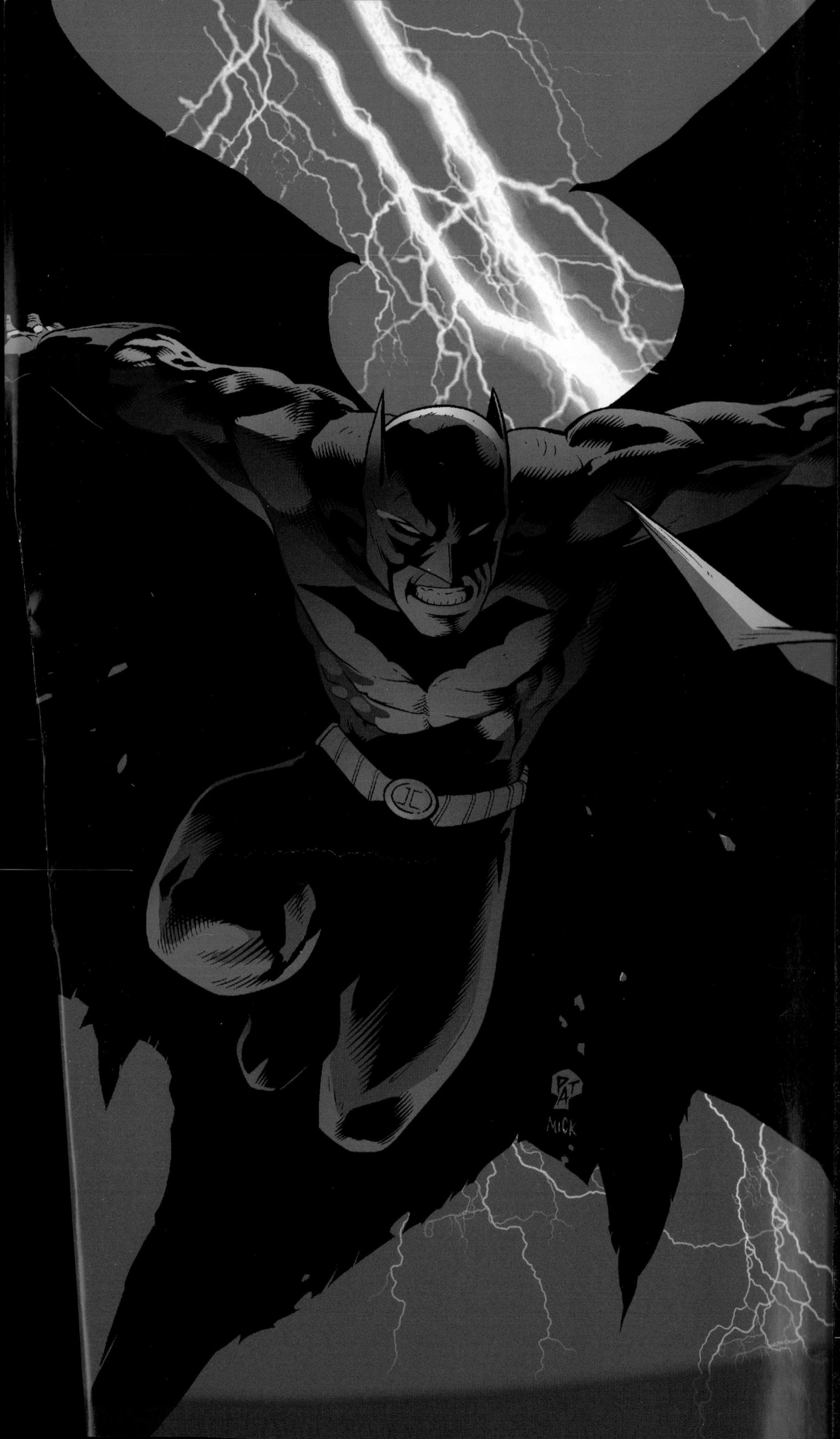

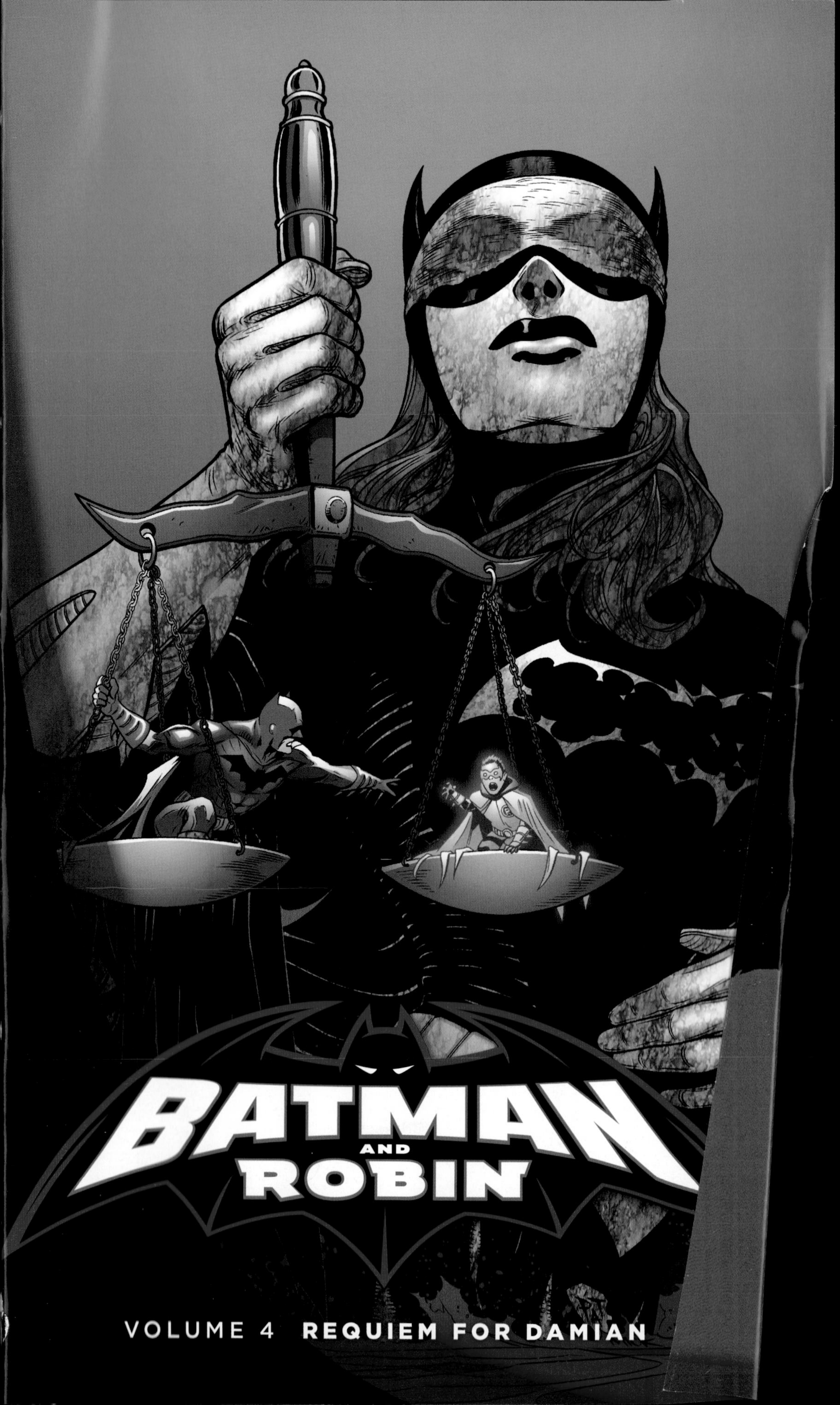
BATMAN
AND
ROBIN
VOLUME 4 REQUIEM FOR DAMIAN

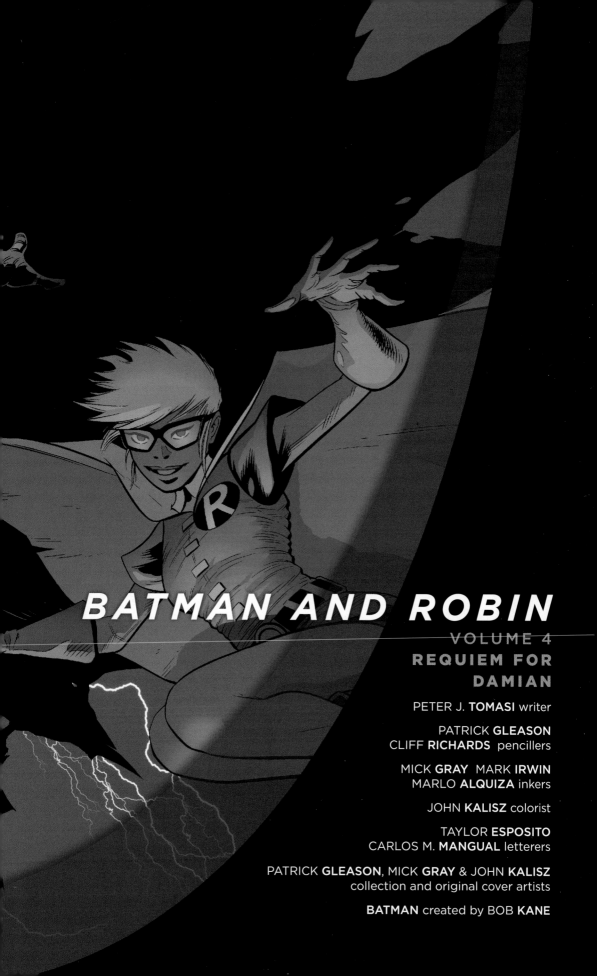

BATMAN AND ROBIN

VOLUME 4
REQUIEM FOR DAMIAN

PETER J. **TOMASI** writer

PATRICK **GLEASON**
CLIFF **RICHARDS** pencillers

MICK **GRAY** MARK **IRWIN**
MARLO **ALQUIZA** inkers

JOHN **KALISZ** colorist

TAYLOR **ESPOSITO**
CARLOS M. **MANGUAL** letterers

PATRICK **GLEASON**, MICK **GRAY** & JOHN **KALISZ**
collection and original cover artists

BATMAN created by BOB **KANE**

RACHEL GLUCKSTERN Editor – Original Series RICKEY PURDIN DARREN SHAN Assistant Editors – Original Series
RACHEL PINNELAS Editor ROBBIN BROSTERMAN Design Director – Books ROBBIE BIEDERMAN Publication Design

BOB HARRAS Senior VP – Editor-in-Chief, DC Comics

DIANE NELSON President DAN DIDIO and JIM LEE Co-Publishers
GEOFF JOHNS Chief Creative Officer
JOHN ROOD Executive VP – Sales, Marketing and Business Development
AMY GENKINS Senior VP – Business and Legal Affairs NAIRI GARDINER Senior VP – Finance
JEFF BOISON VP – Publishing Planning MARK CHIARELLO VP – Art Direction and Design
JOHN CUNNINGHAM VP – Marketing TERRI CUNNINGHAM VP – Editorial Administration
ALISON GILL Senior VP – Manufacturing and Operations
HANK KANALZ Senior VP – Vertigo and Integrated Publishing JAY KOGAN VP – Business and Legal Affairs, Publishing
JACK MAHAN VP – Business Affairs, Talent NICK NAPOLITANO VP – Manufacturing Administration
SUE POHJA VP – Book Sales COURTNEY SIMMONS Senior VP – Publicity
BOB WAYNE Senior VP – Sales

BATMAN AND ROBIN VOLUME 4: REQUIEM FOR DAMIAN

DC Comics, 1700 Broadway, New York, NY 10019
A Warner Bros. Entertainment Company.
Printed by RR Donnelley, Salem, VA, USA. 5/2/14. First Printing.
HC ISBN: 978-1-4012-4618-1
SC ISBN: 978-1-4012-5058-4

Library of Congress Cataloging-in-Publication Data

Tomasi, Peter, author.
Batman and Robin. Vol. 4, Requiem for Damian / Peter Tomasi ; illustrated by Patrick Gleason ; illustrated by Mick Gray.
pages cm. — (The New 52!)
ISBN 978-1-4012-4618-1 (hardback)
1. Graphic novels. I. Gleason, Patrick, illustrator. II. Gray, Mick, illustrator. III. Title. IV. Title: Requiem for Damian.
PN6728.B36T646 2014
741.5'973—dc23
                    2014008595

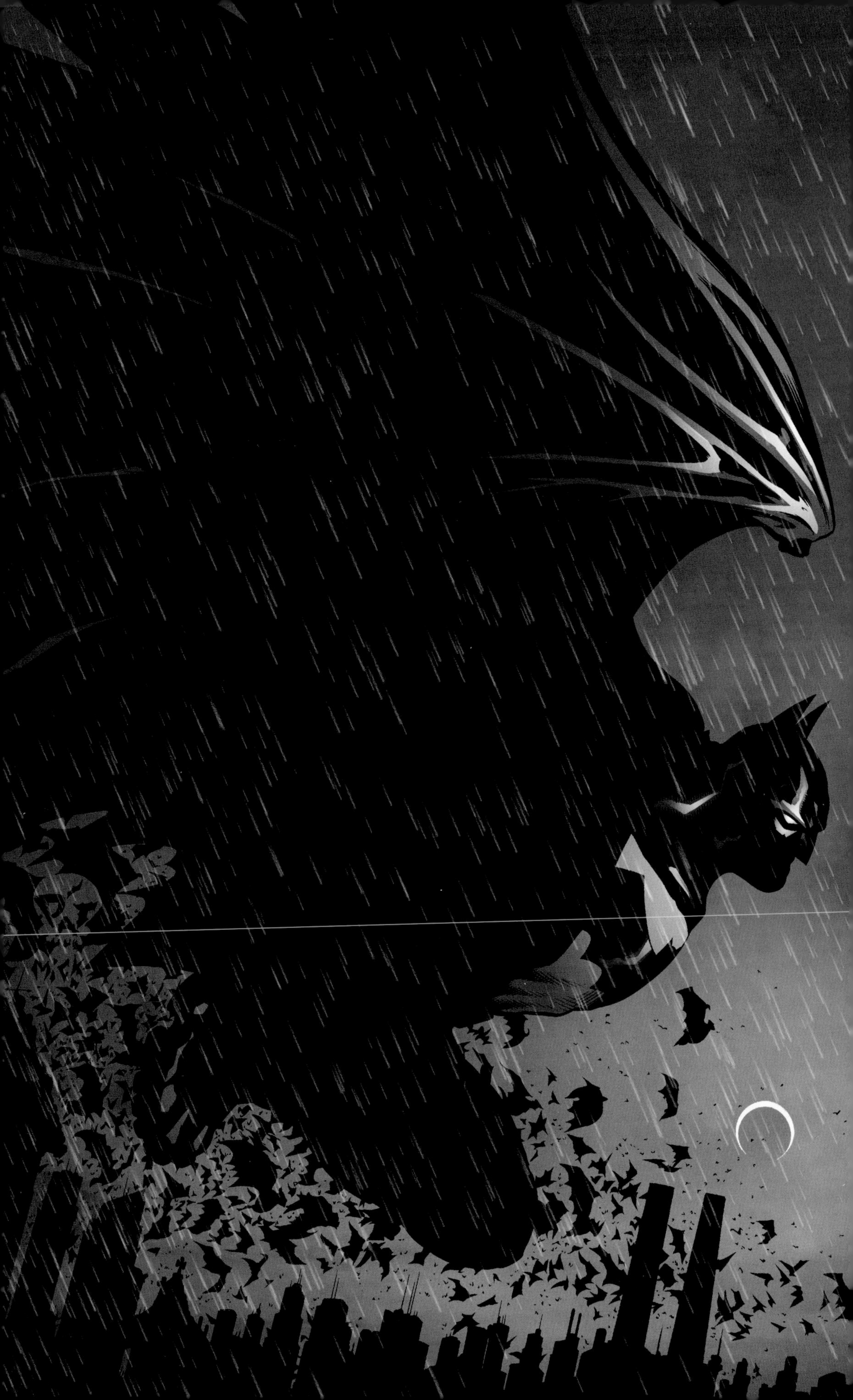

UNDONE

PATRICK GLEASON penciller MICK GRAY inker

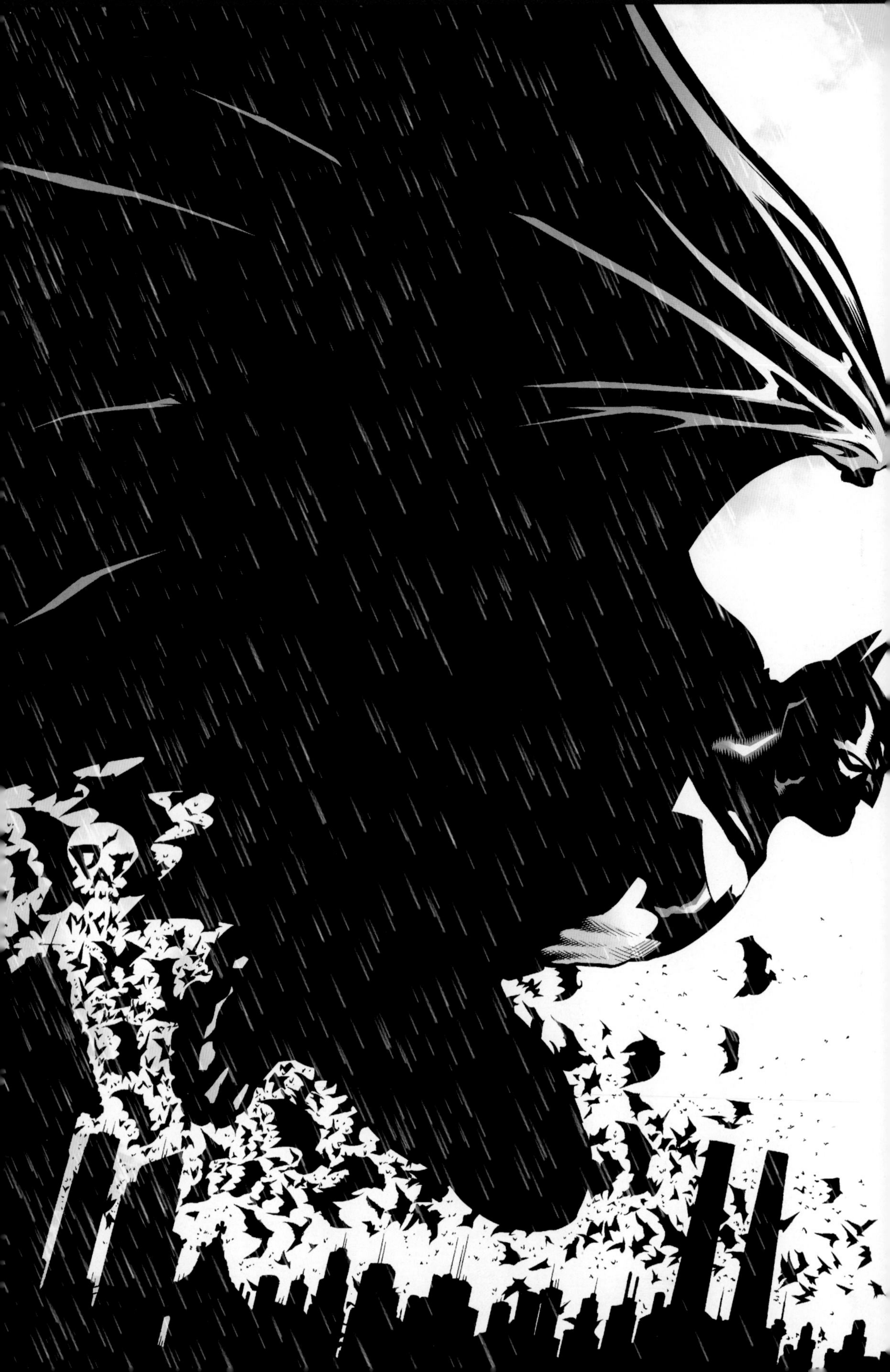

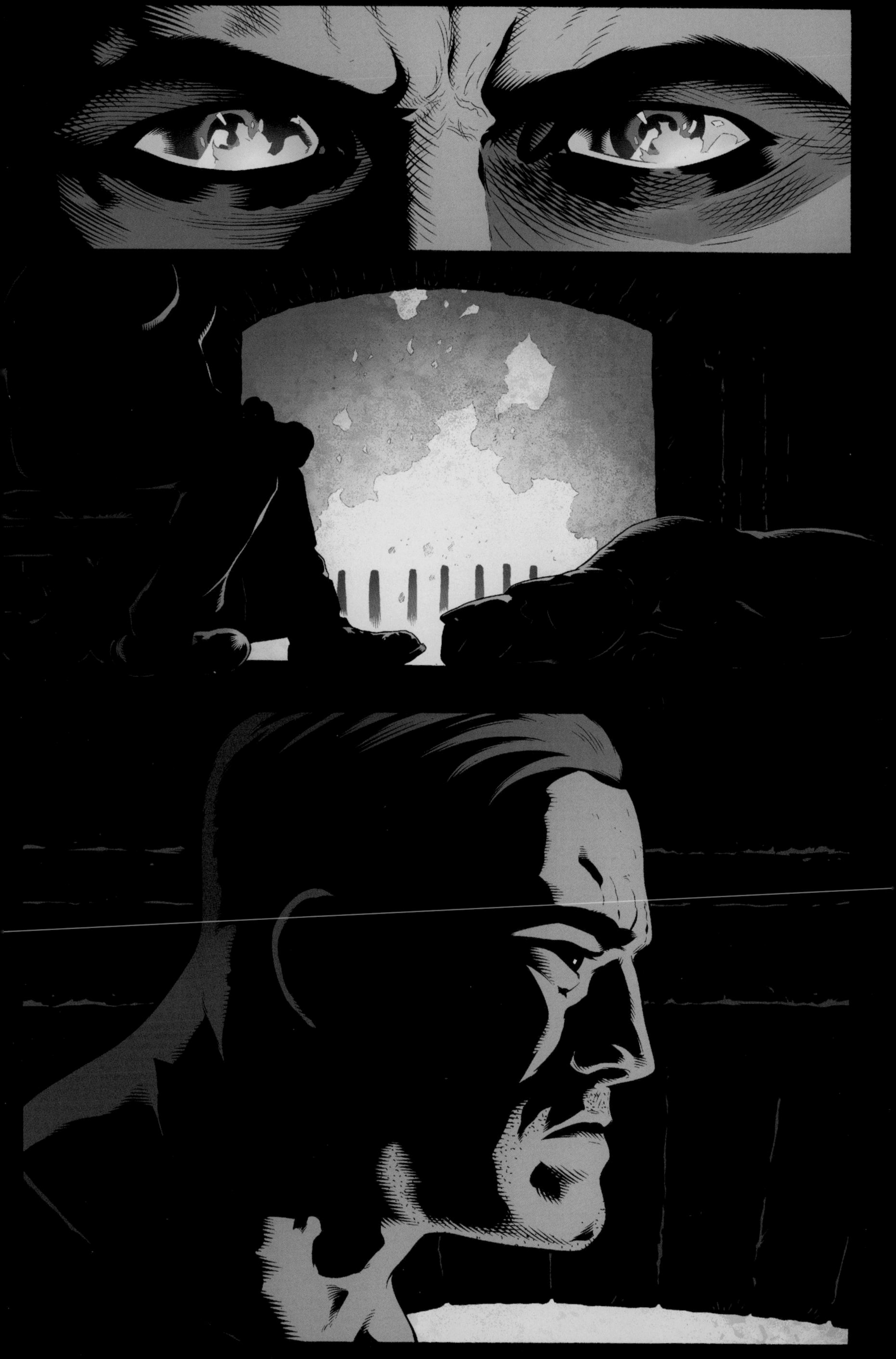

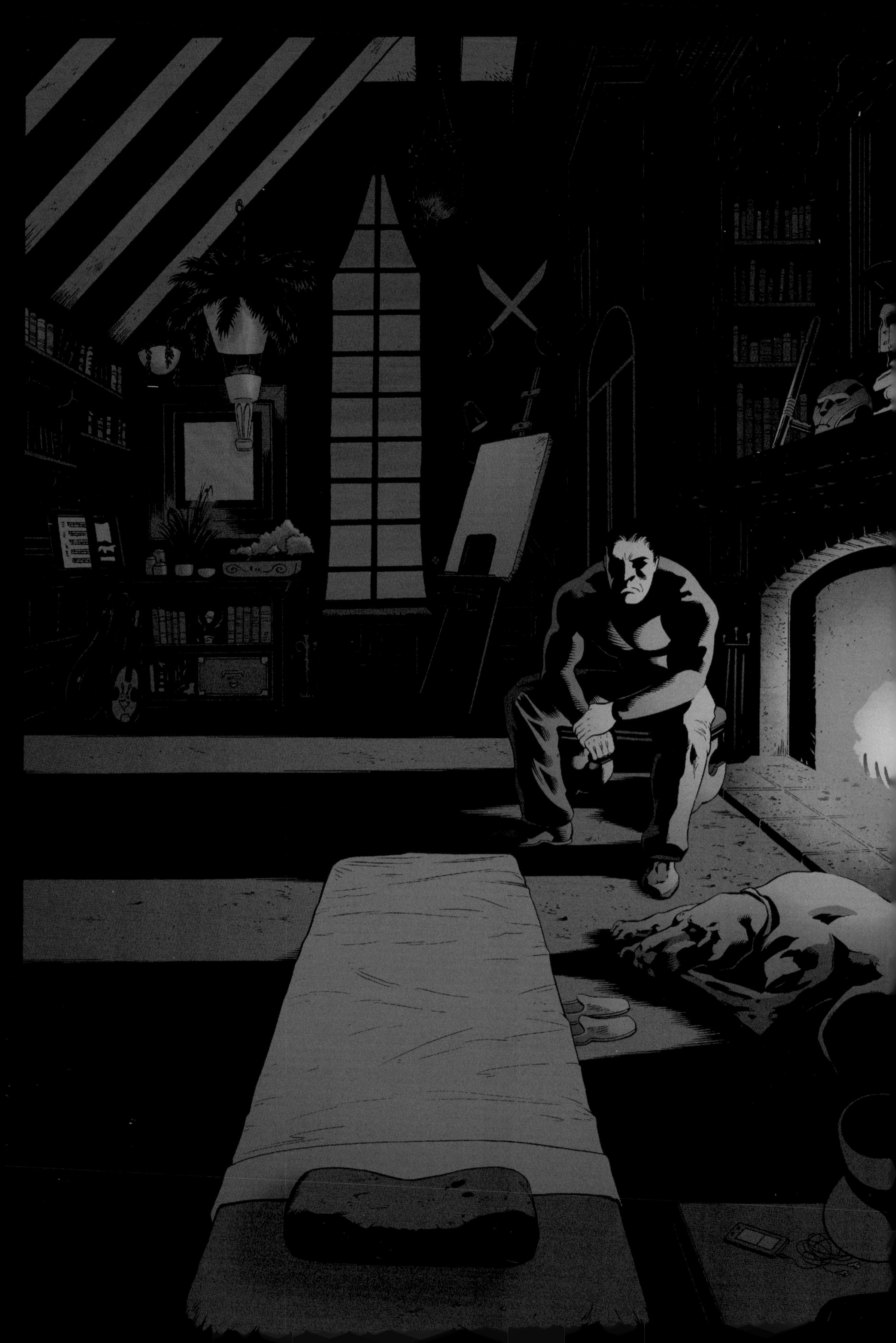

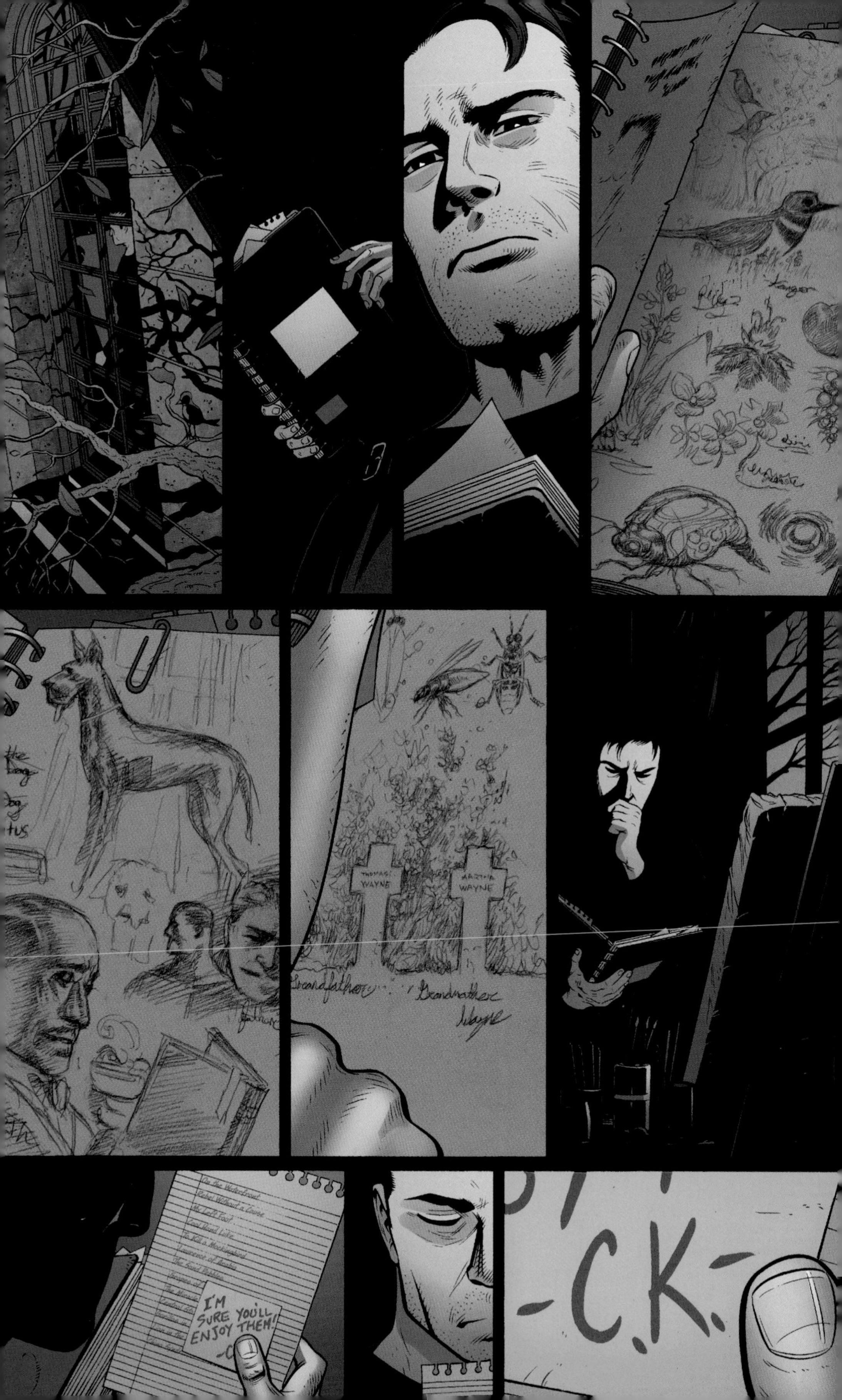
THOMAS WAYNE
MARTHA WAYNE
Grandfather
Grandmother Wayne
On the Waterfront
Rebel Without a Cause
My Left Foot
Cool Hand Luke
To Kill a Mockingbird
Lawrence of Arabia
The Sand Pebbles
I'M SURE YOU'LL ENJOY THEM!
-C
-C.K.-

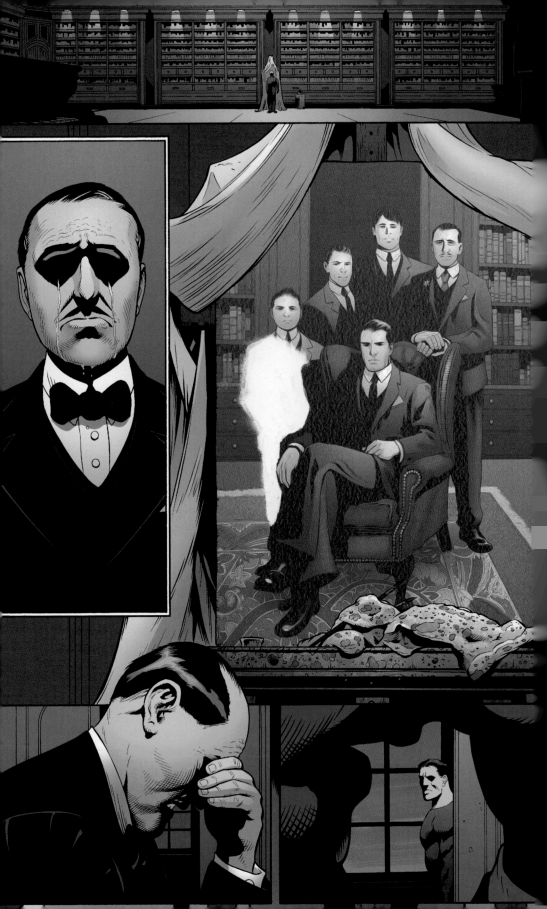

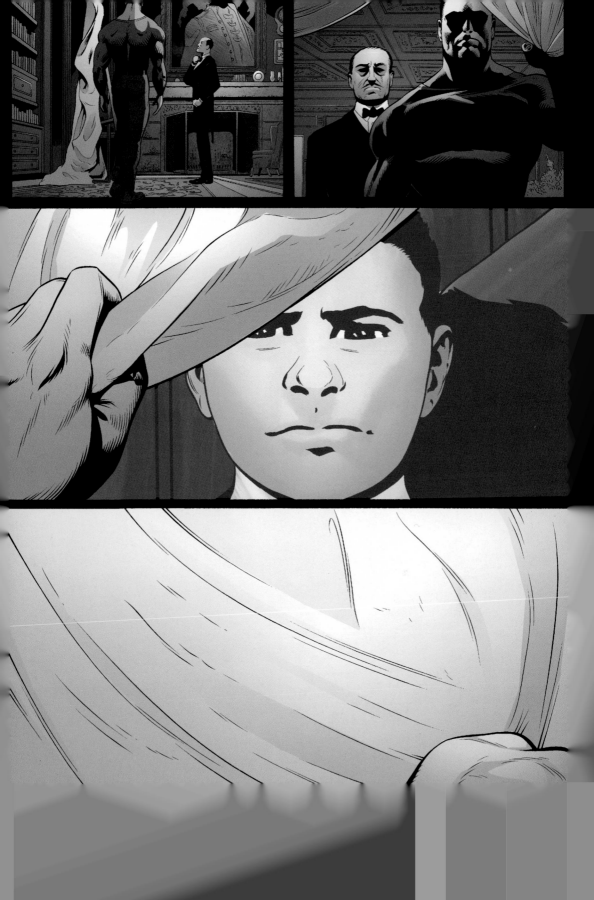

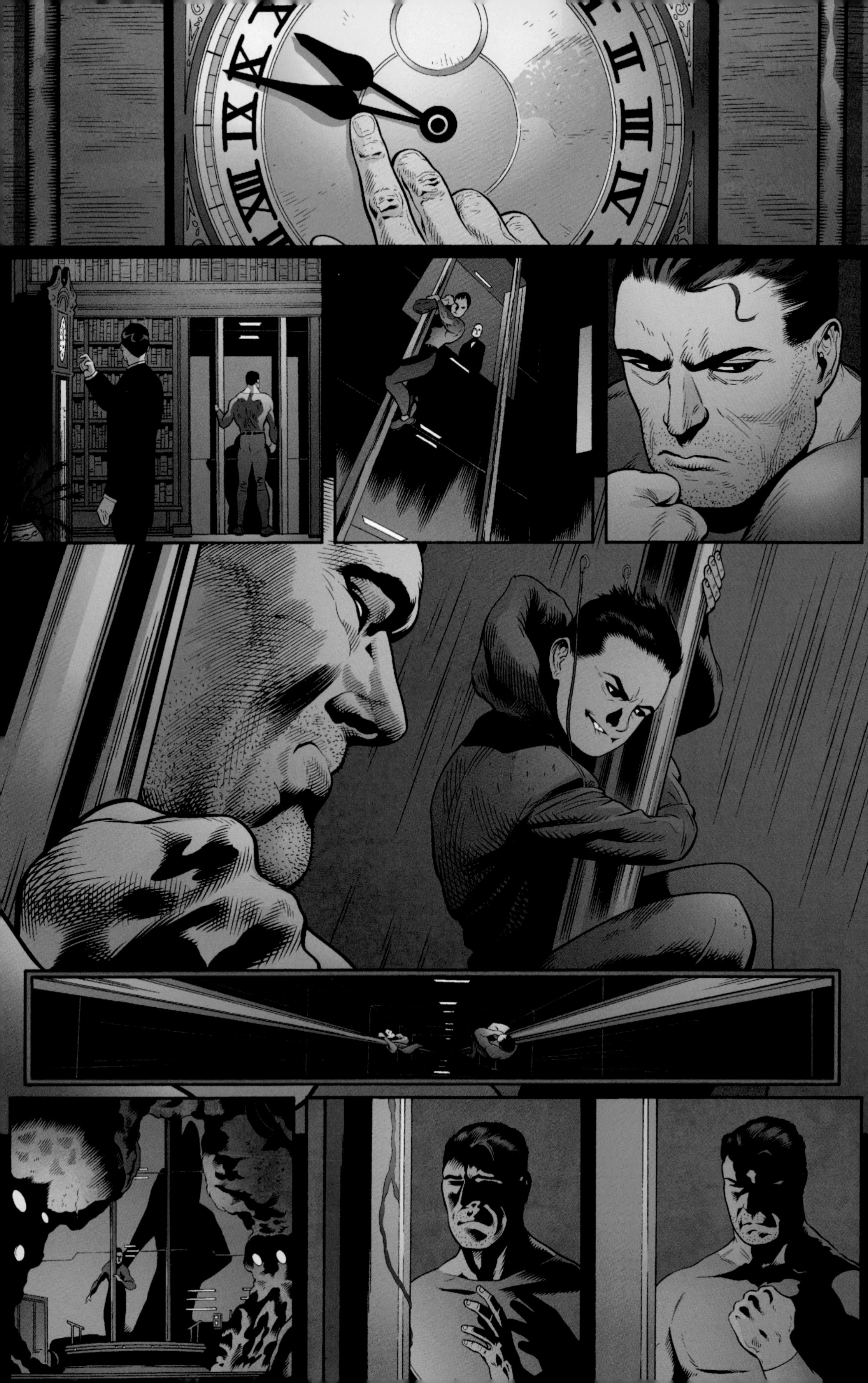

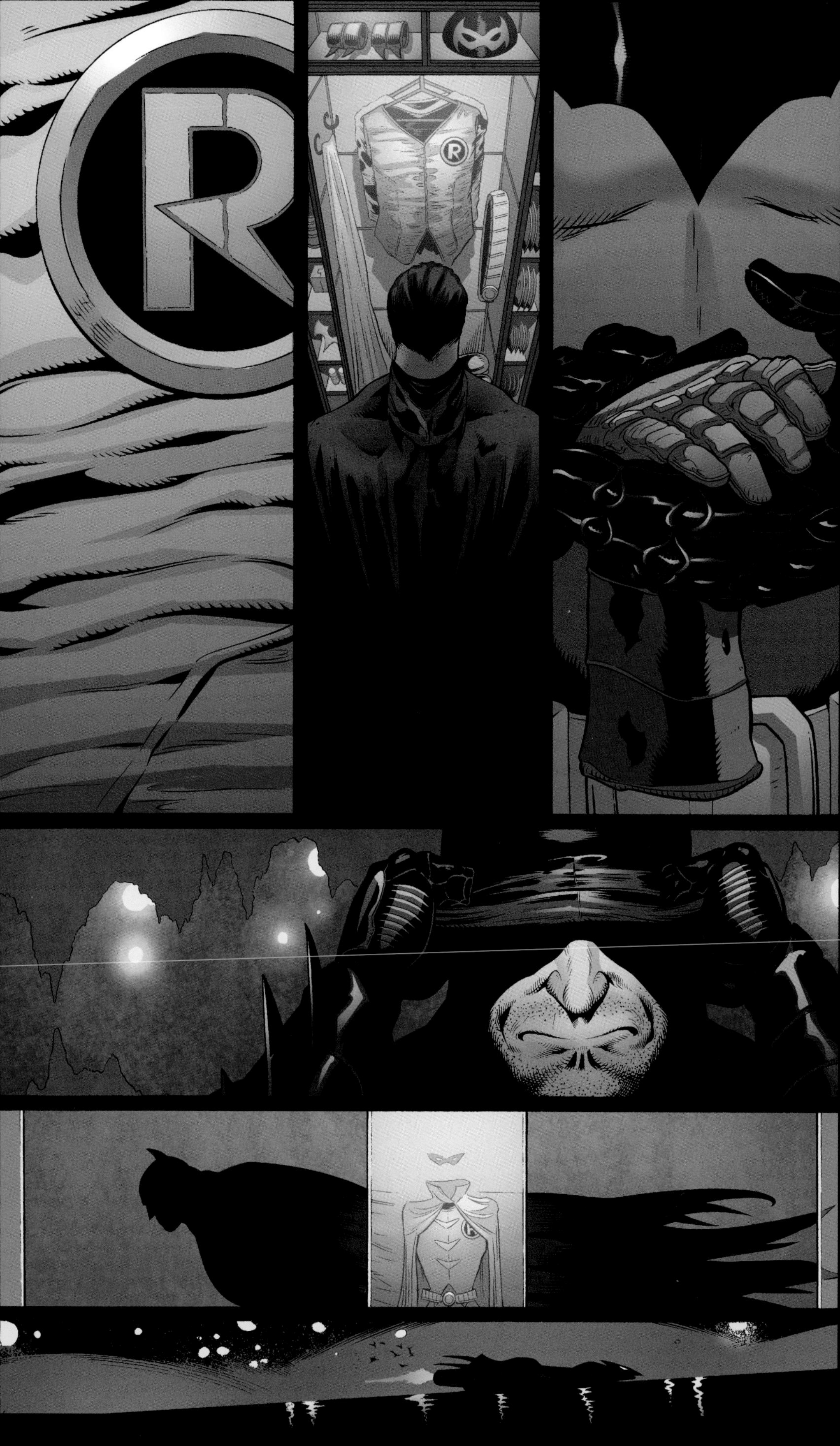

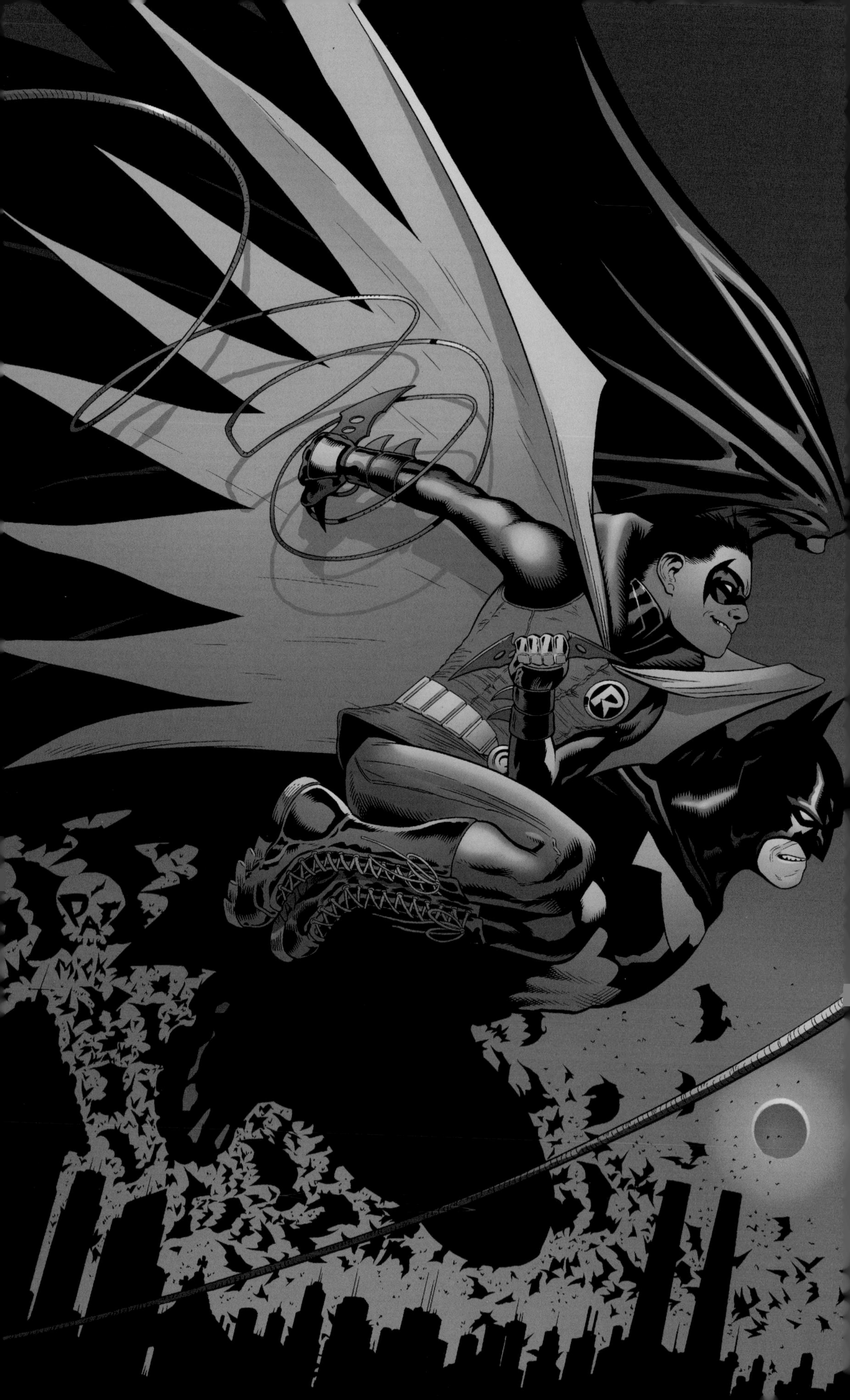

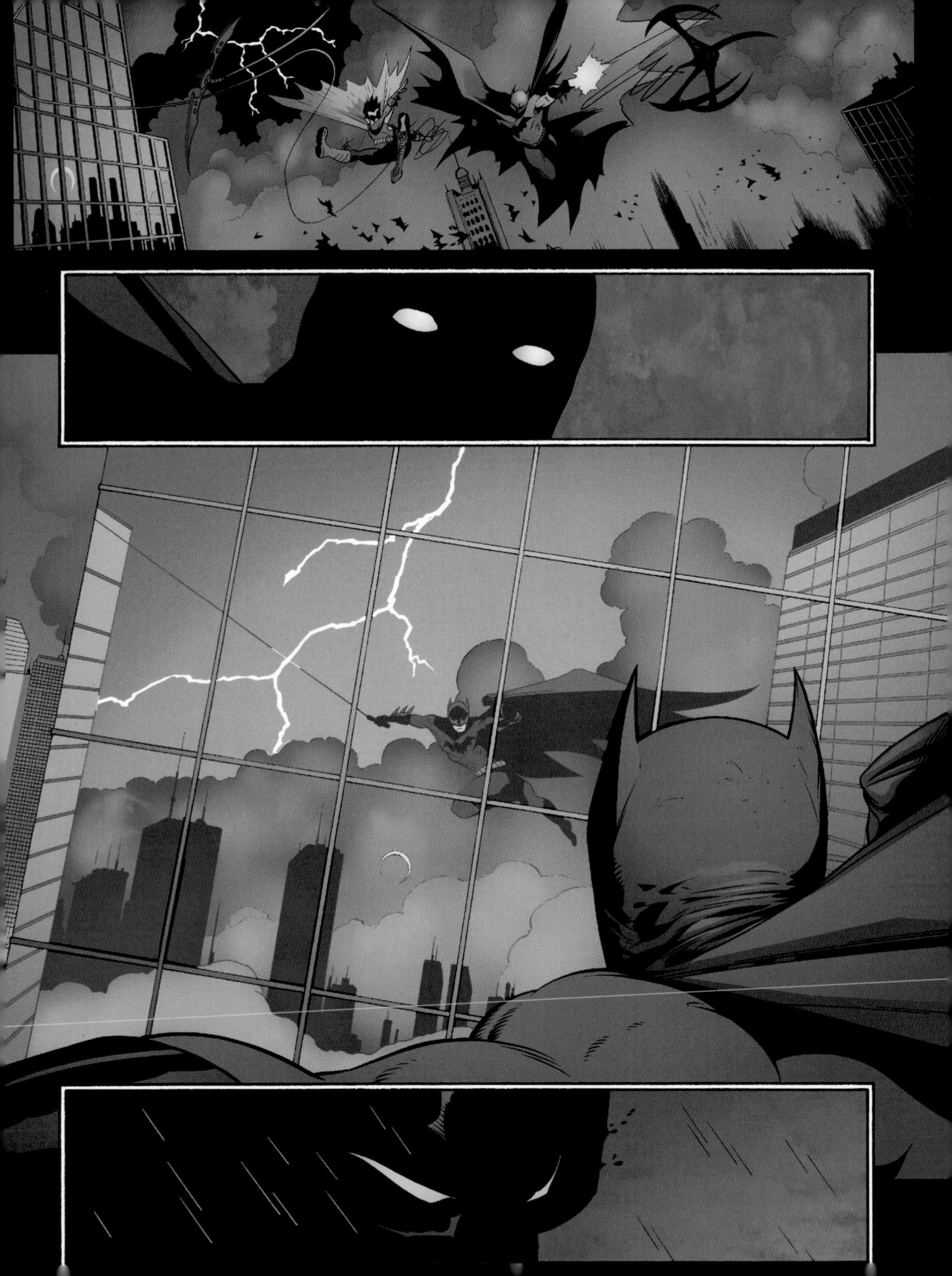

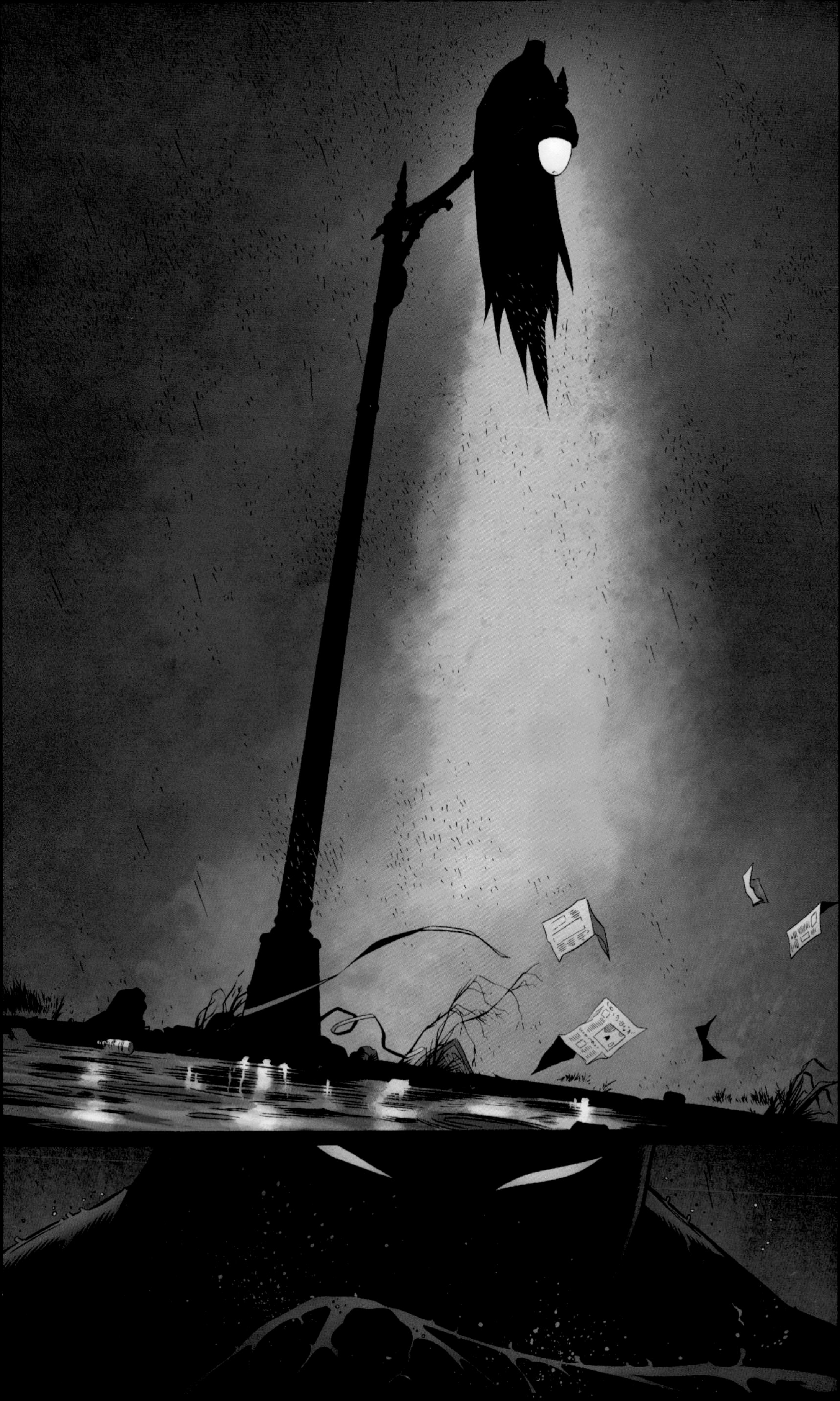

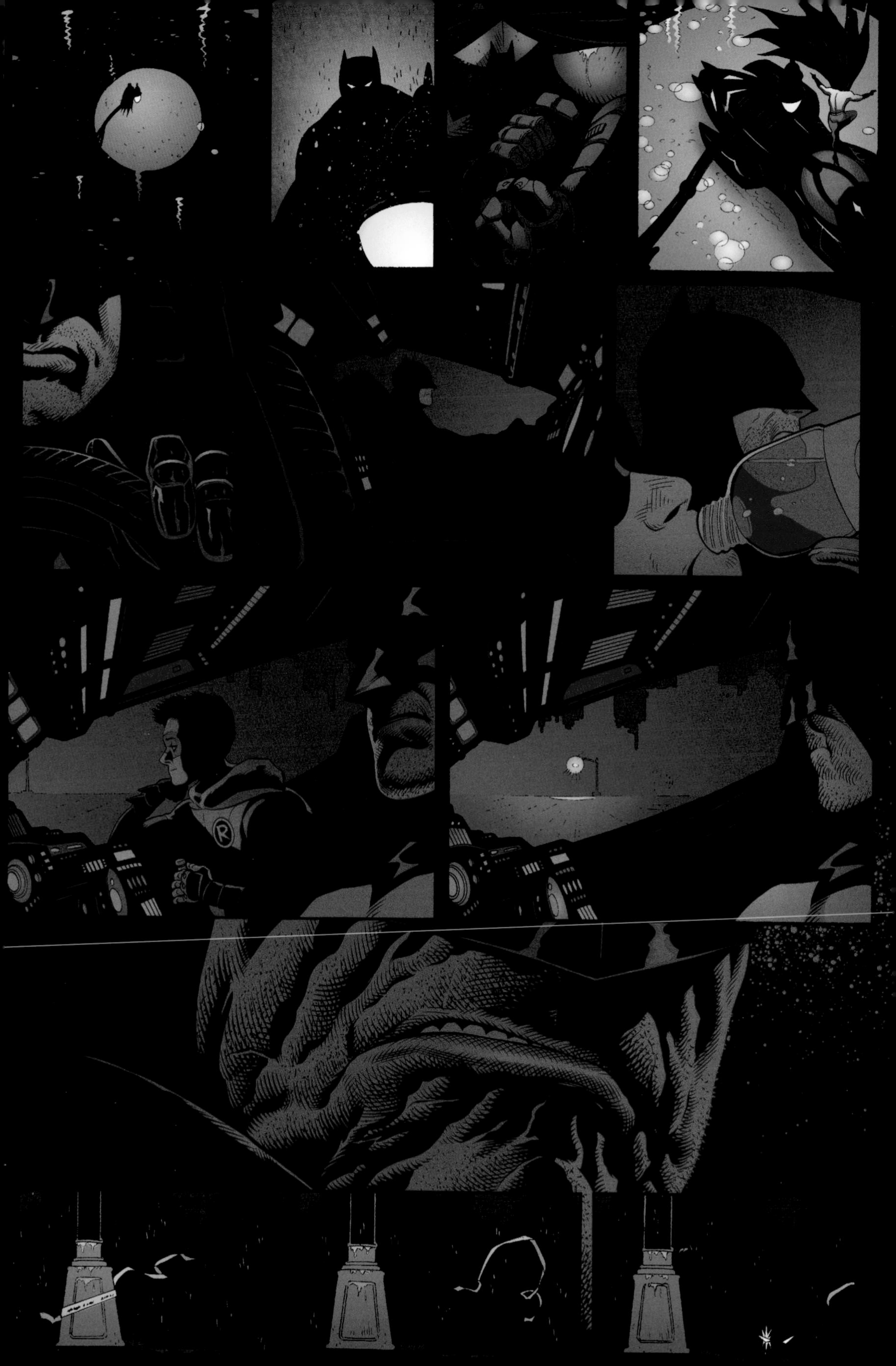

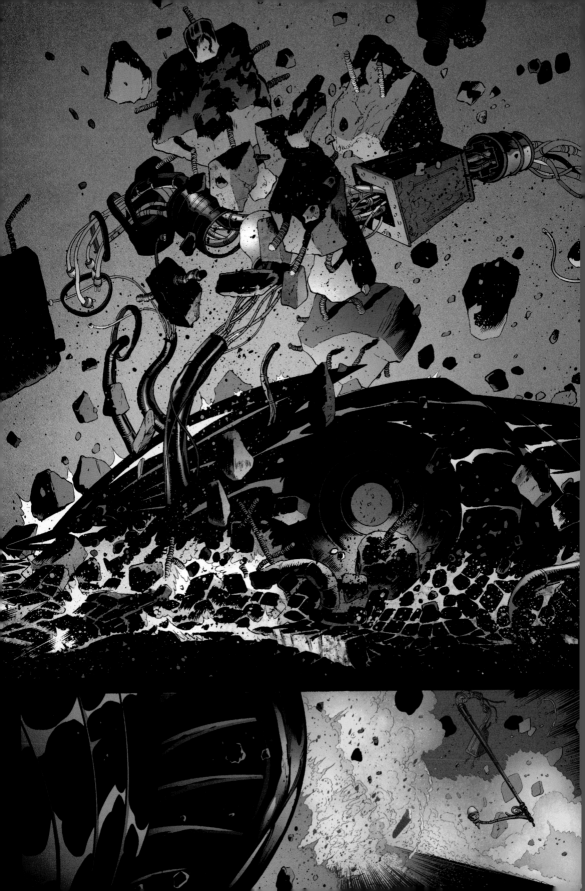

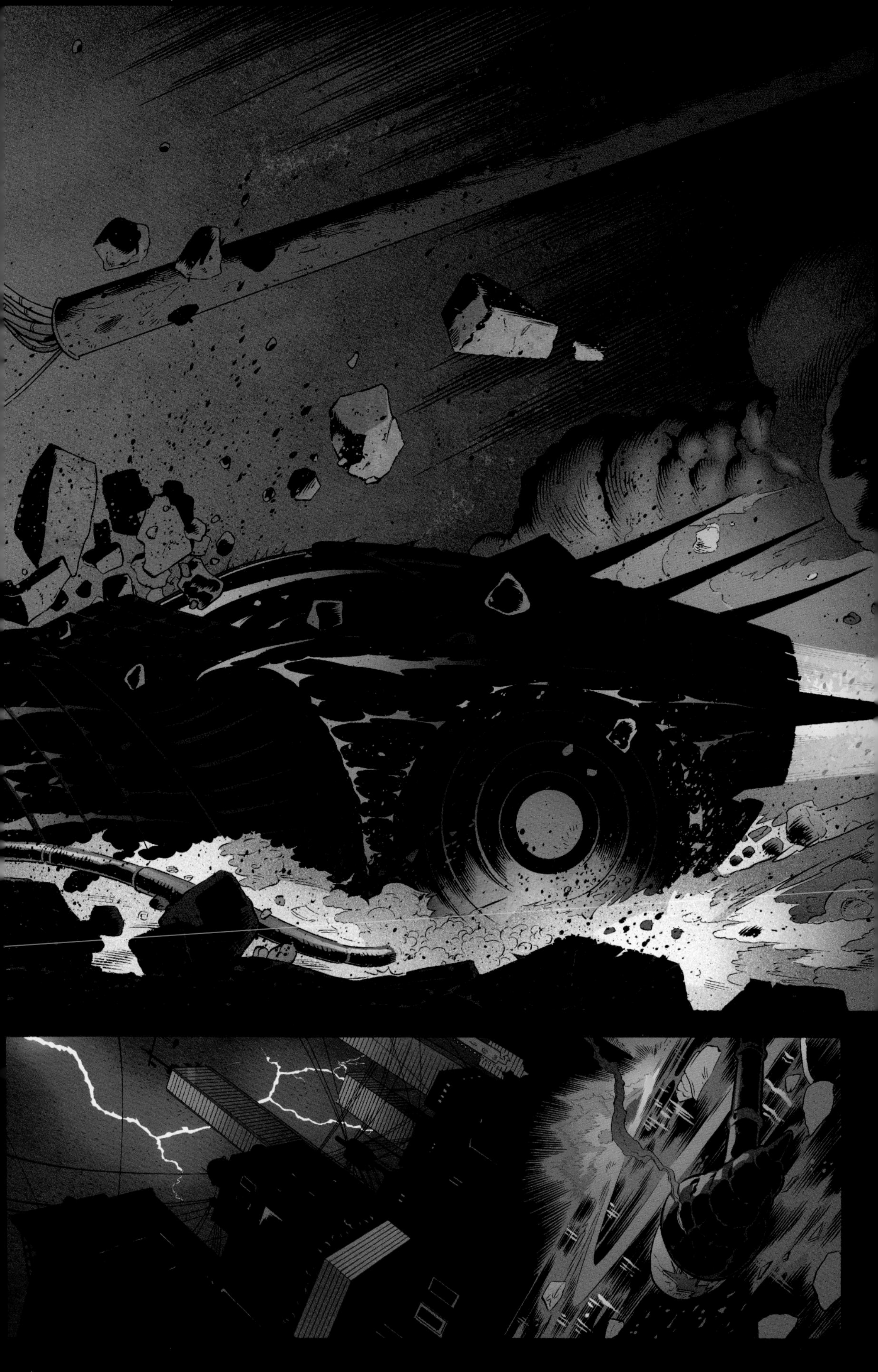

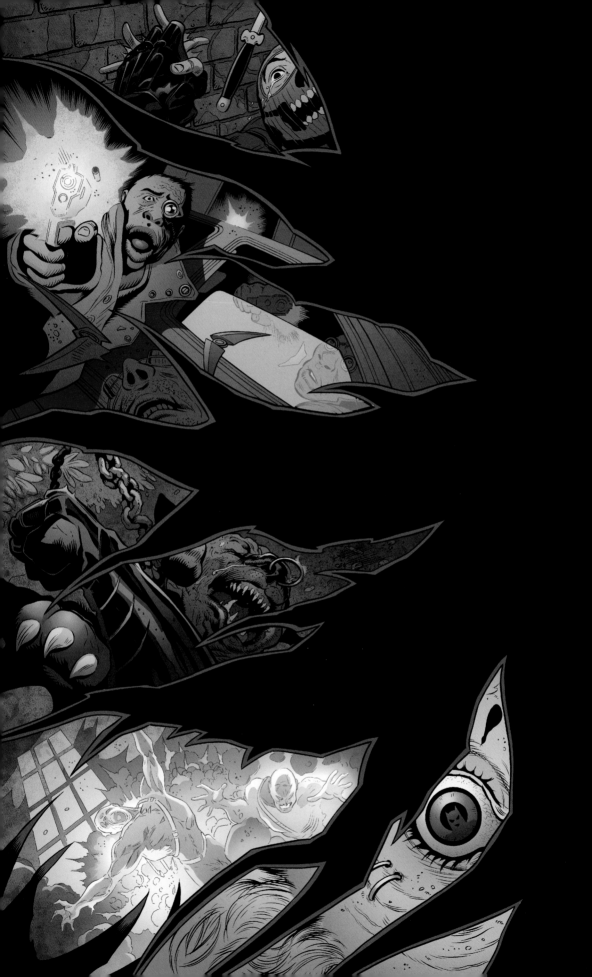

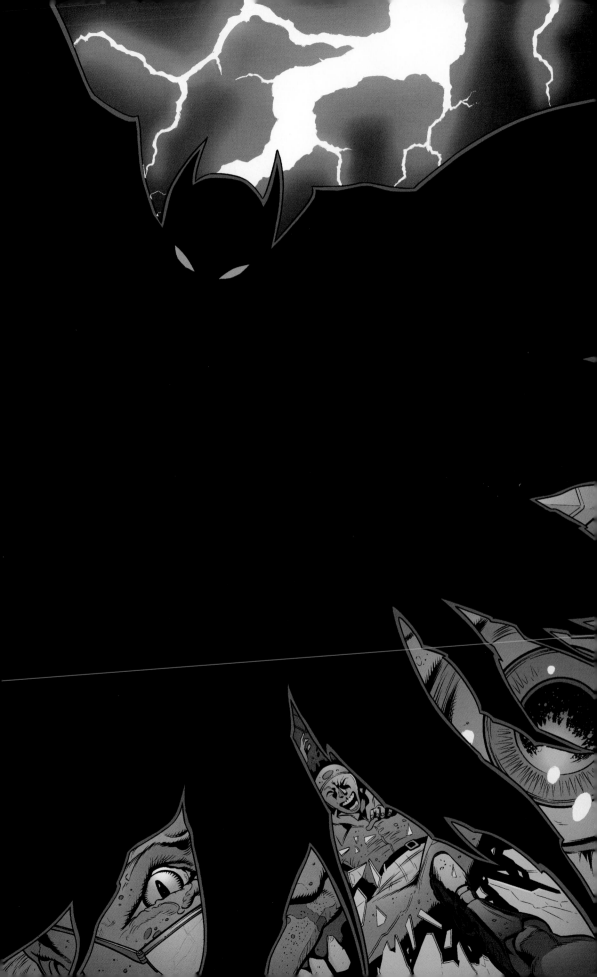

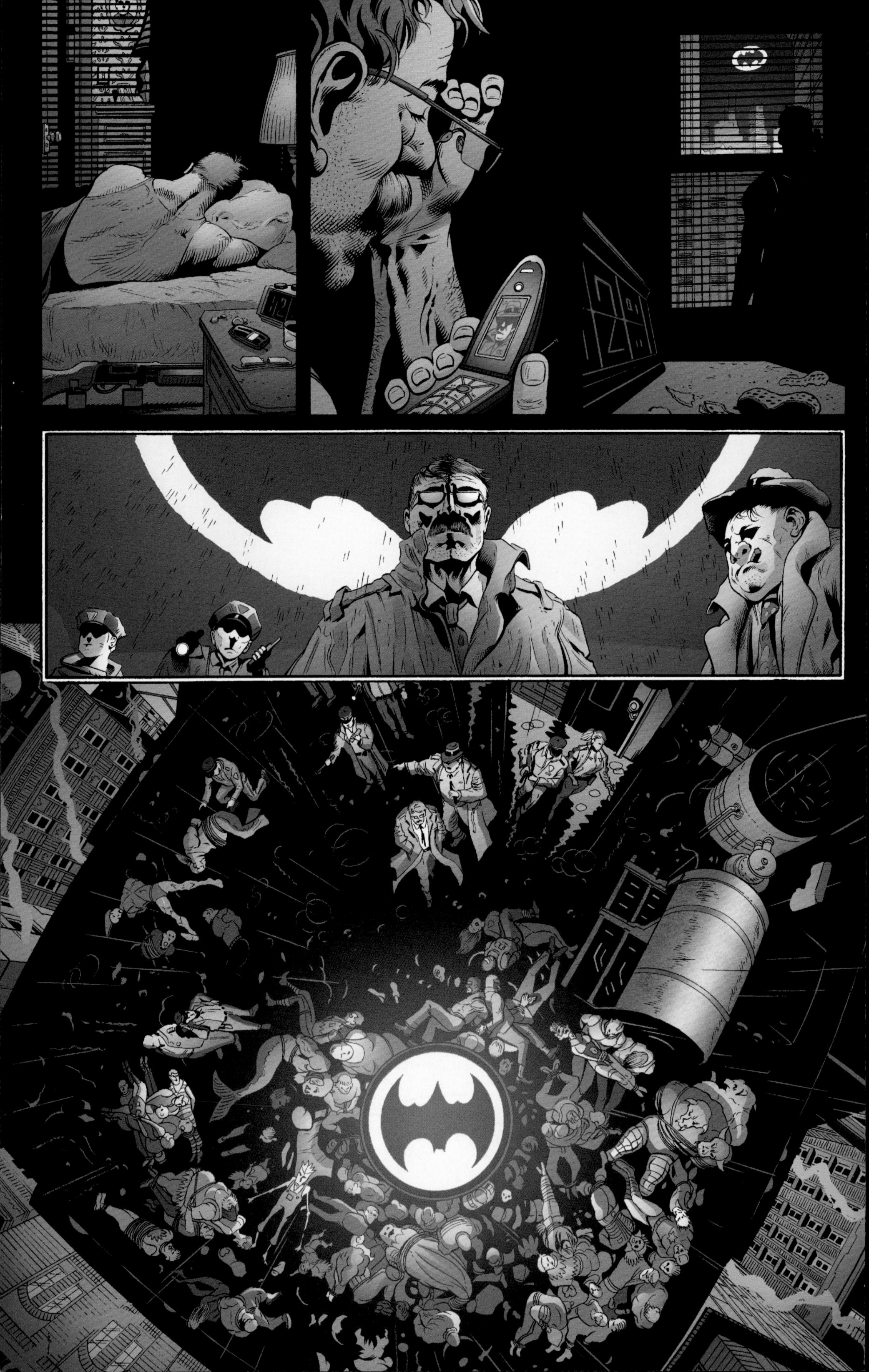

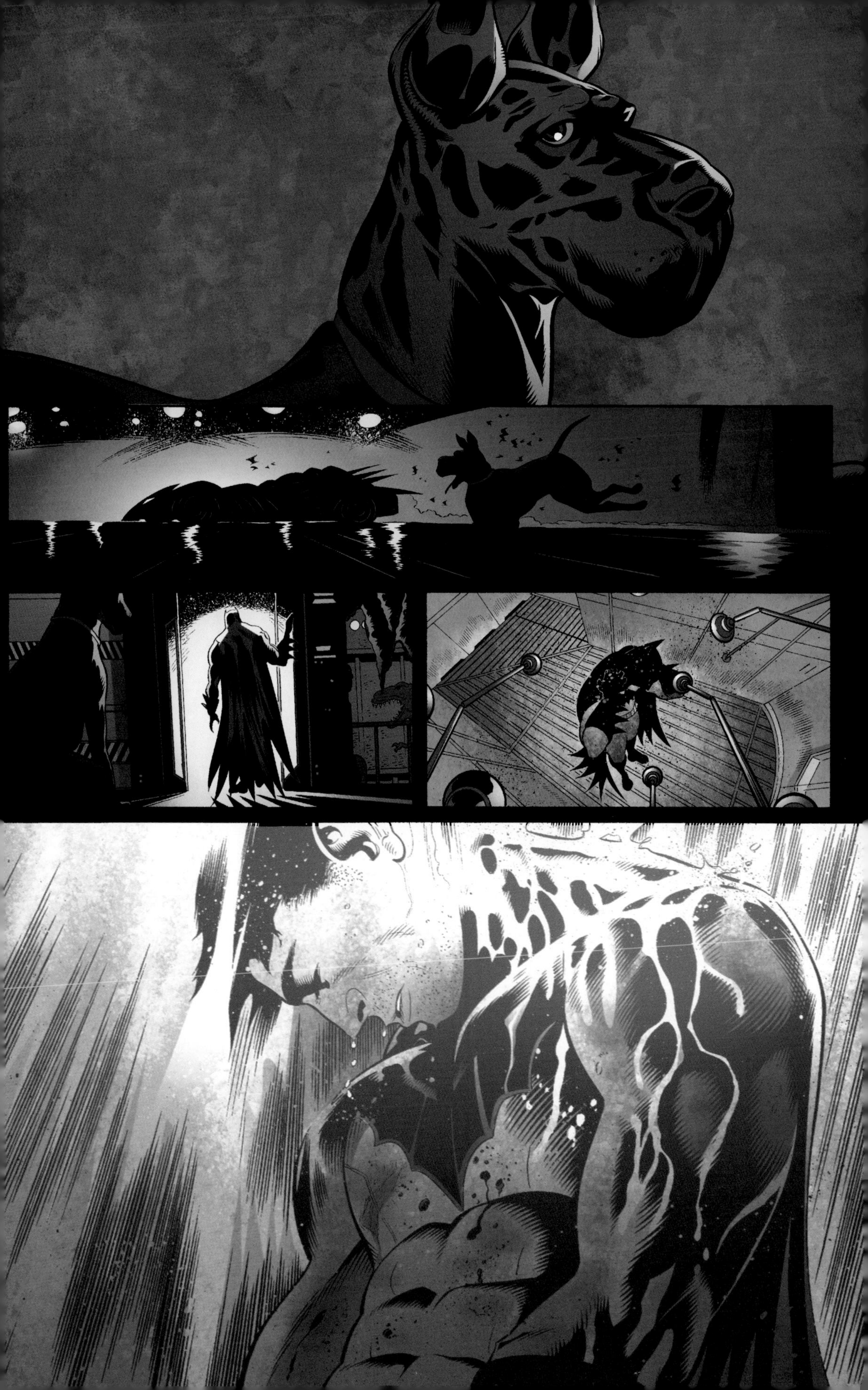

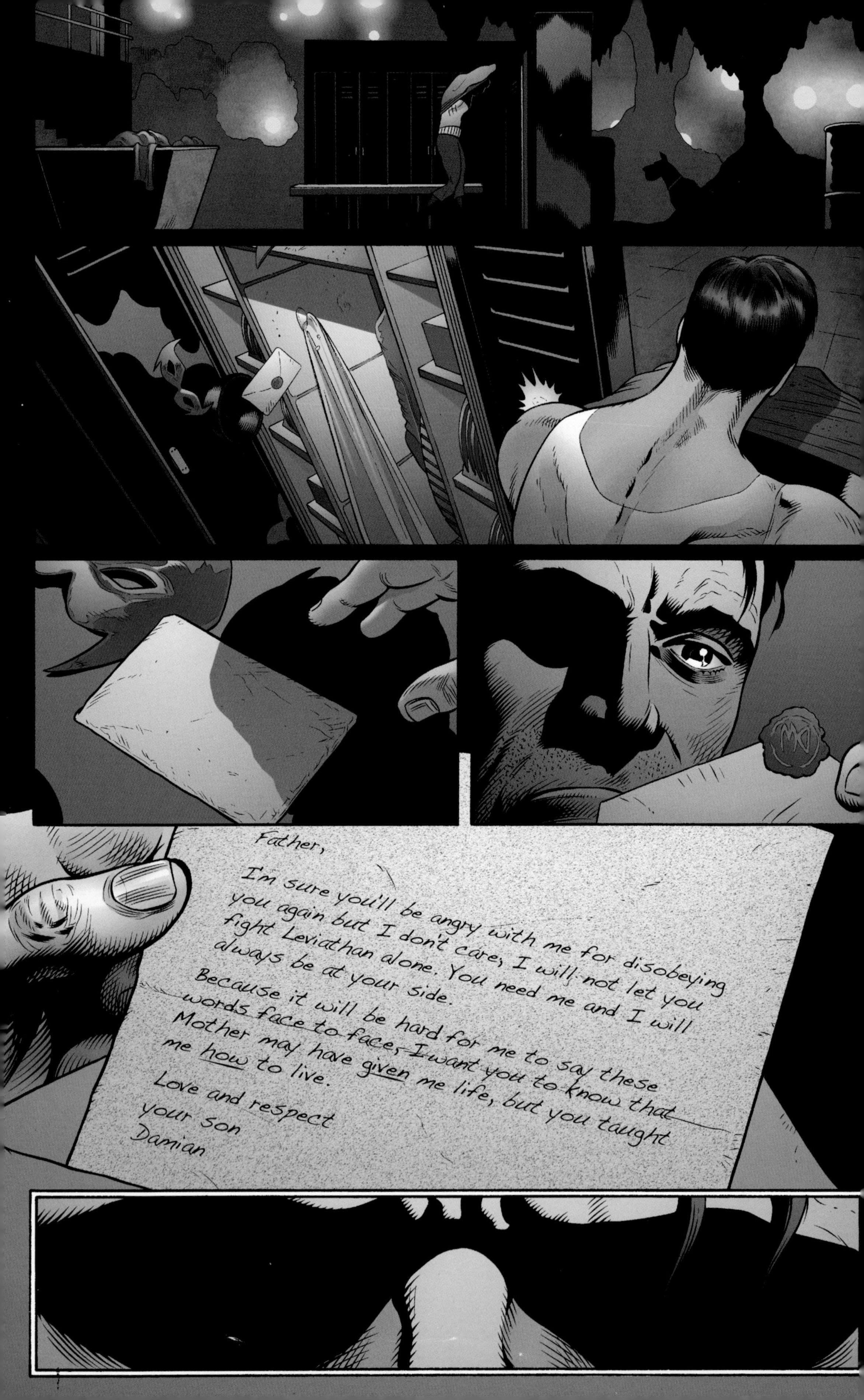
Father,
I'm sure you'll be angry with me for disobeying you again but I don't care, I will not let you fight Leviathan alone. You need me and I will always be at your side.
Because it will be hard for me to say these words face to face, I want you to know that Mother may have given me life, but you taught me how to live.
Love and respect
your son
Damian

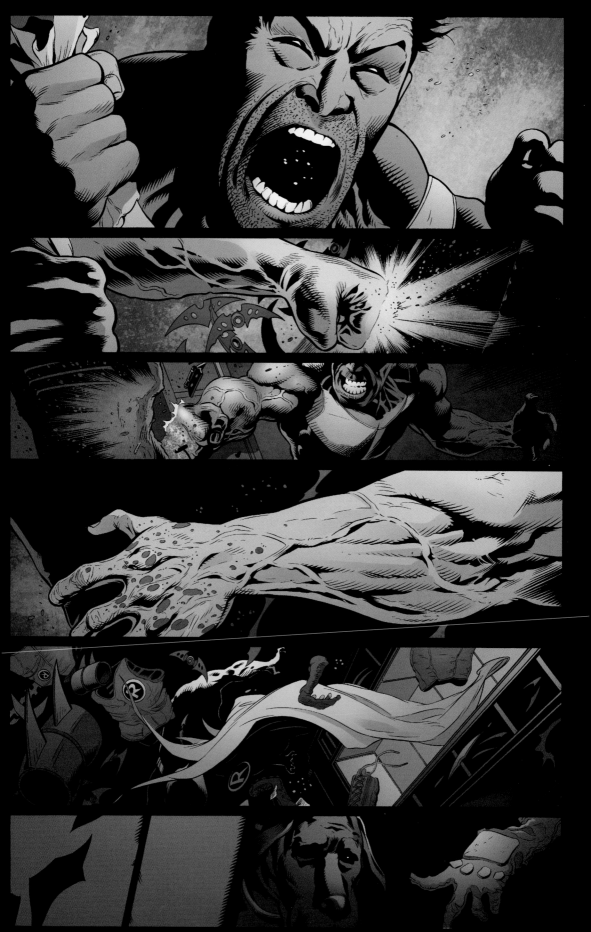

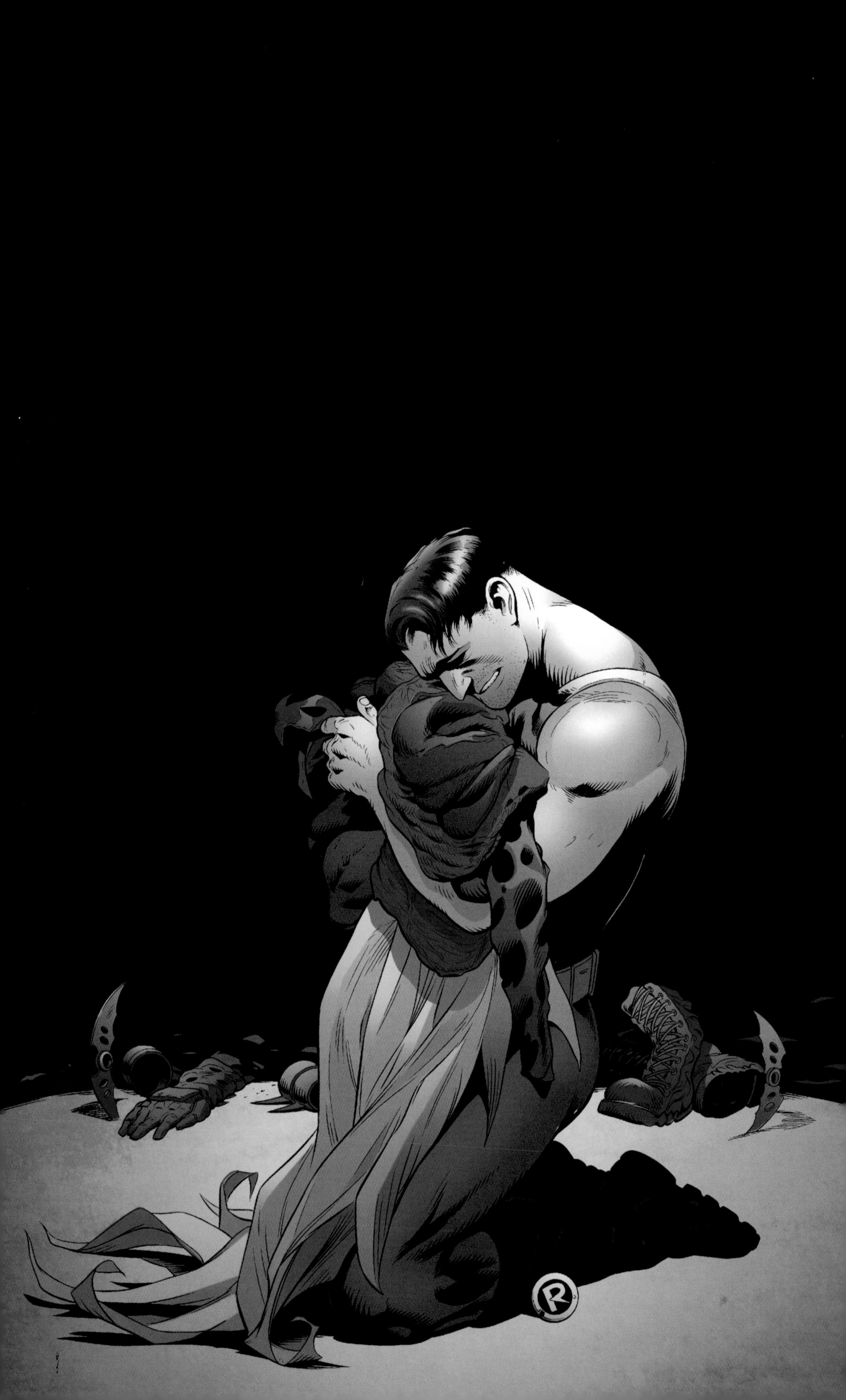

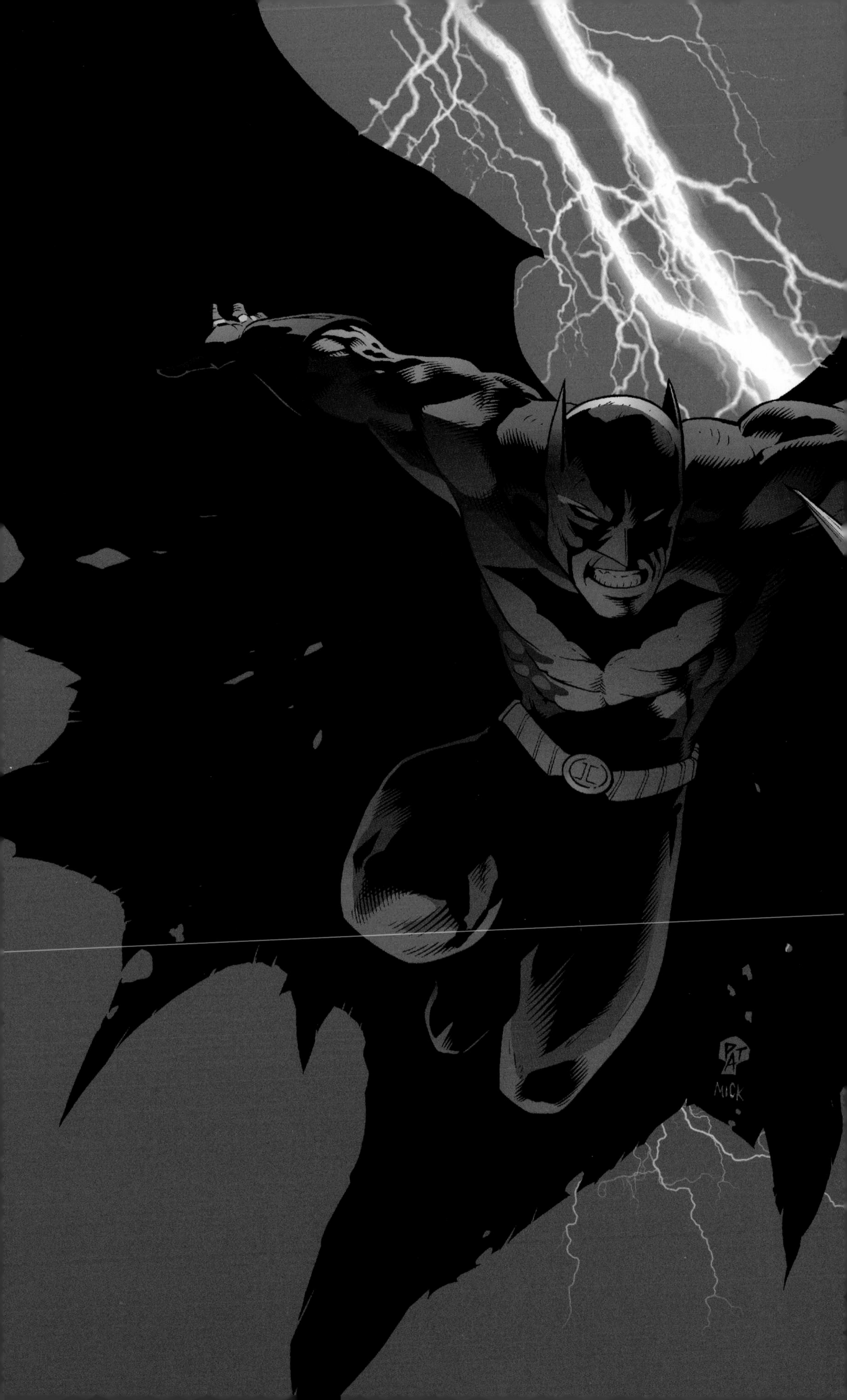
PAT
MICK

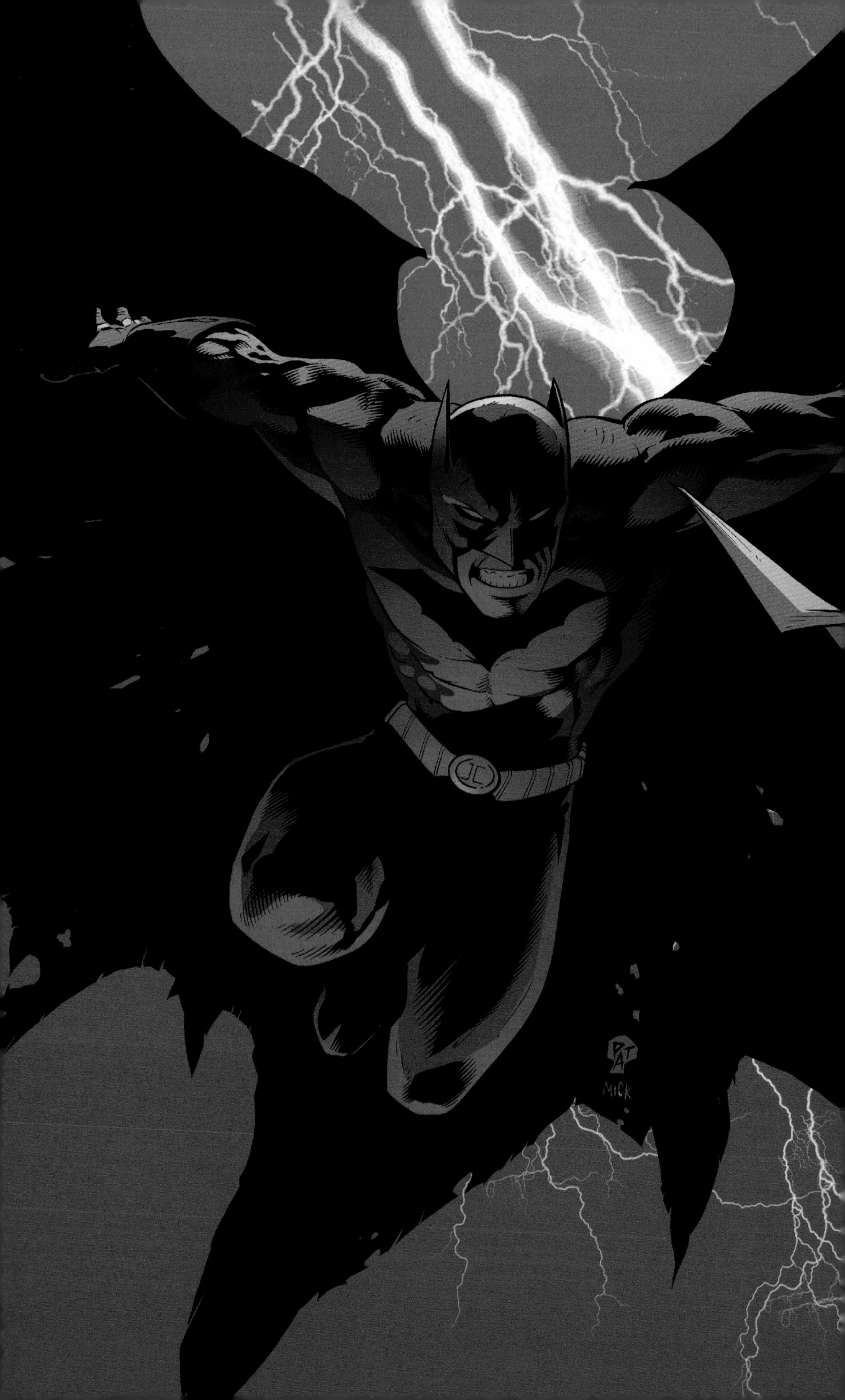
PAT
MICK

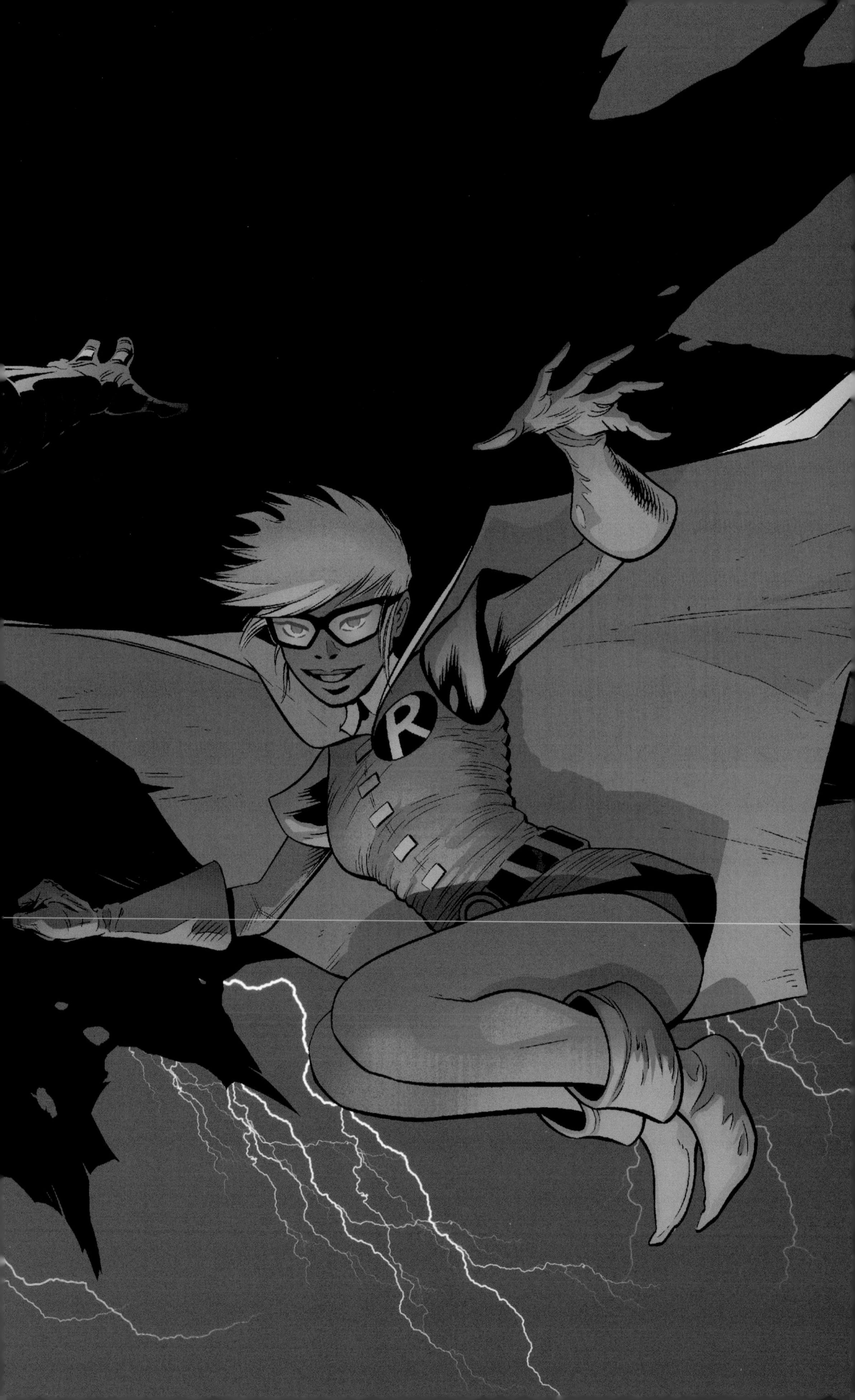

BATMAN AND RED ROBIN: DENIAL

PATRICK GLEASON penciller **MICK GRAY** inker

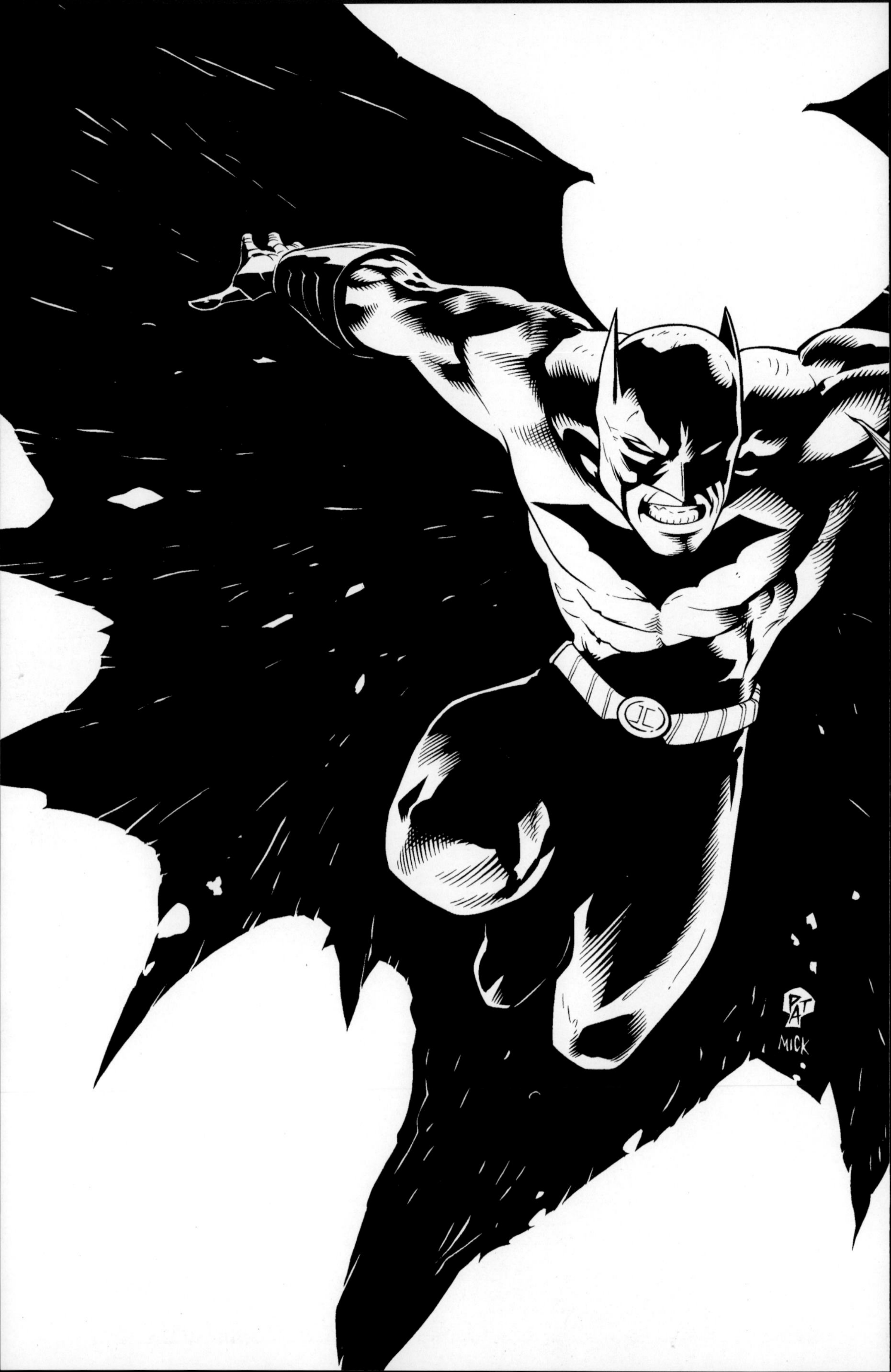
PAT
MICK

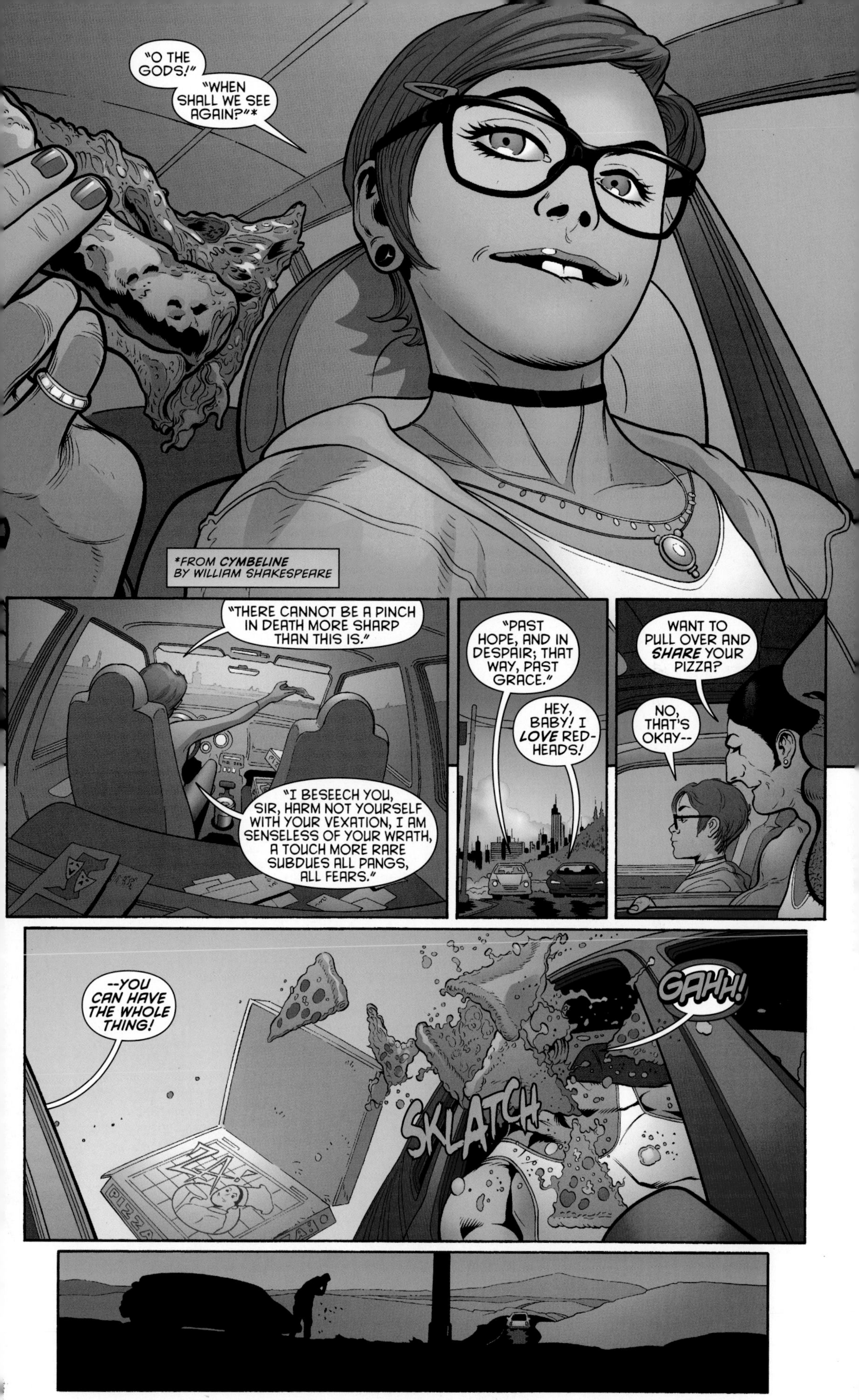
"O THE GODS!"
"WHEN SHALL WE SEE AGAIN?"*
*FROM CYMBELINE BY WILLIAM SHAKESPEARE
"THERE CANNOT BE A PINCH IN DEATH MORE SHARP THAN THIS IS."
"I BESEECH YOU, SIR, HARM NOT YOURSELF WITH YOUR VEXATION, I AM SENSELESS OF YOUR WRATH, A TOUCH MORE RARE SUBDUES ALL PANGS, ALL FEARS."
"PAST HOPE, AND IN DESPAIR; THAT WAY, PAST GRACE."
HEY, BABY! I LOVE RED-HEADS!
WANT TO PULL OVER AND SHARE YOUR PIZZA?
NO, THAT'S OKAY--
--YOU CAN HAVE THE WHOLE THING!
GAHH!
SKLATCH
PIZZA

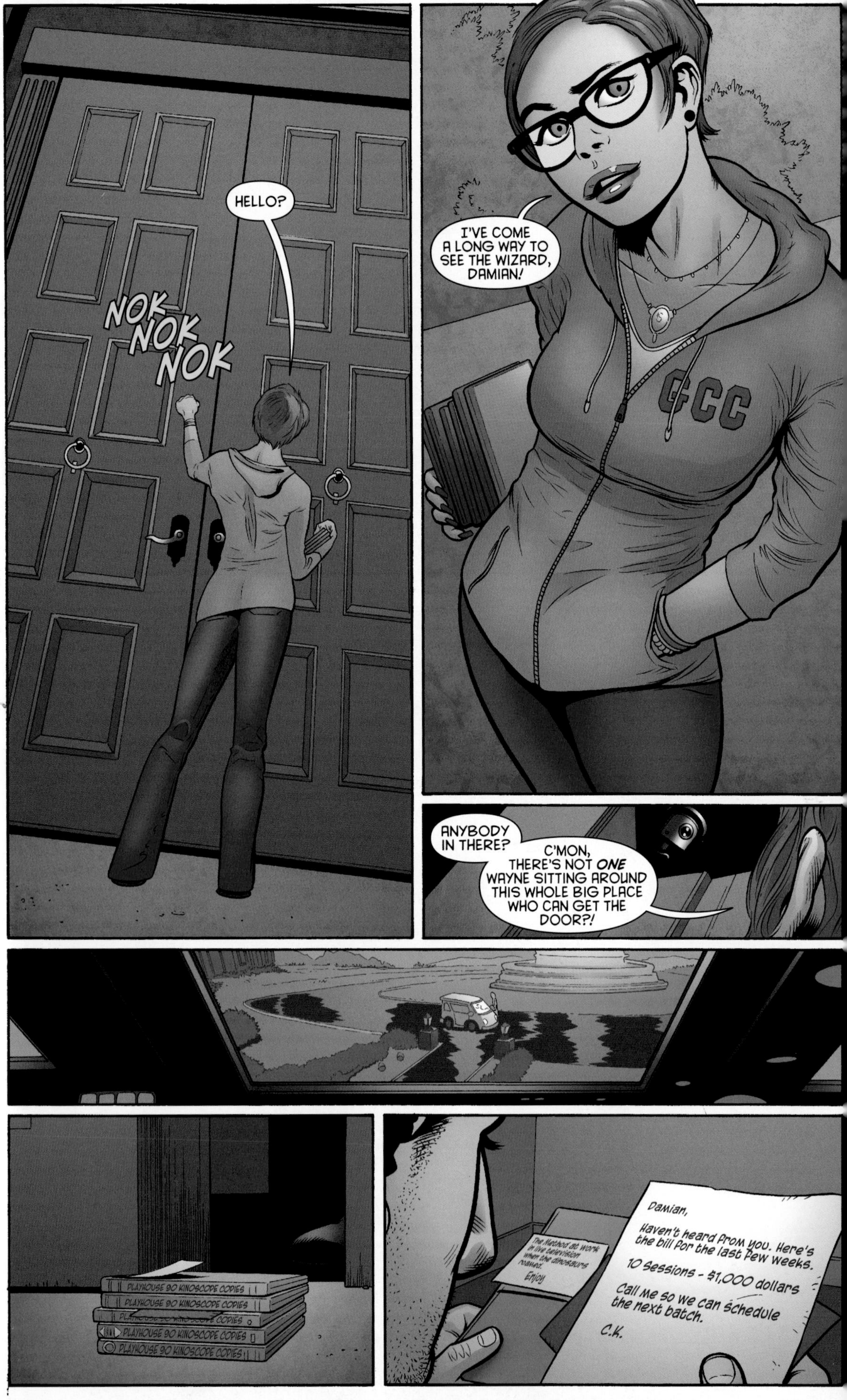
HELLO?
NOK NOK NOK
I'VE COME A LONG WAY TO SEE THE WIZARD, DAMIAN!
ANYBODY IN THERE?
C'MON, THERE'S NOT ONE WAYNE SITTING AROUND THIS WHOLE BIG PLACE WHO CAN GET THE DOOR?!
PLAYHOUSE 90 KINOSCOPE COPIES
PLAYHOUSE 90 KINOSCOPE COPIES
PLAYHOUSE 90 KINOSCOPE COPIES
PLAYHOUSE 90 KINOSCOPE COPIES
PLAYHOUSE 90 KINOSCOPE COPIES
The Method at work in live television when the dinosaurs roamed.
Enjoy
Damian,
Haven't heard from you. Here's the bill for the last few weeks.
10 Sessions - $1,000 dollars
Call me so we can schedule the next batch.
C.K.

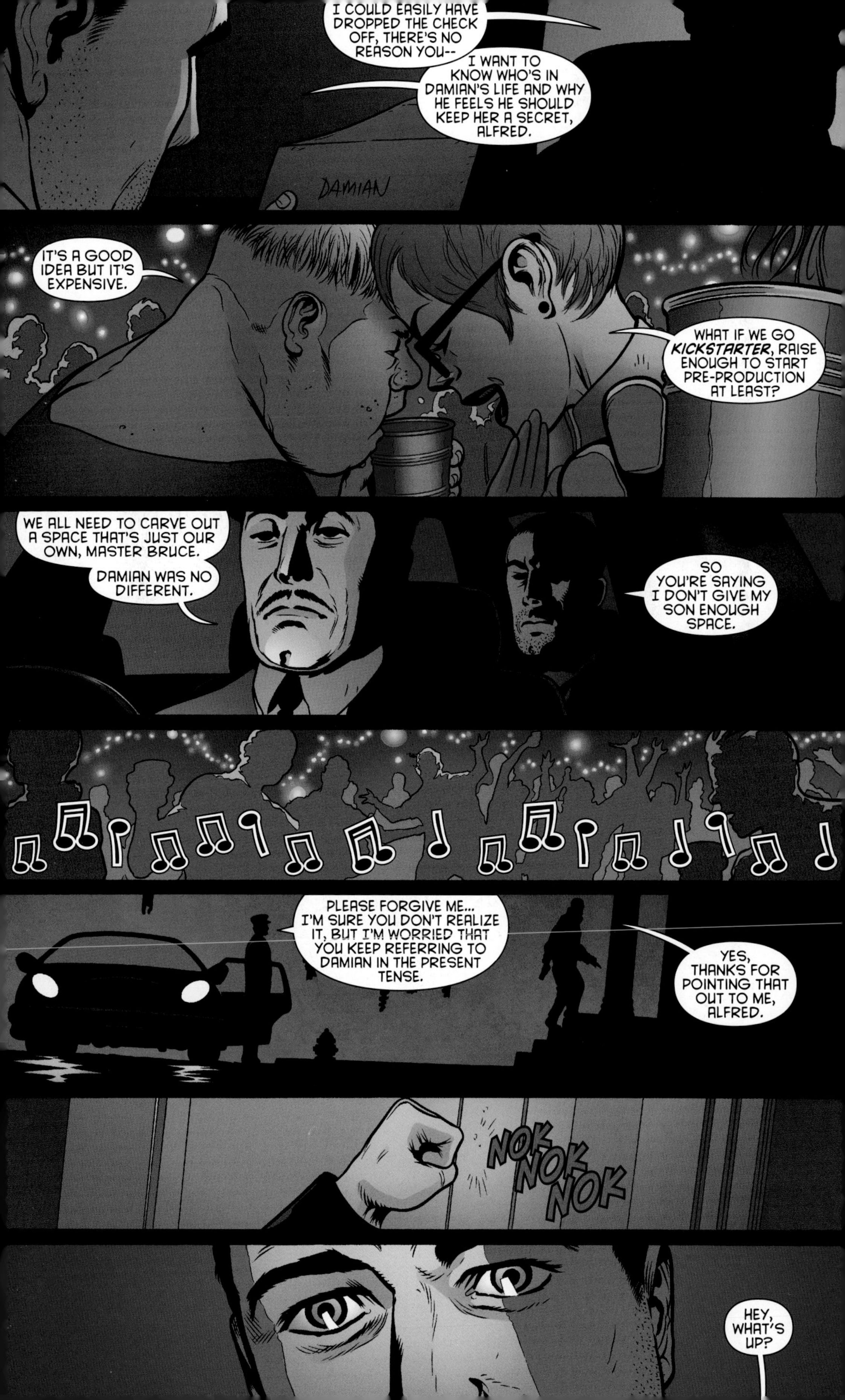
I COULD EASILY HAVE DROPPED THE CHECK OFF, THERE'S NO REASON YOU--
I WANT TO KNOW WHO'S IN DAMIAN'S LIFE AND WHY HE FEELS HE SHOULD KEEP HER A SECRET, ALFRED.
DAMIAN
IT'S A GOOD IDEA BUT IT'S EXPENSIVE.
WHAT IF WE GO KICKSTARTER, RAISE ENOUGH TO START PRE-PRODUCTION AT LEAST?
WE ALL NEED TO CARVE OUT A SPACE THAT'S JUST OUR OWN, MASTER BRUCE.
DAMIAN WAS NO DIFFERENT.
SO YOU'RE SAYING I DON'T GIVE MY SON ENOUGH SPACE.
PLEASE FORGIVE ME... I'M SURE YOU DON'T REALIZE IT, BUT I'M WORRIED THAT YOU KEEP REFERRING TO DAMIAN IN THE PRESENT TENSE.
YES, THANKS FOR POINTING THAT OUT TO ME, ALFRED.
NOK NOK NOK
HEY, WHAT'S UP?

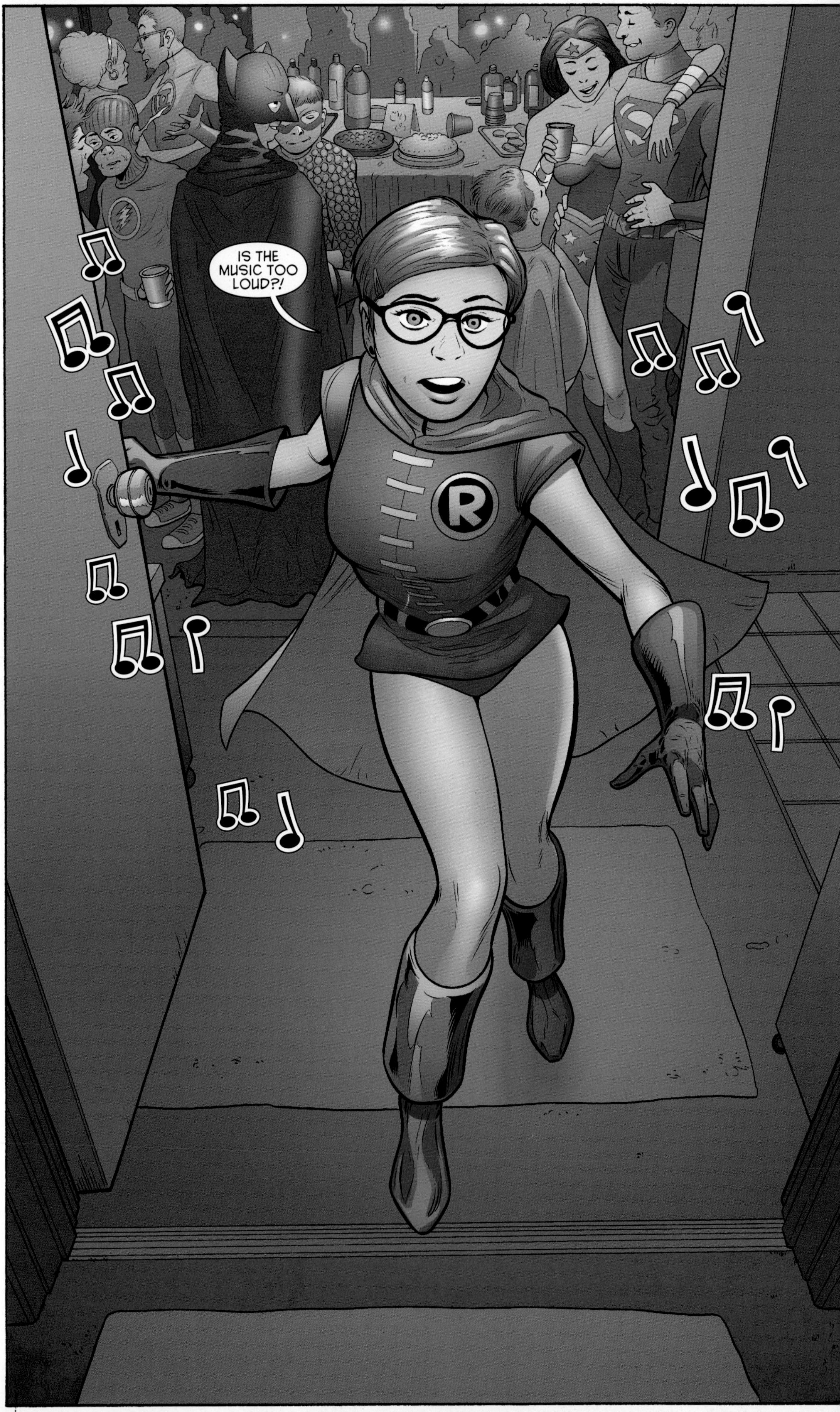
IS THE MUSIC TOO LOUD?!

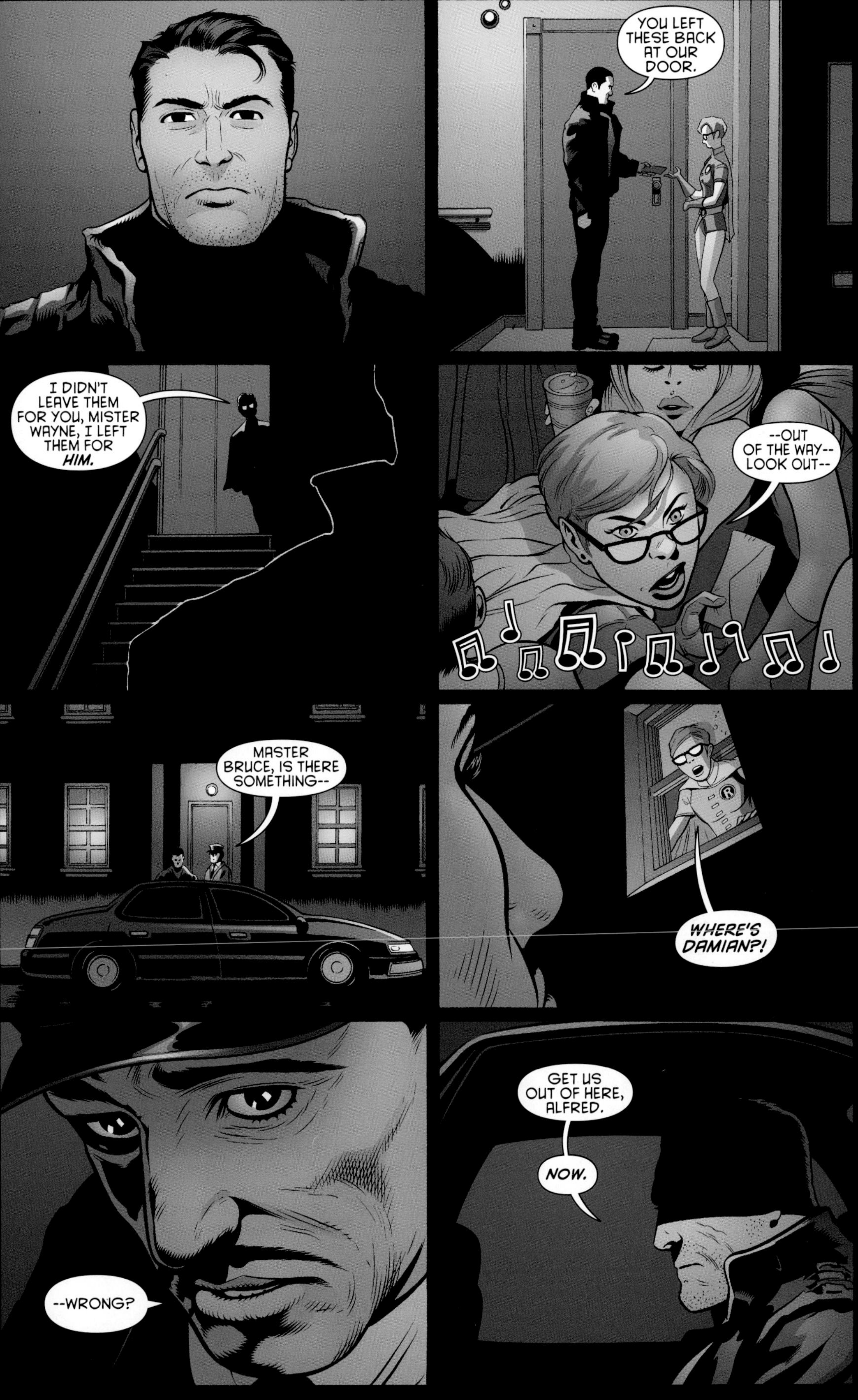
YOU LEFT THESE BACK AT OUR DOOR.
I DIDN'T LEAVE THEM FOR YOU, MISTER WAYNE, I LEFT THEM FOR *HIM.*
--OUT OF THE WAY-- LOOK OUT--
MASTER BRUCE, IS THERE SOMETHING--
WHERE'S DAMIAN?!
--WRONG?
GET US OUT OF HERE, ALFRED.
NOW.

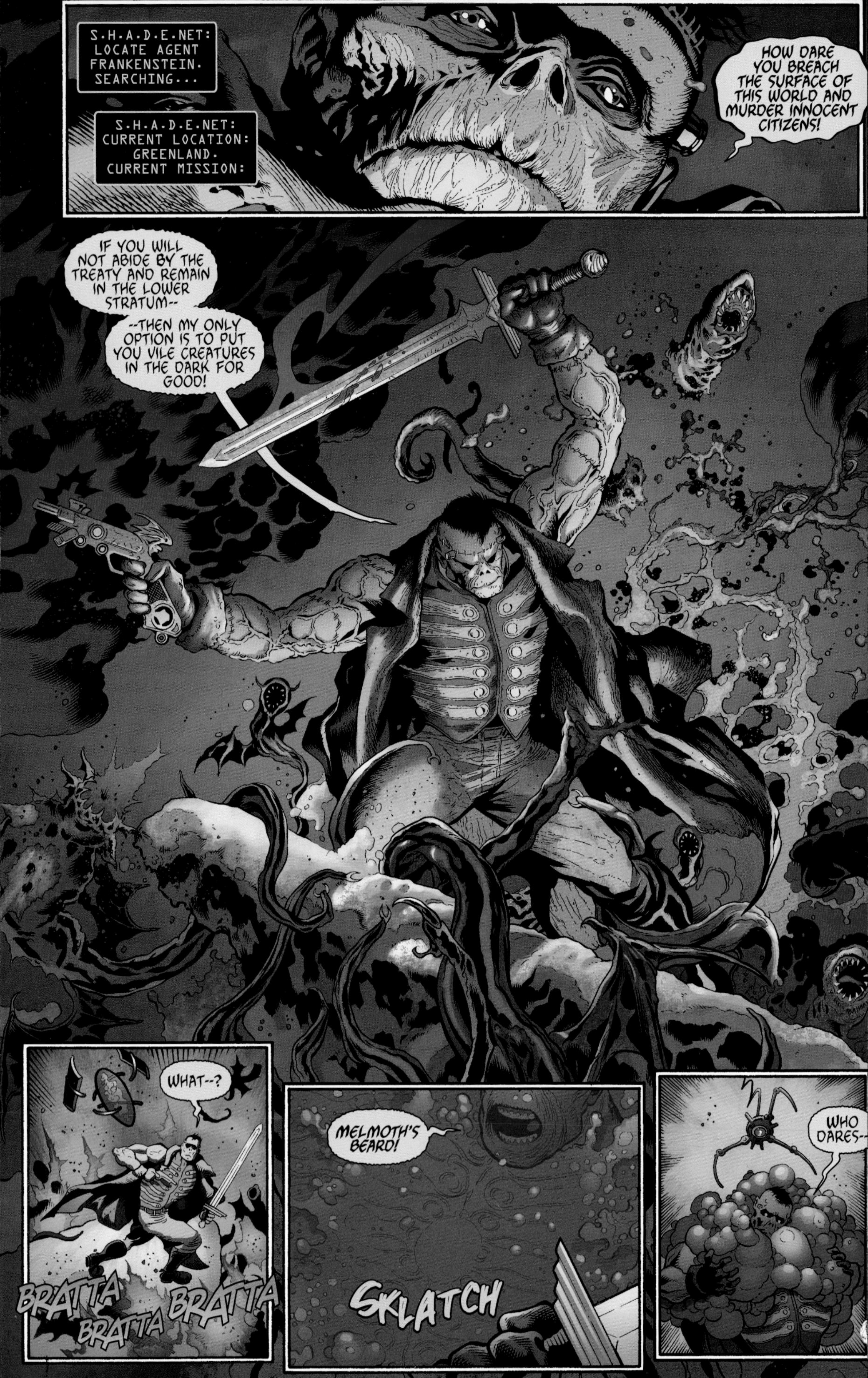
S.H.A.D.E.NET: LOCATE AGENT FRANKENSTEIN. SEARCHING...
S.H.A.D.E.NET: CURRENT LOCATION: GREENLAND. CURRENT MISSION:
HOW DARE YOU BREACH THE SURFACE OF THIS WORLD AND MURDER INNOCENT CITIZENS!
IF YOU WILL NOT ABIDE BY THE TREATY AND REMAIN IN THE LOWER STRATUM--
--THEN MY ONLY OPTION IS TO PUT YOU VILE CREATURES IN THE DARK FOR GOOD!
WHAT--?
BRATTA BRATTA BRATTA
MELMOTH'S BEARD!
SKLATCH
WHO DARES--

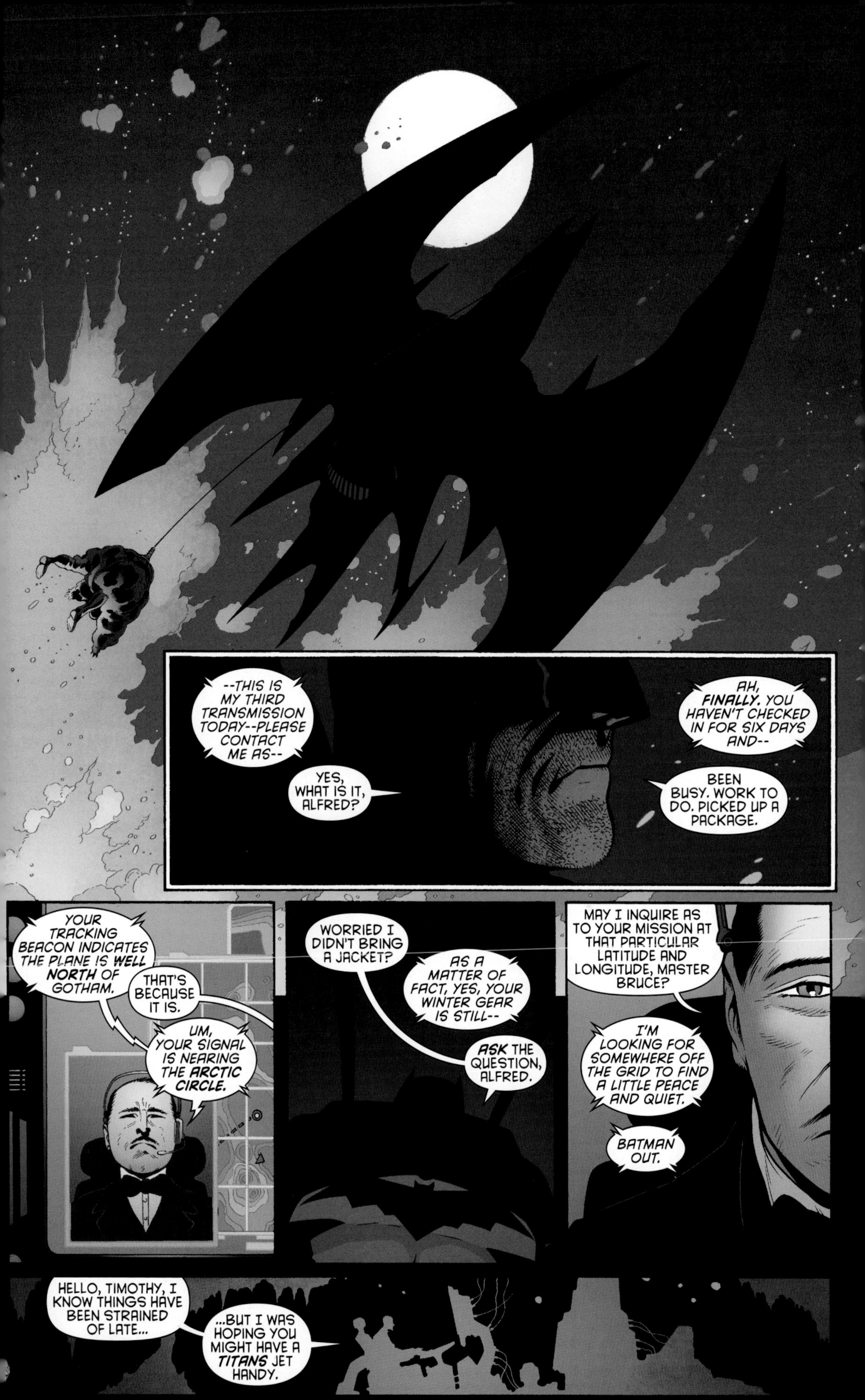
--THIS IS MY THIRD TRANSMISSION TODAY--PLEASE CONTACT ME AS--
AH, FINALLY. YOU HAVEN'T CHECKED IN FOR SIX DAYS AND--
YES, WHAT IS IT, ALFRED?
BEEN BUSY. WORK TO DO. PICKED UP A PACKAGE.
YOUR TRACKING BEACON INDICATES THE PLANE IS WELL NORTH OF GOTHAM.
THAT'S BECAUSE IT IS.
UM, YOUR SIGNAL IS NEARING THE ARCTIC CIRCLE.
WORRIED I DIDN'T BRING A JACKET?
AS A MATTER OF FACT, YES, YOUR WINTER GEAR IS STILL--
ASK THE QUESTION, ALFRED.
MAY I INQUIRE AS TO YOUR MISSION AT THAT PARTICULAR LATITUDE AND LONGITUDE, MASTER BRUCE?
I'M LOOKING FOR SOMEWHERE OFF THE GRID TO FIND A LITTLE PEACE AND QUIET.
BATMAN OUT.
HELLO, TIMOTHY, I KNOW THINGS HAVE BEEN STRAINED OF LATE...
...BUT I WAS HOPING YOU MIGHT HAVE A TITANS JET HANDY.

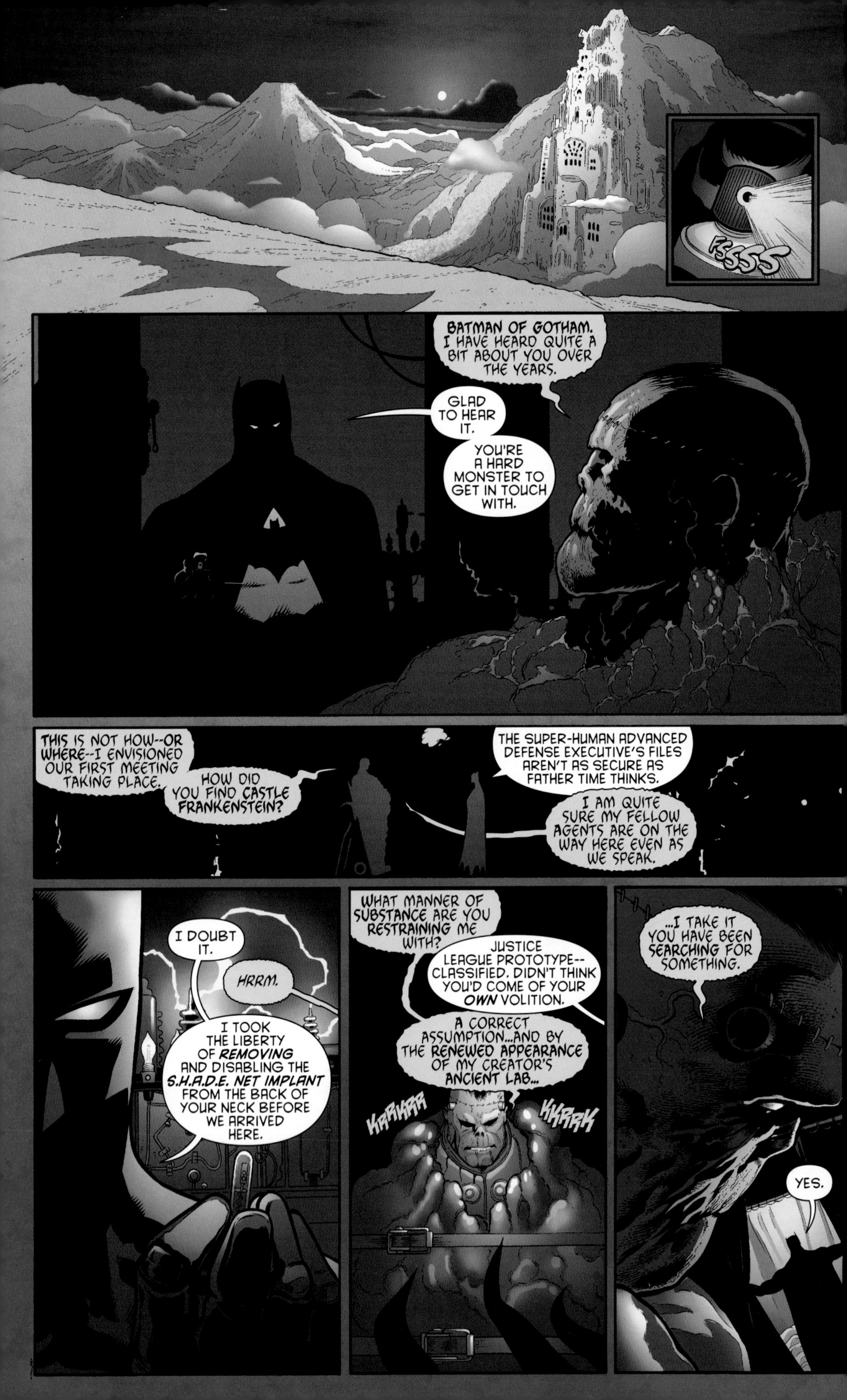
FSSSS
BATMAN OF GOTHAM. I HAVE HEARD QUITE A BIT ABOUT YOU OVER THE YEARS.
GLAD TO HEAR IT.
YOU'RE A HARD MONSTER TO GET IN TOUCH WITH.
THIS IS NOT HOW--OR WHERE--I ENVISIONED OUR FIRST MEETING TAKING PLACE.
HOW DID YOU FIND CASTLE FRANKENSTEIN?
THE SUPER-HUMAN ADVANCED DEFENSE EXECUTIVE'S FILES AREN'T AS SECURE AS FATHER TIME THINKS.
I AM QUITE SURE MY FELLOW AGENTS ARE ON THE WAY HERE EVEN AS WE SPEAK.
I DOUBT IT.
HRRM.
I TOOK THE LIBERTY OF REMOVING AND DISABLING THE S.H.A.D.E. NET IMPLANT FROM THE BACK OF YOUR NECK BEFORE WE ARRIVED HERE.
WHAT MANNER OF SUBSTANCE ARE YOU RESTRAINING ME WITH?
JUSTICE LEAGUE PROTOTYPE--CLASSIFIED. DIDN'T THINK YOU'D COME OF YOUR OWN VOLITION.
A CORRECT ASSUMPTION...AND BY THE RENEWED APPEARANCE OF MY CREATOR'S ANCIENT LAB...
KRRKRR
KKRRK
...I TAKE IT YOU HAVE BEEN SEARCHING FOR SOMETHING.
YES.

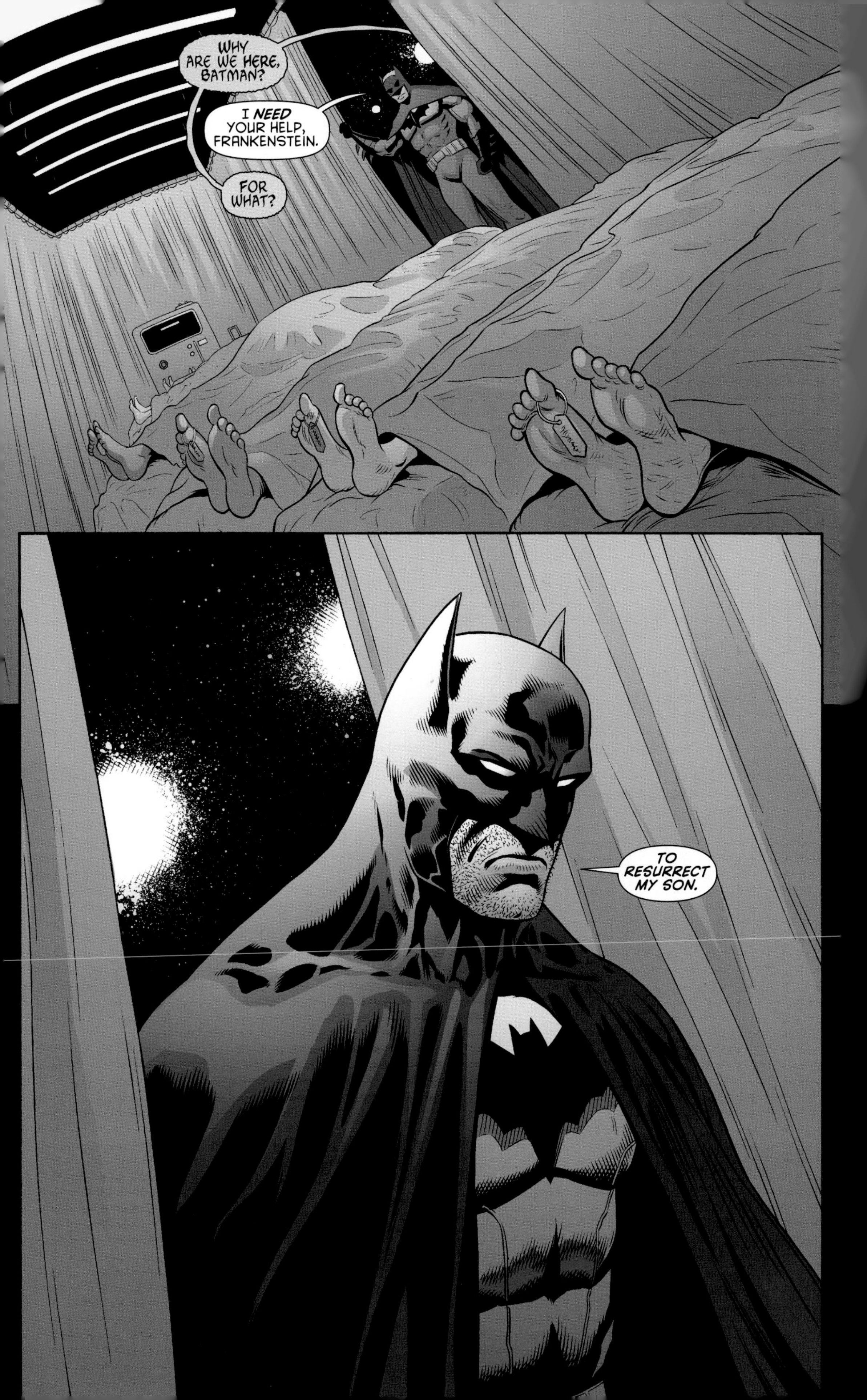
WHY ARE WE HERE, BATMAN?
I NEED YOUR HELP, FRANKENSTEIN.
FOR WHAT?
TO RESURRECT MY SON.

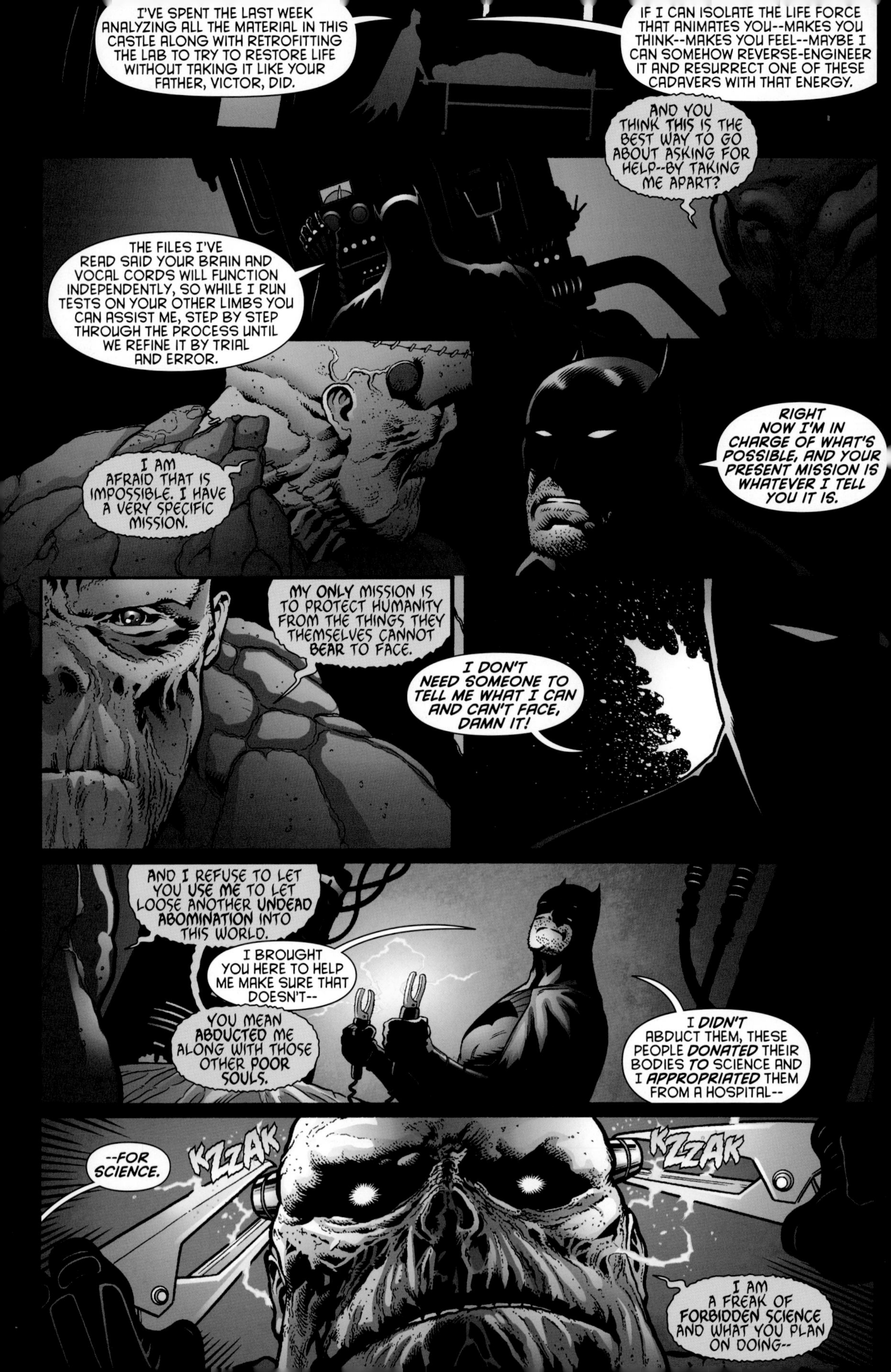

I'VE SPENT THE LAST WEEK ANALYZING ALL THE MATERIAL IN THIS CASTLE ALONG WITH RETROFITTING THE LAB TO TRY TO RESTORE LIFE WITHOUT TAKING IT LIKE YOUR FATHER, VICTOR, DID.
IF I CAN ISOLATE THE LIFE FORCE THAT ANIMATES YOU--MAKES YOU THINK--MAKES YOU FEEL--MAYBE I CAN SOMEHOW REVERSE-ENGINEER IT AND RESURRECT ONE OF THESE CADAVERS WITH THAT ENERGY.
AND YOU THINK THIS IS THE BEST WAY TO GO ABOUT ASKING FOR HELP--BY TAKING ME APART?
THE FILES I'VE READ SAID YOUR BRAIN AND VOCAL CORDS WILL FUNCTION INDEPENDENTLY, SO WHILE I RUN TESTS ON YOUR OTHER LIMBS YOU CAN ASSIST ME, STEP BY STEP THROUGH THE PROCESS UNTIL WE REFINE IT BY TRIAL AND ERROR.
I AM AFRAID THAT IS IMPOSSIBLE. I HAVE A VERY SPECIFIC MISSION.
RIGHT NOW I'M IN CHARGE OF WHAT'S POSSIBLE, AND YOUR PRESENT MISSION IS WHATEVER I TELL YOU IT IS.
MY ONLY MISSION IS TO PROTECT HUMANITY FROM THE THINGS THEY THEMSELVES CANNOT BEAR TO FACE.
I DON'T NEED SOMEONE TO TELL ME WHAT I CAN AND CAN'T FACE, DAMN IT!
AND I REFUSE TO LET YOU USE ME TO LET LOOSE ANOTHER UNDEAD ABOMINATION INTO THIS WORLD.
I BROUGHT YOU HERE TO HELP ME MAKE SURE THAT DOESN'T--
YOU MEAN ABDUCTED ME ALONG WITH THOSE OTHER POOR SOULS.
I DIDN'T ABDUCT THEM, THESE PEOPLE DONATED THEIR BODIES TO SCIENCE AND I APPROPRIATED THEM FROM A HOSPITAL--
--FOR SCIENCE.
KZZAK
KZZAK
I AM A FREAK OF FORBIDDEN SCIENCE AND WHAT YOU PLAN ON DOING--

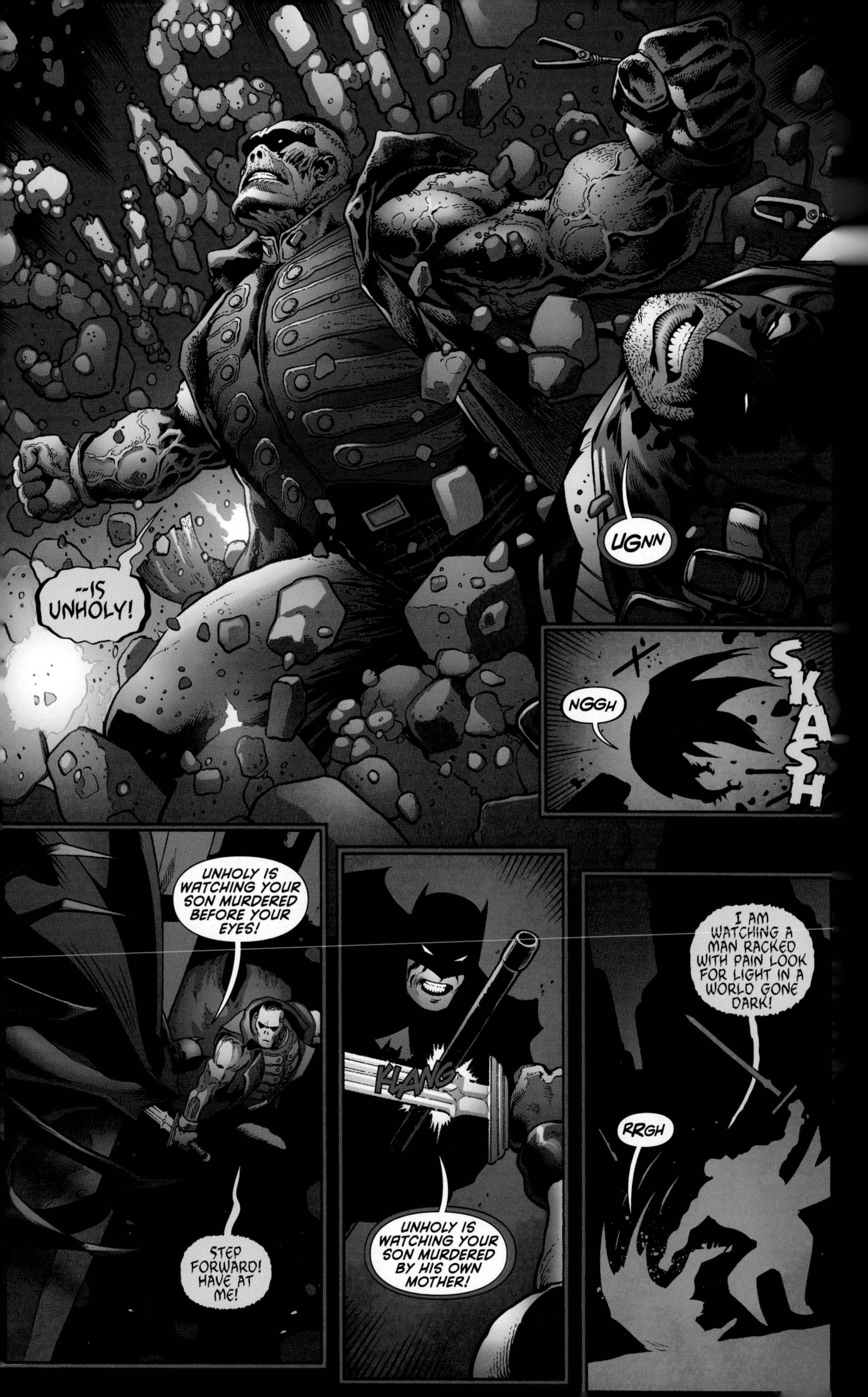
--IS UNHOLY!
UGNN
NGGH
SKASH
UNHOLY IS WATCHING YOUR SON MURDERED BEFORE YOUR EYES!
STEP FORWARD! HAVE AT ME!
KLANG
UNHOLY IS WATCHING YOUR SON MURDERED BY HIS OWN MOTHER!
I AM WATCHING A MAN RACKED WITH PAIN LOOK FOR LIGHT IN A WORLD GONE DARK!
RRGH

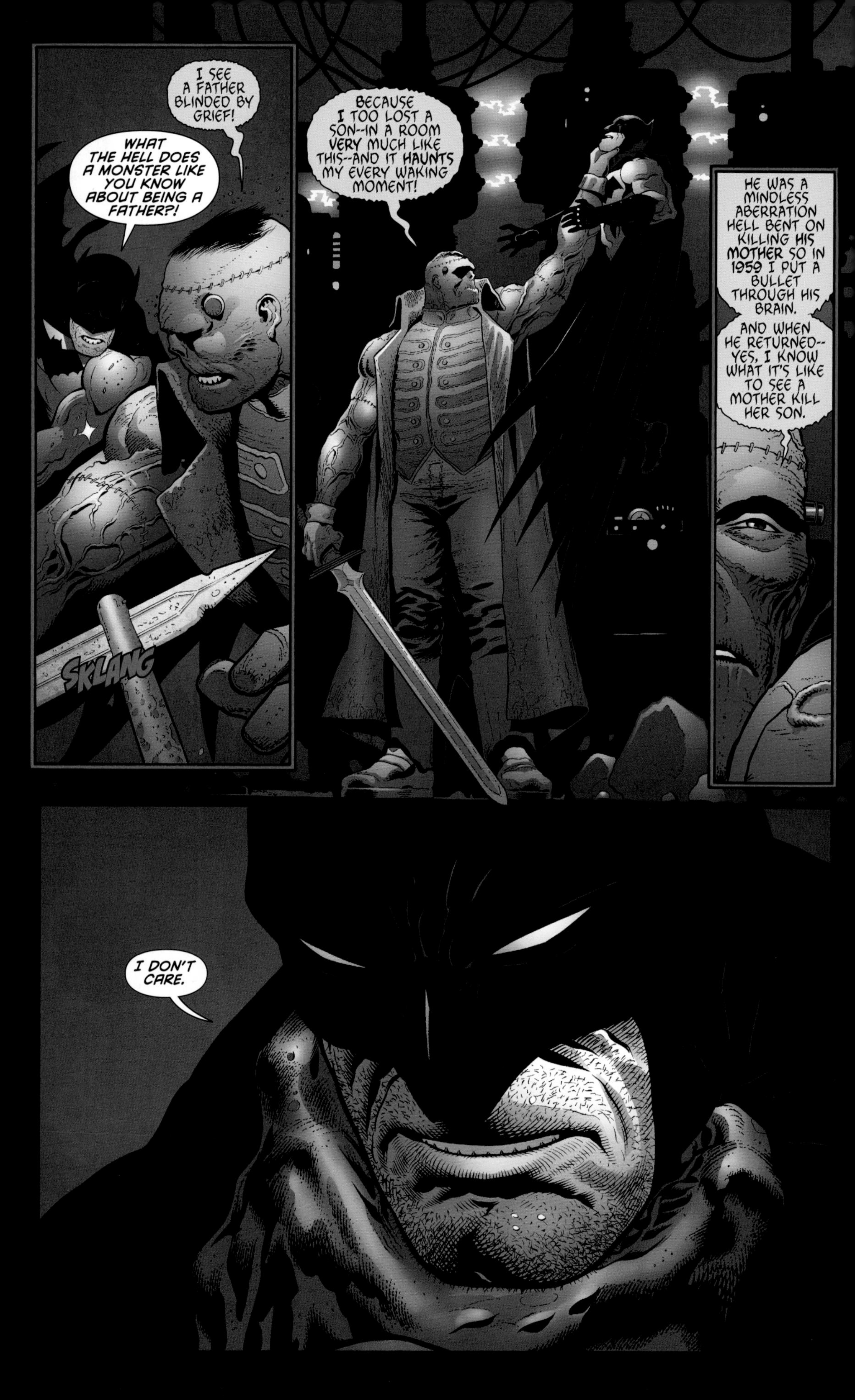
WHAT THE HELL DOES A MONSTER LIKE YOU KNOW ABOUT BEING A FATHER?!
I SEE A FATHER BLINDED BY GRIEF!
SKLANG
BECAUSE I TOO LOST A SON--IN A ROOM VERY MUCH LIKE THIS--AND IT HAUNTS MY EVERY WAKING MOMENT!
HE WAS A MINDLESS ABERRATION HELL BENT ON KILLING HIS MOTHER SO IN 1959 I PUT A BULLET THROUGH HIS BRAIN.
AND WHEN HE RETURNED--YES, I KNOW WHAT IT'S LIKE TO SEE A MOTHER KILL HER SON.
I DON'T CARE.

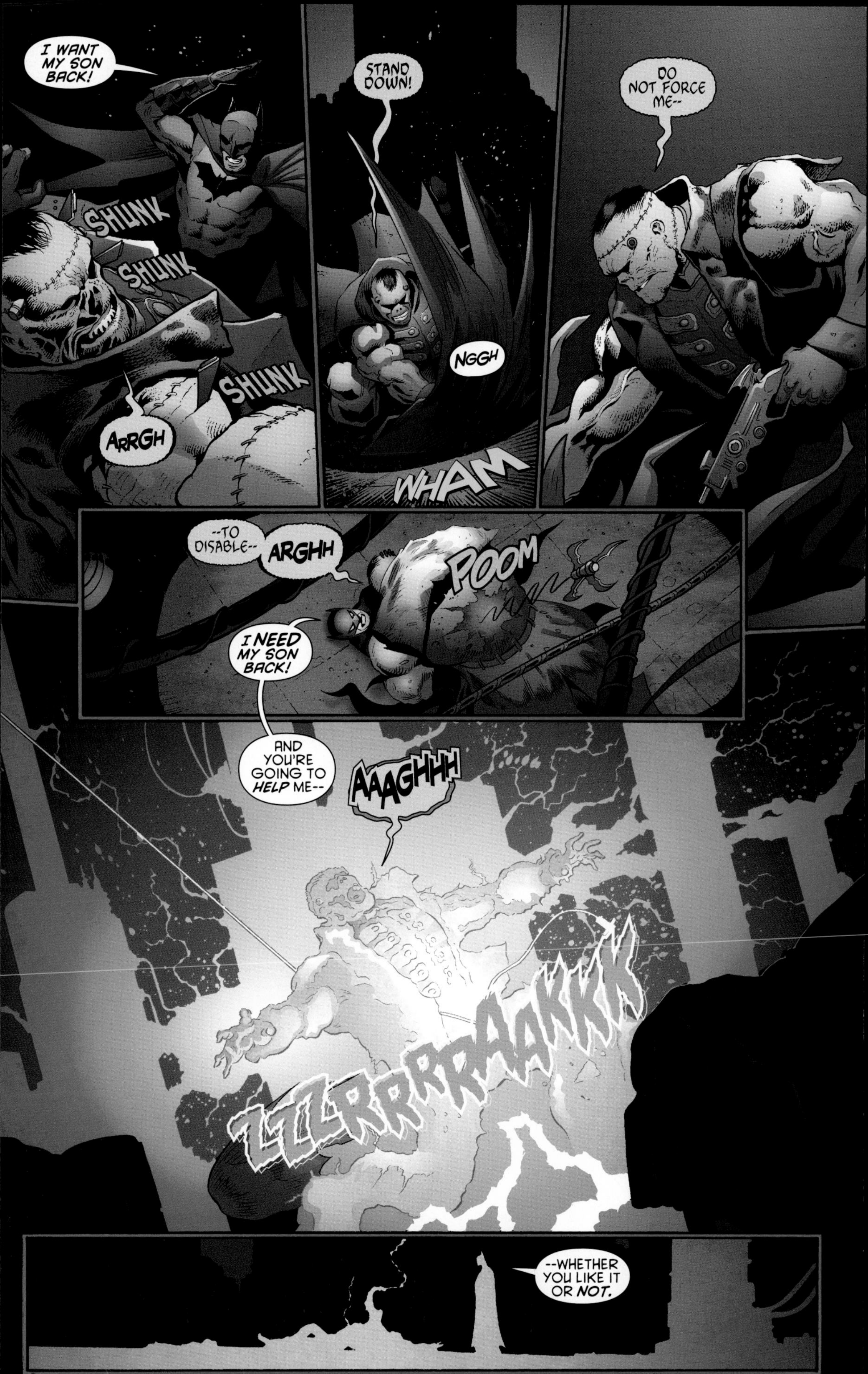
I WANT MY SON BACK!
SHUNK
SHUNK
SHUNK
ARRGH
STAND DOWN!
NGGH
WHAM
DO NOT FORCE ME--
--TO DISABLE--
ARGHH
POOM
I NEED MY SON BACK!
AND YOU'RE GOING TO HELP ME--
AAAGHHH
ZZZRRRRAAKKK
--WHETHER YOU LIKE IT OR NOT.

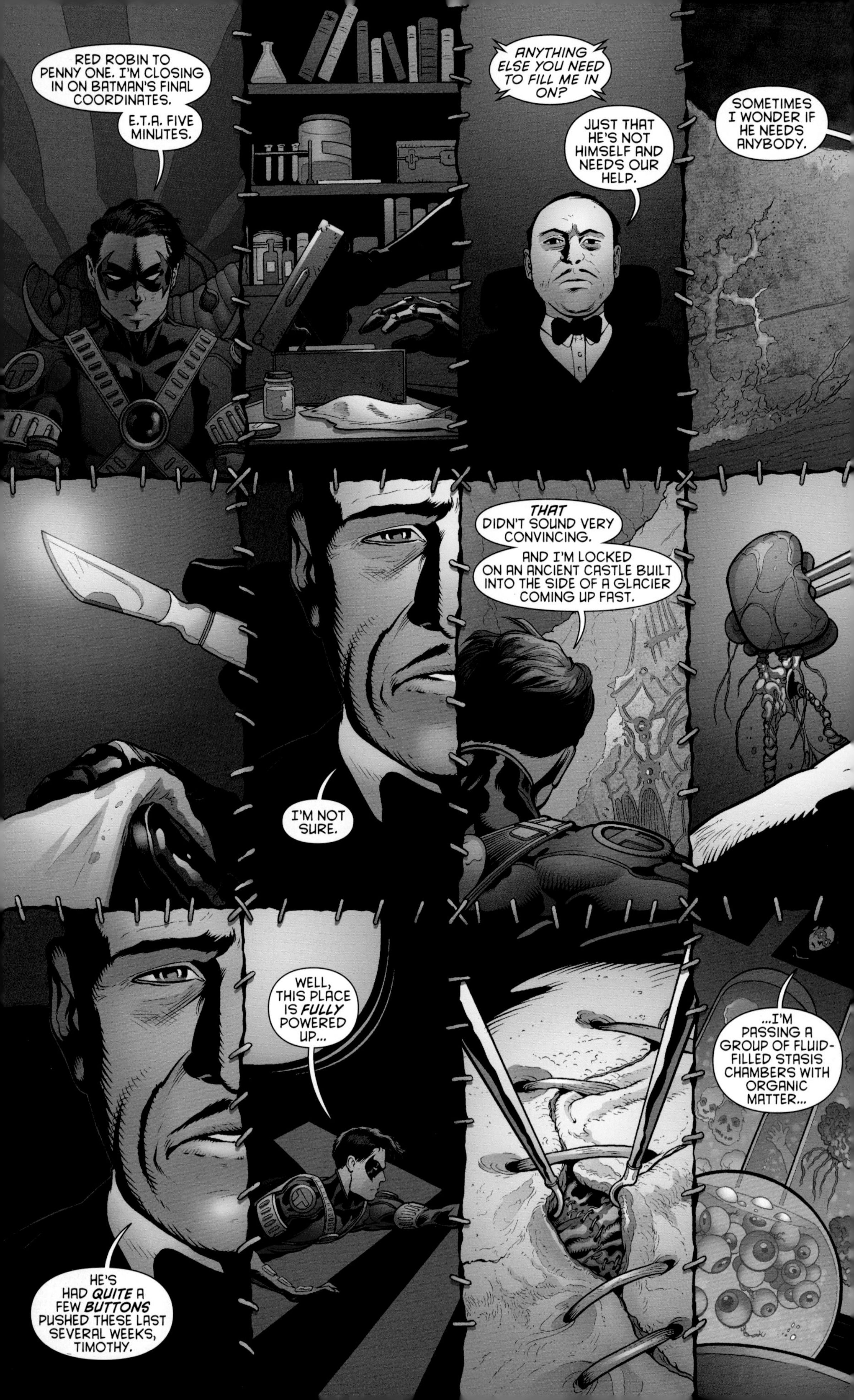
RED ROBIN TO PENNY ONE. I'M CLOSING IN ON BATMAN'S FINAL COORDINATES.
E.T.A. FIVE MINUTES.
ANYTHING ELSE YOU NEED TO FILL ME IN ON?
JUST THAT HE'S NOT HIMSELF AND NEEDS OUR HELP.
SOMETIMES I WONDER IF HE NEEDS ANYBODY.
THAT DIDN'T SOUND VERY CONVINCING.
AND I'M LOCKED ON AN ANCIENT CASTLE BUILT INTO THE SIDE OF A GLACIER COMING UP FAST.
I'M NOT SURE.
HE'S HAD QUITE A FEW BUTTONS PUSHED THESE LAST SEVERAL WEEKS, TIMOTHY.
WELL, THIS PLACE IS FULLY POWERED UP...
...I'M PASSING A GROUP OF FLUID-FILLED STASIS CHAMBERS WITH ORGANIC MATTER...

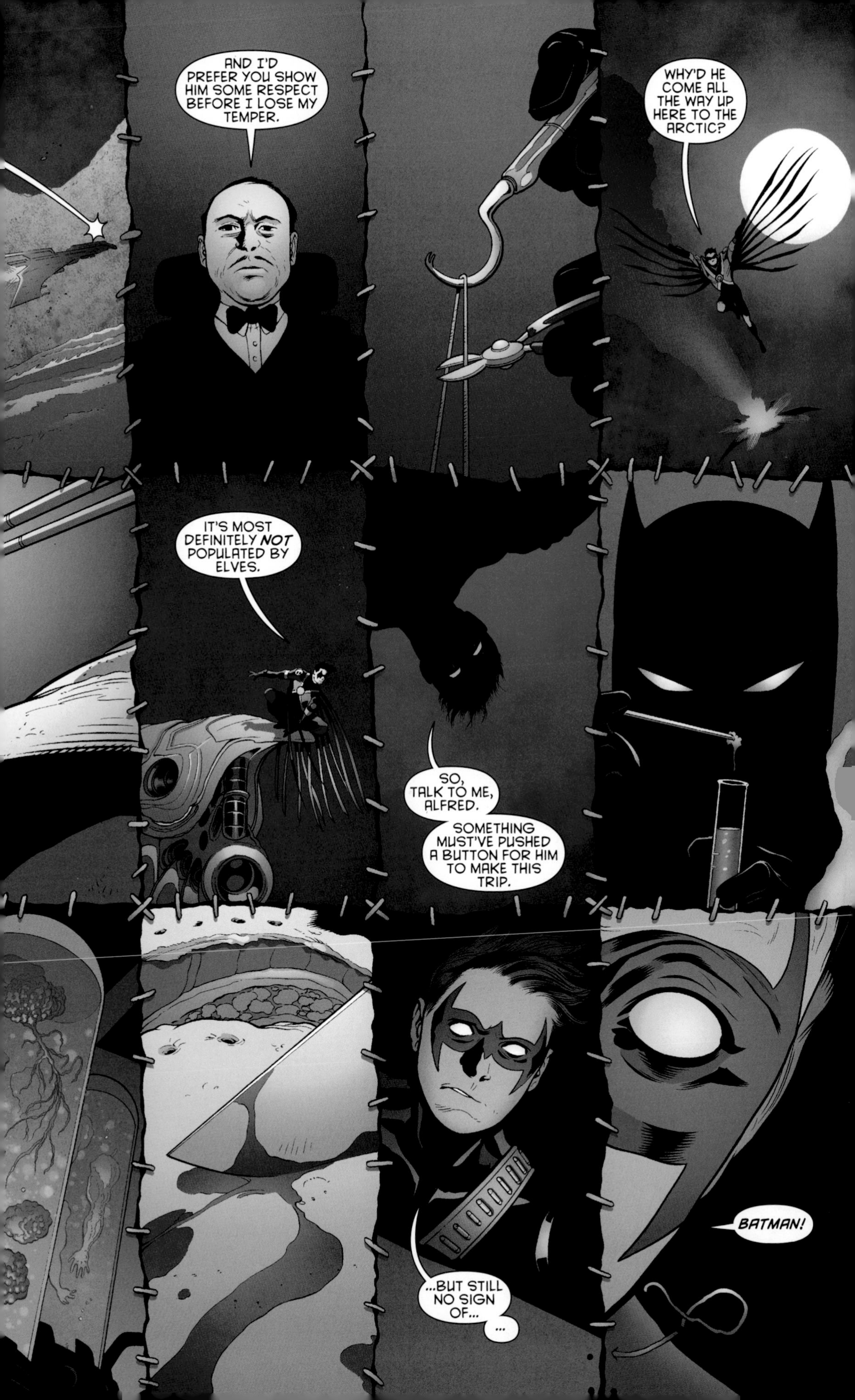
AND I'D PREFER YOU SHOW HIM SOME RESPECT BEFORE I LOSE MY TEMPER.
WHY'D HE COME ALL THE WAY UP HERE TO THE ARCTIC?
IT'S MOST DEFINITELY *NOT* POPULATED BY ELVES.
SO, TALK TO ME, ALFRED.
SOMETHING MUST'VE PUSHED A BUTTON FOR HIM TO MAKE THIS TRIP.
...BUT STILL NO SIGN OF...
...
BATMAN!

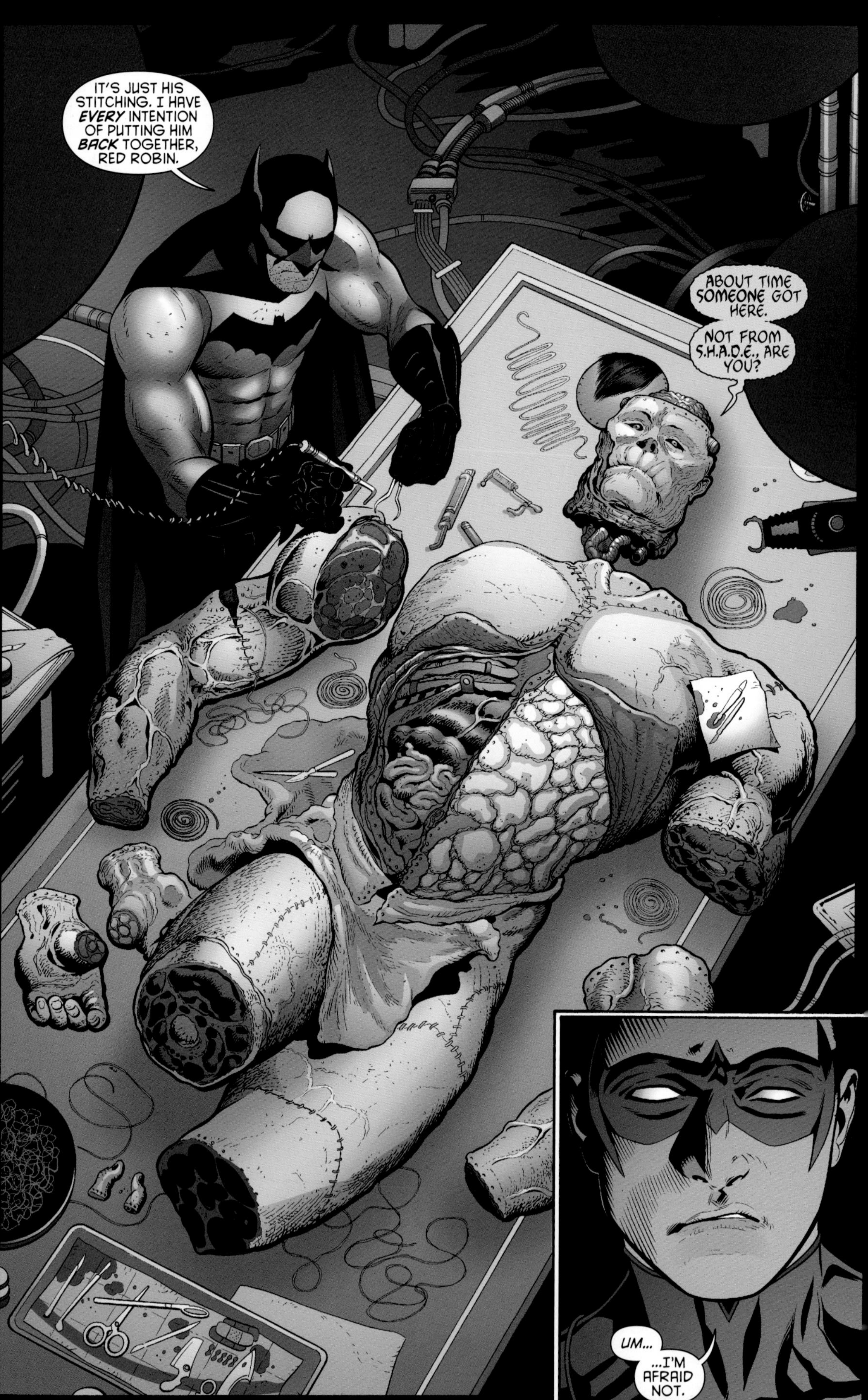
IT'S JUST HIS STITCHING. I HAVE **EVERY** INTENTION OF PUTTING HIM **BACK** TOGETHER, RED ROBIN.
ABOUT TIME SOMEONE GOT HERE.
NOT FROM S.H.A.D.E., ARE YOU?
UM...
...I'M AFRAID NOT.

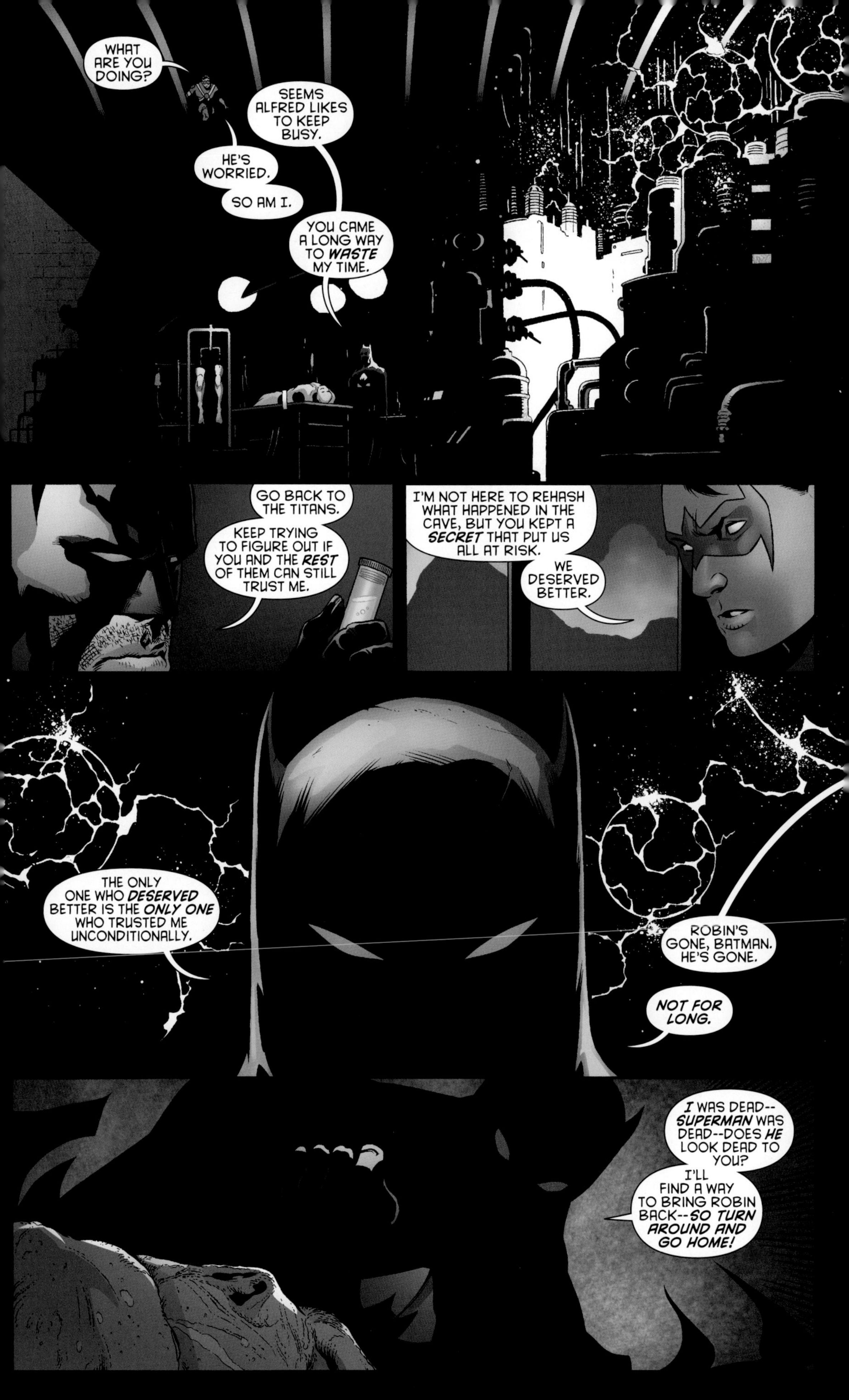
WHAT ARE YOU DOING?
SEEMS ALFRED LIKES TO KEEP BUSY.
HE'S WORRIED.
SO AM I.
YOU CAME A LONG WAY TO *WASTE* MY TIME.
GO BACK TO THE TITANS.
KEEP TRYING TO FIGURE OUT IF YOU AND THE *REST* OF THEM CAN STILL TRUST ME.
I'M NOT HERE TO REHASH WHAT HAPPENED IN THE CAVE, BUT YOU KEPT A *SECRET* THAT PUT US ALL AT RISK.
WE DESERVED BETTER.
THE ONLY ONE WHO *DESERVED* BETTER IS THE *ONLY ONE* WHO TRUSTED ME UNCONDITIONALLY.
ROBIN'S GONE, BATMAN. HE'S GONE.
NOT FOR LONG.
I WAS DEAD--*SUPERMAN* WAS DEAD--DOES *HE* LOOK DEAD TO YOU?
I'LL FIND A WAY TO BRING ROBIN BACK--*SO TURN AROUND AND GO HOME!*

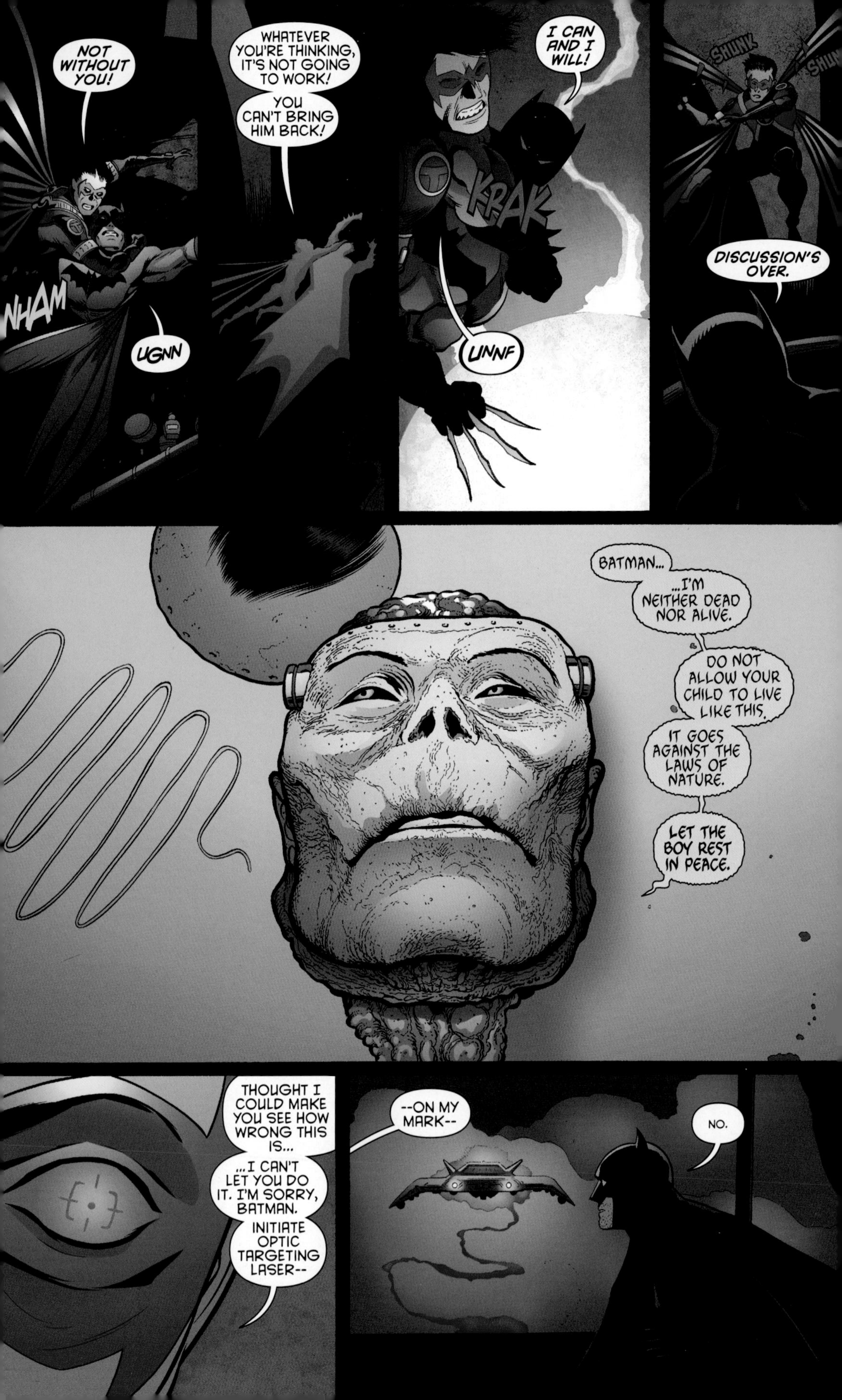
NOT WITHOUT YOU!
NHAM
UGNN
WHATEVER YOU'RE THINKING, IT'S NOT GOING TO WORK!
YOU CAN'T BRING HIM BACK!
I CAN AND I WILL!
KRAK
UNNF
SHUNK
SHUNK
DISCUSSION'S OVER.
BATMAN...
...I'M NEITHER DEAD NOR ALIVE.
DO NOT ALLOW YOUR CHILD TO LIVE LIKE THIS.
IT GOES AGAINST THE LAWS OF NATURE.
LET THE BOY REST IN PEACE.
THOUGHT I COULD MAKE YOU SEE HOW WRONG THIS IS...
...I CAN'T LET YOU DO IT. I'M SORRY, BATMAN.
INITIATE OPTIC TARGETING LASER--
--ON MY MARK--
NO.

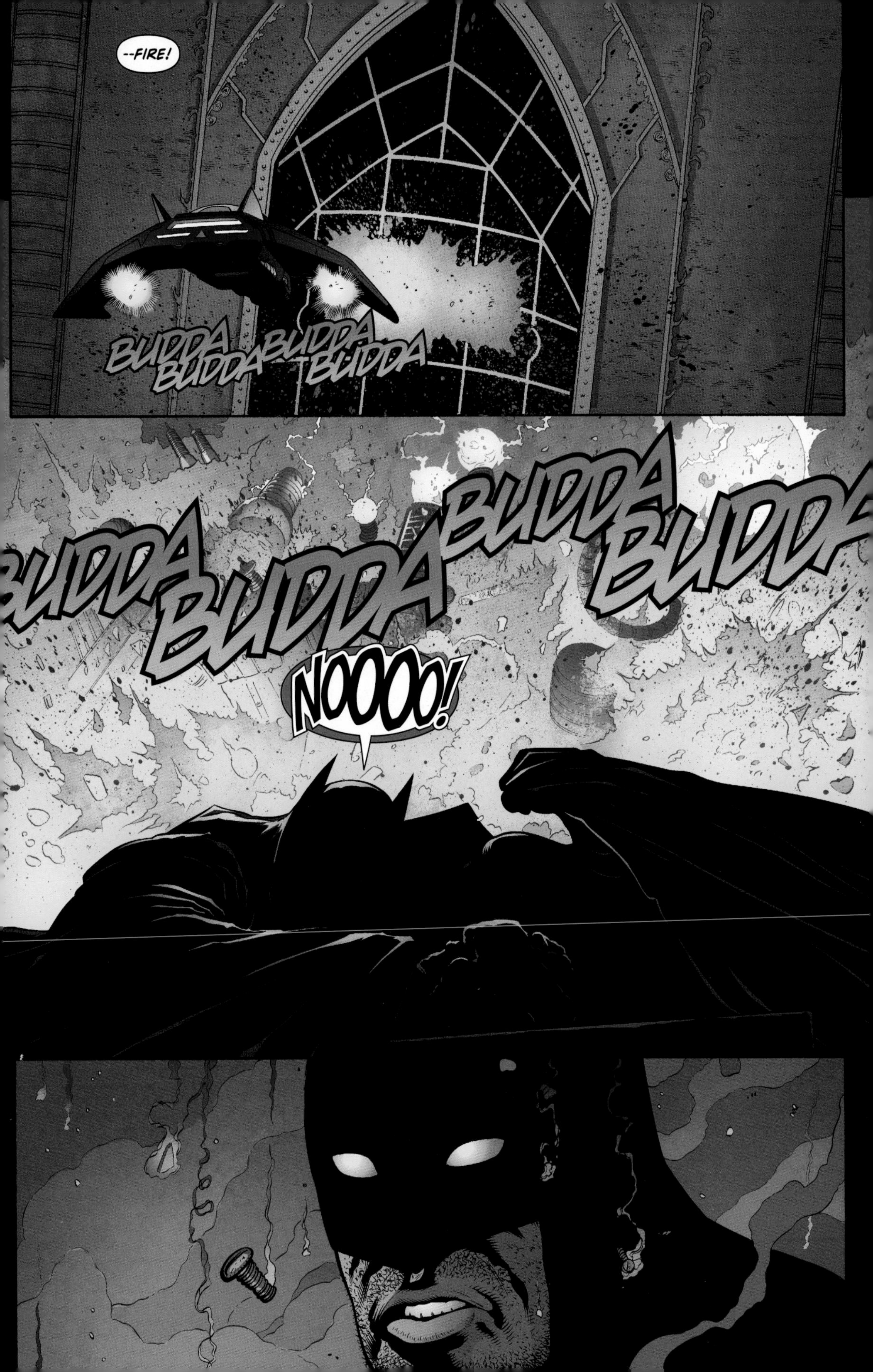
--FIRE!
BUDDA BUDDA BUDDA BUDDA
BUDDA BUDDA BUDDA BUDDA
NOOOO!

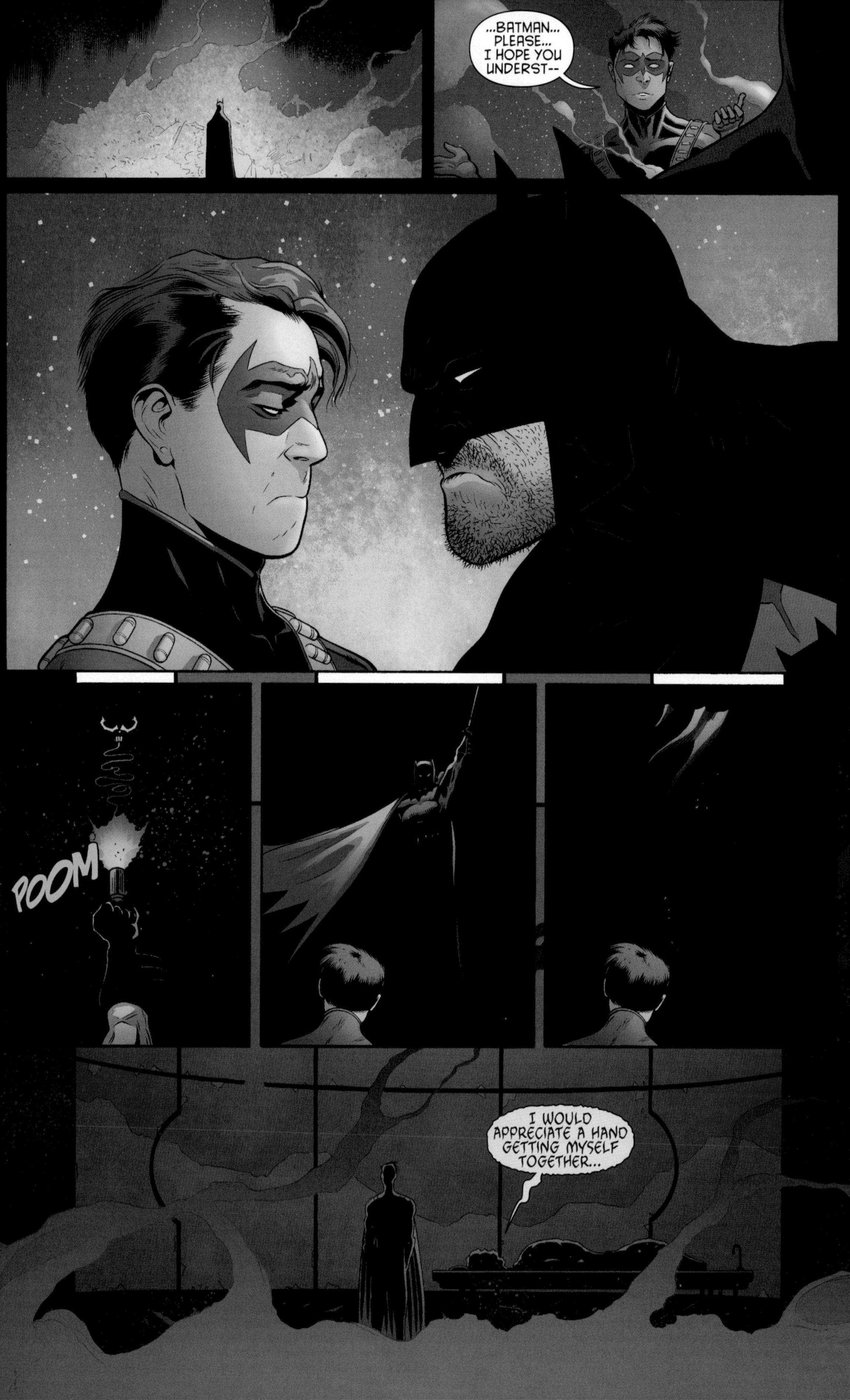
...BATMAN... PLEASE... I HOPE YOU UNDERST--
POOM
I WOULD APPRECIATE A HAND GETTING MYSELF TOGETHER...

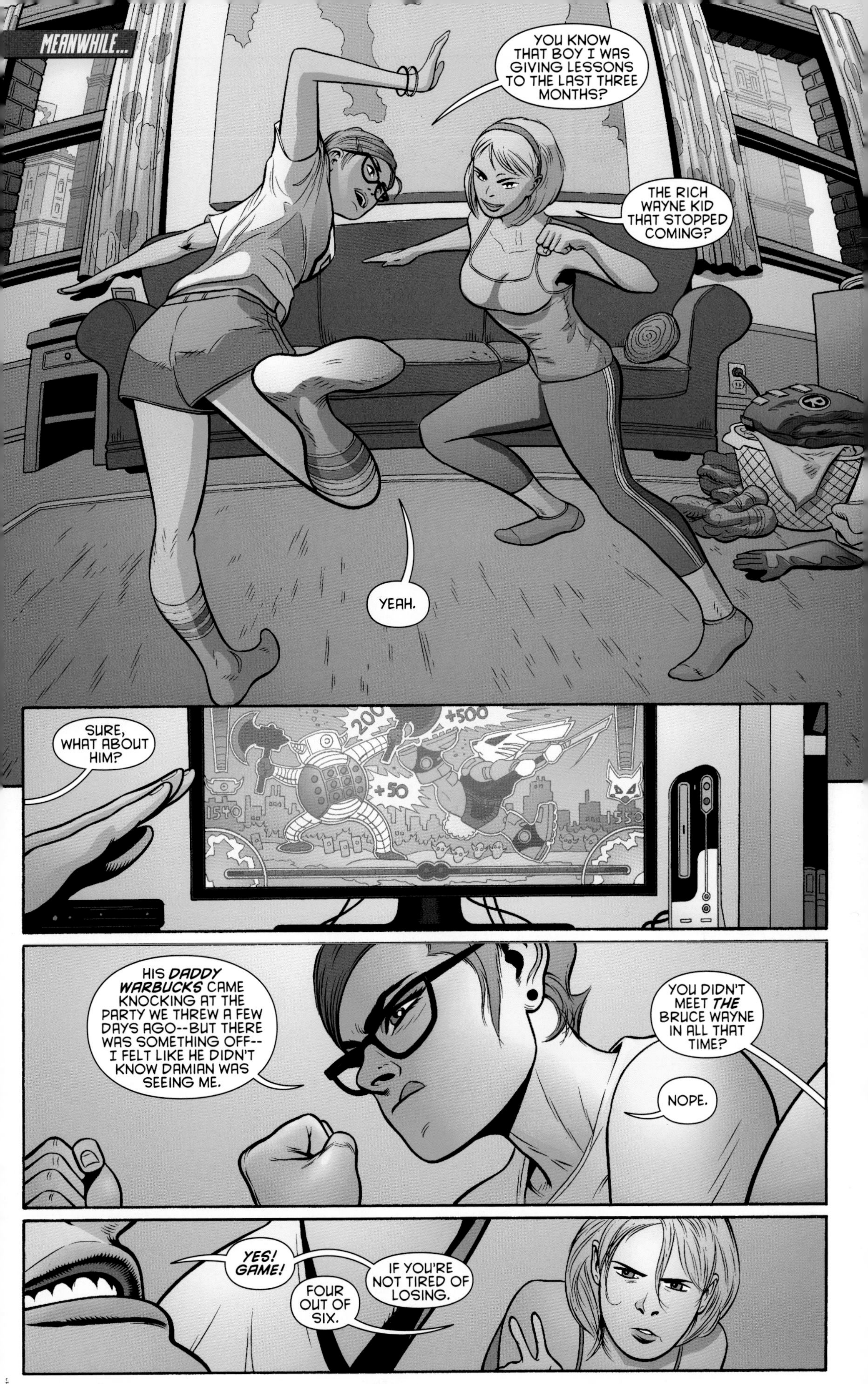
MEANWHILE...
YOU KNOW THAT BOY I WAS GIVING LESSONS TO THE LAST THREE MONTHS?
THE RICH WAYNE KID THAT STOPPED COMING?
YEAH.
SURE, WHAT ABOUT HIM?
200
+500
+50
1540
1550
HIS *DADDY WARBUCKS* CAME KNOCKING AT THE PARTY WE THREW A FEW DAYS AGO--BUT THERE WAS SOMETHING OFF-- I FELT LIKE HE DIDN'T KNOW DAMIAN WAS SEEING ME.
YOU DIDN'T MEET *THE* BRUCE WAYNE IN ALL THAT TIME?
NOPE.
YES! GAME!
IF YOU'RE NOT TIRED OF LOSING.
FOUR OUT OF SIX.

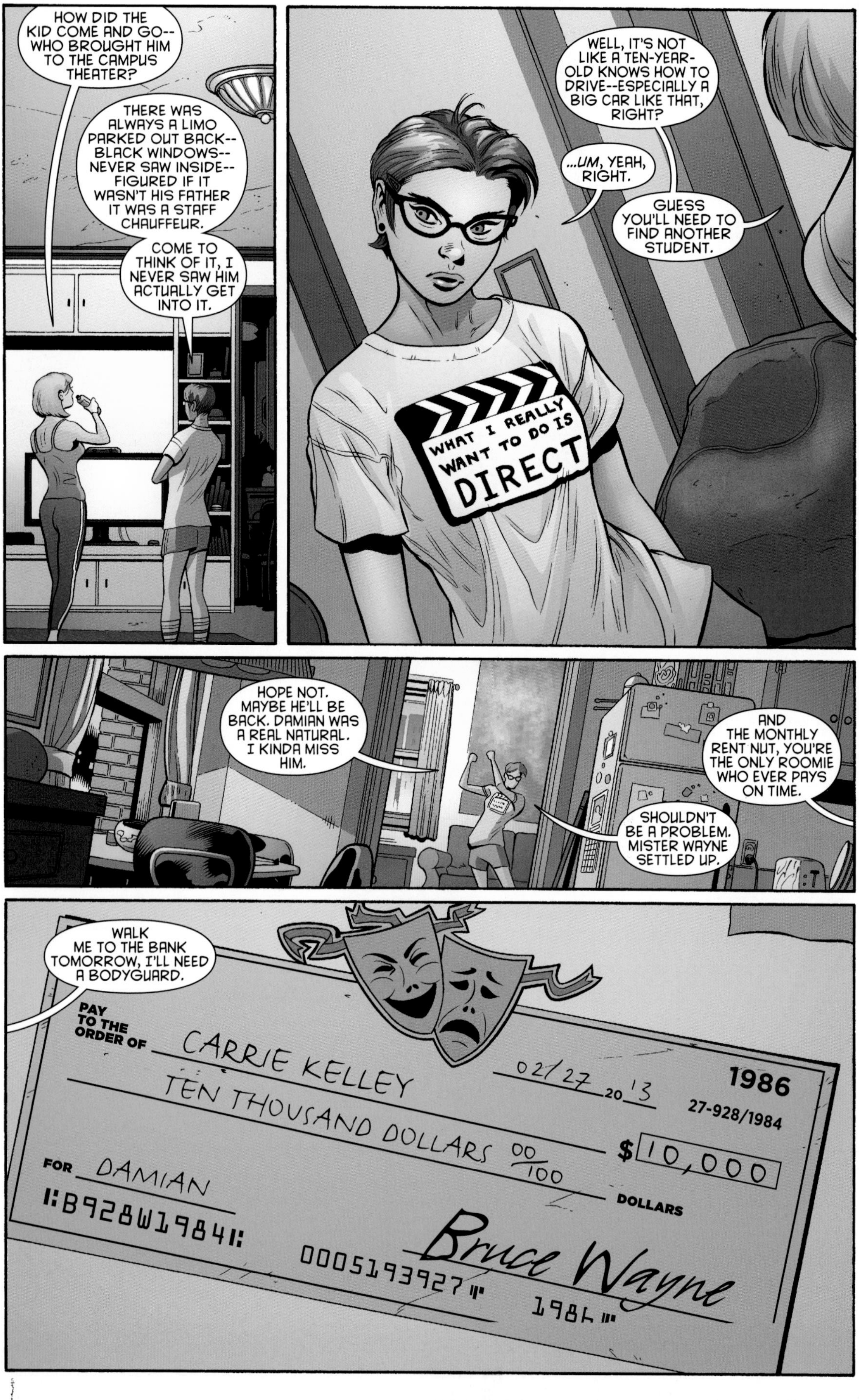
HOW DID THE KID COME AND GO--WHO BROUGHT HIM TO THE CAMPUS THEATER?
THERE WAS ALWAYS A LIMO PARKED OUT BACK--BLACK WINDOWS--NEVER SAW INSIDE--FIGURED IF IT WASN'T HIS FATHER IT WAS A STAFF CHAUFFEUR.
COME TO THINK OF IT, I NEVER SAW HIM ACTUALLY GET INTO IT.
WELL, IT'S NOT LIKE A TEN-YEAR-OLD KNOWS HOW TO DRIVE--ESPECIALLY A BIG CAR LIKE THAT, RIGHT?
...UM, YEAH, RIGHT.
GUESS YOU'LL NEED TO FIND ANOTHER STUDENT.
WHAT I REALLY WANT TO DO IS DIRECT
HOPE NOT. MAYBE HE'LL BE BACK. DAMIAN WAS A REAL NATURAL. I KINDA MISS HIM.
AND THE MONTHLY RENT NUT, YOU'RE THE ONLY ROOMIE WHO EVER PAYS ON TIME.
SHOULDN'T BE A PROBLEM. MISTER WAYNE SETTLED UP.
WALK ME TO THE BANK TOMORROW, I'LL NEED A BODYGUARD.
PAY TO THE ORDER OF CARRIE KELLEY
02/27 20 13
1986
27-928/1984
TEN THOUSAND DOLLARS 00/100
$ 10,000
DOLLARS
FOR DAMIAN
⑆B928W1984⑆
0005193927⑈ 1986⑈
Bruce Wayne

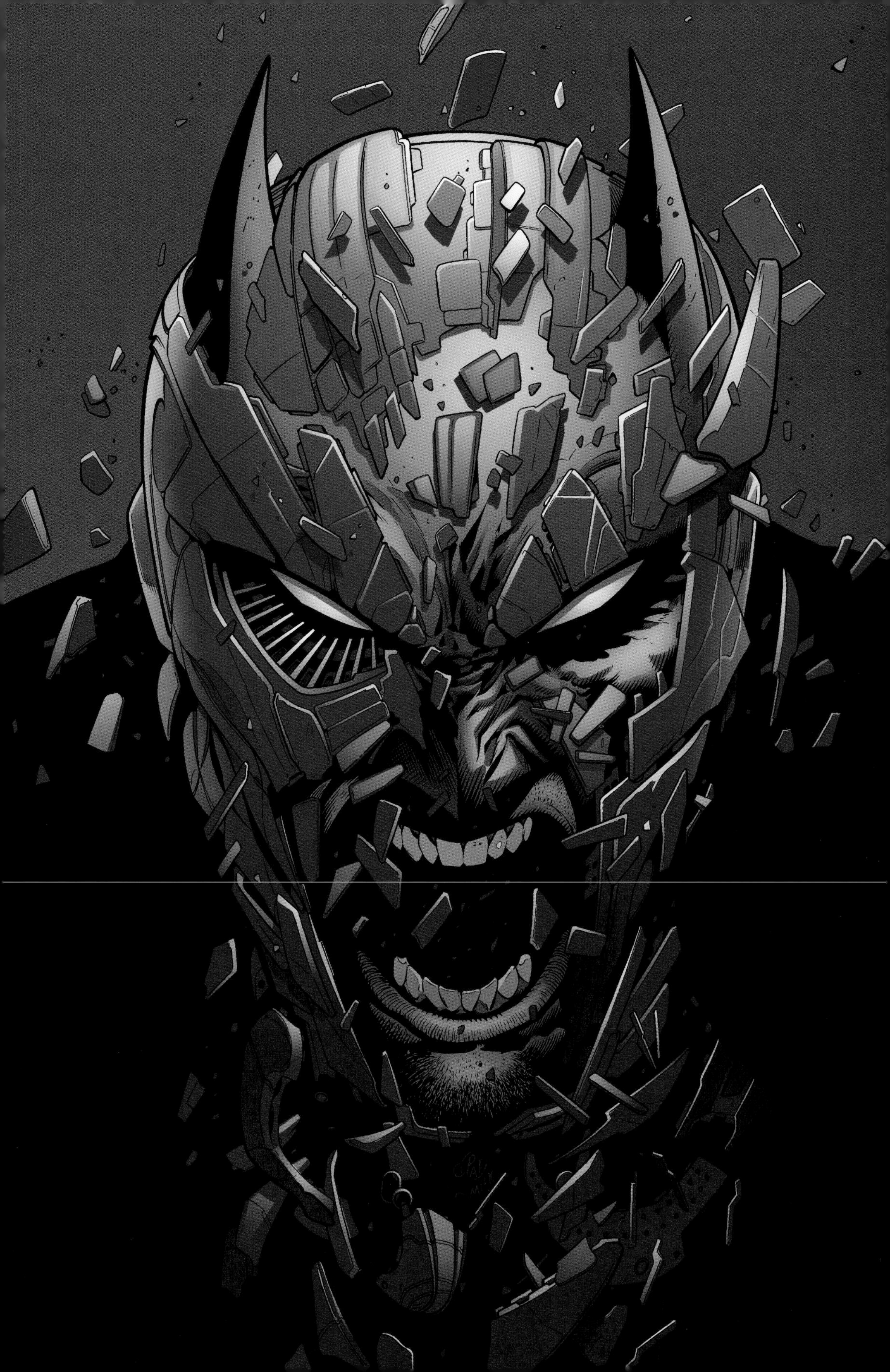

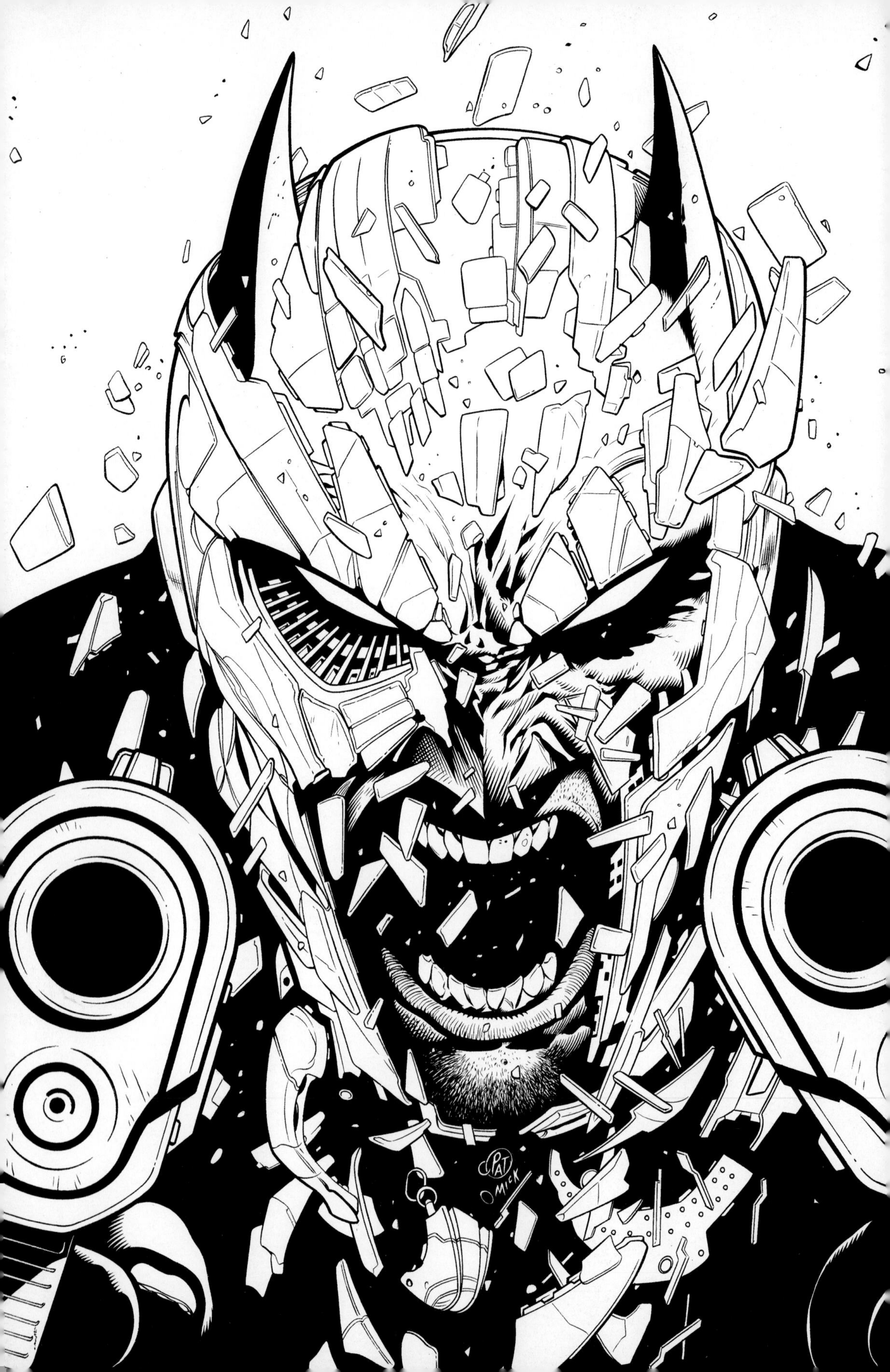

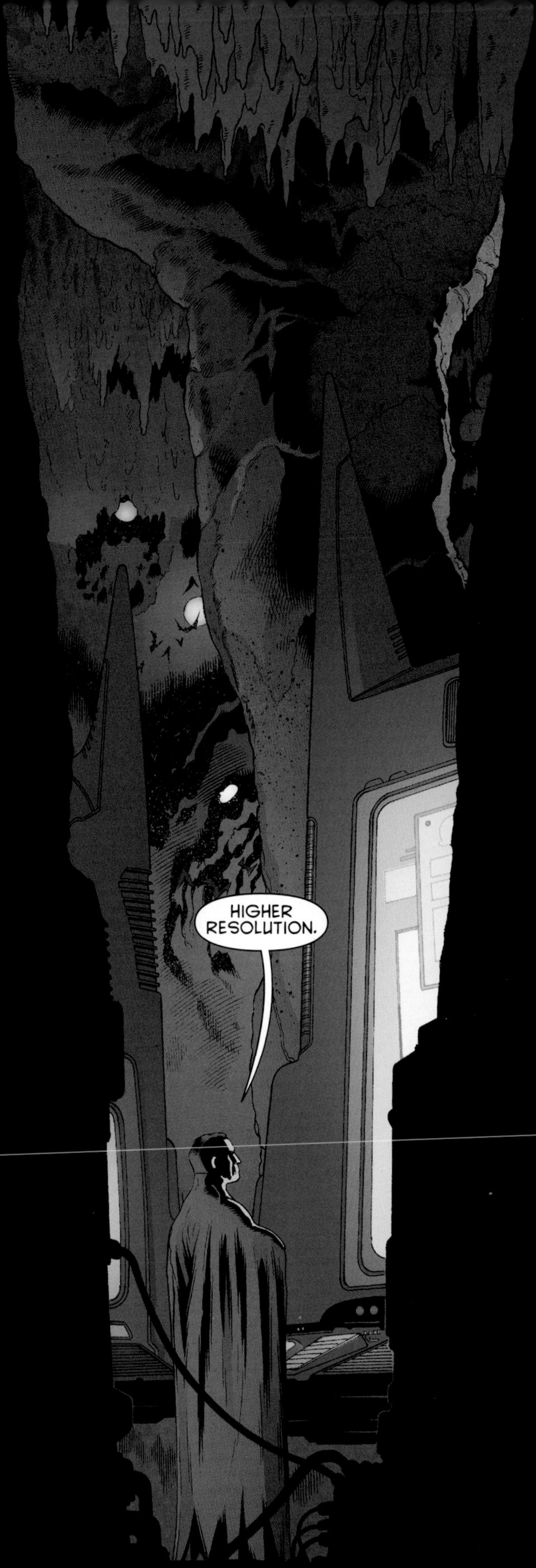
HIGHER RESOLUTION.

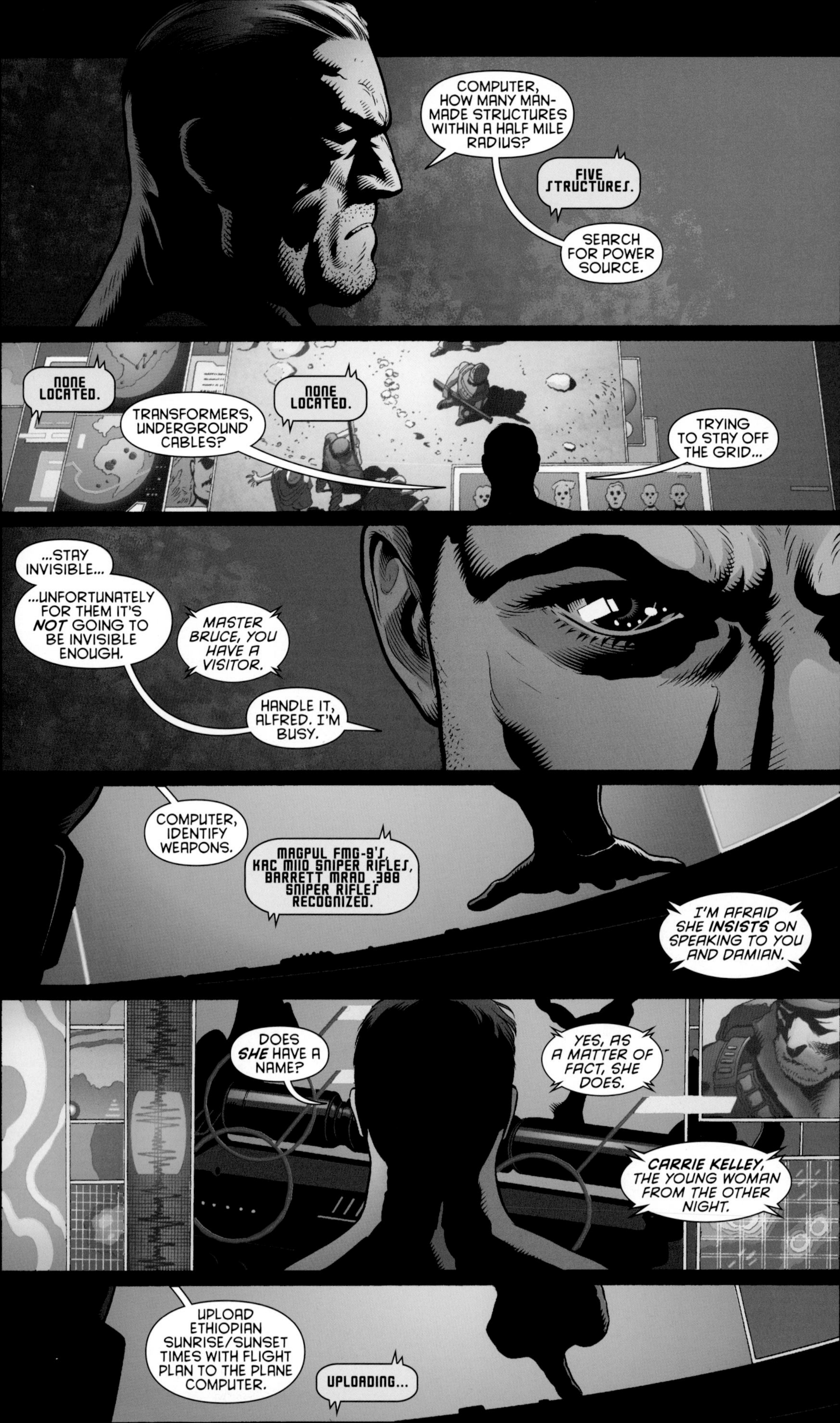
COMPUTER, HOW MANY MAN-MADE STRUCTURES WITHIN A HALF MILE RADIUS?
FIVE STRUCTURES.
SEARCH FOR POWER SOURCE.
NONE LOCATED.
TRANSFORMERS, UNDERGROUND CABLES?
NONE LOCATED.
TRYING TO STAY OFF THE GRID...
...STAY INVISIBLE...
...UNFORTUNATELY FOR THEM IT'S NOT GOING TO BE INVISIBLE ENOUGH.
MASTER BRUCE, YOU HAVE A VISITOR.
HANDLE IT, ALFRED. I'M BUSY.
COMPUTER, IDENTIFY WEAPONS.
MAGPUL FMG-9'S, KAC M110 SNIPER RIFLES, BARRETT MRAD .308 SNIPER RIFLES RECOGNIZED.
I'M AFRAID SHE INSISTS ON SPEAKING TO YOU AND DAMIAN.
DOES SHE HAVE A NAME?
YES, AS A MATTER OF FACT, SHE DOES.
CARRIE KELLEY, THE YOUNG WOMAN FROM THE OTHER NIGHT.
UPLOAD ETHIOPIAN SUNRISE/SUNSET TIMES WITH FLIGHT PLAN TO THE PLANE COMPUTER.
UPLOADING...

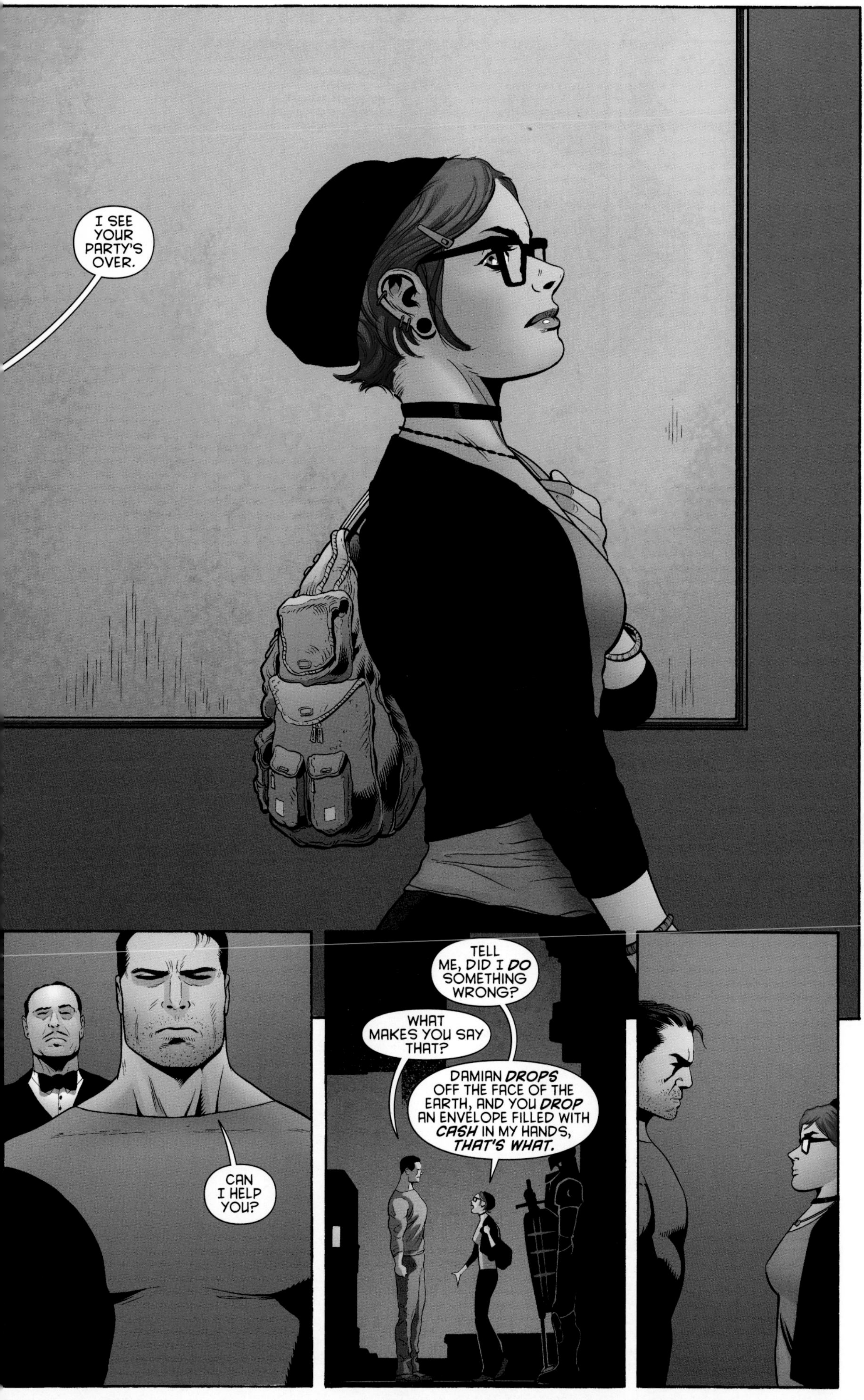
I SEE YOUR PARTY'S OVER.
CAN I HELP YOU?
TELL ME, DID I *DO* SOMETHING WRONG?
WHAT MAKES YOU SAY THAT?
DAMIAN *DROPS* OFF THE FACE OF THE EARTH, AND YOU *DROP* AN ENVELOPE FILLED WITH *CASH* IN MY HANDS, *THAT'S WHAT.*

I SEE YOU'RE **WORKING** TO KEEP YOUR CARBON FOOTPRINT SMALL.

CAN I ASK YOU SOMETHING?

SURE, WHAT?

WHY WAS DAMIAN TAKING *ACTING* LESSONS?

HE SAID HE WANTED TO SEE WHAT IT WAS LIKE BEING *SOMEONE ELSE.*

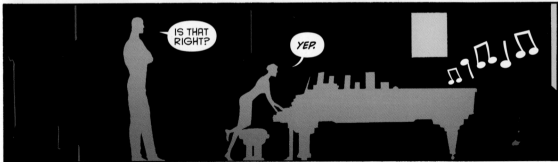

IS THAT RIGHT?

YEP.

NICE-LOOKING FAMILY.

WOW, *HOBSON'S* BEEN HERE FOREVER-- LOOK HOW *YOUNG* HE IS IN THIS ONE.

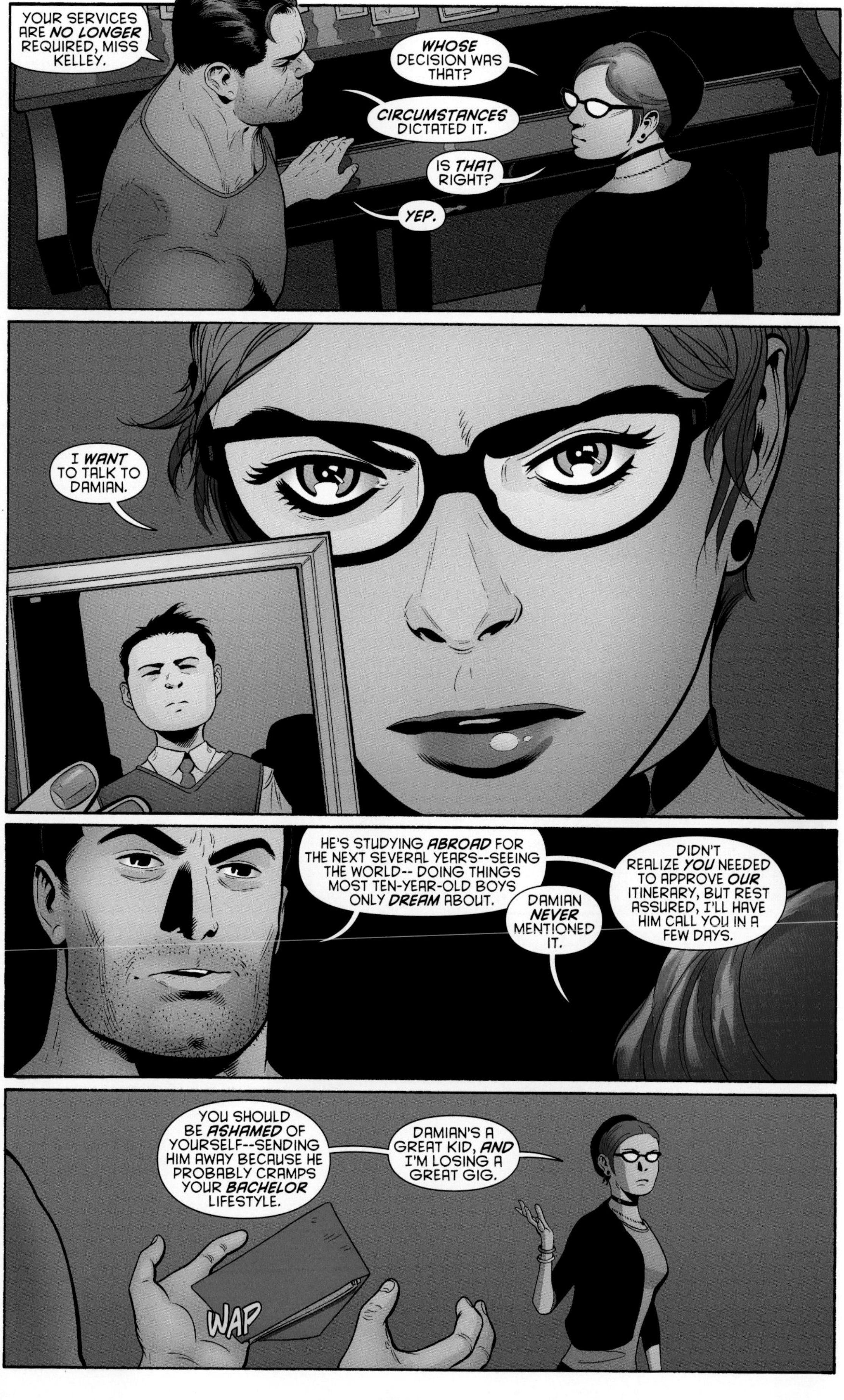
YOUR SERVICES ARE NO LONGER REQUIRED, MISS KELLEY.
WHOSE DECISION WAS THAT?
CIRCUMSTANCES DICTATED IT.
IS THAT RIGHT?
YEP.
I WANT TO TALK TO DAMIAN.
HE'S STUDYING ABROAD FOR THE NEXT SEVERAL YEARS--SEEING THE WORLD-- DOING THINGS MOST TEN-YEAR-OLD BOYS ONLY DREAM ABOUT.
DAMIAN NEVER MENTIONED IT.
DIDN'T REALIZE YOU NEEDED TO APPROVE OUR ITINERARY, BUT REST ASSURED, I'LL HAVE HIM CALL YOU IN A FEW DAYS.
YOU SHOULD BE ASHAMED OF YOURSELF--SENDING HIM AWAY BECAUSE HE PROBABLY CRAMPS YOUR BACHELOR LIFESTYLE.
DAMIAN'S A GREAT KID, AND I'M LOSING A GREAT GIG.
WAP

THIS MONEY I GAVE YOU IS FOR LESSONS OWED ALONG WITH COMPENSATING YOU FOR NOT GIVING NOTICE.

I PULLED OUT THE THOUSAND I EARNED--THE REST IS YOURS--I DON'T TAKE MONEY FOR WORK I HAVEN'T DONE, MISTER WAYNE.

RRFF

TITUS USUALLY DOESN'T TAKE TO STRANGERS VERY WELL.

"I HAVE DOGS, MY LORD, WILL ROUSE THE PROUDEST PANTHER IN THE CHASE, AND CLIMB THE HIGHEST PROMONTORY TOP."

RRRM

GREAT DANES WERE BRED TO HUNT WILD BOAR IN GERMANY OVER A THOUSAND YEARS AGO. A NICE COMBO OF AN IRISH WOLFHOUND AND ENGLISH MASTIFF.

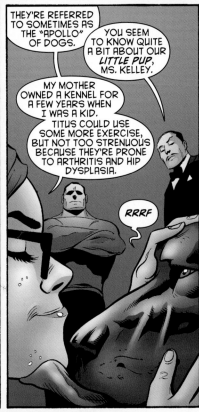

THEY'RE REFERRED TO SOMETIMES AS THE "APOLLO" OF DOGS.

YOU SEEM TO KNOW QUITE A BIT ABOUT OUR LITTLE PUP, MS. KELLEY.

MY MOTHER OWNED A KENNEL FOR A FEW YEARS WHEN I WAS A KID. TITUS COULD USE SOME MORE EXERCISE, BUT NOT TOO STRENUOUS BECAUSE THEY'RE PRONE TO ARTHRITIS AND HIP DYSPLASIA.

RRRF

ALFRED CAN HANDLE TITUS AND ALSO SHOW YOU TO THE DOOR.

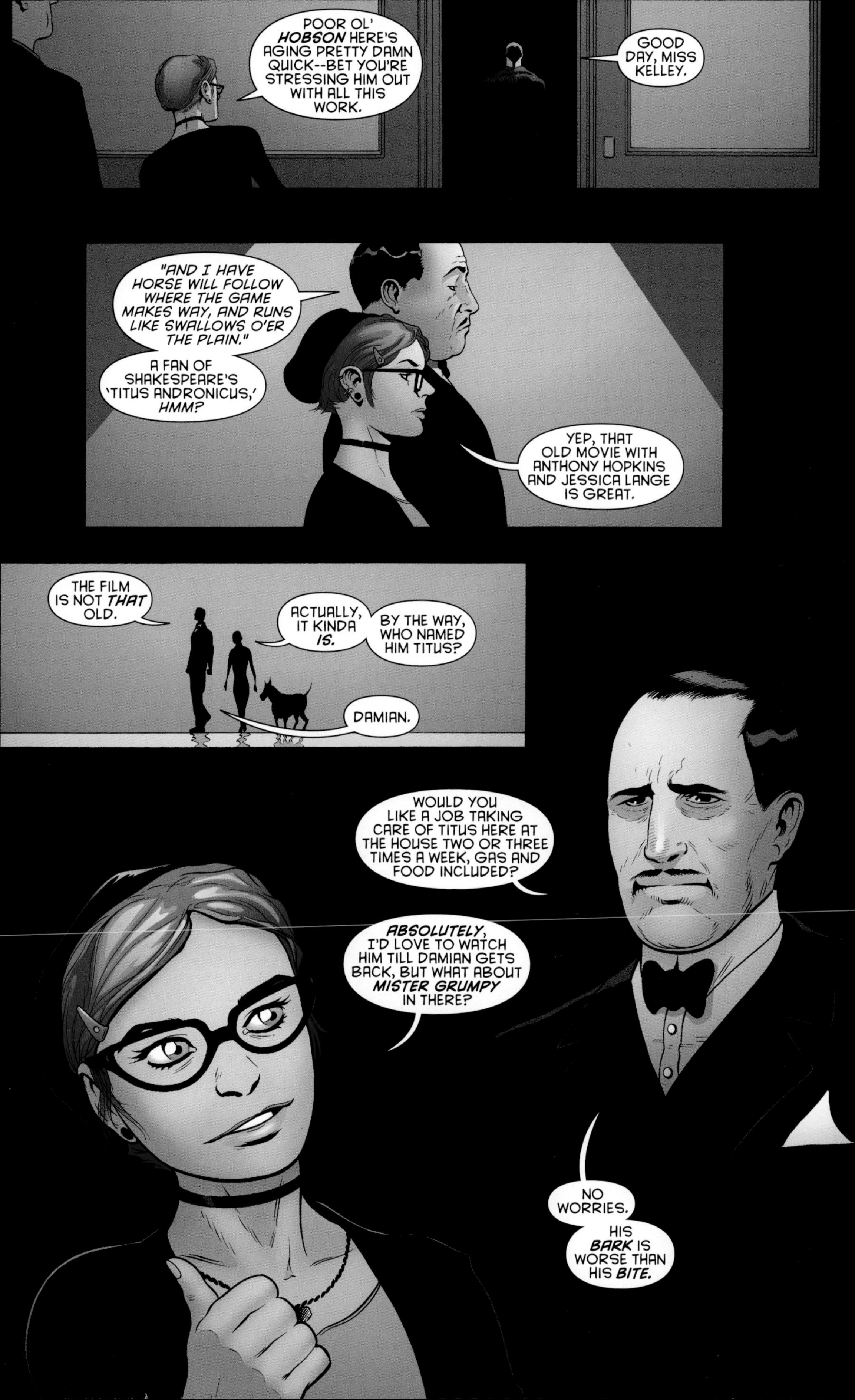
POOR OL' *HOBSON* HERE'S AGING PRETTY DAMN QUICK--BET YOU'RE STRESSING HIM OUT WITH ALL THIS WORK.
GOOD DAY, MISS KELLEY.
"AND I HAVE HORSE WILL FOLLOW WHERE THE GAME MAKES WAY, AND RUNS LIKE SWALLOWS O'ER THE PLAIN."
A FAN OF SHAKESPEARE'S 'TITUS ANDRONICUS,' *HMM?*
YEP, THAT OLD MOVIE WITH ANTHONY HOPKINS AND JESSICA LANGE IS GREAT.
THE FILM IS NOT *THAT* OLD.
ACTUALLY, IT KINDA *IS.*
BY THE WAY, WHO NAMED HIM TITUS?
DAMIAN.
WOULD YOU LIKE A JOB TAKING CARE OF TITUS HERE AT THE HOUSE TWO OR THREE TIMES A WEEK, GAS AND FOOD INCLUDED?
ABSOLUTELY, I'D LOVE TO WATCH HIM TILL DAMIAN GETS BACK, BUT WHAT ABOUT *MISTER GRUMPY* IN THERE?
NO WORRIES.
HIS *BARK* IS WORSE THAN HIS *BITE.*

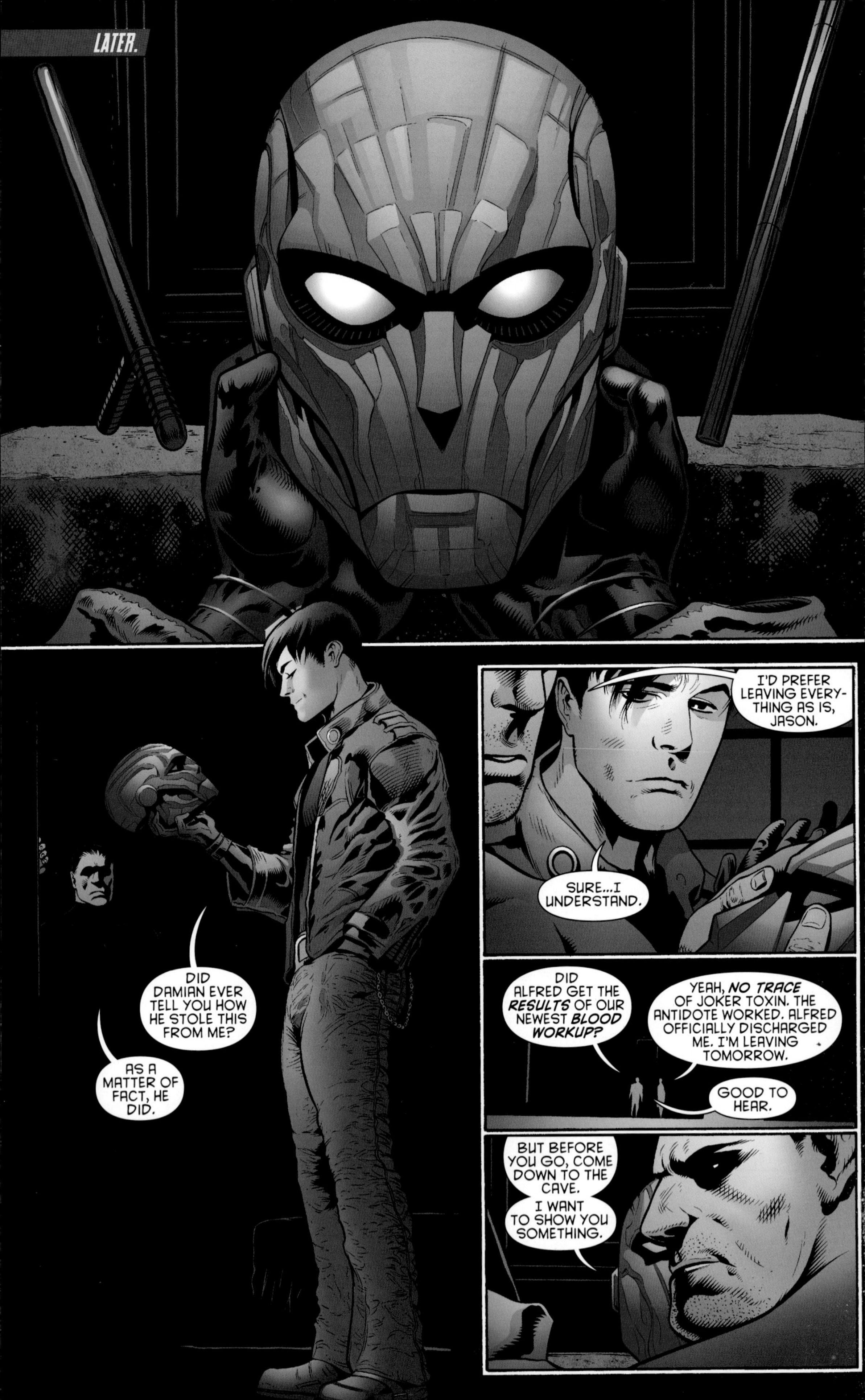
LATER.
DID DAMIAN EVER TELL YOU HOW HE STOLE THIS FROM ME?
AS A MATTER OF FACT, HE DID.
I'D PREFER LEAVING EVERY-THING AS IS, JASON.
SURE...I UNDERSTAND.
DID ALFRED GET THE RESULTS OF OUR NEWEST BLOOD WORKUP?
YEAH, NO TRACE OF JOKER TOXIN. THE ANTIDOTE WORKED. ALFRED OFFICIALLY DISCHARGED ME. I'M LEAVING TOMORROW.
GOOD TO HEAR.
BUT BEFORE YOU GO, COME DOWN TO THE CAVE.
I WANT TO SHOW YOU SOMETHING.

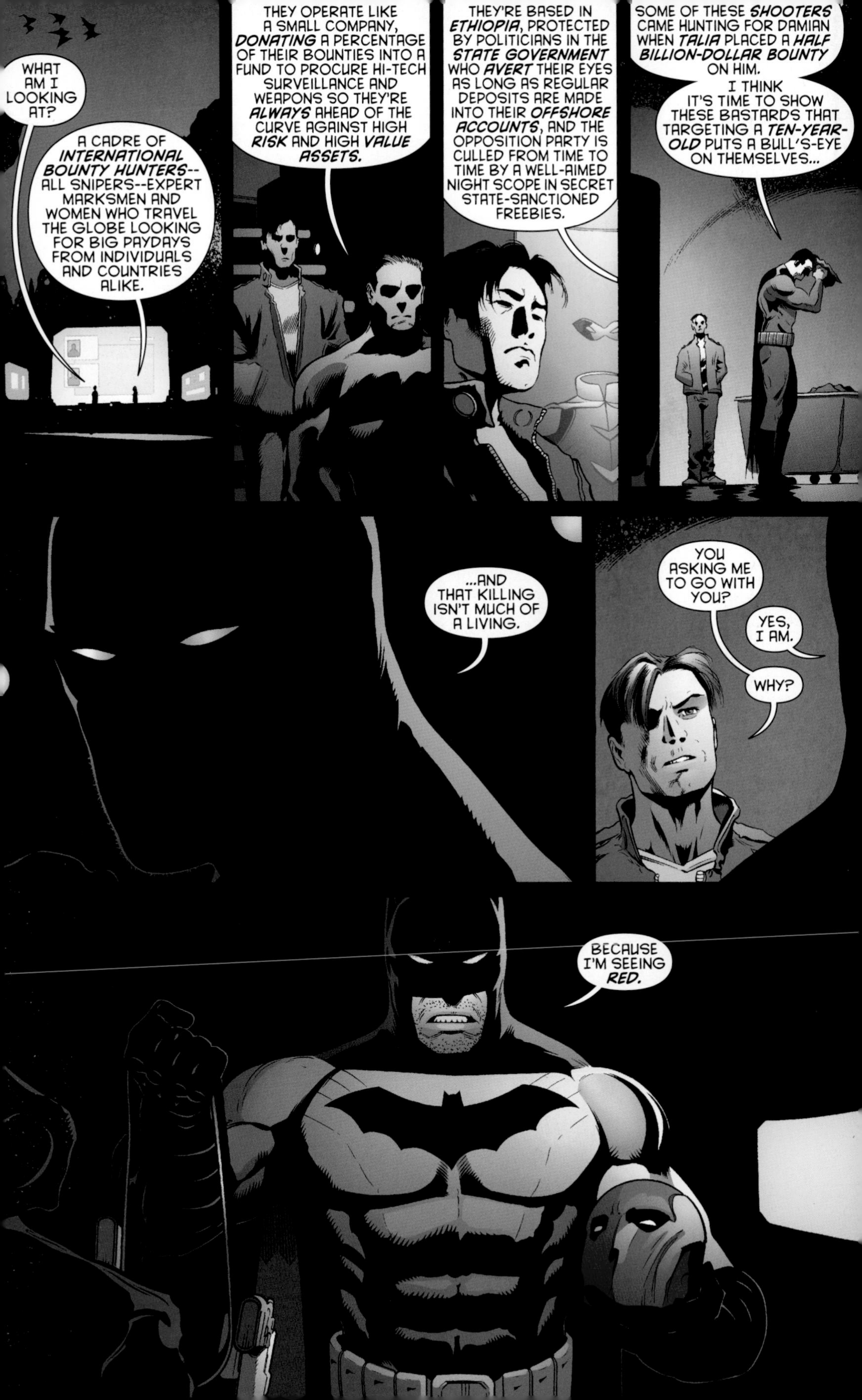
WHAT AM I LOOKING AT?
A CADRE OF INTERNATIONAL BOUNTY HUNTERS--ALL SNIPERS--EXPERT MARKSMEN AND WOMEN WHO TRAVEL THE GLOBE LOOKING FOR BIG PAYDAYS FROM INDIVIDUALS AND COUNTRIES ALIKE.
THEY OPERATE LIKE A SMALL COMPANY, DONATING A PERCENTAGE OF THEIR BOUNTIES INTO A FUND TO PROCURE HI-TECH SURVEILLANCE AND WEAPONS SO THEY'RE ALWAYS AHEAD OF THE CURVE AGAINST HIGH RISK AND HIGH VALUE ASSETS.
THEY'RE BASED IN ETHIOPIA, PROTECTED BY POLITICIANS IN THE STATE GOVERNMENT WHO AVERT THEIR EYES AS LONG AS REGULAR DEPOSITS ARE MADE INTO THEIR OFFSHORE ACCOUNTS, AND THE OPPOSITION PARTY IS CULLED FROM TIME TO TIME BY A WELL-AIMED NIGHT SCOPE IN SECRET STATE-SANCTIONED FREEBIES.
SOME OF THESE SHOOTERS CAME HUNTING FOR DAMIAN WHEN TALIA PLACED A HALF BILLION-DOLLAR BOUNTY ON HIM.
I THINK IT'S TIME TO SHOW THESE BASTARDS THAT TARGETING A TEN-YEAR-OLD PUTS A BULL'S-EYE ON THEMSELVES...
...AND THAT KILLING ISN'T MUCH OF A LIVING.
YOU ASKING ME TO GO WITH YOU?
YES, I AM.
WHY?
BECAUSE I'M SEEING RED.

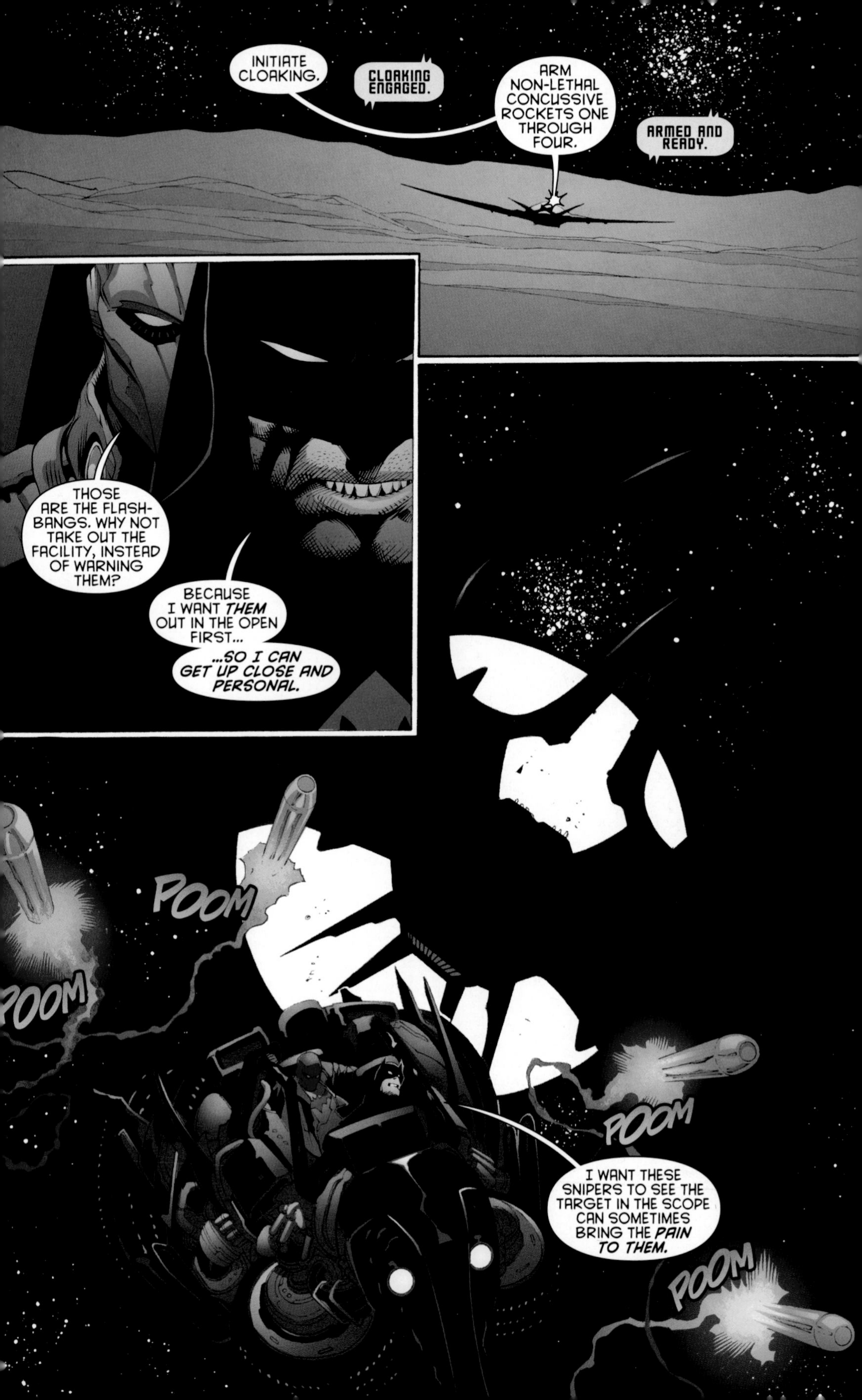
INITIATE CLOAKING.
CLOAKING ENGAGED.
ARM NON-LETHAL CONCUSSIVE ROCKETS ONE THROUGH FOUR.
ARMED AND READY.
THOSE ARE THE FLASH-BANGS. WHY NOT TAKE OUT THE FACILITY, INSTEAD OF WARNING THEM?
BECAUSE I WANT *THEM* OUT IN THE OPEN FIRST...
...SO I CAN GET UP CLOSE AND PERSONAL.
POOM
POOM
POOM
I WANT THESE SNIPERS TO SEE THE TARGET IN THE SCOPE CAN SOMETIMES BRING THE *PAIN TO THEM.*
POOM

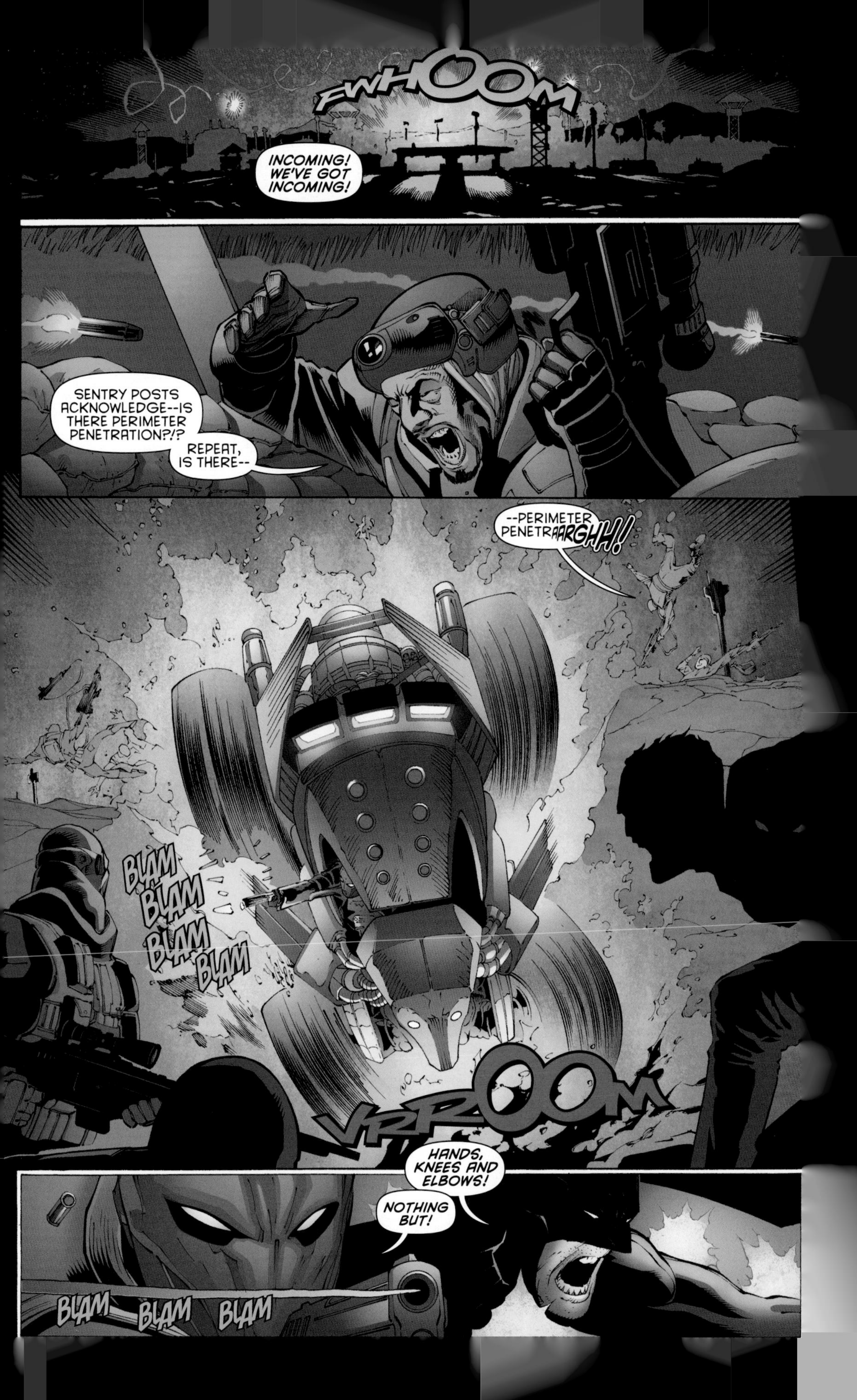
FWHOOOM
INCOMING! WE'VE GOT INCOMING!
SENTRY POSTS ACKNOWLEDGE--IS THERE PERIMETER PENETRATION?!?
REPEAT, IS THERE--
--PERIMETER PENETRAARGHH!
BLAM BLAM BLAM BLAM
VRROOOM
HANDS, KNEES AND ELBOWS!
NOTHING BUT!
BLAM BLAM BLAM

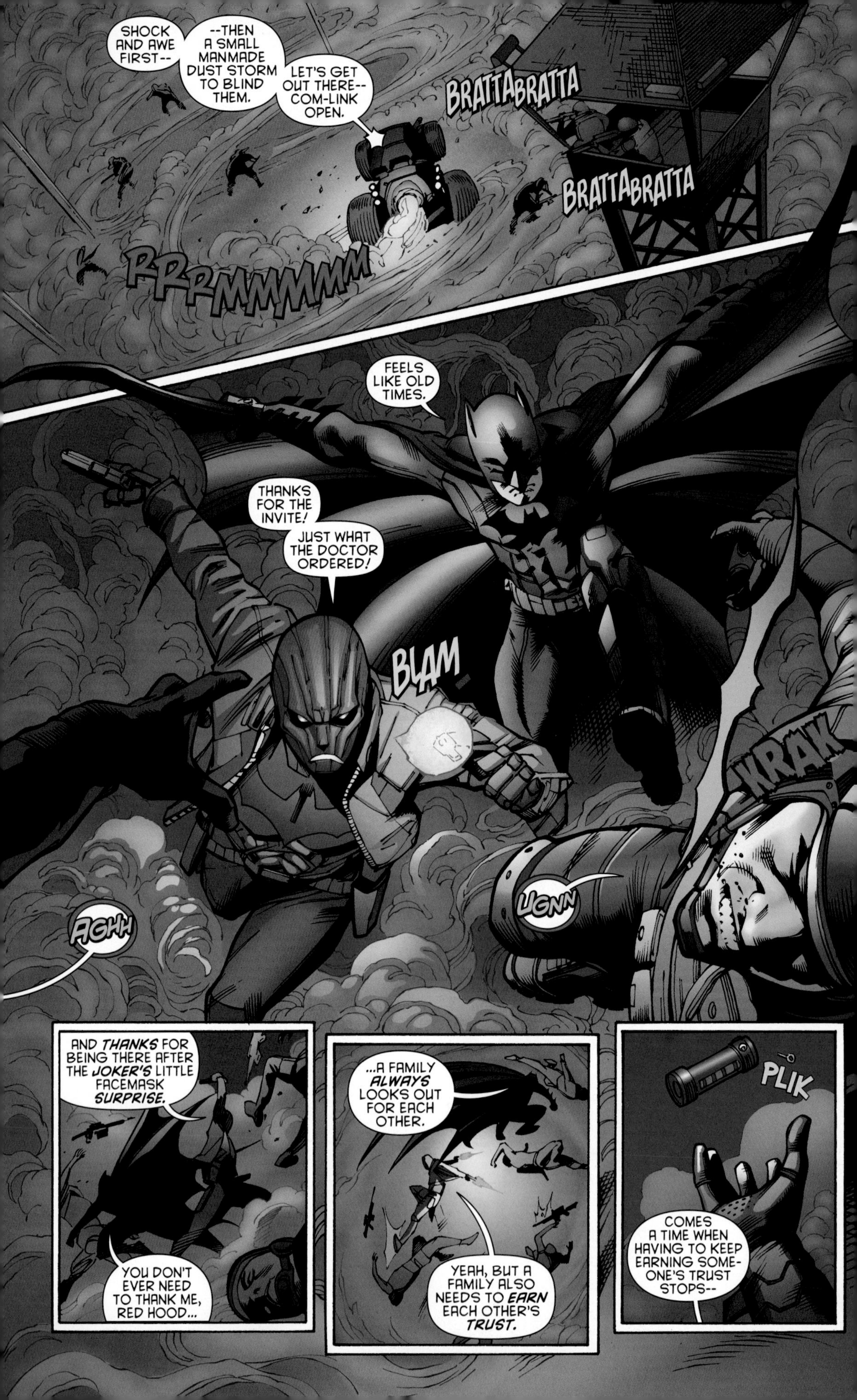
SHOCK AND AWE FIRST--
--THEN A SMALL MANMADE DUST STORM TO BLIND THEM.
LET'S GET OUT THERE-- COM-LINK OPEN.
BRATTABRATTA
BRATTABRATTA
RRRMMMMMM
FEELS LIKE OLD TIMES.
THANKS FOR THE INVITE!
JUST WHAT THE DOCTOR ORDERED!
BLAM
KRAK
UGNN
AGHH
AND THANKS FOR BEING THERE AFTER THE JOKER'S LITTLE FACEMASK SURPRISE.
YOU DON'T EVER NEED TO THANK ME, RED HOOD...
...A FAMILY ALWAYS LOOKS OUT FOR EACH OTHER.
YEAH, BUT A FAMILY ALSO NEEDS TO EARN EACH OTHER'S TRUST.
PLIK
COMES A TIME WHEN HAVING TO KEEP EARNING SOME-ONE'S TRUST STOPS--

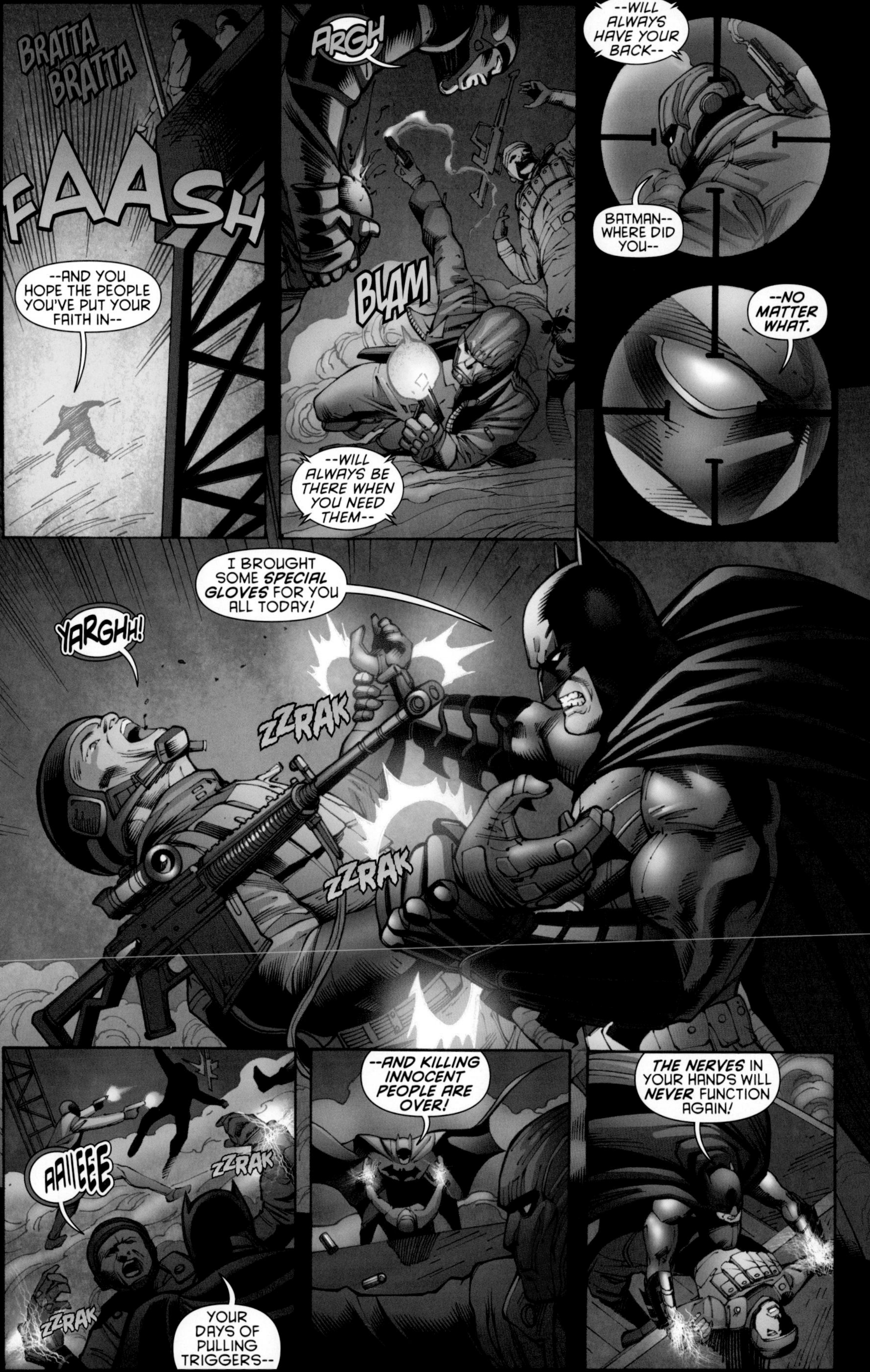
BRATTA BRATTA
FAASH
--AND YOU HOPE THE PEOPLE YOU'VE PUT YOUR FAITH IN--
ARGH
BLAM
--WILL ALWAYS BE THERE WHEN YOU NEED THEM--
--WILL ALWAYS HAVE YOUR BACK--
BATMAN-- WHERE DID YOU--
--NO MATTER WHAT.
I BROUGHT SOME SPECIAL GLOVES FOR YOU ALL TODAY!
YARGHH!
ZZRAK
ZZRAK
AAIIEEEE
ZZRAK
ZZRAK
YOUR DAYS OF PULLING TRIGGERS--
--AND KILLING INNOCENT PEOPLE ARE OVER!
THE NERVES IN YOUR HANDS WILL NEVER FUNCTION AGAIN!

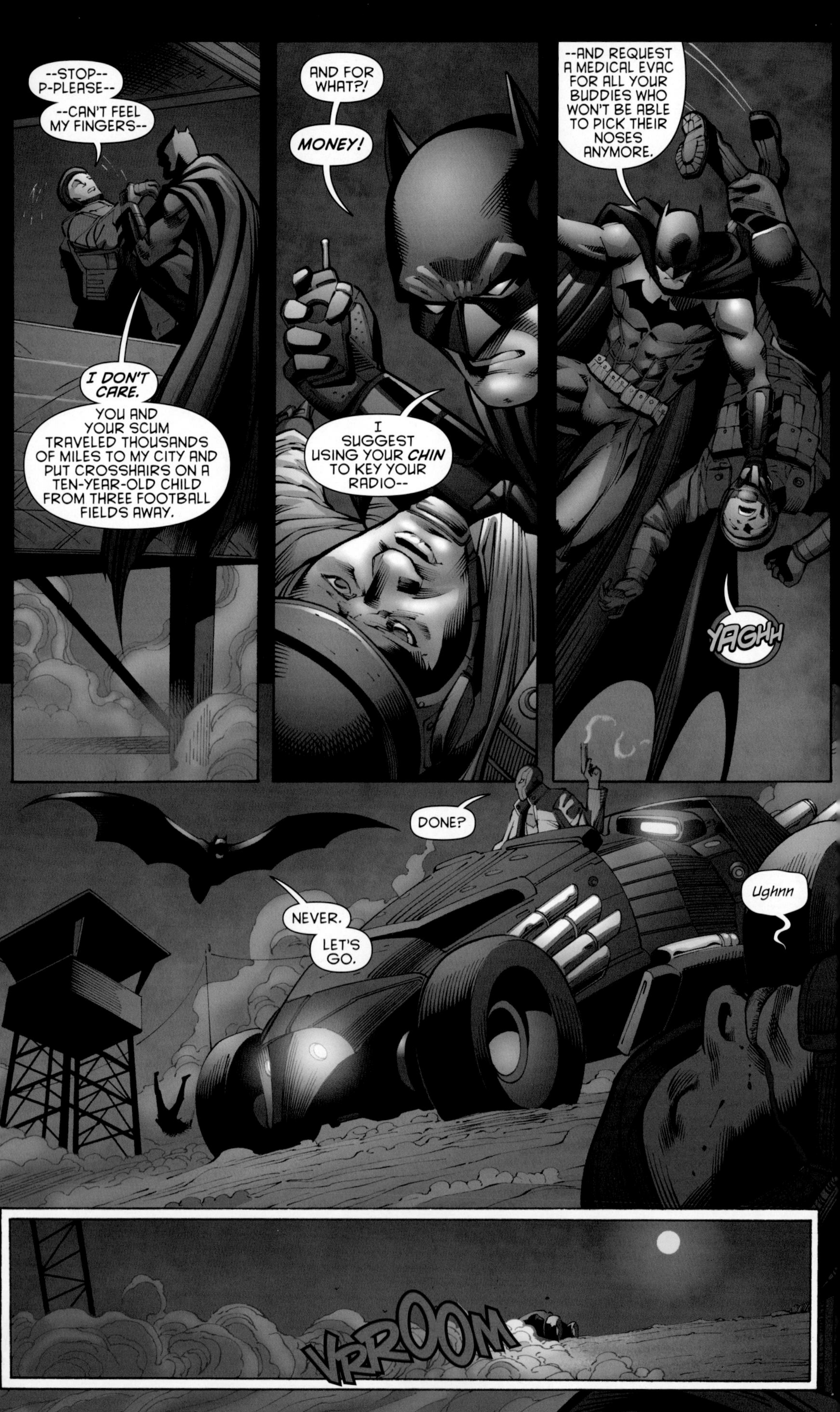

--STOP-- P-PLEASE--
--CAN'T FEEL MY FINGERS--
I DON'T CARE.
YOU AND YOUR SCUM TRAVELED THOUSANDS OF MILES TO MY CITY AND PUT CROSSHAIRS ON A TEN-YEAR-OLD CHILD FROM THREE FOOTBALL FIELDS AWAY.
AND FOR WHAT?!
MONEY!
I SUGGEST USING YOUR CHIN TO KEY YOUR RADIO--
--AND REQUEST A MEDICAL EVAC FOR ALL YOUR BUDDIES WHO WON'T BE ABLE TO PICK THEIR NOSES ANYMORE.
YAGHH
DONE?
NEVER.
LET'S GO.
Ughnn
VRROOM

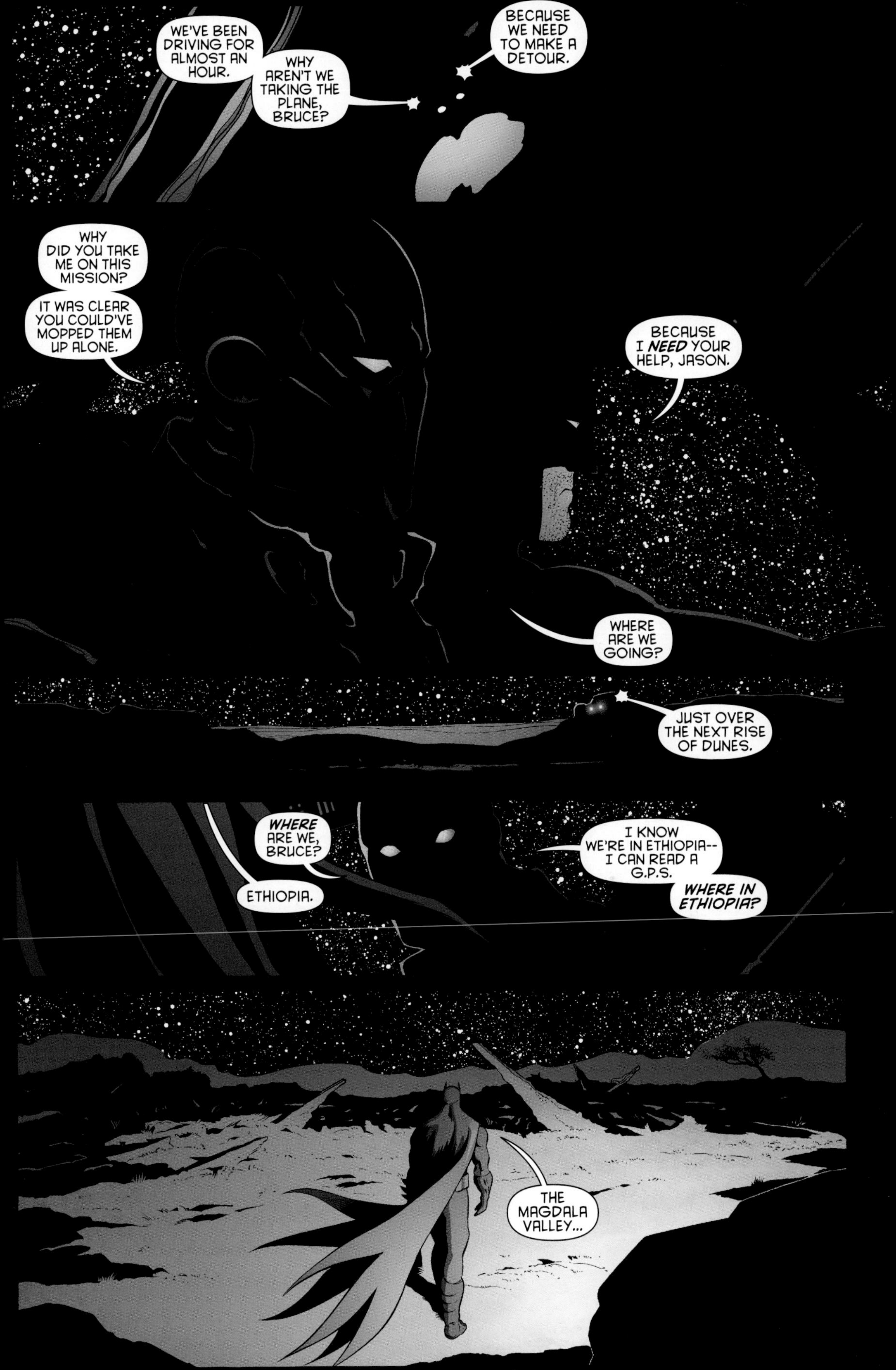

WE'VE BEEN DRIVING FOR ALMOST AN HOUR.
WHY AREN'T WE TAKING THE PLANE, BRUCE?
BECAUSE WE NEED TO MAKE A DETOUR.
WHY DID YOU TAKE ME ON THIS MISSION?
IT WAS CLEAR YOU COULD'VE MOPPED THEM UP ALONE.
BECAUSE I NEED YOUR HELP, JASON.
WHERE ARE WE GOING?
JUST OVER THE NEXT RISE OF DUNES.
WHERE ARE WE, BRUCE?
ETHIOPIA.
I KNOW WE'RE IN ETHIOPIA-- I CAN READ A G.P.S.
WHERE IN ETHIOPIA?
THE MAGDALA VALLEY...

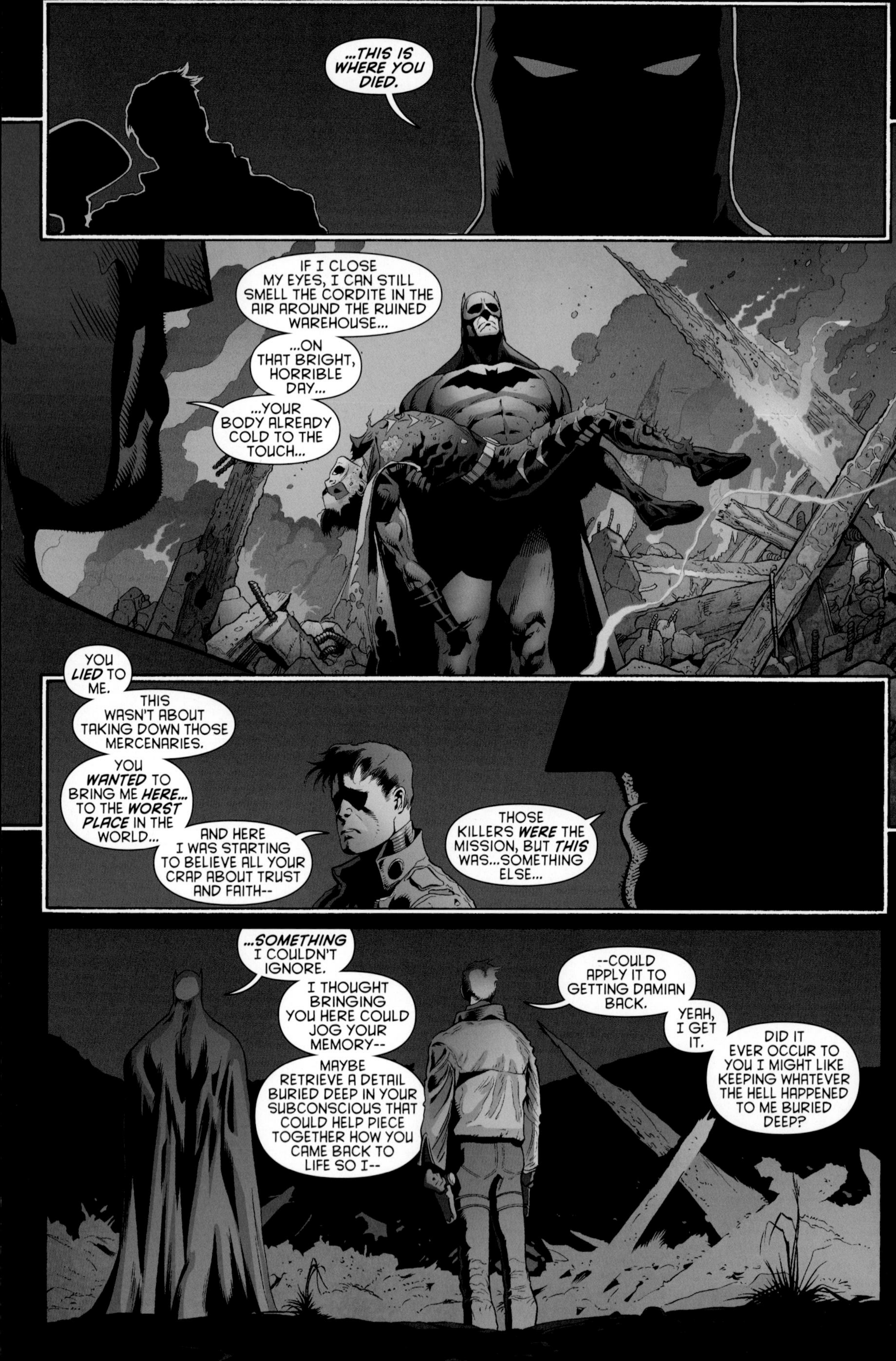
...THIS IS WHERE YOU DIED.
IF I CLOSE MY EYES, I CAN STILL SMELL THE CORDITE IN THE AIR AROUND THE RUINED WAREHOUSE...
...ON THAT BRIGHT, HORRIBLE DAY...
...YOUR BODY ALREADY COLD TO THE TOUCH...
YOU *LIED* TO ME.
THIS WASN'T ABOUT TAKING DOWN THOSE MERCENARIES.
YOU *WANTED* TO BRING ME *HERE*... TO THE *WORST PLACE* IN THE WORLD...
AND HERE I WAS STARTING TO BELIEVE ALL YOUR CRAP ABOUT TRUST AND FAITH--
THOSE KILLERS *WERE* THE MISSION, BUT *THIS* WAS...SOMETHING ELSE...
...*SOMETHING* I COULDN'T IGNORE.
I THOUGHT BRINGING YOU HERE COULD JOG YOUR MEMORY--
MAYBE RETRIEVE A DETAIL BURIED DEEP IN YOUR SUBCONSCIOUS THAT COULD HELP PIECE TOGETHER HOW YOU CAME BACK TO LIFE SO I--
--COULD APPLY IT TO GETTING DAMIAN BACK.
YEAH, I GET IT.
DID IT EVER OCCUR TO YOU I MIGHT LIKE KEEPING WHATEVER THE HELL HAPPENED TO ME BURIED DEEP?

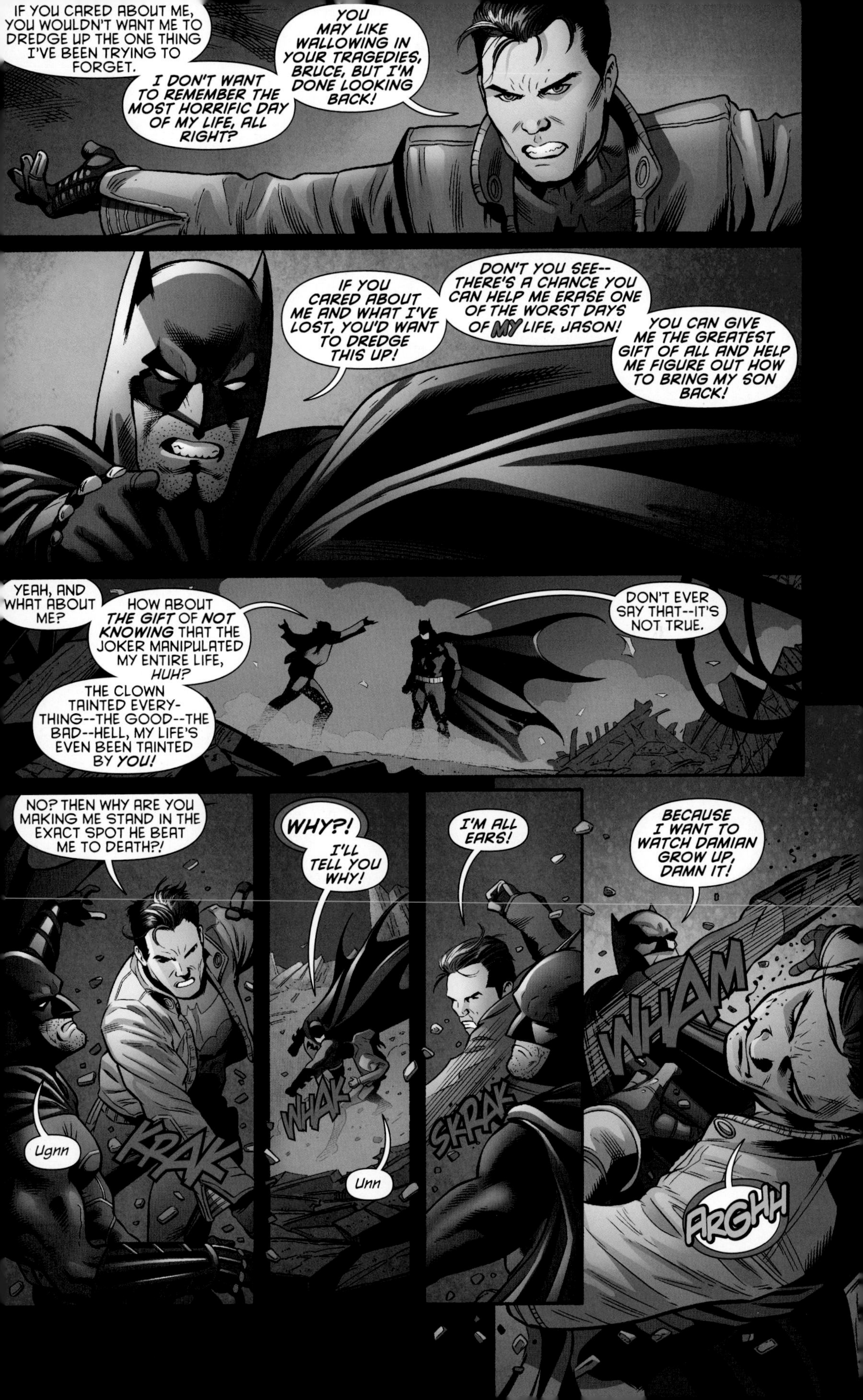
IF YOU CARED ABOUT ME, YOU WOULDN'T WANT ME TO DREDGE UP THE ONE THING I'VE BEEN TRYING TO FORGET.
I DON'T WANT TO REMEMBER THE MOST HORRIFIC DAY OF MY LIFE, ALL RIGHT?
YOU MAY LIKE WALLOWING IN YOUR TRAGEDIES, BRUCE, BUT I'M DONE LOOKING BACK!
IF YOU CARED ABOUT ME AND WHAT I'VE LOST, YOU'D WANT TO DREDGE THIS UP!
DON'T YOU SEE--THERE'S A CHANCE YOU CAN HELP ME ERASE ONE OF THE WORST DAYS OF MY LIFE, JASON!
YOU CAN GIVE ME THE GREATEST GIFT OF ALL AND HELP ME FIGURE OUT HOW TO BRING MY SON BACK!
YEAH, AND WHAT ABOUT ME?
HOW ABOUT THE GIFT OF NOT KNOWING THAT THE JOKER MANIPULATED MY ENTIRE LIFE, HUH?
THE CLOWN TAINTED EVERY-THING--THE GOOD--THE BAD--HELL, MY LIFE'S EVEN BEEN TAINTED BY YOU!
DON'T EVER SAY THAT--IT'S NOT TRUE.
NO? THEN WHY ARE YOU MAKING ME STAND IN THE EXACT SPOT HE BEAT ME TO DEATH?!
Ugnn
KRAK
WHY?!
I'LL TELL YOU WHY!
WHAK
Unn
I'M ALL EARS!
SKRAK
BECAUSE I WANT TO WATCH DAMIAN GROW UP, DAMN IT!
WHAM
ARGHH

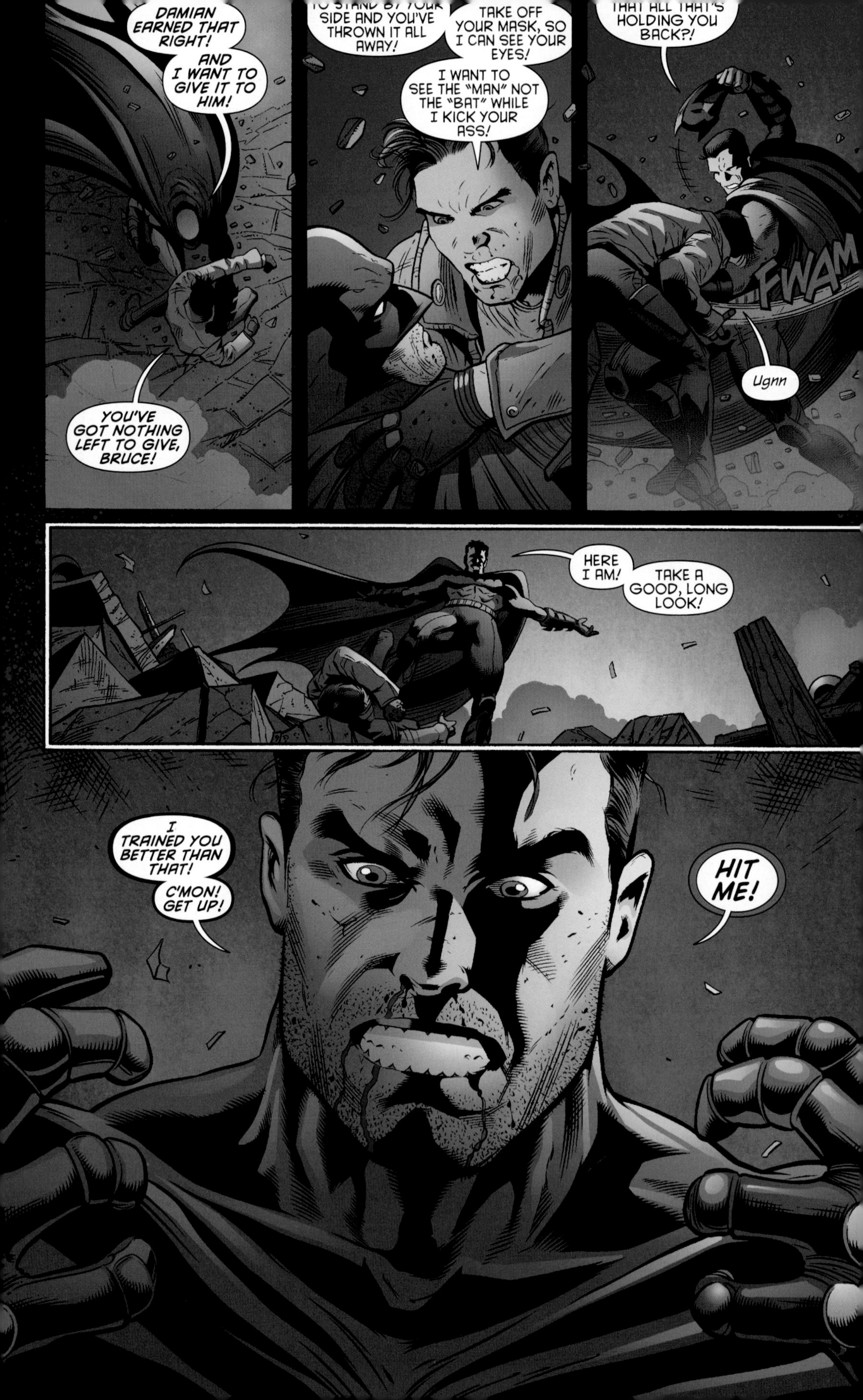
DAMIAN EARNED THAT RIGHT!
AND I WANT TO GIVE IT TO HIM!
YOU'VE GOT NOTHING LEFT TO GIVE, BRUCE!
SIDE AND YOU'VE THROWN IT ALL AWAY!
TAKE OFF YOUR MASK, SO I CAN SEE YOUR EYES!
I WANT TO SEE THE "MAN" NOT THE "BAT" WHILE I KICK YOUR ASS!
HOLDING YOU BACK?!
FWAM
Ugnn
HERE I AM!
TAKE A GOOD, LONG LOOK!
I TRAINED YOU BETTER THAN THAT!
C'MON! GET UP!
HIT ME!

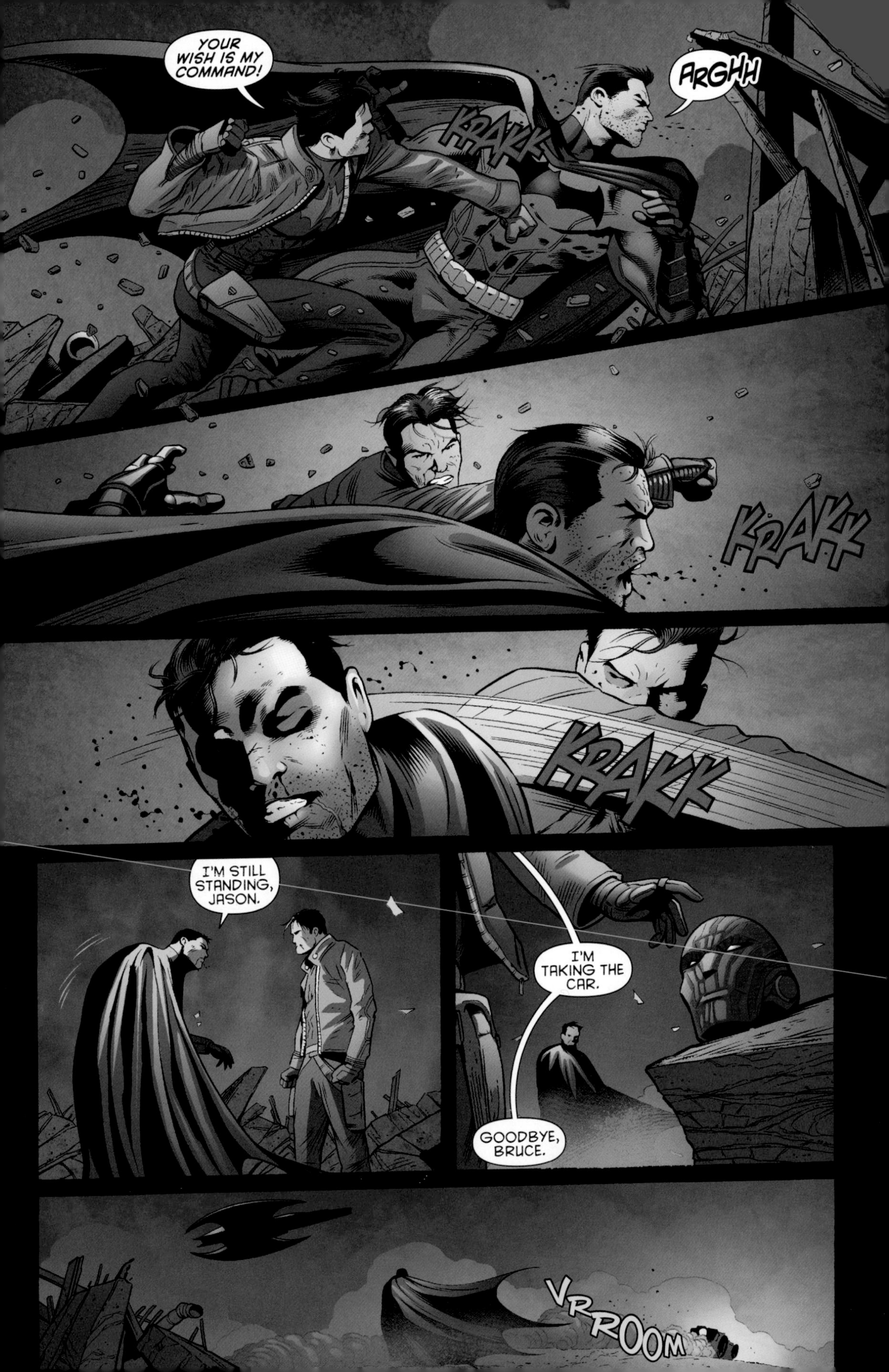
YOUR WISH IS MY COMMAND!
ARGHH
KRAKK
KRAKK
KRAKK
I'M STILL STANDING, JASON.
I'M TAKING THE CAR.
GOODBYE, BRUCE.
VRROOM

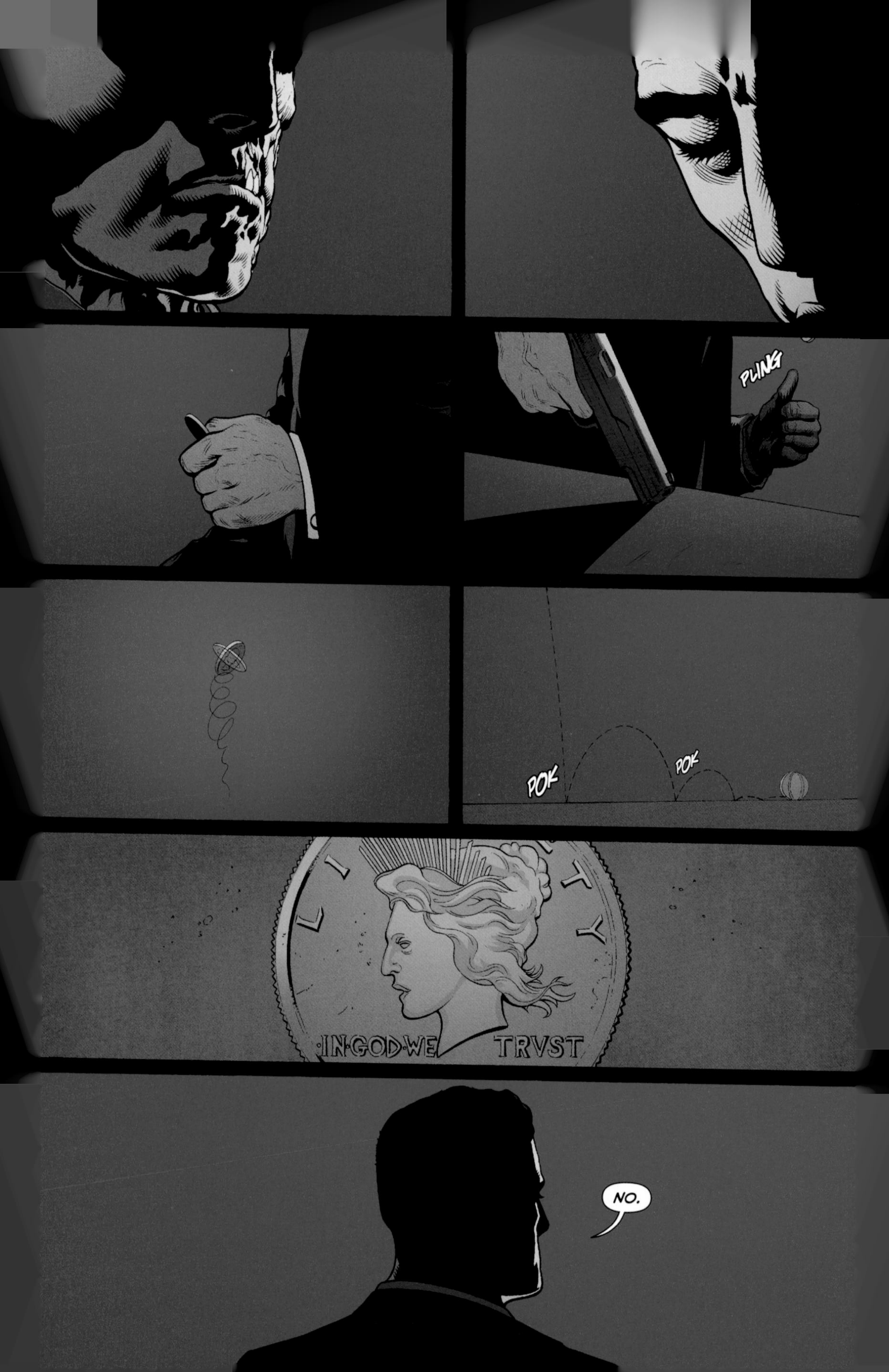
PLING
POK
POK
LIBERTY
IN GOD WE TRVST
NO.

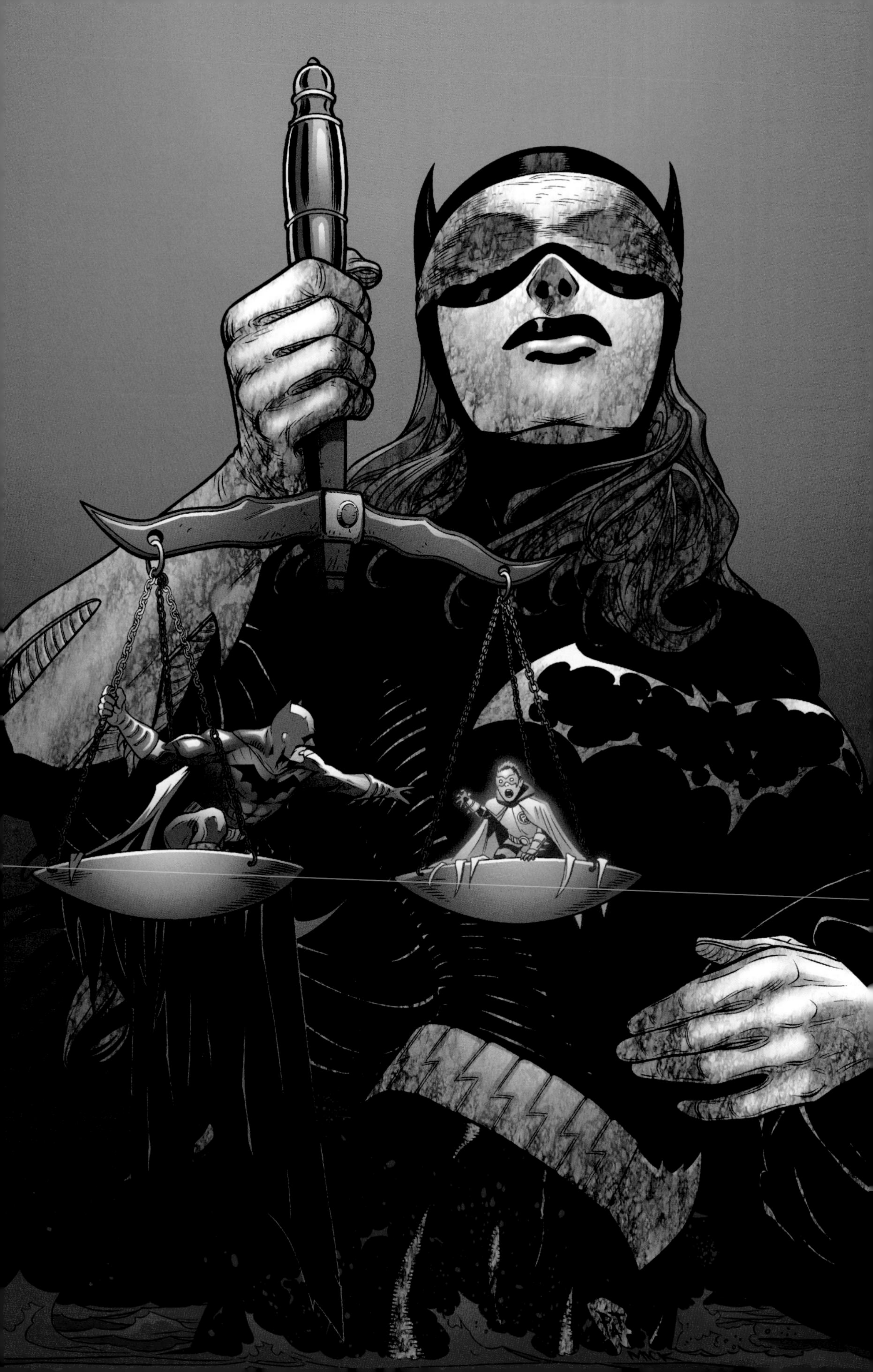

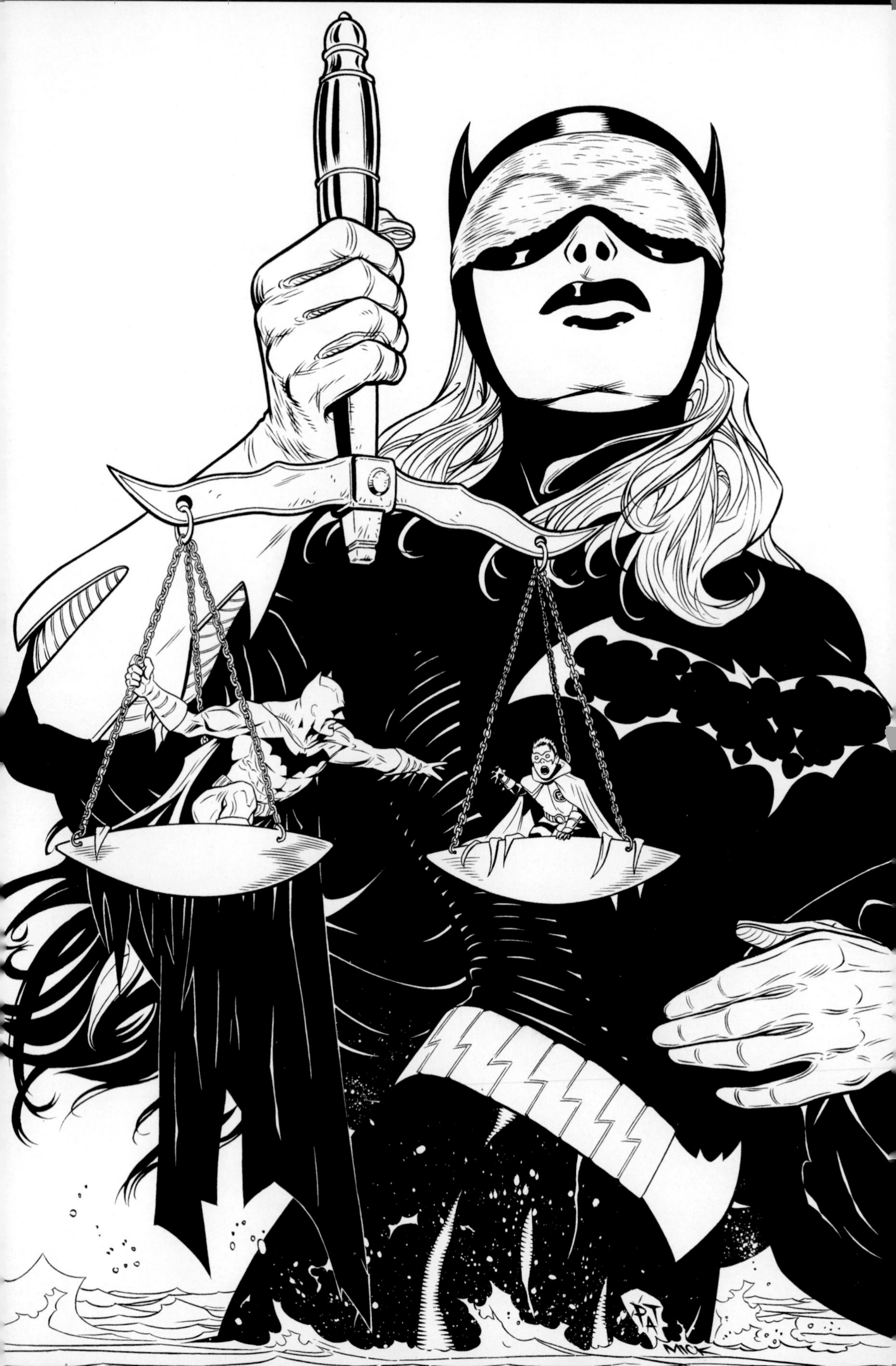

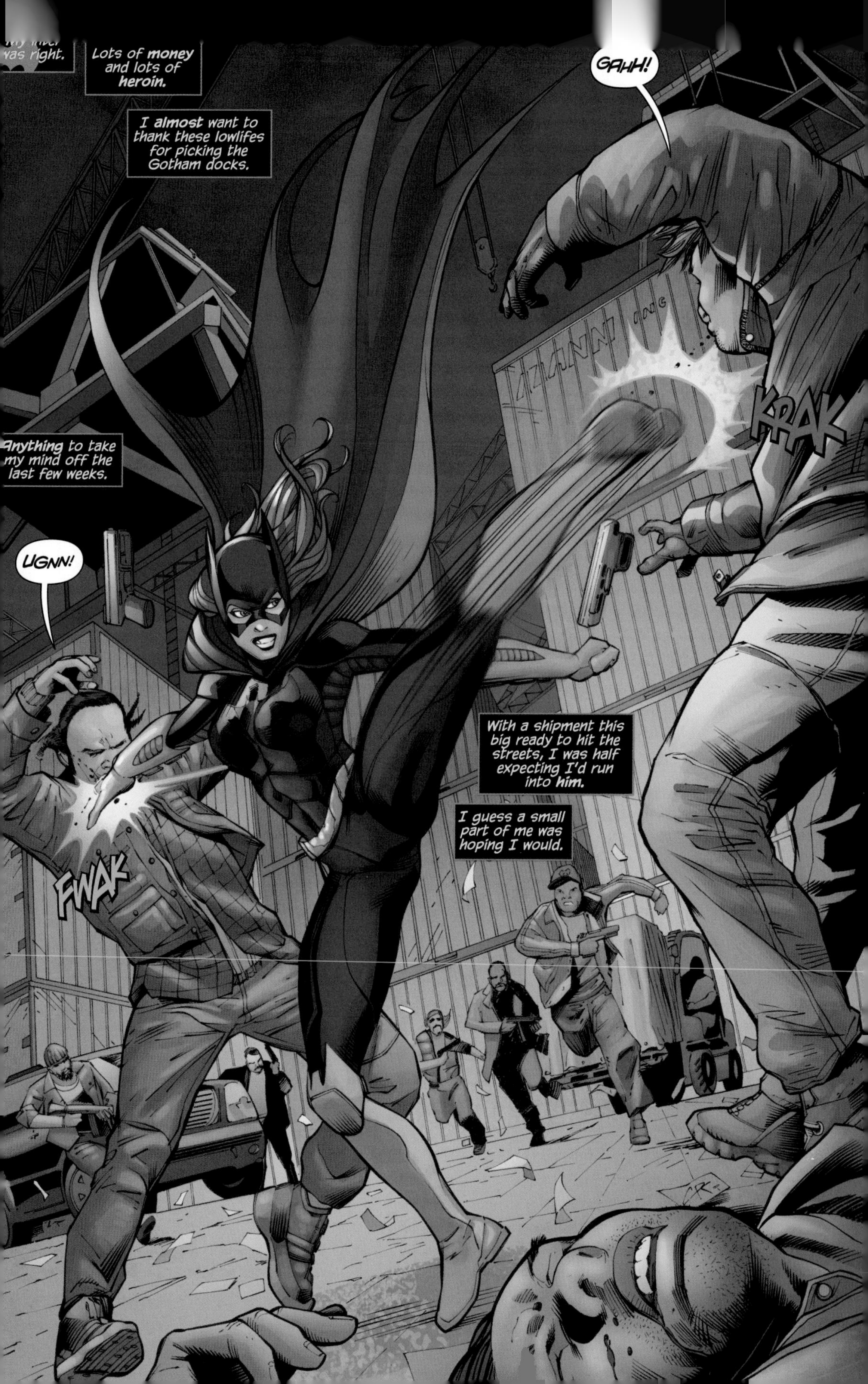
Lots of money and lots of heroin.
I almost want to thank these lowlifes for picking the Gotham docks.
GAHH!
KRAK
Anything to take my mind off the last few weeks.
UGNN!
With a shipment this big ready to hit the streets, I was half expecting I'd run into him.
I guess a small part of me was hoping I would.
FWAK

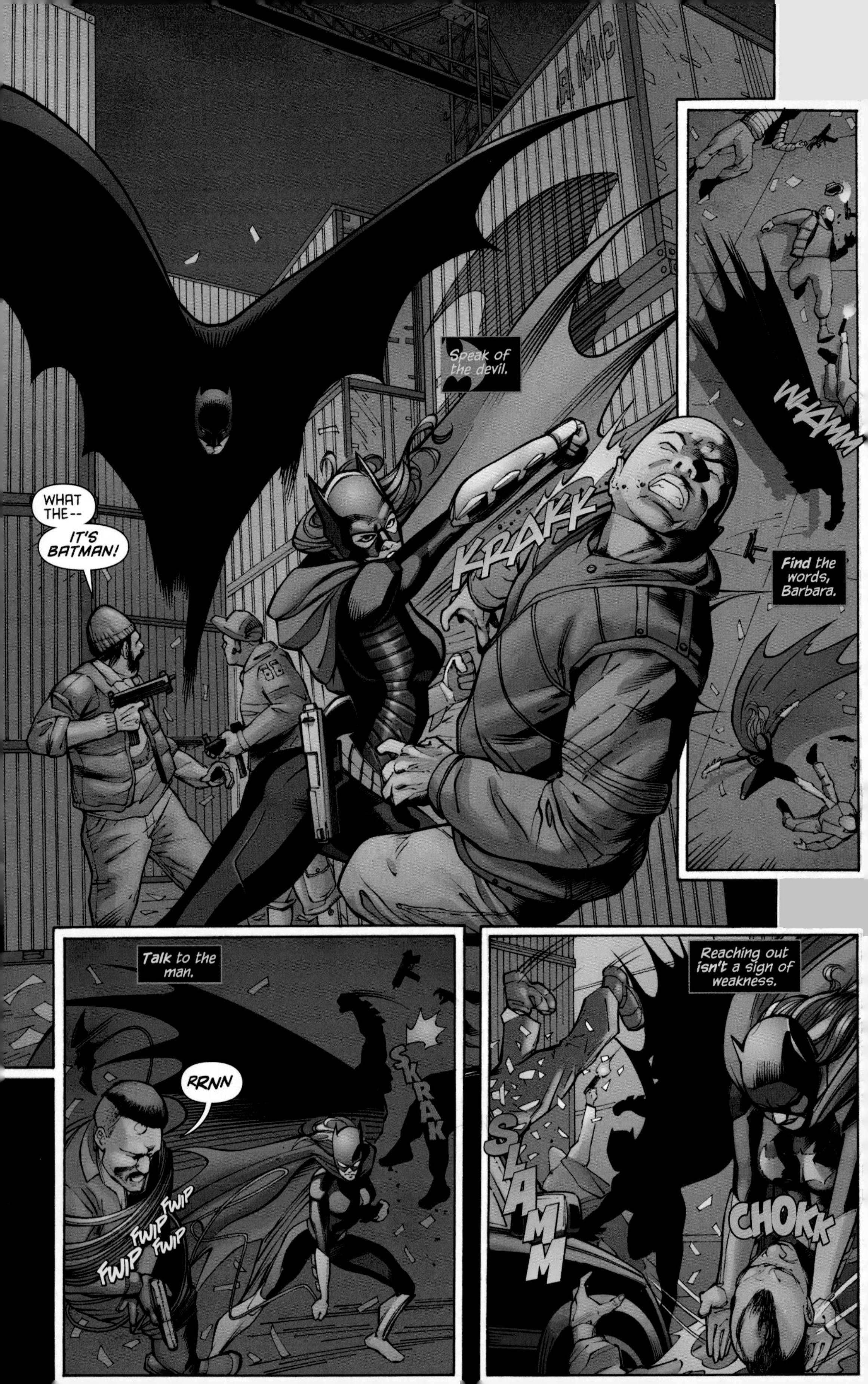
Speak of the devil.
WHAT THE--
IT'S BATMAN!
KRAKK
WHAMM
Find the words, Barbara.
Talk to the man.
RRNN
SKRAK
FWIP FWIP FWIP FWIP
Reaching out isn't a sign of weakness.
SLAMM
CHOKK

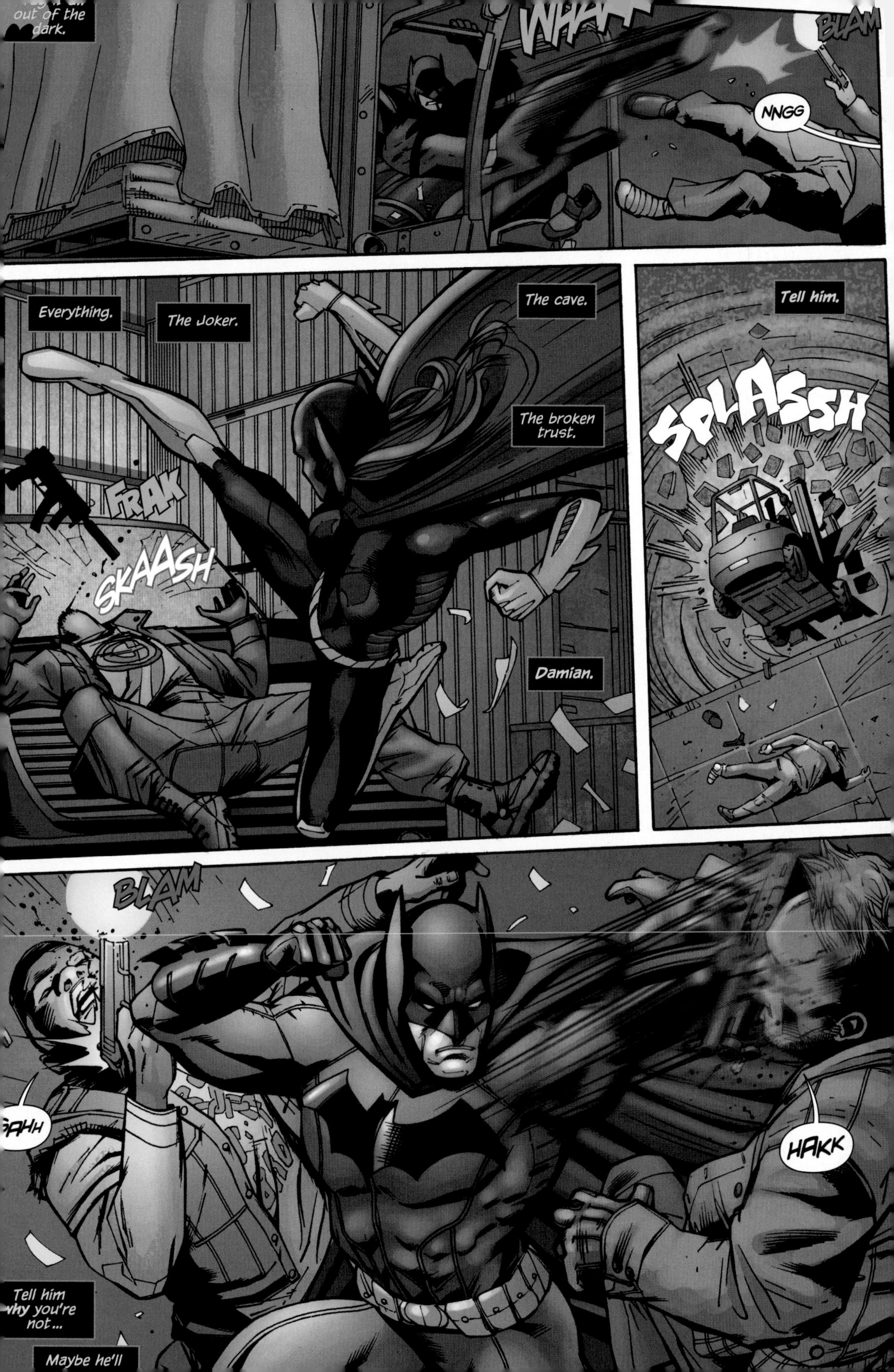

out of the
dark.
BLAM
NNGG
Everything.
The Joker.
The cave.
The broken trust.
FRAK
SKAASH
Damian.
Tell him.
SPLASSH
BLAM
HAKK
Tell him why you're not...
Maybe he'll

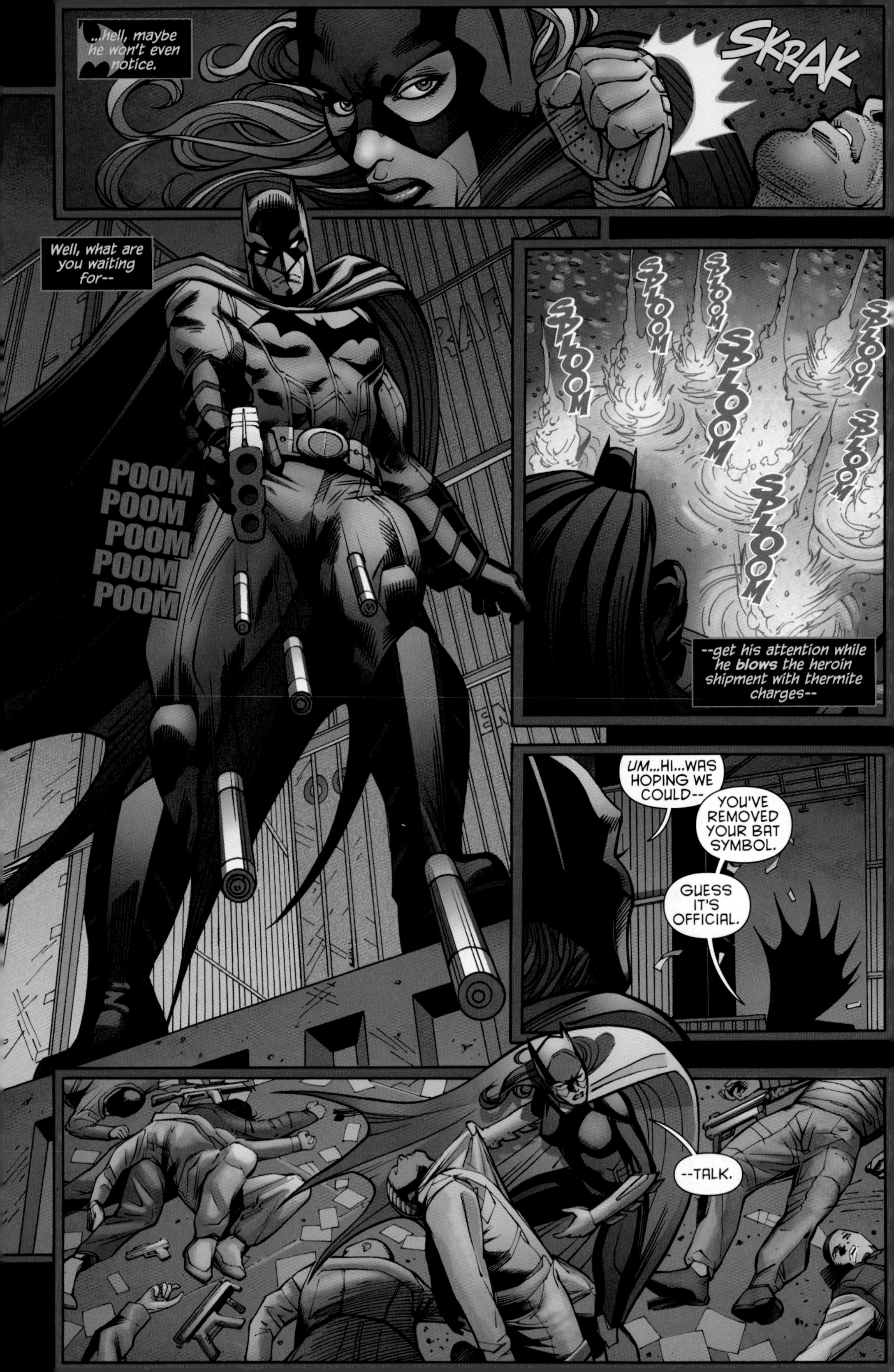

..hell, maybe he won't even notice.
SKRAK
Well, what are you waiting for--
POOM POOM POOM POOM POOM
SPLOOM SPLOOM SPLOOM SPLOOM SPLOOM SPLOOM SPLOOM SPLOOM
--get his attention while he **blows** the heroin shipment with thermite charges--
UM...HI...WAS HOPING WE COULD--
YOU'VE REMOVED YOUR BAT SYMBOL.
GUESS IT'S OFFICIAL.
--TALK.

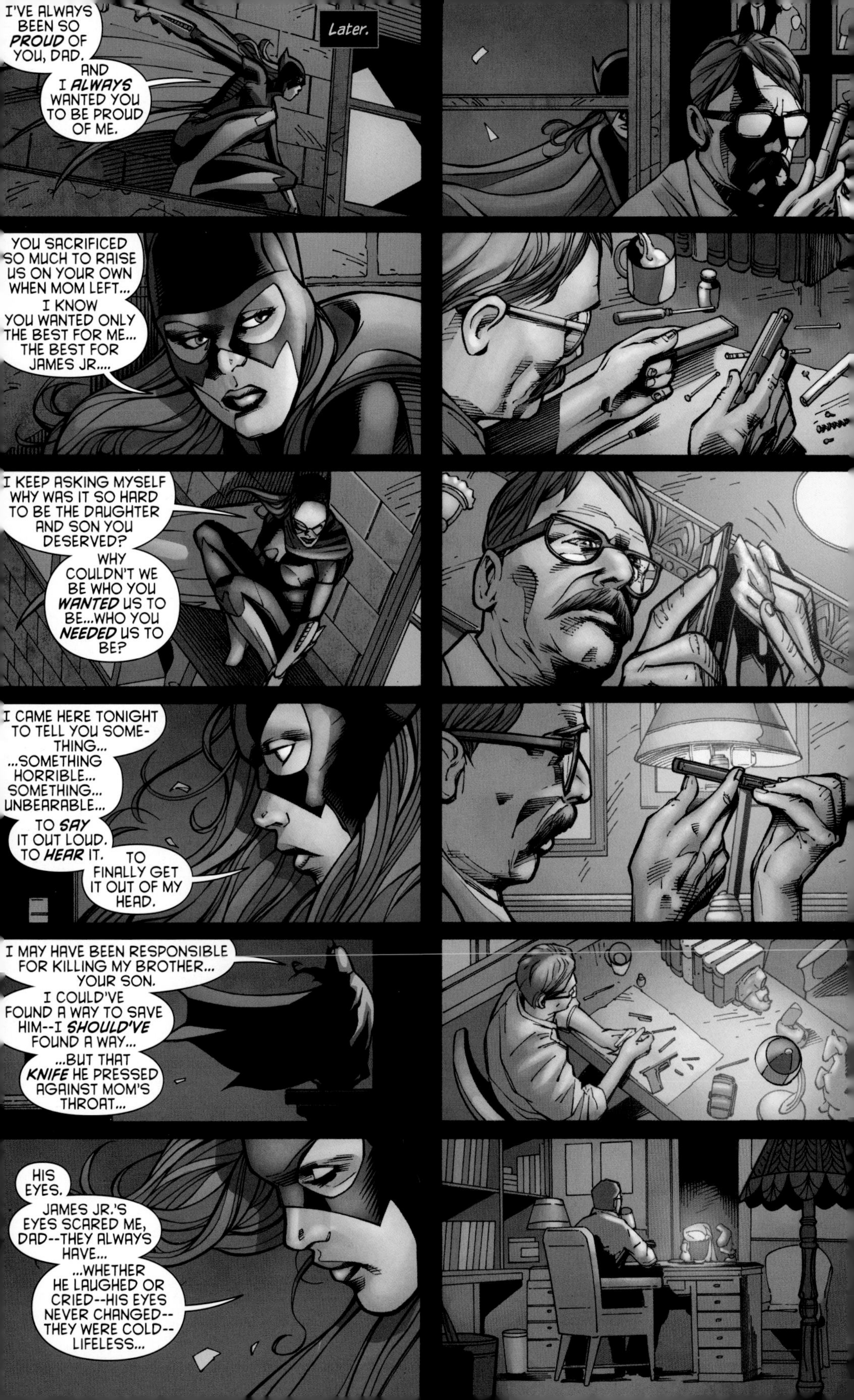
I'VE ALWAYS BEEN SO PROUD OF YOU, DAD.
AND I ALWAYS WANTED YOU TO BE PROUD OF ME.
Later.
YOU SACRIFICED SO MUCH TO RAISE US ON YOUR OWN WHEN MOM LEFT...
I KNOW YOU WANTED ONLY THE BEST FOR ME... THE BEST FOR JAMES JR....
I KEEP ASKING MYSELF WHY WAS IT SO HARD TO BE THE DAUGHTER AND SON YOU DESERVED?
WHY COULDN'T WE BE WHO YOU WANTED US TO BE...WHO YOU NEEDED US TO BE?
I CAME HERE TONIGHT TO TELL YOU SOME-THING...
...SOMETHING HORRIBLE... SOMETHING... UNBEARABLE...
TO SAY IT OUT LOUD. TO HEAR IT.
TO FINALLY GET IT OUT OF MY HEAD.
I MAY HAVE BEEN RESPONSIBLE FOR KILLING MY BROTHER... YOUR SON.
I COULD'VE FOUND A WAY TO SAVE HIM--I SHOULD'VE FOUND A WAY...
...BUT THAT KNIFE HE PRESSED AGAINST MOM'S THROAT...
HIS EYES.
JAMES JR.'S EYES SCARED ME, DAD--THEY ALWAYS HAVE...
...WHETHER HE LAUGHED OR CRIED--HIS EYES NEVER CHANGED--THEY WERE COLD--LIFELESS...

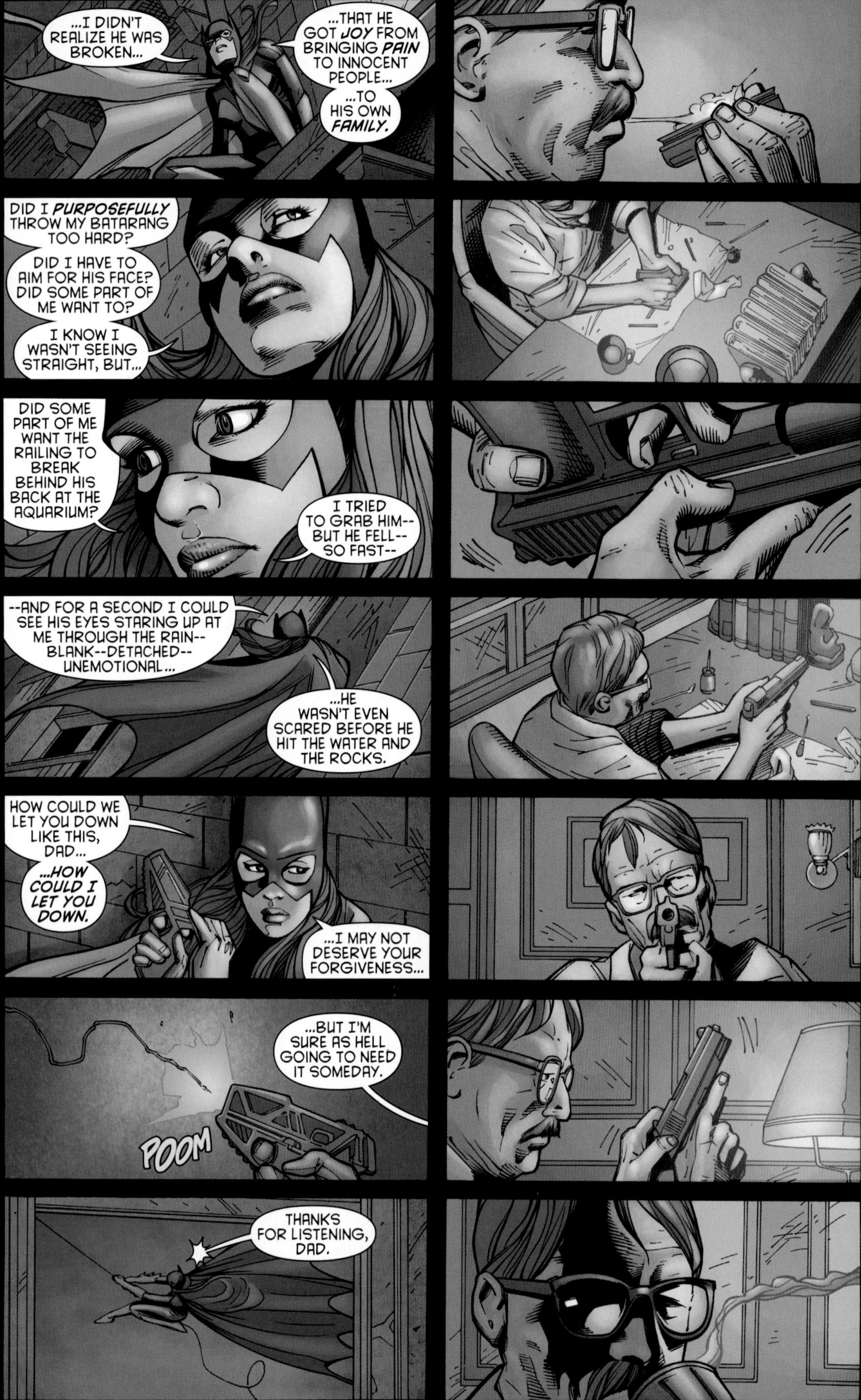
...I DIDN'T REALIZE HE WAS BROKEN...
...THAT HE GOT JOY FROM BRINGING PAIN TO INNOCENT PEOPLE...
...TO HIS OWN FAMILY.
DID I PURPOSEFULLY THROW MY BATARANG TOO HARD?
DID I HAVE TO AIM FOR HIS FACE? DID SOME PART OF ME WANT TO?
I KNOW I WASN'T SEEING STRAIGHT, BUT...
DID SOME PART OF ME WANT THE RAILING TO BREAK BEHIND HIS BACK AT THE AQUARIUM?
I TRIED TO GRAB HIM--BUT HE FELL--SO FAST--
--AND FOR A SECOND I COULD SEE HIS EYES STARING UP AT ME THROUGH THE RAIN--BLANK--DETACHED--UNEMOTIONAL...
...HE WASN'T EVEN SCARED BEFORE HE HIT THE WATER AND THE ROCKS.
HOW COULD WE LET YOU DOWN LIKE THIS, DAD...
...HOW COULD I LET YOU DOWN.
...I MAY NOT DESERVE YOUR FORGIVENESS...
...BUT I'M SURE AS HELL GOING TO NEED IT SOMEDAY.
POOM
THANKS FOR LISTENING, DAD.

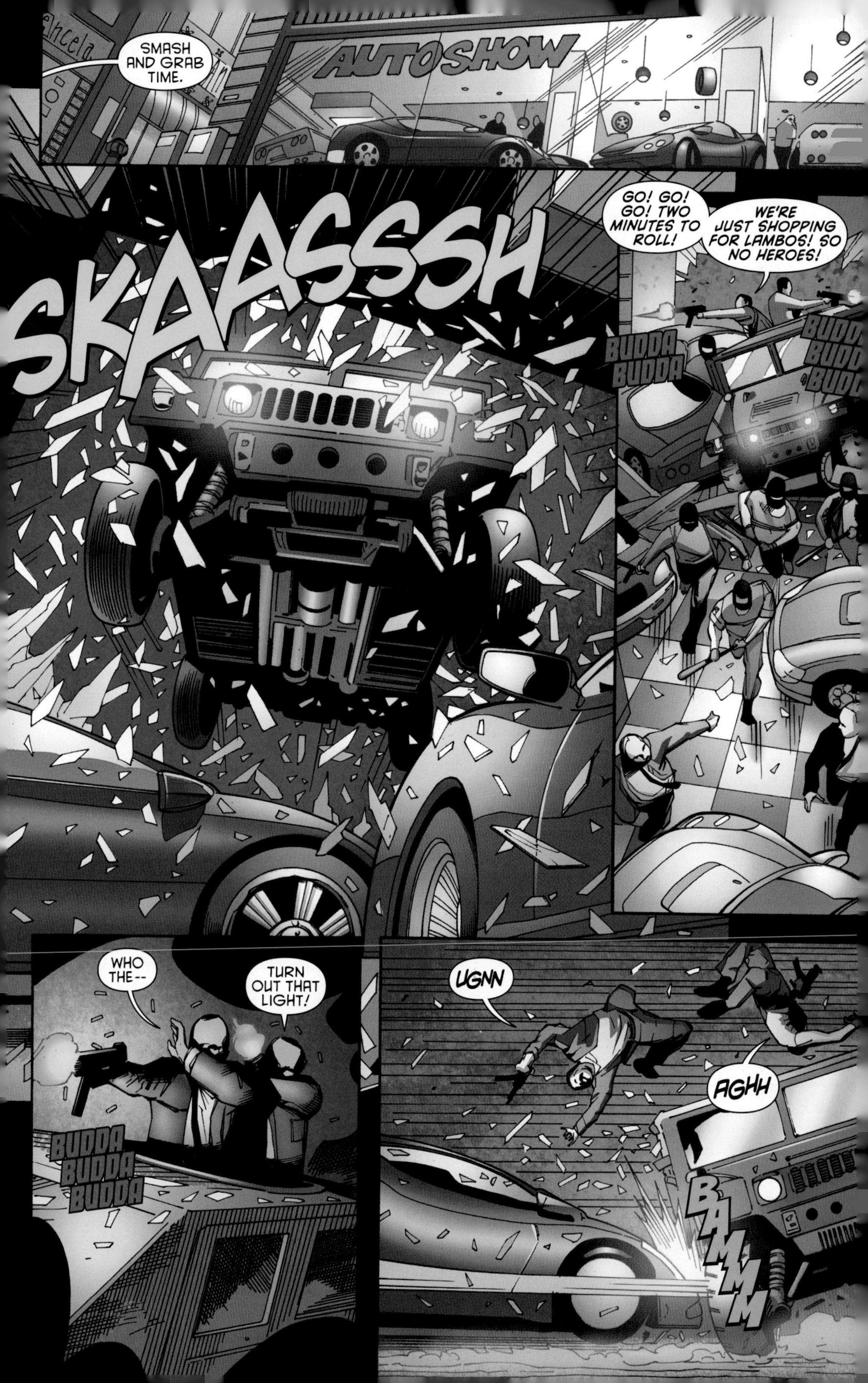
SMASH AND GRAB TIME.
AUTO SHOW
SKAASSSH
GO! GO! GO! TWO MINUTES TO ROLL!
WE'RE JUST SHOPPING FOR LAMBOS! SO NO HEROES!
BUDDA BUDDA
BUDDA BUDDA BUDDA
WHO THE--
TURN OUT THAT LIGHT!
BUDDA BUDDA BUDDA
UGNN
AGHH
BAMMMM

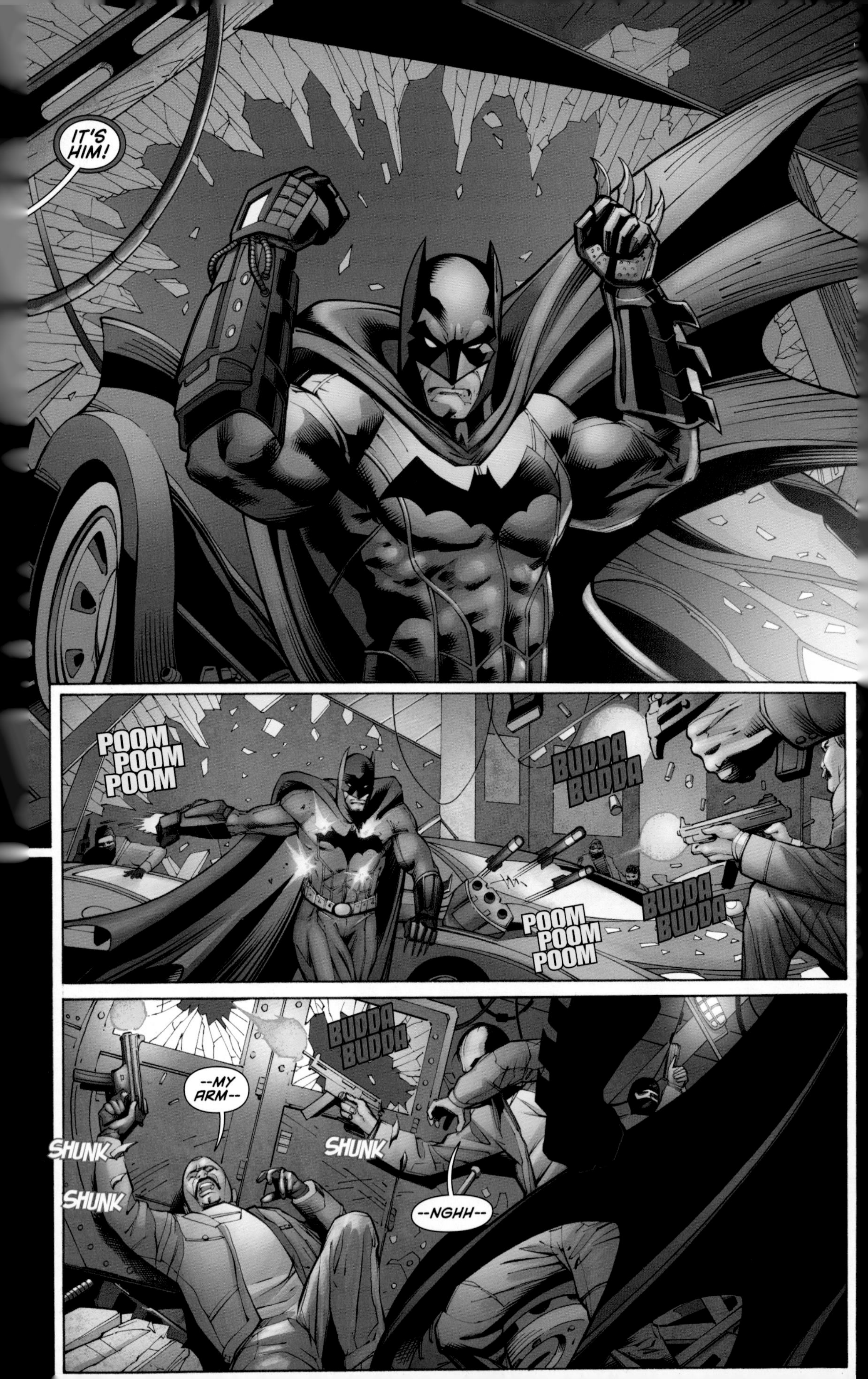

IT'S HIM!
POOM POOM POOM
BUDDA BUDDA
BUDDA BUDDA
POOM POOM POOM
BUDDA BUDDA
--MY ARM--
SHUNK
SHUNK
SHUNK
--NGHH--

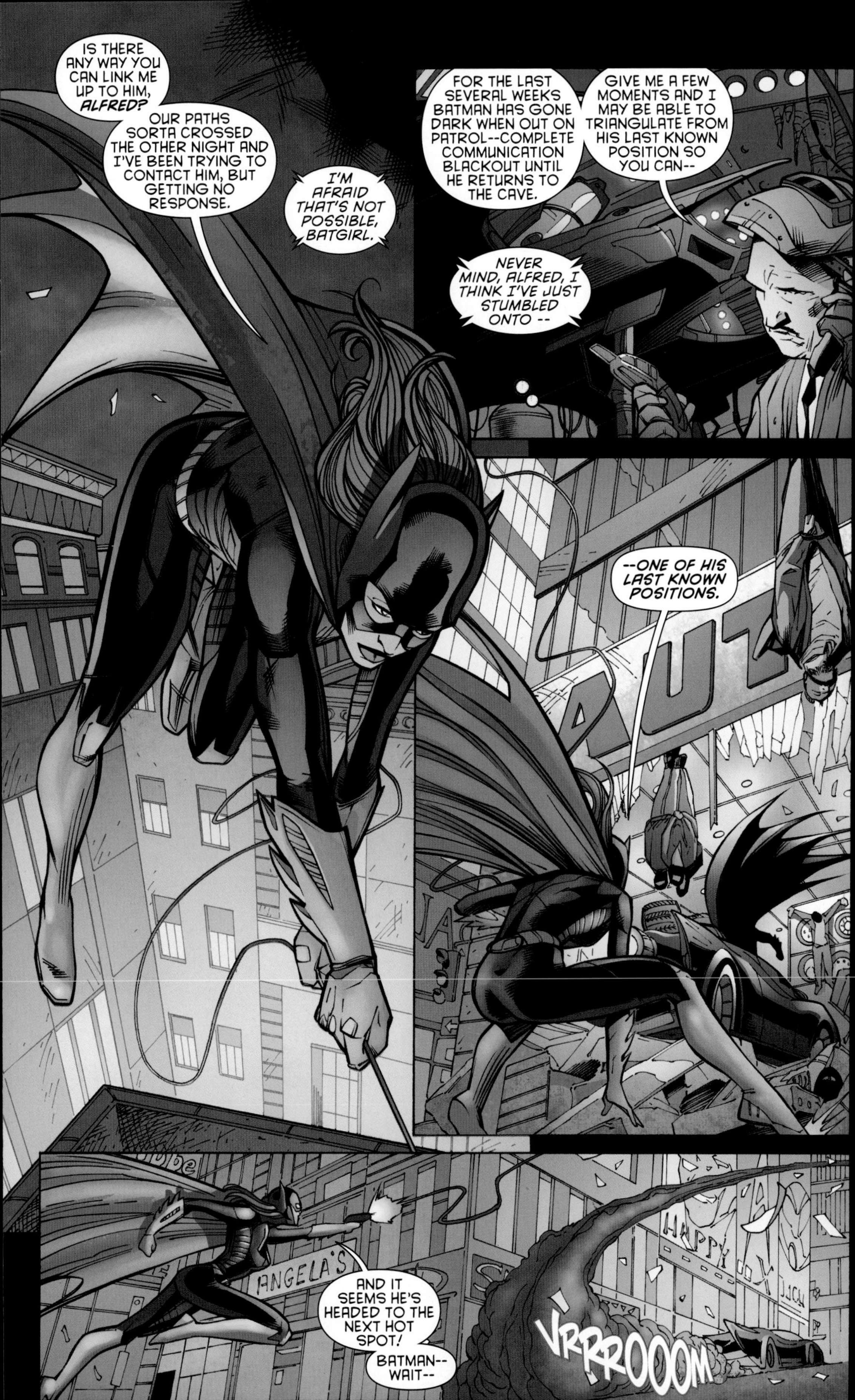
IS THERE ANY WAY YOU CAN LINK ME UP TO HIM, ALFRED?
OUR PATHS SORTA CROSSED THE OTHER NIGHT AND I'VE BEEN TRYING TO CONTACT HIM, BUT GETTING NO RESPONSE.
I'M AFRAID THAT'S NOT POSSIBLE, BATGIRL.
FOR THE LAST SEVERAL WEEKS BATMAN HAS GONE DARK WHEN OUT ON PATROL--COMPLETE COMMUNICATION BLACKOUT UNTIL HE RETURNS TO THE CAVE.
GIVE ME A FEW MOMENTS AND I MAY BE ABLE TO TRIANGULATE FROM HIS LAST KNOWN POSITION SO YOU CAN--
NEVER MIND, ALFRED, I THINK I'VE JUST STUMBLED ONTO --
--ONE OF HIS LAST KNOWN POSITIONS.
ANGELA'S
HAPPY
AND IT SEEMS HE'S HEADED TO THE NEXT HOT SPOT!
BATMAN-- WAIT--
VRRROOOM

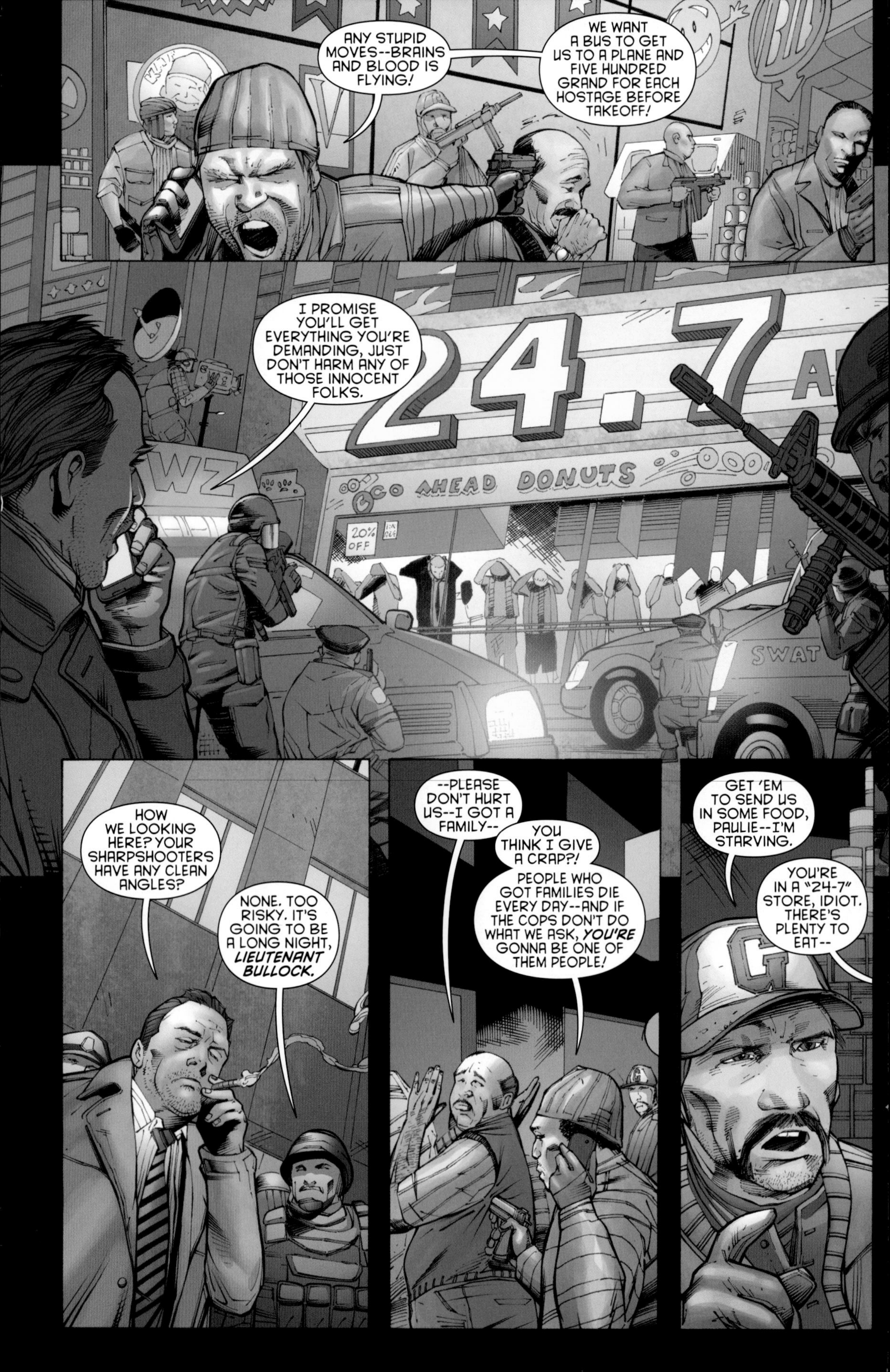
ANY STUPID MOVES--BRAINS AND BLOOD IS FLYING!
WE WANT A BUS TO GET US TO A PLANE AND FIVE HUNDRED GRAND FOR EACH HOSTAGE BEFORE TAKEOFF!
I PROMISE YOU'LL GET EVERYTHING YOU'RE DEMANDING, JUST DON'T HARM ANY OF THOSE INNOCENT FOLKS.
24.7
GO AHEAD DONUTS
20% OFF
SWAT
HOW WE LOOKING HERE? YOUR SHARPSHOOTERS HAVE ANY CLEAN ANGLES?
NONE. TOO RISKY. IT'S GOING TO BE A LONG NIGHT, LIEUTENANT BULLOCK.
--PLEASE DON'T HURT US--I GOT A FAMILY--
YOU THINK I GIVE A CRAP?!
PEOPLE WHO GOT FAMILIES DIE EVERY DAY--AND IF THE COPS DON'T DO WHAT WE ASK, YOU'RE GONNA BE ONE OF THEM PEOPLE!
GET 'EM TO SEND US IN SOME FOOD, PAULIE--I'M STARVING.
YOU'RE IN A "24-7" STORE, IDIOT. THERE'S PLENTY TO EAT--

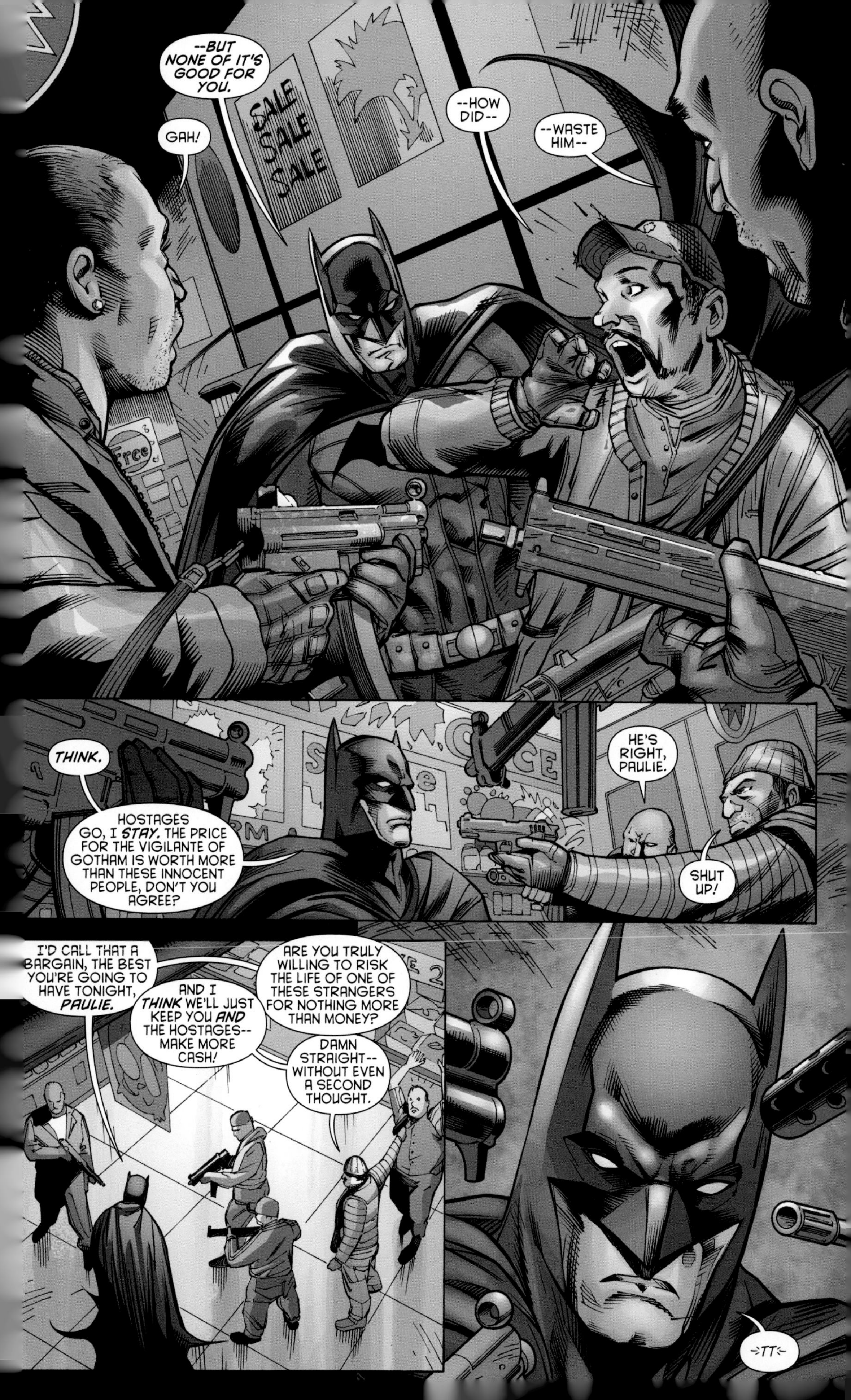
--BUT NONE OF IT'S GOOD FOR YOU.
GAH!
--HOW DID--
--WASTE HIM--
SALE SALE SALE
THINK.
HOSTAGES GO, I STAY. THE PRICE FOR THE VIGILANTE OF GOTHAM IS WORTH MORE THAN THESE INNOCENT PEOPLE, DON'T YOU AGREE?
HE'S RIGHT, PAULIE.
SHUT UP!
I'D CALL THAT A BARGAIN, THE BEST YOU'RE GOING TO HAVE TONIGHT, PAULIE.
AND I THINK WE'LL JUST KEEP YOU AND THE HOSTAGES-- MAKE MORE CASH!
ARE YOU TRULY WILLING TO RISK THE LIFE OF ONE OF THESE STRANGERS FOR NOTHING MORE THAN MONEY?
DAMN STRAIGHT-- WITHOUT EVEN A SECOND THOUGHT.
TT

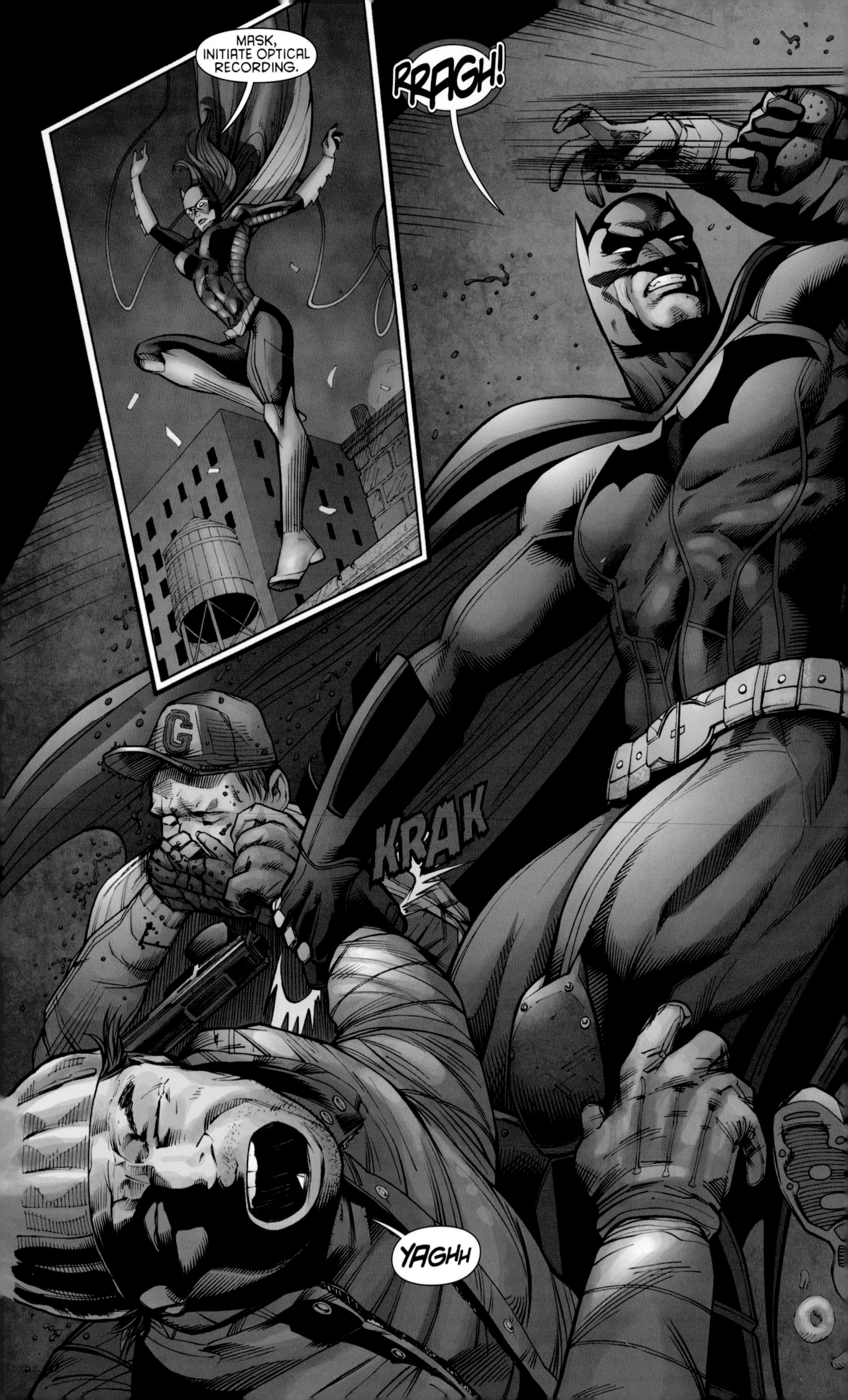
MASK, INITIATE OPTICAL RECORDING.
RRAGH!
KRAK
YAGHH

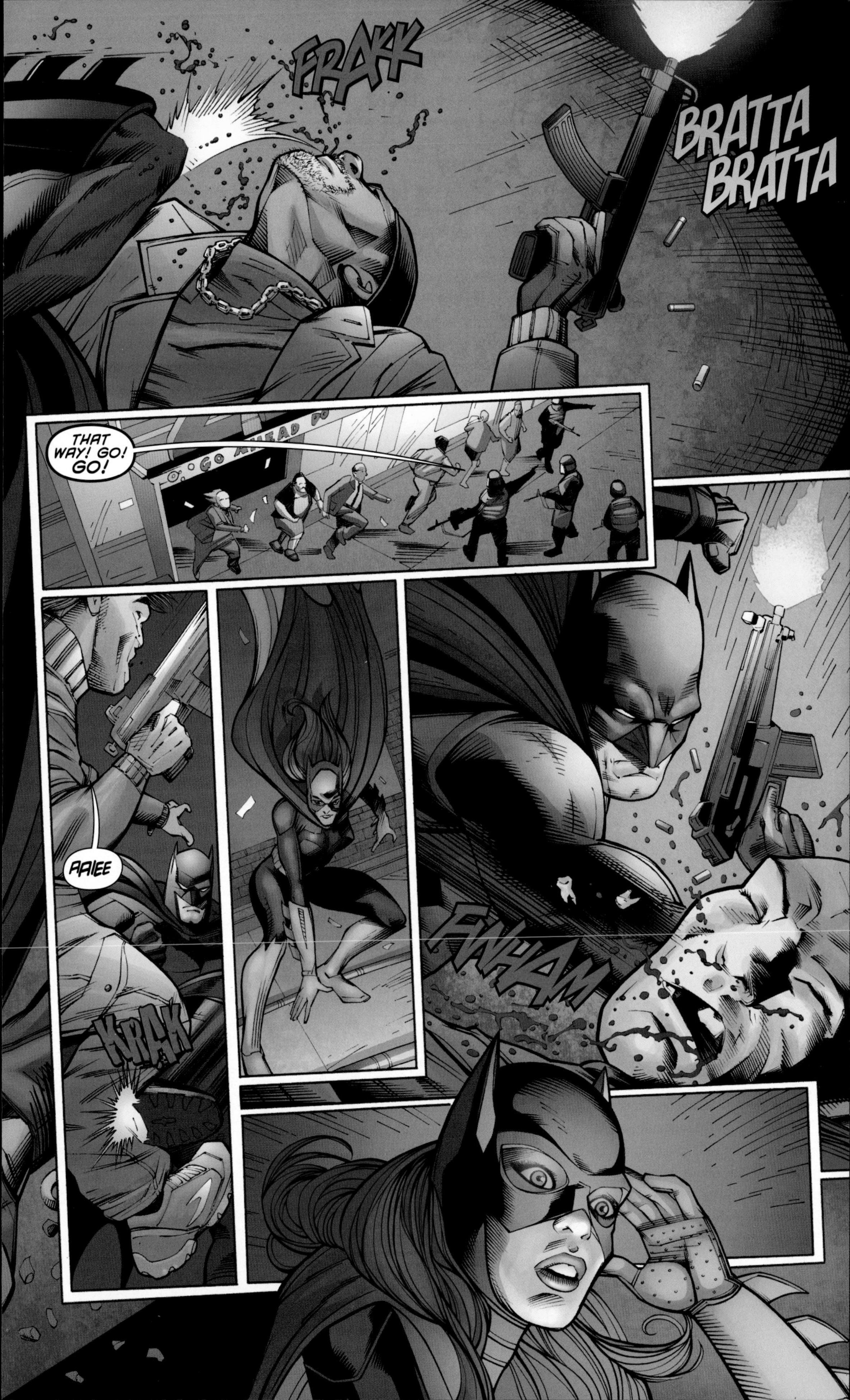
FRAKK
BRATTA BRATTA
THAT WAY! GO! GO!
AAIEE
KRAK
FWHAM

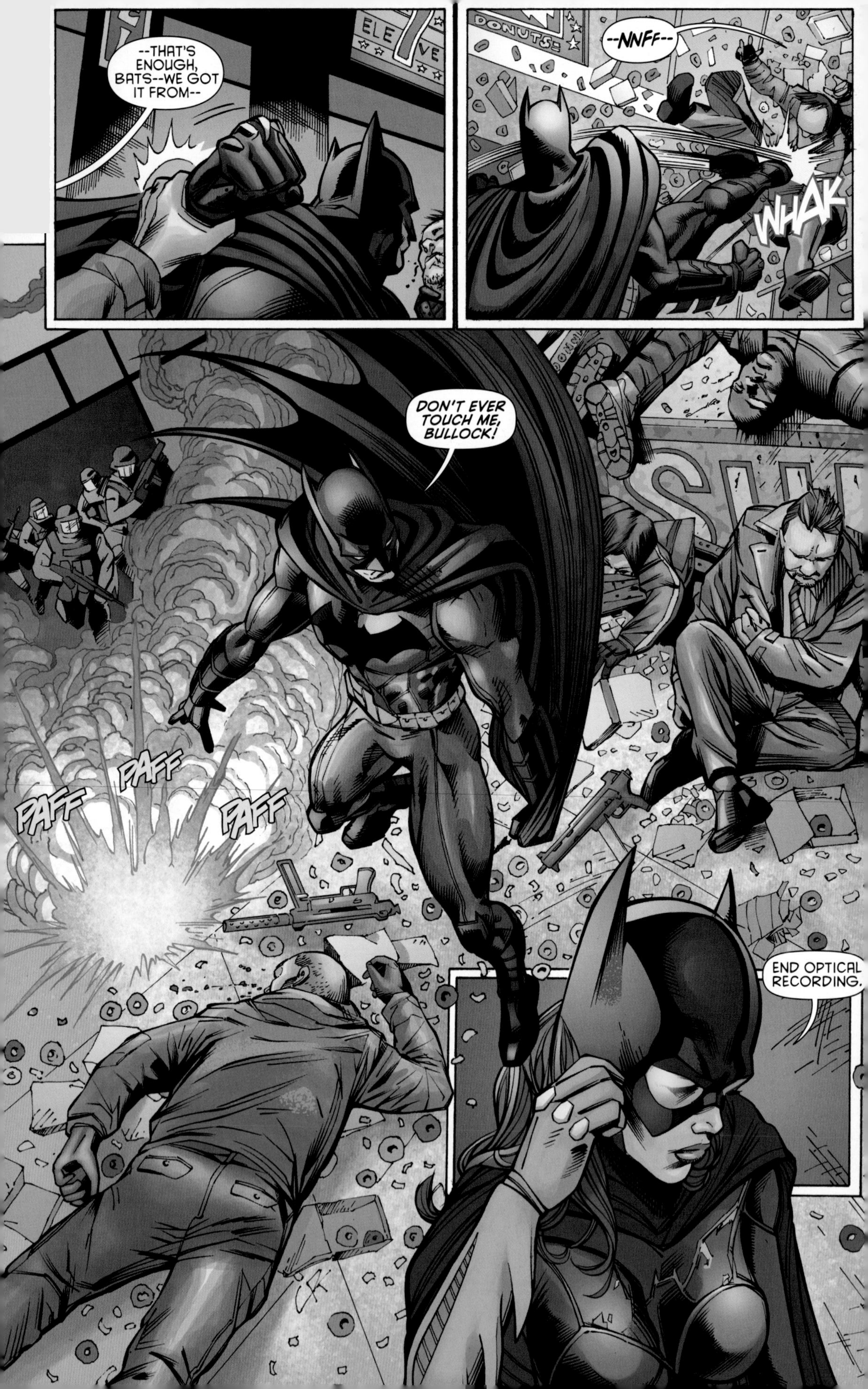
--THAT'S ENOUGH, BATS--WE GOT IT FROM--
--NNFF--
WHAK
DON'T EVER TOUCH ME, BULLOCK!
PAFF
PAFF
PAFF
END OPTICAL RECORDING.

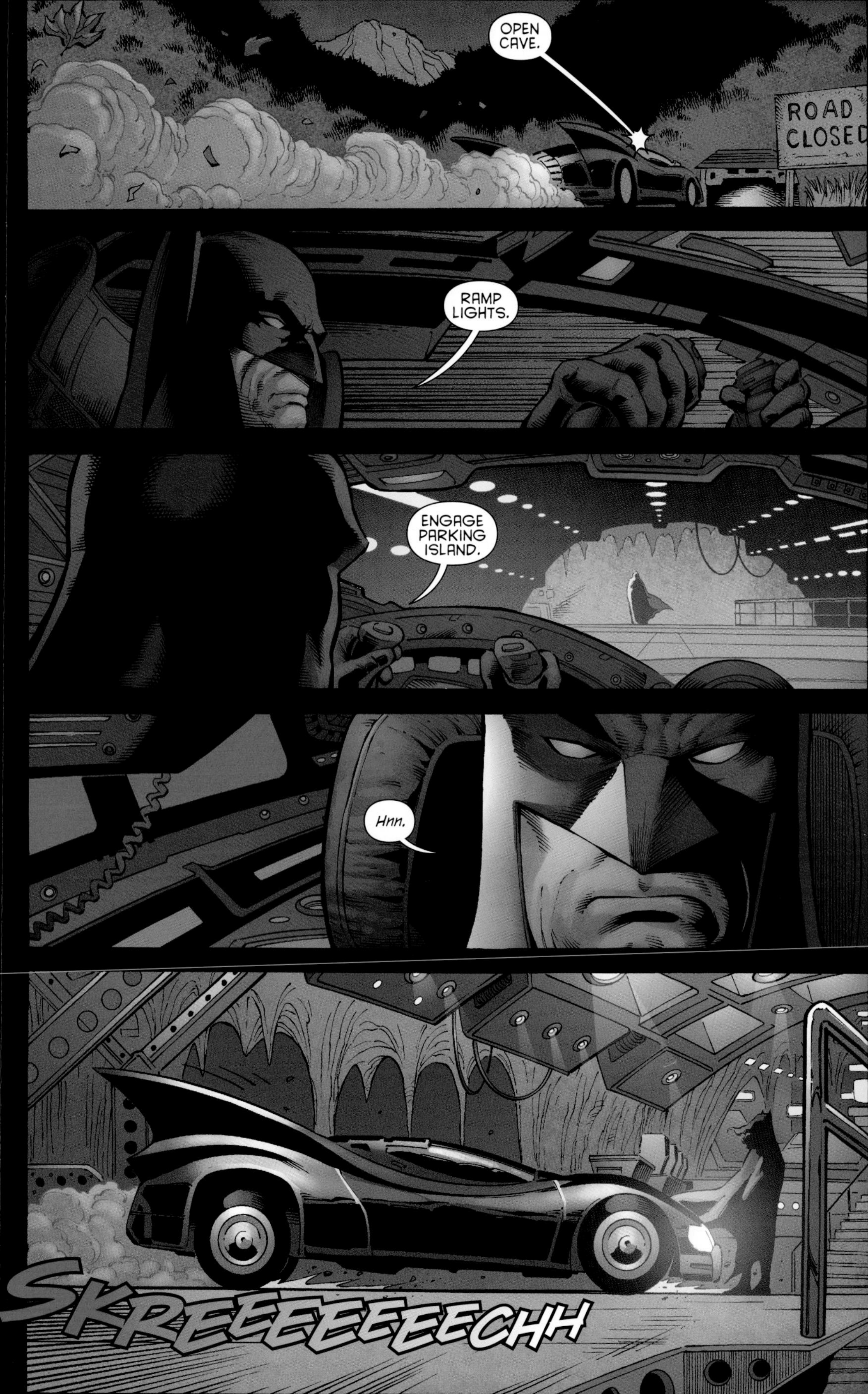
OPEN CAVE.
ROAD CLOSED
RAMP LIGHTS.
ENGAGE PARKING ISLAND.
Hnn.
SKREEEEEEEEECHH

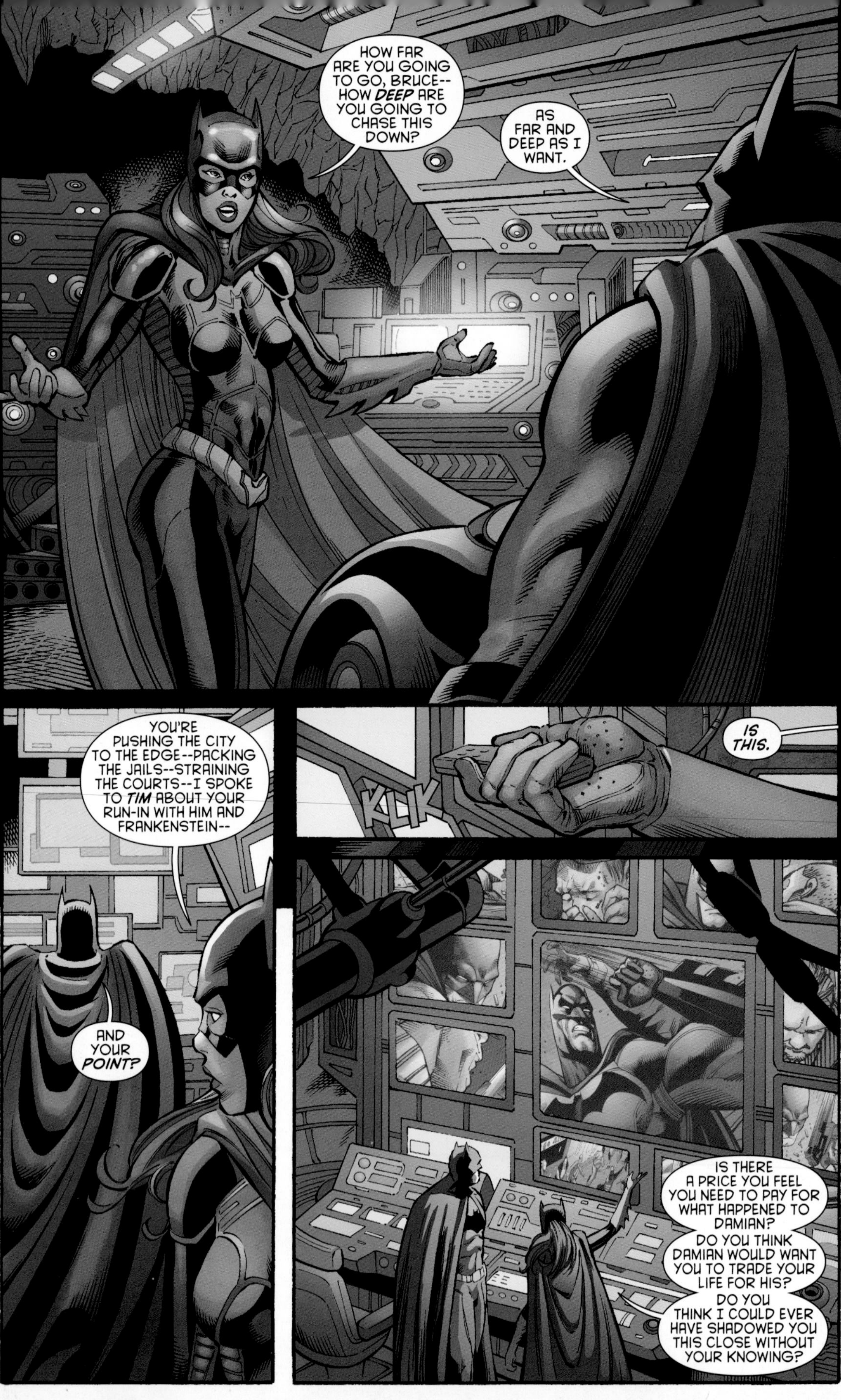
HOW FAR ARE YOU GOING TO GO, BRUCE-- HOW *DEEP* ARE YOU GOING TO CHASE THIS DOWN?
AS FAR AND DEEP AS I WANT.
YOU'RE PUSHING THE CITY TO THE EDGE--PACKING THE JAILS--STRAINING THE COURTS--I SPOKE TO *TIM* ABOUT YOUR RUN-IN WITH HIM AND FRANKENSTEIN--
AND YOUR *POINT?*
KLIK
IS THIS.
IS THERE A PRICE YOU FEEL YOU NEED TO PAY FOR WHAT HAPPENED TO DAMIAN?
DO YOU THINK DAMIAN WOULD WANT YOU TO TRADE YOUR LIFE FOR HIS?
DO YOU THINK I COULD EVER HAVE SHADOWED YOU THIS CLOSE WITHOUT YOUR KNOWING?

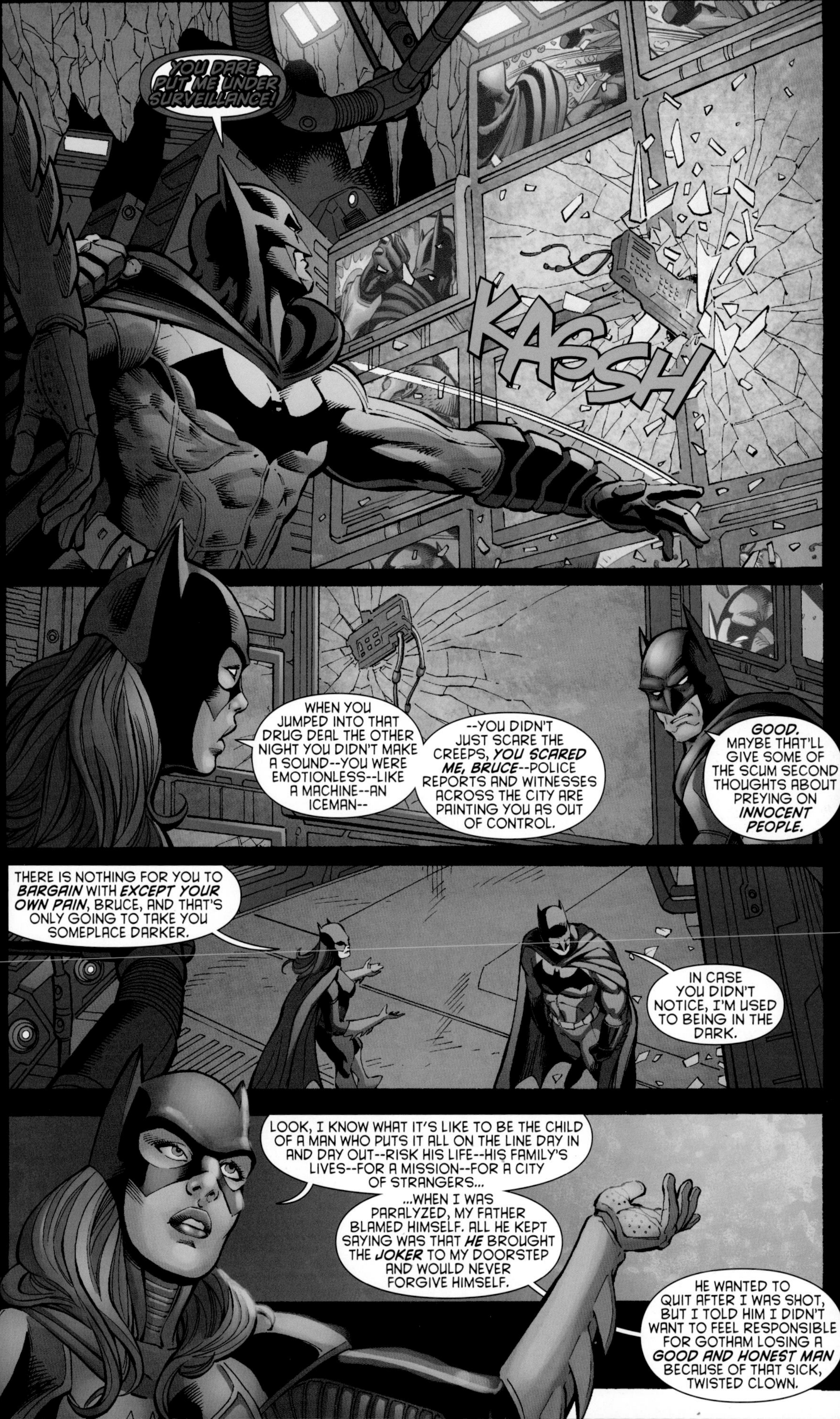
YOU DARE PUT ME UNDER SURVEILLANCE!
KASSH
WHEN YOU JUMPED INTO THAT DRUG DEAL THE OTHER NIGHT YOU DIDN'T MAKE A SOUND--YOU WERE EMOTIONLESS--LIKE A MACHINE--AN ICEMAN--
--YOU DIDN'T JUST SCARE THE CREEPS, YOU SCARED ME, BRUCE--POLICE REPORTS AND WITNESSES ACROSS THE CITY ARE PAINTING YOU AS OUT OF CONTROL.
GOOD. MAYBE THAT'LL GIVE SOME OF THE SCUM SECOND THOUGHTS ABOUT PREYING ON INNOCENT PEOPLE.
THERE IS NOTHING FOR YOU TO BARGAIN WITH EXCEPT YOUR OWN PAIN, BRUCE, AND THAT'S ONLY GOING TO TAKE YOU SOMEPLACE DARKER.
IN CASE YOU DIDN'T NOTICE, I'M USED TO BEING IN THE DARK.
LOOK, I KNOW WHAT IT'S LIKE TO BE THE CHILD OF A MAN WHO PUTS IT ALL ON THE LINE DAY IN AND DAY OUT--RISK HIS LIFE--HIS FAMILY'S LIVES--FOR A MISSION--FOR A CITY OF STRANGERS...
...WHEN I WAS PARALYZED, MY FATHER BLAMED HIMSELF. ALL HE KEPT SAYING WAS THAT HE BROUGHT THE JOKER TO MY DOORSTEP AND WOULD NEVER FORGIVE HIMSELF.
HE WANTED TO QUIT AFTER I WAS SHOT, BUT I TOLD HIM I DIDN'T WANT TO FEEL RESPONSIBLE FOR GOTHAM LOSING A GOOD AND HONEST MAN BECAUSE OF THAT SICK, TWISTED CLOWN.

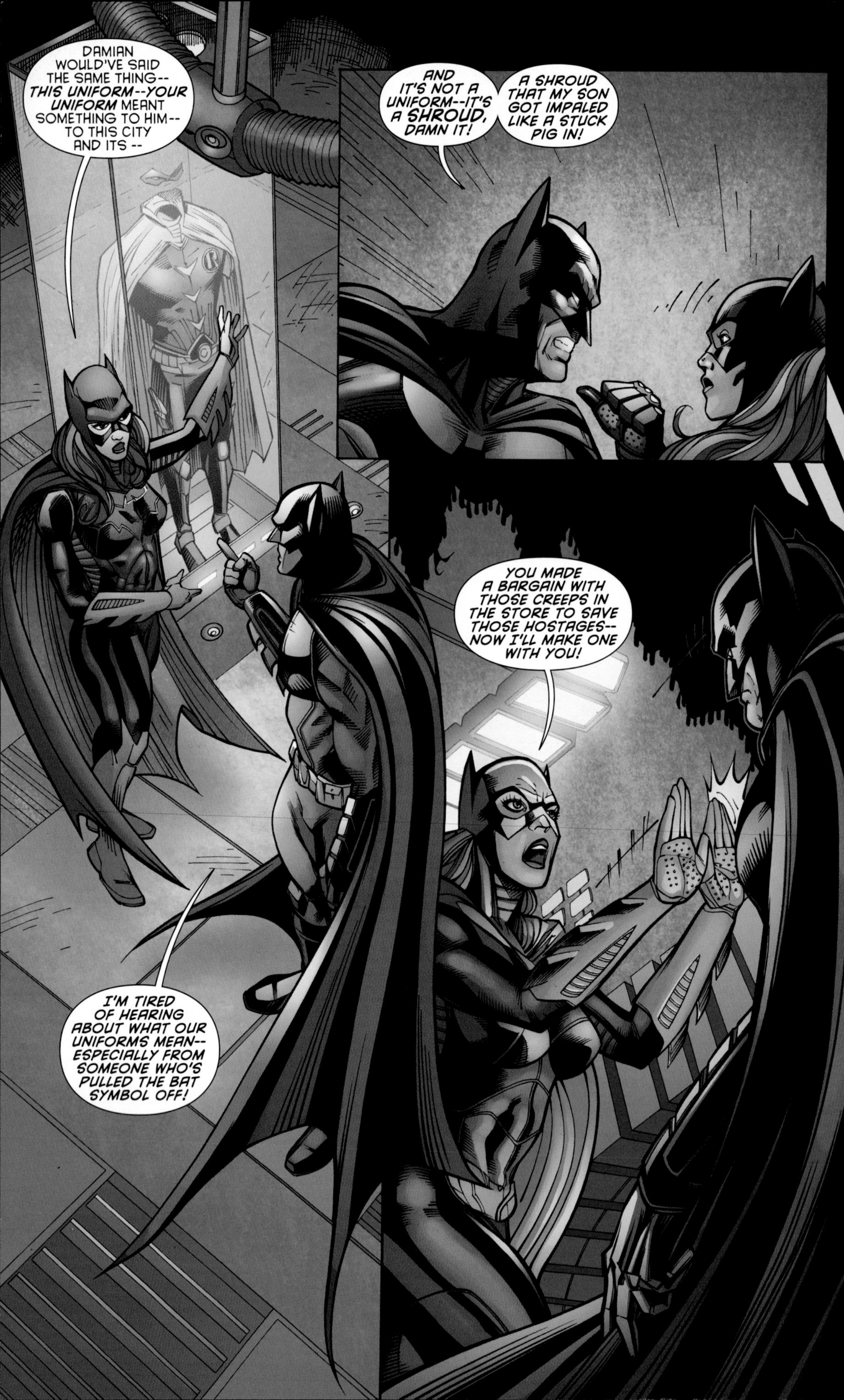
DAMIAN WOULD'VE SAID THE SAME THING-- THIS UNIFORM--YOUR UNIFORM MEANT SOMETHING TO HIM-- TO THIS CITY AND ITS --
I'M TIRED OF HEARING ABOUT WHAT OUR UNIFORMS MEAN-- ESPECIALLY FROM SOMEONE WHO'S PULLED THE BAT SYMBOL OFF!
AND IT'S NOT A UNIFORM--IT'S A SHROUD, DAMN IT!
A SHROUD THAT MY SON GOT IMPALED LIKE A STUCK PIG IN!
YOU MADE A BARGAIN WITH THOSE CREEPS IN THE STORE TO SAVE THOSE HOSTAGES-- NOW I'LL MAKE ONE WITH YOU!

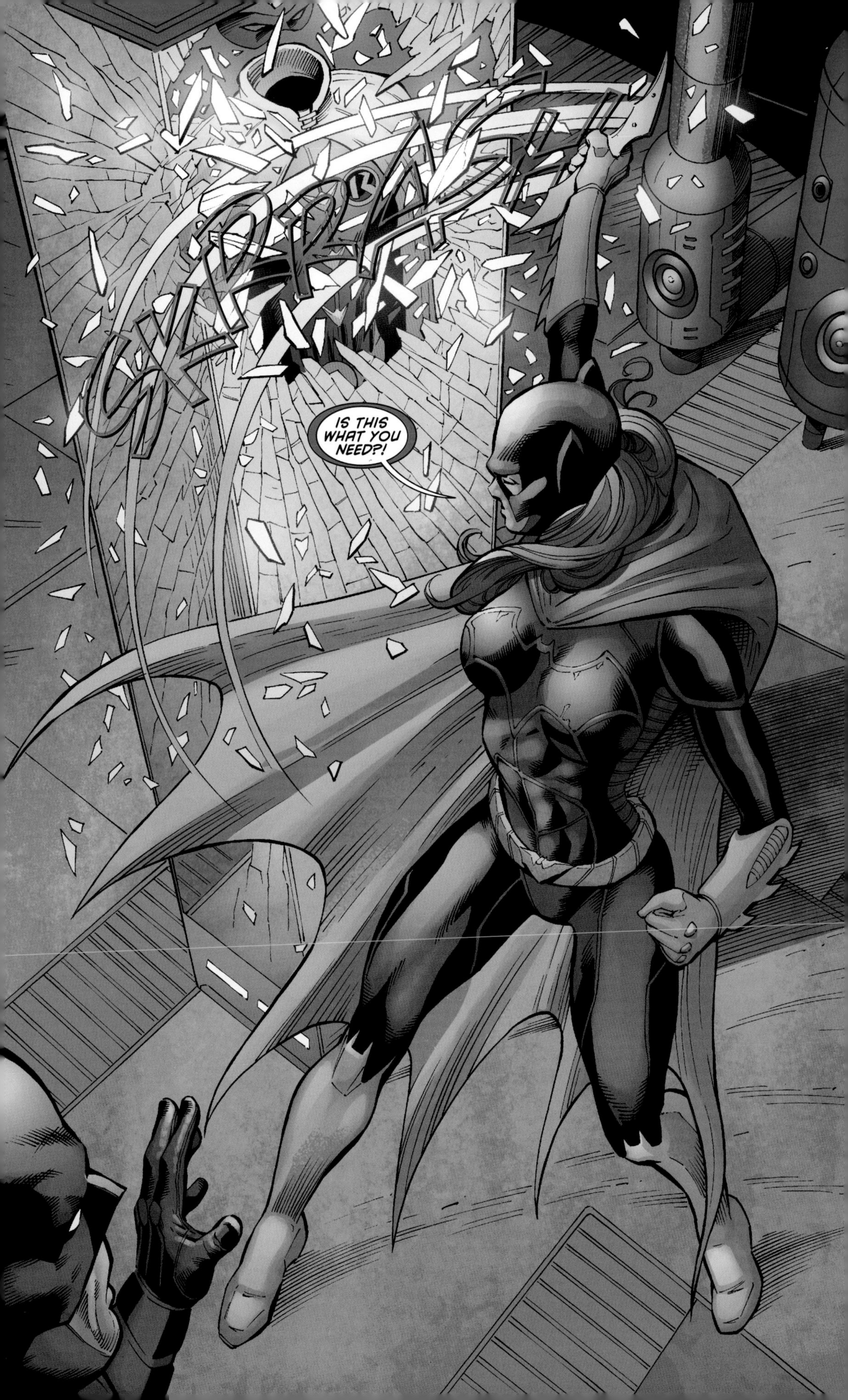
SKRRASH!
IS THIS WHAT YOU NEED?!

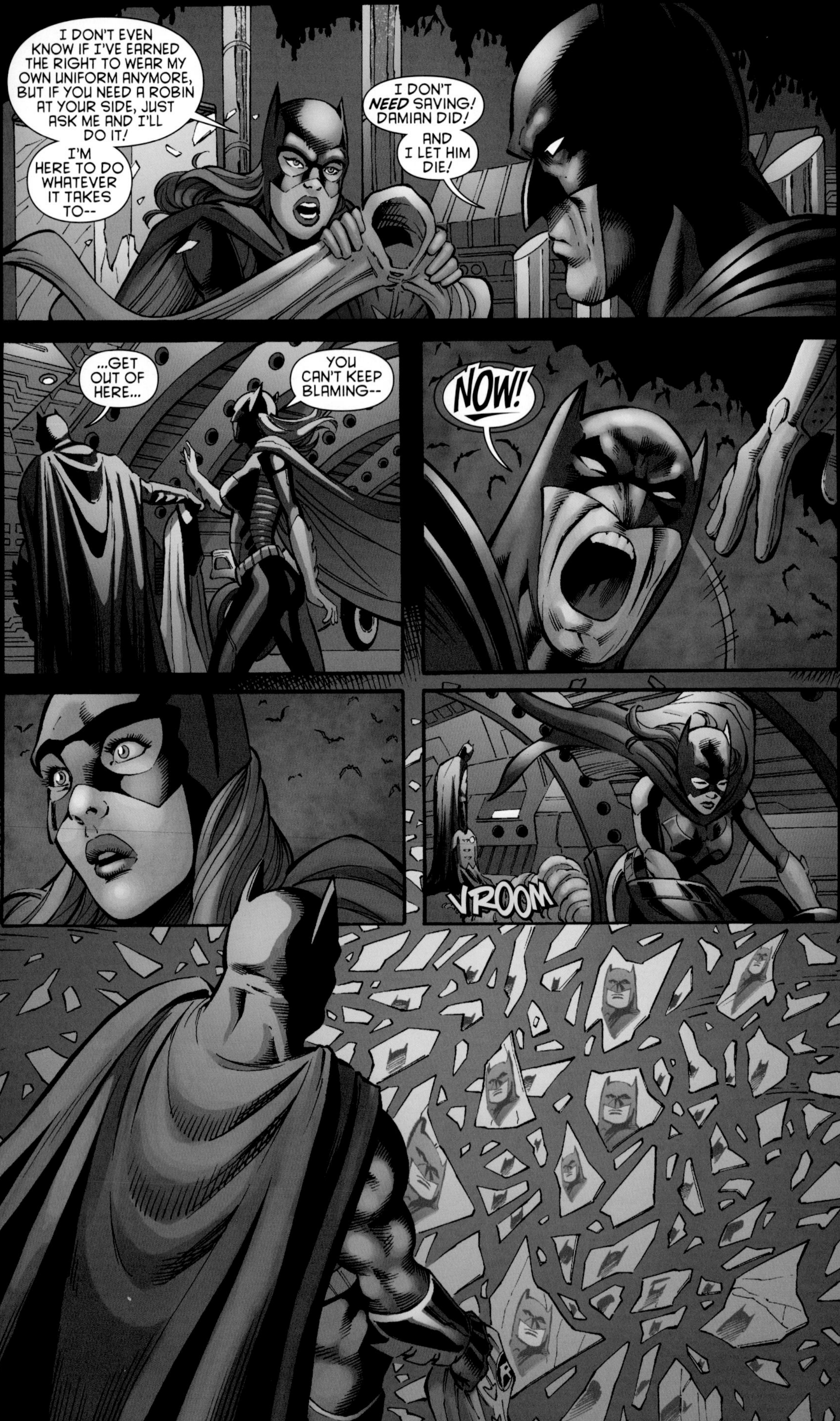
I DON'T EVEN KNOW IF I'VE EARNED THE RIGHT TO WEAR MY OWN UNIFORM ANYMORE, BUT IF YOU NEED A ROBIN AT YOUR SIDE, JUST ASK ME AND I'LL DO IT!
I'M HERE TO DO WHATEVER IT TAKES TO--
I DON'T **NEED** SAVING! DAMIAN DID!
AND I LET HIM DIE!
...GET OUT OF HERE...
YOU CAN'T KEEP BLAMING--
NOW!
VROOM

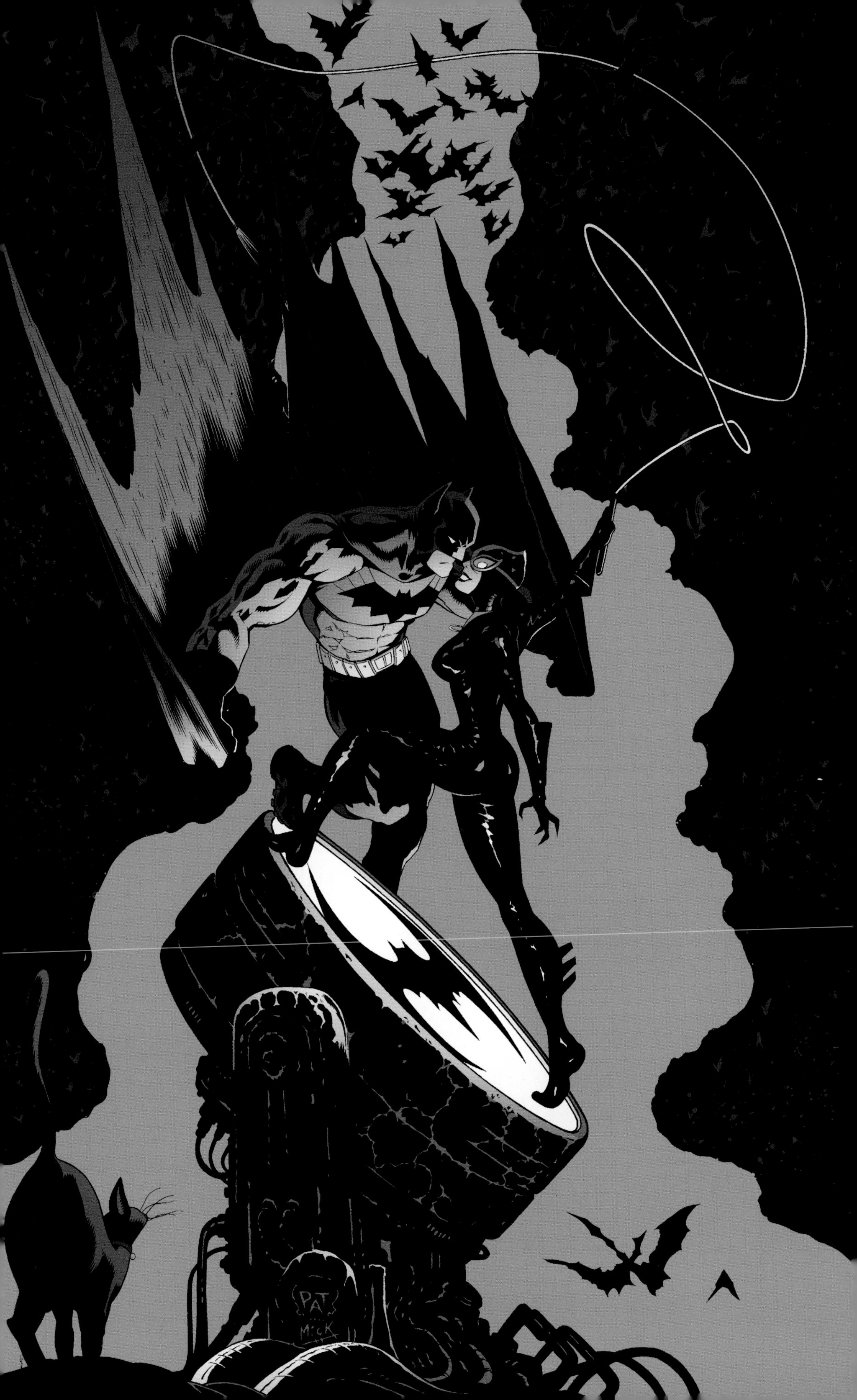

BATMAN AND CATWOMAN: DESPAIR

PATRICK GLEASON penciller MICK GRAY inker

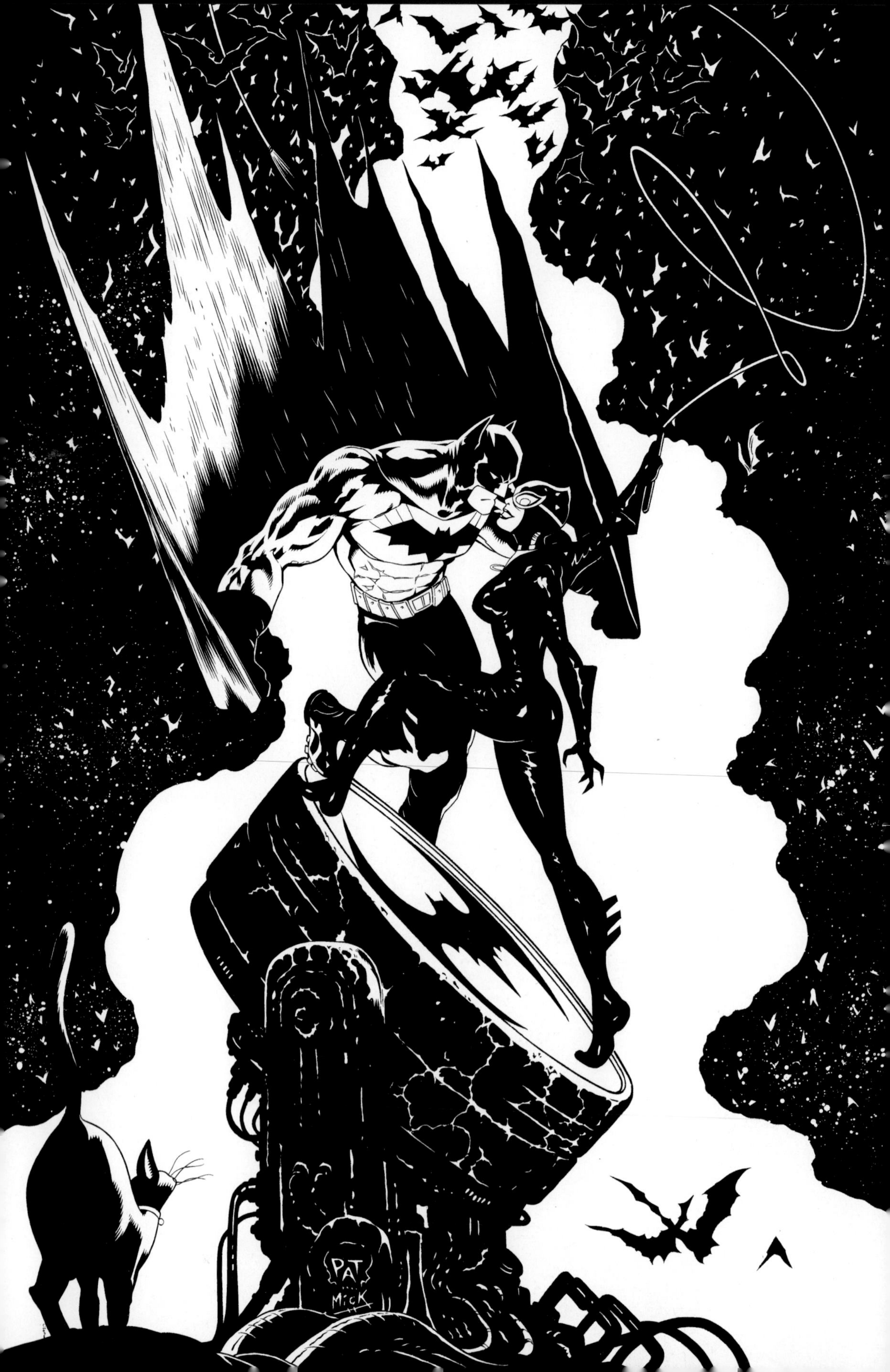
PAT
MICK

Best part of my job's the quiet. The sounds of silence.

Splendid isolation, no one to answer to.

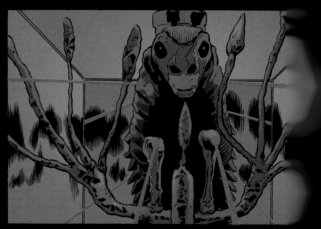

Just me being me and getting the thing that needs getting...

...which tonight is something called the "Ram in a Thicket," a golden figurine that dates back to 2400 B.C.

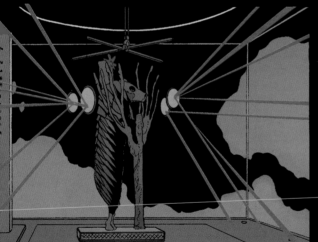

Got its name from a guy named Woolley who exca[v]... it from the Royal Cemete[ry] at Ur in Southern Iraq ba[ck] in 1928.

My client's 4-1-1 sai[d] called it that becaus[e it] reminded him of the [time] Abraham all set to k[ill his] son, Isaac, in the B[ook of] Genesis until he was [saved] by a ram tangled in [the] bushes.

Sure was Isaac's lucky day.

And mine too, since this'll be a nice payout if I keep Penguin from getting a peck of the action.

INCOMING JLA TRANSMISSION.

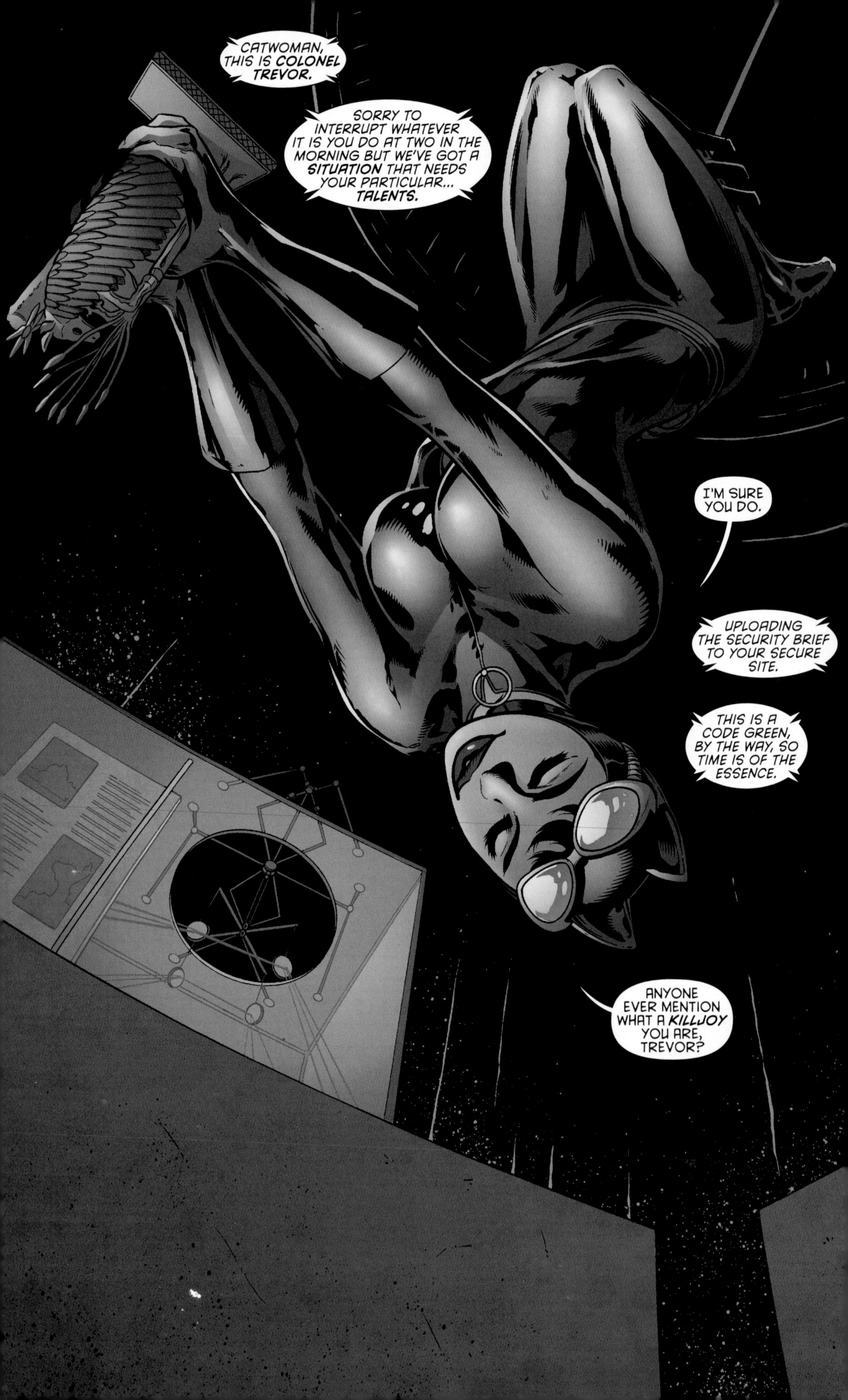
CATWOMAN, THIS IS COLONEL TREVOR.
SORRY TO INTERRUPT WHATEVER IT IS YOU DO AT TWO IN THE MORNING BUT WE'VE GOT A SITUATION THAT NEEDS YOUR PARTICULAR... TALENTS.
I'M SURE YOU DO.
UPLOADING THE SECURITY BRIEF TO YOUR SECURE SITE.
THIS IS A CODE GREEN, BY THE WAY, SO TIME IS OF THE ESSENCE.
ANYONE EVER MENTION WHAT A KILLJOY YOU ARE, TREVOR?

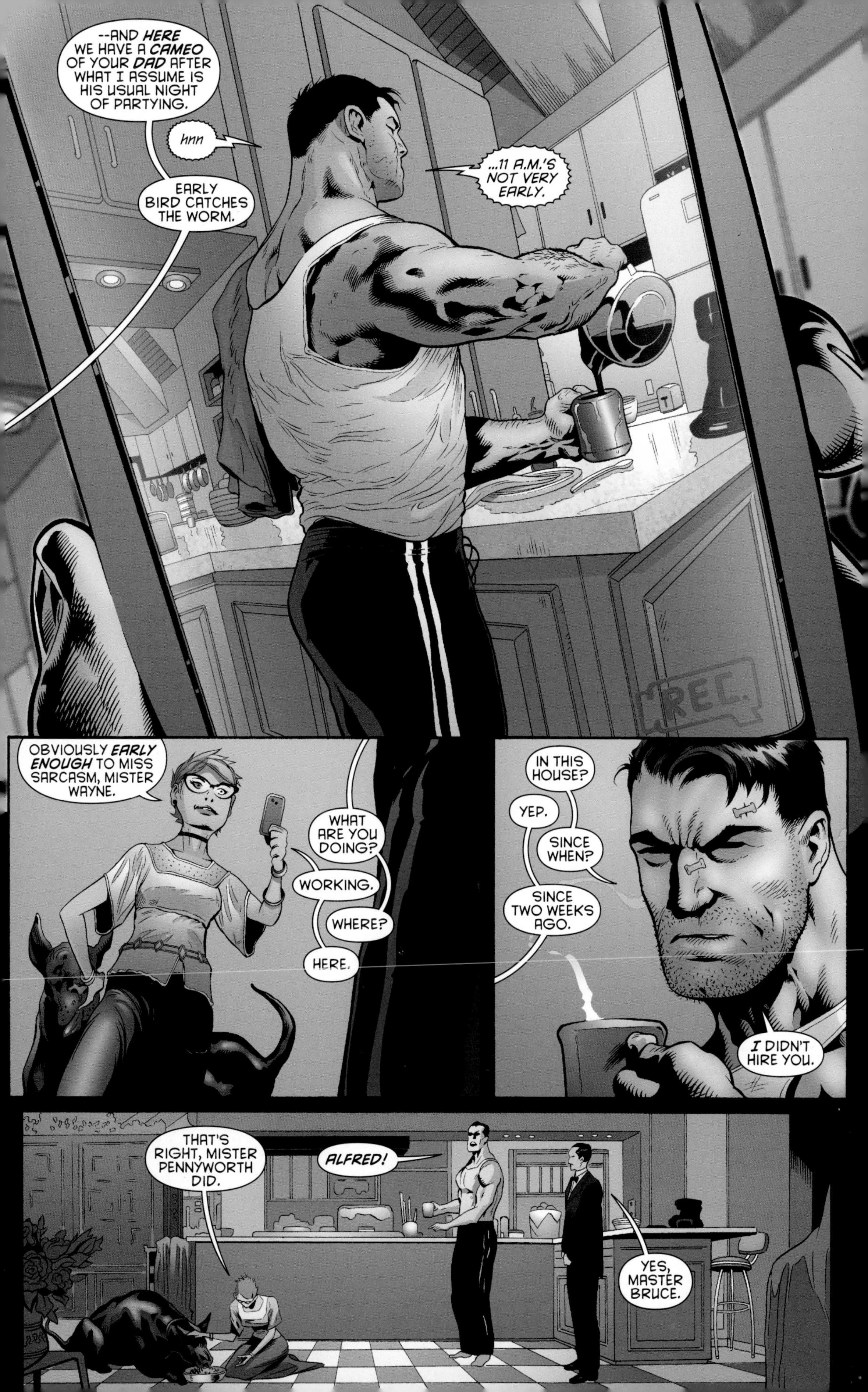
--AND HERE WE HAVE A CAMEO OF YOUR DAD AFTER WHAT I ASSUME IS HIS USUAL NIGHT OF PARTYING.
hnn
EARLY BIRD CATCHES THE WORM.
...11 A.M.'S NOT VERY EARLY.
REC.
OBVIOUSLY EARLY ENOUGH TO MISS SARCASM, MISTER WAYNE.
WHAT ARE YOU DOING?
WORKING.
WHERE?
HERE.
IN THIS HOUSE?
YEP.
SINCE WHEN?
SINCE TWO WEEKS AGO.
I DIDN'T HIRE YOU.
THAT'S RIGHT, MISTER PENNYWORTH DID.
ALFRED!
YES, MASTER BRUCE.

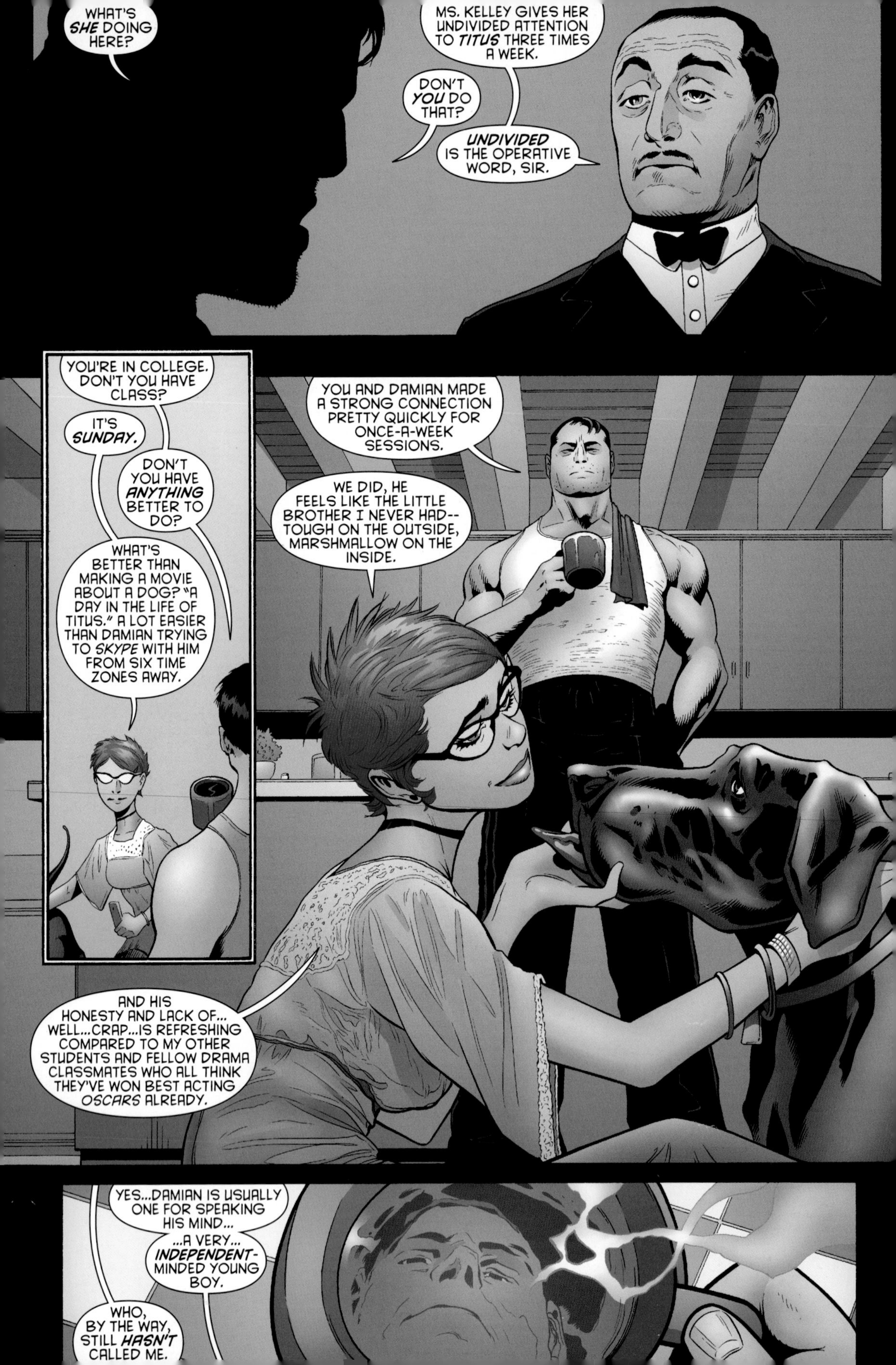
WHAT'S *SHE* DOING HERE?
MS. KELLEY GIVES HER UNDIVIDED ATTENTION TO *TITUS* THREE TIMES A WEEK.
DON'T *YOU* DO THAT?
UNDIVIDED IS THE OPERATIVE WORD, SIR.
YOU'RE IN COLLEGE. DON'T YOU HAVE CLASS?
IT'S *SUNDAY.*
DON'T YOU HAVE *ANYTHING* BETTER TO DO?
WHAT'S BETTER THAN MAKING A MOVIE ABOUT A DOG? "A DAY IN THE LIFE OF TITUS." A LOT EASIER THAN DAMIAN TRYING TO *SKYPE* WITH HIM FROM SIX TIME ZONES AWAY.
YOU AND DAMIAN MADE A STRONG CONNECTION PRETTY QUICKLY FOR ONCE-A-WEEK SESSIONS.
WE DID, HE FEELS LIKE THE LITTLE BROTHER I NEVER HAD-- TOUGH ON THE OUTSIDE, MARSHMALLOW ON THE INSIDE.
AND HIS HONESTY AND LACK OF... WELL...CRAP...IS REFRESHING COMPARED TO MY OTHER STUDENTS AND FELLOW DRAMA CLASSMATES WHO ALL THINK THEY'VE WON BEST ACTING *OSCARS* ALREADY.
YES...DAMIAN IS USUALLY ONE FOR SPEAKING HIS MIND...
...A VERY... *INDEPENDENT*-MINDED YOUNG BOY.
WHO, BY THE WAY, STILL *HASN'T* CALLED ME.

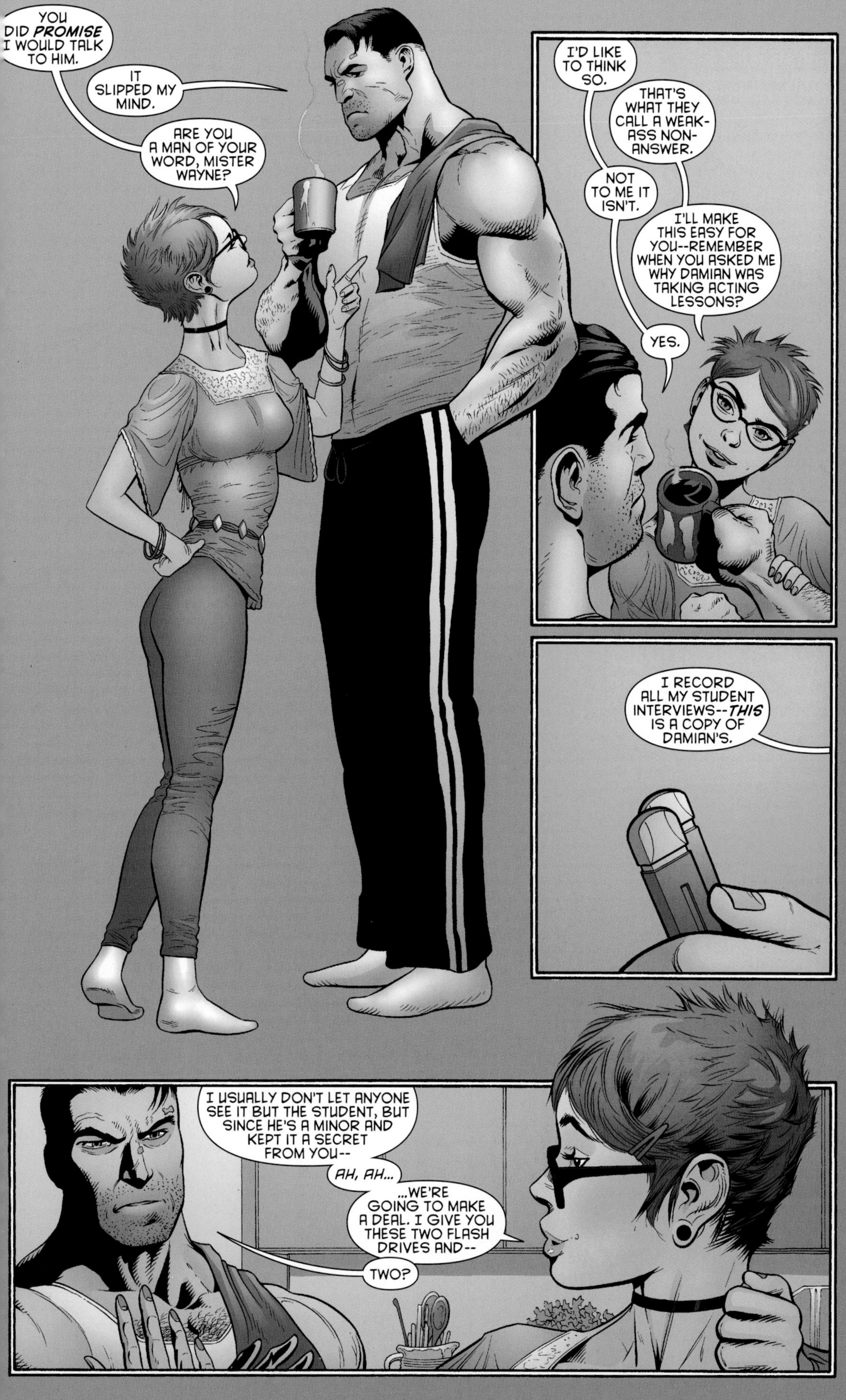

YOU DID *PROMISE* I WOULD TALK TO HIM.
IT SLIPPED MY MIND.
ARE YOU A MAN OF YOUR WORD, MISTER WAYNE?
I'D LIKE TO THINK SO.
THAT'S WHAT THEY CALL A WEAK-ASS NON-ANSWER.
NOT TO ME IT ISN'T.
I'LL MAKE THIS EASY FOR YOU--REMEMBER WHEN YOU ASKED ME WHY DAMIAN WAS TAKING ACTING LESSONS?
YES.
I RECORD ALL MY STUDENT INTERVIEWS--*THIS* IS A COPY OF DAMIAN'S.
I USUALLY DON'T LET ANYONE SEE IT BUT THE STUDENT, BUT SINCE HE'S A MINOR AND KEPT IT A SECRET FROM YOU--
AH, AH...
...WE'RE GOING TO MAKE A DEAL. I GIVE YOU THESE TWO FLASH DRIVES AND--
TWO?

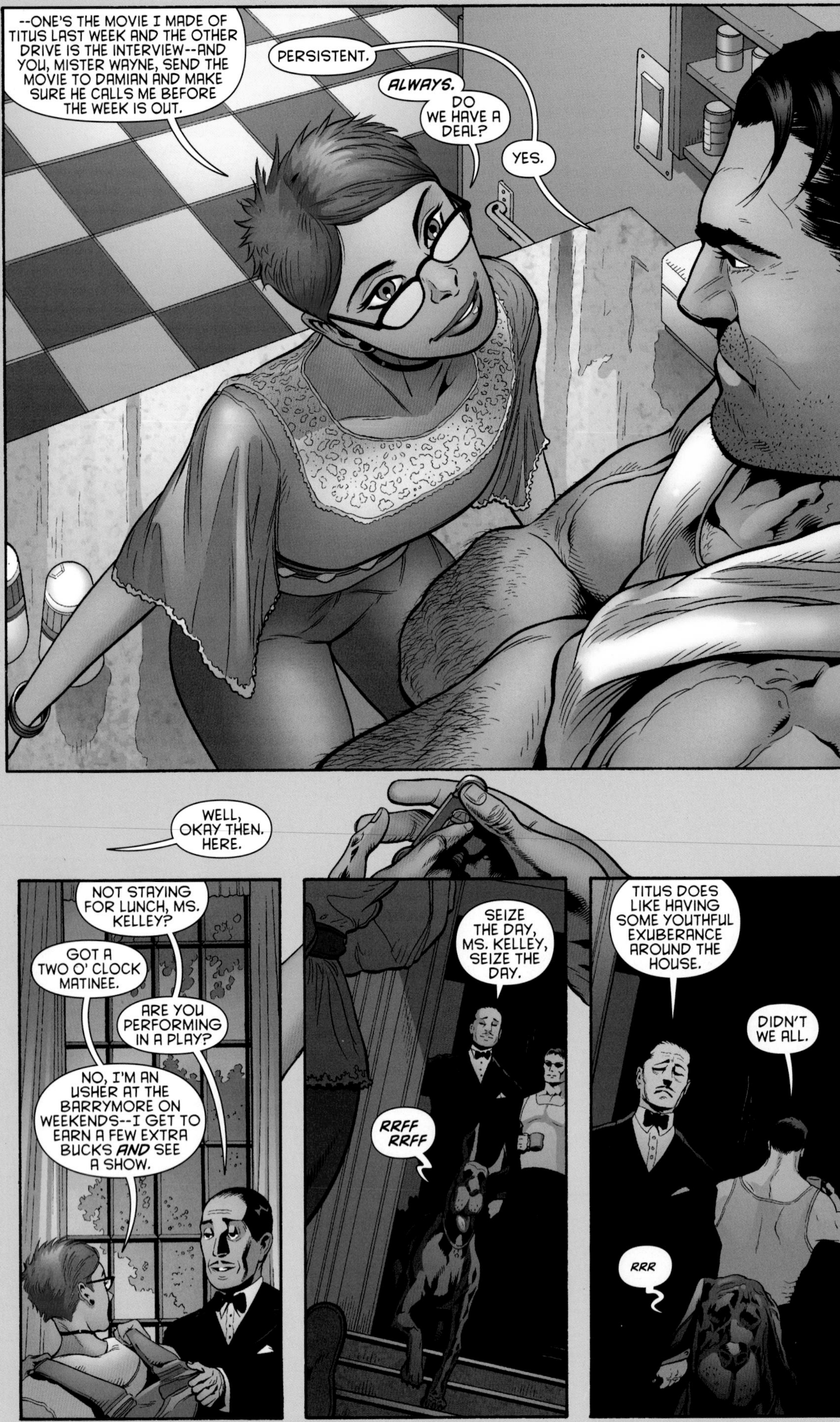
--ONE'S THE MOVIE I MADE OF TITUS LAST WEEK AND THE OTHER DRIVE IS THE INTERVIEW--AND YOU, MISTER WAYNE, SEND THE MOVIE TO DAMIAN AND MAKE SURE HE CALLS ME BEFORE THE WEEK IS OUT.
PERSISTENT.
ALWAYS.
DO WE HAVE A DEAL?
YES.
WELL, OKAY THEN. HERE.
NOT STAYING FOR LUNCH, MS. KELLEY?
GOT A TWO O' CLOCK MATINEE.
ARE YOU PERFORMING IN A PLAY?
NO, I'M AN USHER AT THE BARRYMORE ON WEEKENDS--I GET TO EARN A FEW EXTRA BUCKS AND SEE A SHOW.
SEIZE THE DAY, MS. KELLEY, SEIZE THE DAY.
RRFF RRFF
TITUS DOES LIKE HAVING SOME YOUTHFUL EXUBERANCE AROUND THE HOUSE.
DIDN'T WE ALL.
RRR

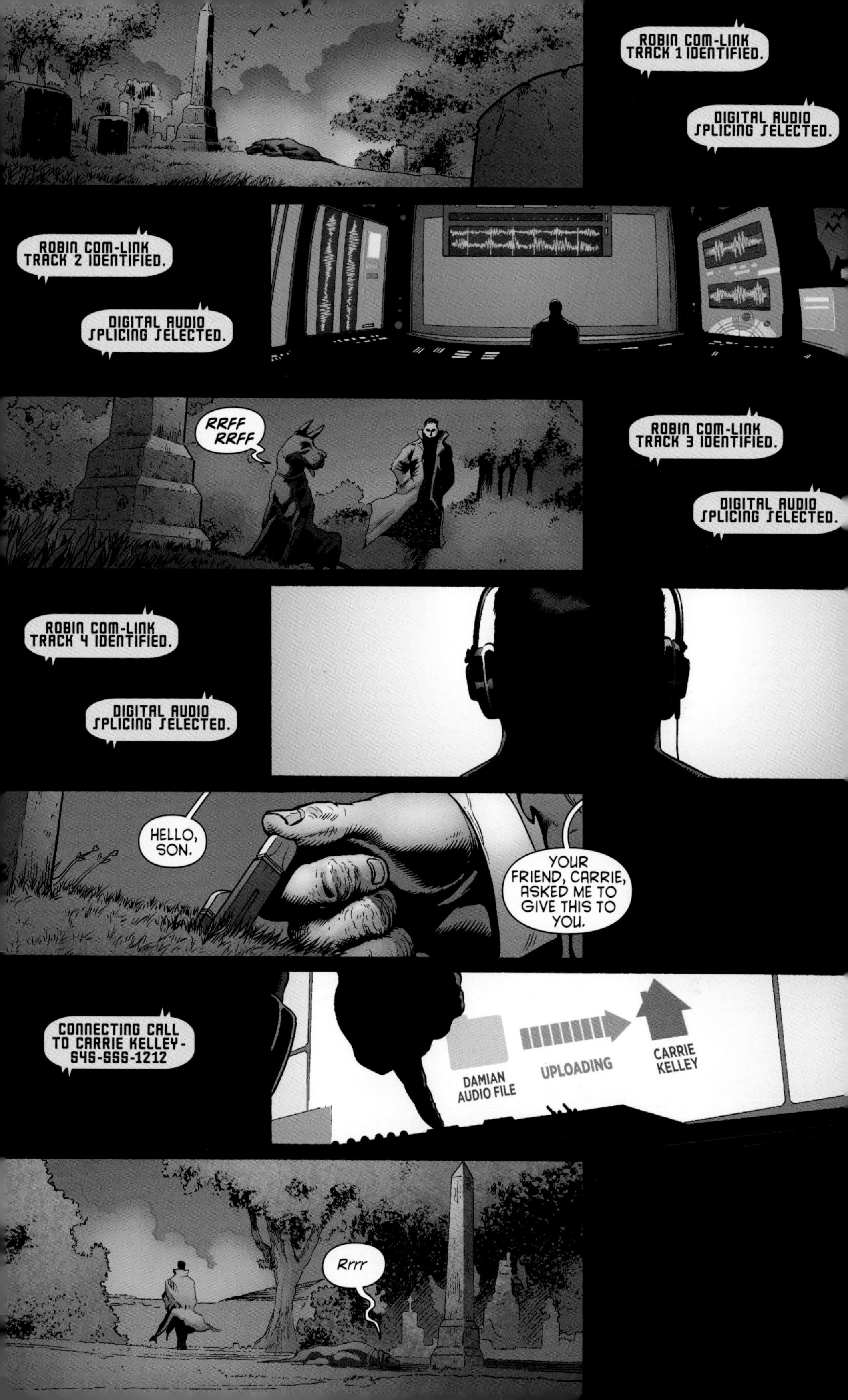
ROBIN COM-LINK TRACK 1 IDENTIFIED.
DIGITAL AUDIO SPLICING SELECTED.
ROBIN COM-LINK TRACK 2 IDENTIFIED.
DIGITAL AUDIO SPLICING SELECTED.
RRFF RRFF
ROBIN COM-LINK TRACK 3 IDENTIFIED.
DIGITAL AUDIO SPLICING SELECTED.
ROBIN COM-LINK TRACK 4 IDENTIFIED.
DIGITAL AUDIO SPLICING SELECTED.
HELLO, SON.
YOUR FRIEND, CARRIE, ASKED ME TO GIVE THIS TO YOU.
CONNECTING CALL TO CARRIE KELLEY - 545-555-1212
DAMIAN AUDIO FILE
UPLOADING
CARRIE KELLEY
Rrrr

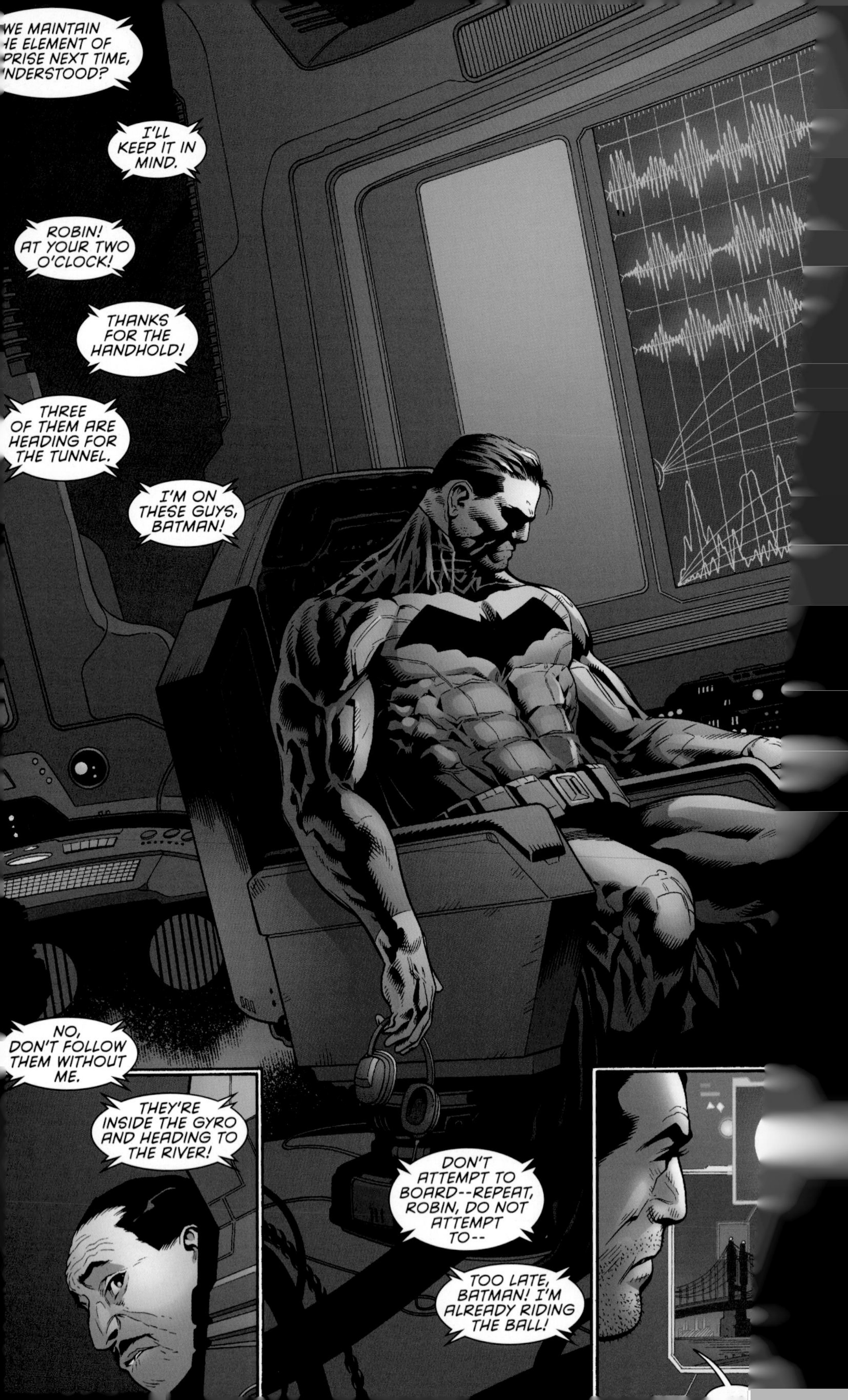
WE MAINTAIN
HE ELEMENT OF
PRISE NEXT TIME,
NDERSTOOD?
I'LL KEEP IT IN MIND.
ROBIN! AT YOUR TWO O'CLOCK!
THANKS FOR THE HANDHOLD!
THREE OF THEM ARE HEADING FOR THE TUNNEL.
I'M ON THESE GUYS, BATMAN!
NO, DON'T FOLLOW THEM WITHOUT ME.
THEY'RE INSIDE THE GYRO AND HEADING TO THE RIVER!
DON'T ATTEMPT TO BOARD--REPEAT, ROBIN, DO NOT ATTEMPT TO--
TOO LATE, BATMAN! I'M ALREADY RIDING THE BALL!

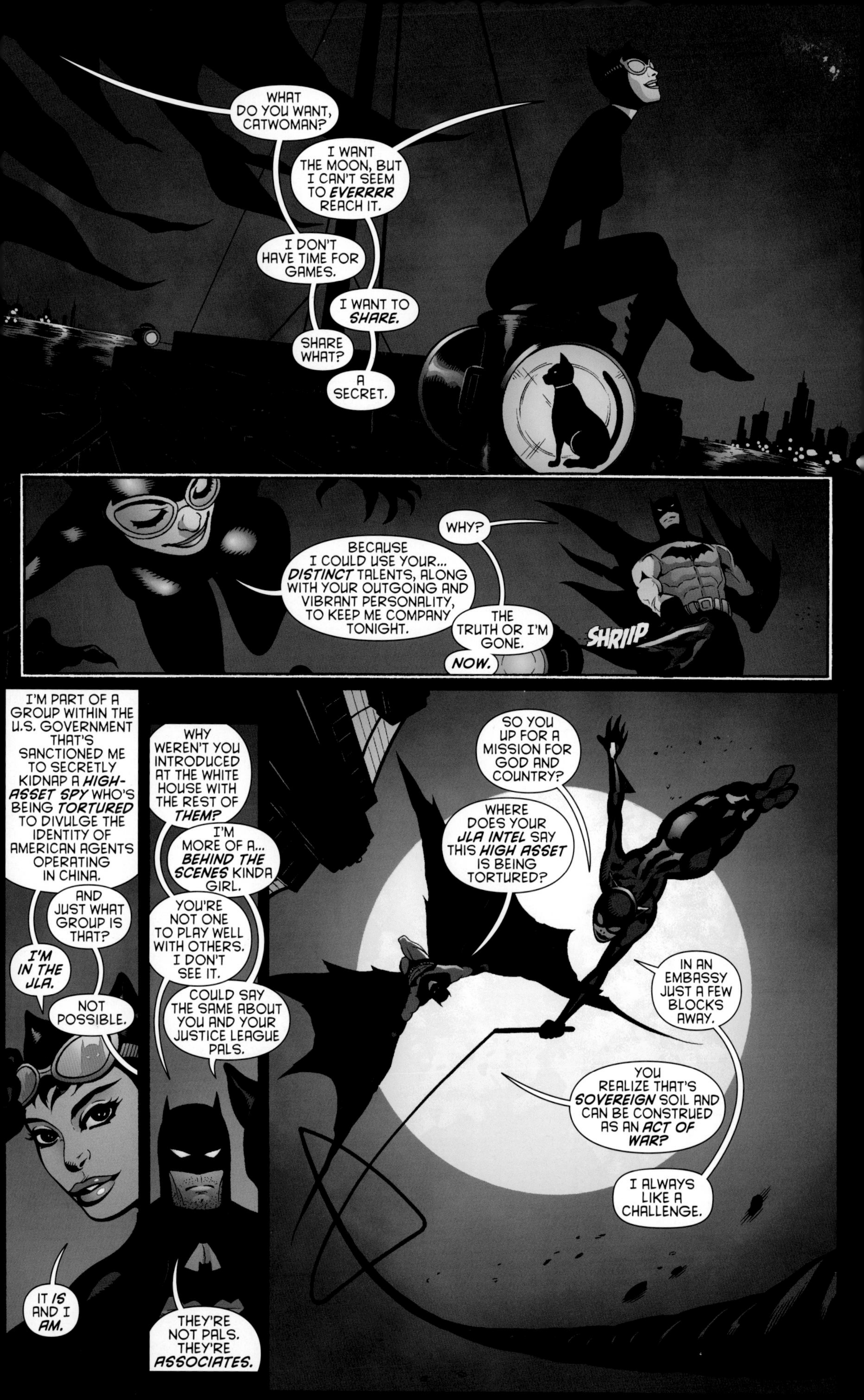
WHAT DO YOU WANT, CATWOMAN?
I WANT THE MOON, BUT I CAN'T SEEM TO EVERRRR REACH IT.
I DON'T HAVE TIME FOR GAMES.
I WANT TO SHARE.
SHARE WHAT?
A SECRET.
WHY?
BECAUSE I COULD USE YOUR... DISTINCT TALENTS, ALONG WITH YOUR OUTGOING AND VIBRANT PERSONALITY, TO KEEP ME COMPANY TONIGHT.
THE TRUTH OR I'M GONE.
NOW.
SHRIIP
I'M PART OF A GROUP WITHIN THE U.S. GOVERNMENT THAT'S SANCTIONED ME TO SECRETLY KIDNAP A HIGH-ASSET SPY WHO'S BEING TORTURED TO DIVULGE THE IDENTITY OF AMERICAN AGENTS OPERATING IN CHINA.
AND JUST WHAT GROUP IS THAT?
I'M IN THE JLA.
NOT POSSIBLE.
IT IS AND I AM.
WHY WEREN'T YOU INTRODUCED AT THE WHITE HOUSE WITH THE REST OF THEM?
I'M MORE OF A... BEHIND THE SCENES KINDA GIRL.
YOU'RE NOT ONE TO PLAY WELL WITH OTHERS. I DON'T SEE IT.
COULD SAY THE SAME ABOUT YOU AND YOUR JUSTICE LEAGUE PALS.
THEY'RE NOT PALS. THEY'RE ASSOCIATES.
SO YOU UP FOR A MISSION FOR GOD AND COUNTRY?
WHERE DOES YOUR JLA INTEL SAY THIS HIGH ASSET IS BEING TORTURED?
IN AN EMBASSY JUST A FEW BLOCKS AWAY.
YOU REALIZE THAT'S SOVEREIGN SOIL AND CAN BE CONSTRUED AS AN ACT OF WAR?
I ALWAYS LIKE A CHALLENGE.

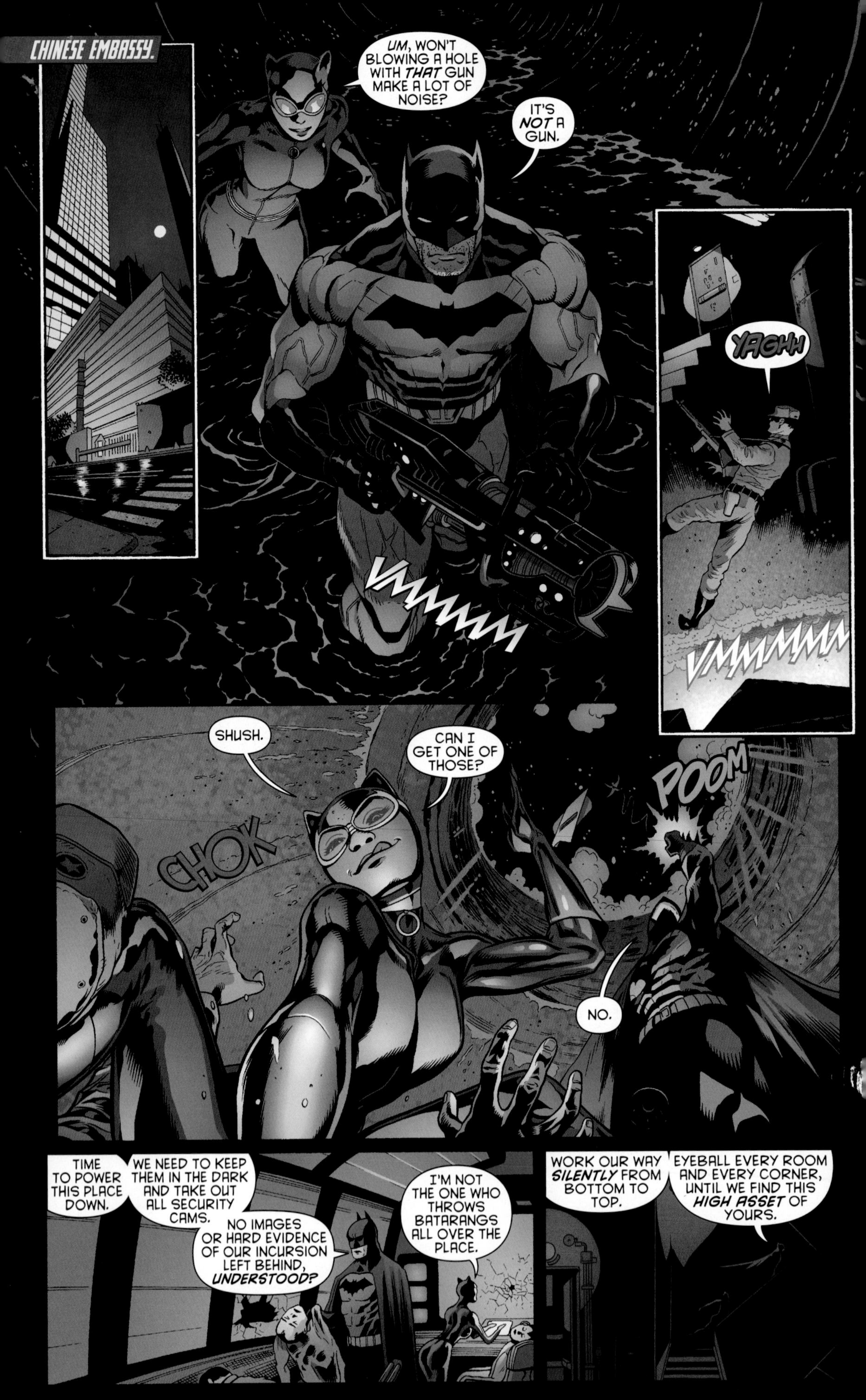
CHINESE EMBASSY.
UM, WON'T BLOWING A HOLE WITH THAT GUN MAKE A LOT OF NOISE?
IT'S NOT A GUN.
VMMMMM
YAGHH
VMMMMM
SHUSH.
CAN I GET ONE OF THOSE?
POOM
CHOK
NO.
TIME TO POWER THIS PLACE DOWN.
WE NEED TO KEEP THEM IN THE DARK AND TAKE OUT ALL SECURITY CAMS.
NO IMAGES OR HARD EVIDENCE OF OUR INCURSION LEFT BEHIND, UNDERSTOOD?
I'M NOT THE ONE WHO THROWS BATARANGS ALL OVER THE PLACE.
WORK OUR WAY SILENTLY FROM BOTTOM TO TOP.
EYEBALL EVERY ROOM AND EVERY CORNER, UNTIL WE FIND THIS HIGH ASSET OF YOURS.

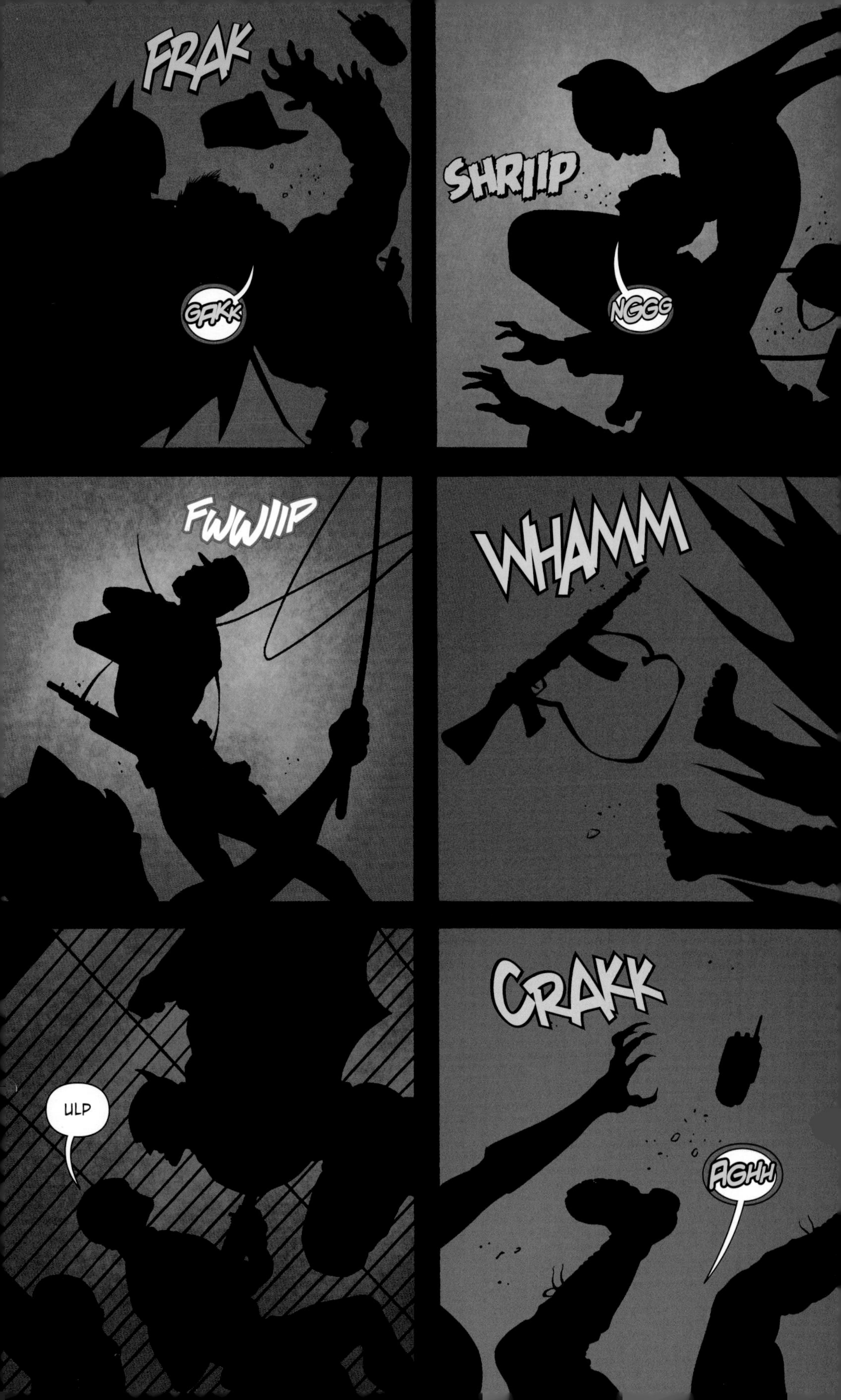
FRAK
GAKK
SHRIIP
NGGG
FWWIIP
WHAMM
ULP
CRAKK
AGHH

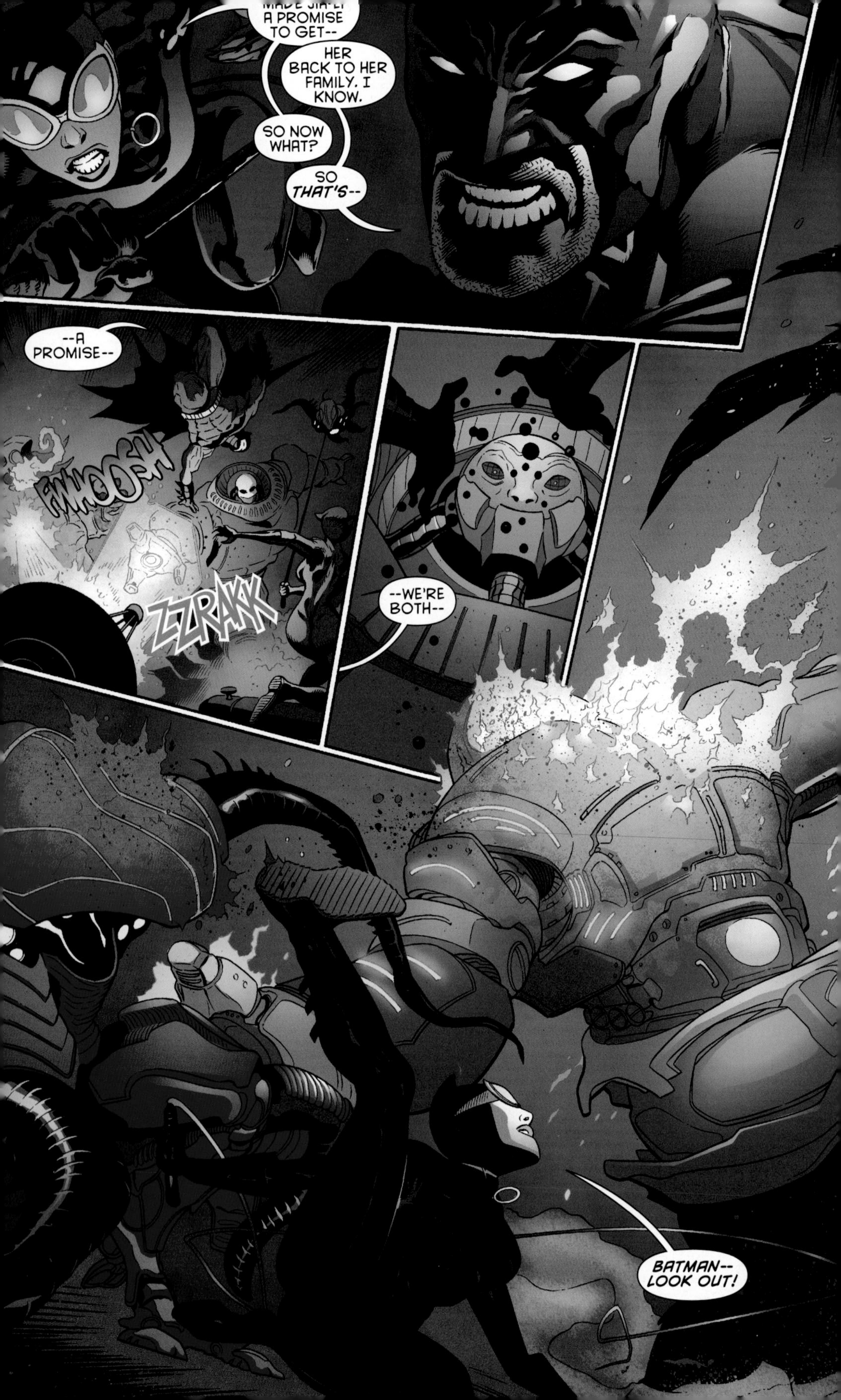
A PROMISE TO GET--
HER BACK TO HER FAMILY. I KNOW.
SO NOW WHAT?
SO THAT'S--
--A PROMISE--
FWHOOSH
ZZRAKK
--WE'RE BOTH--
BATMAN-- LOOK OUT!

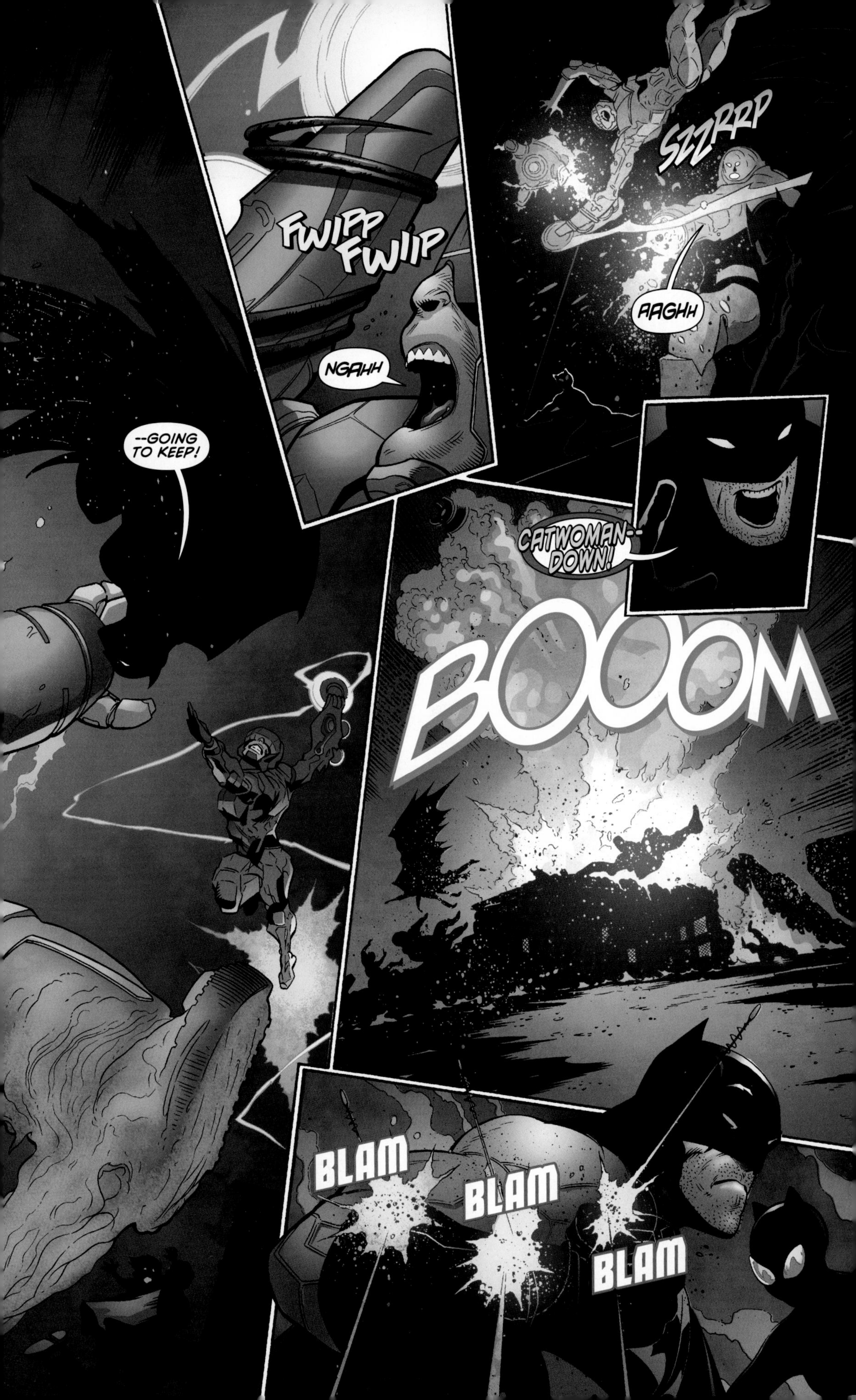
FWIPP FWIIP
NGAHH
SZZRRP
AAGHH
--GOING TO KEEP!
CATWOMAN-- DOWN!
BOOOM
BLAM
BLAM
BLAM

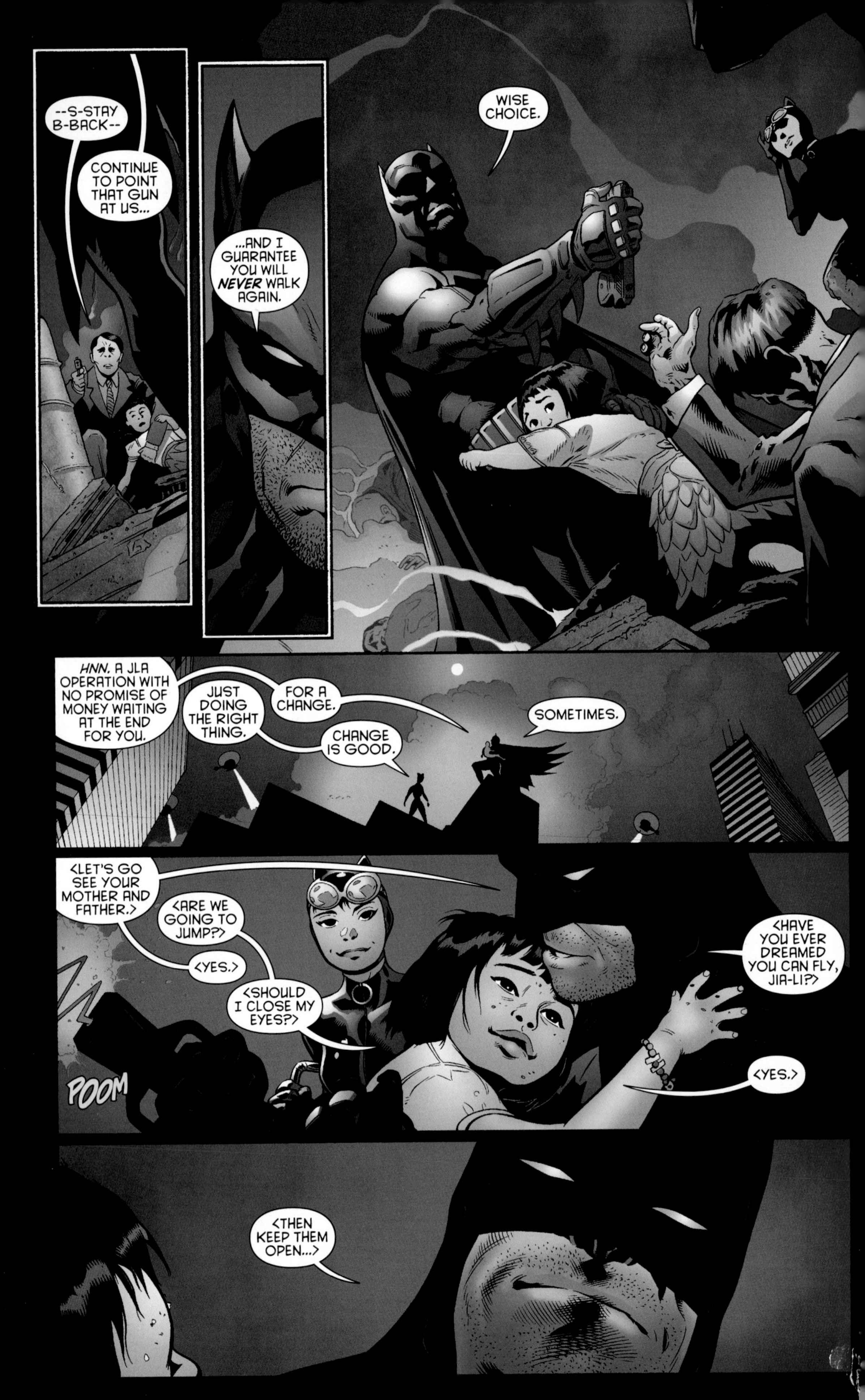
--S-STAY B-BACK--
CONTINUE TO POINT THAT GUN AT US...
...AND I GUARANTEE YOU WILL NEVER WALK AGAIN.
WISE CHOICE.
HNN. A JLA OPERATION WITH NO PROMISE OF MONEY WAITING AT THE END FOR YOU.
JUST DOING THE RIGHT THING.
FOR A CHANGE.
CHANGE IS GOOD.
SOMETIMES.
<LET'S GO SEE YOUR MOTHER AND FATHER.>
<ARE WE GOING TO JUMP?>
<YES.>
<SHOULD I CLOSE MY EYES?>
<HAVE YOU EVER DREAMED YOU CAN FLY, JIA-LI?>
<YES.>
POOM
<THEN KEEP THEM OPEN...>

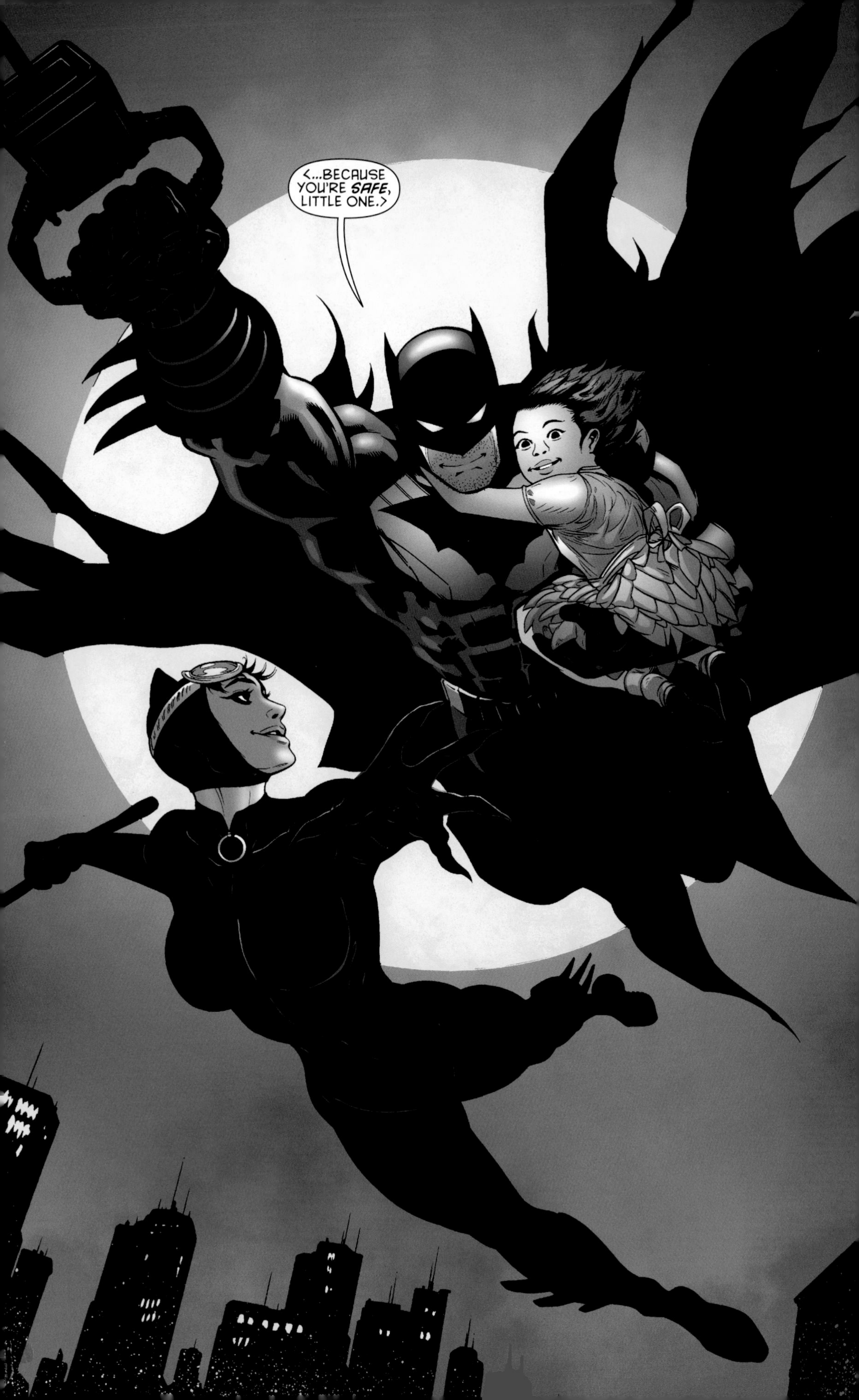
<...BECAUSE YOU'RE SAFE, LITTLE ONE.>

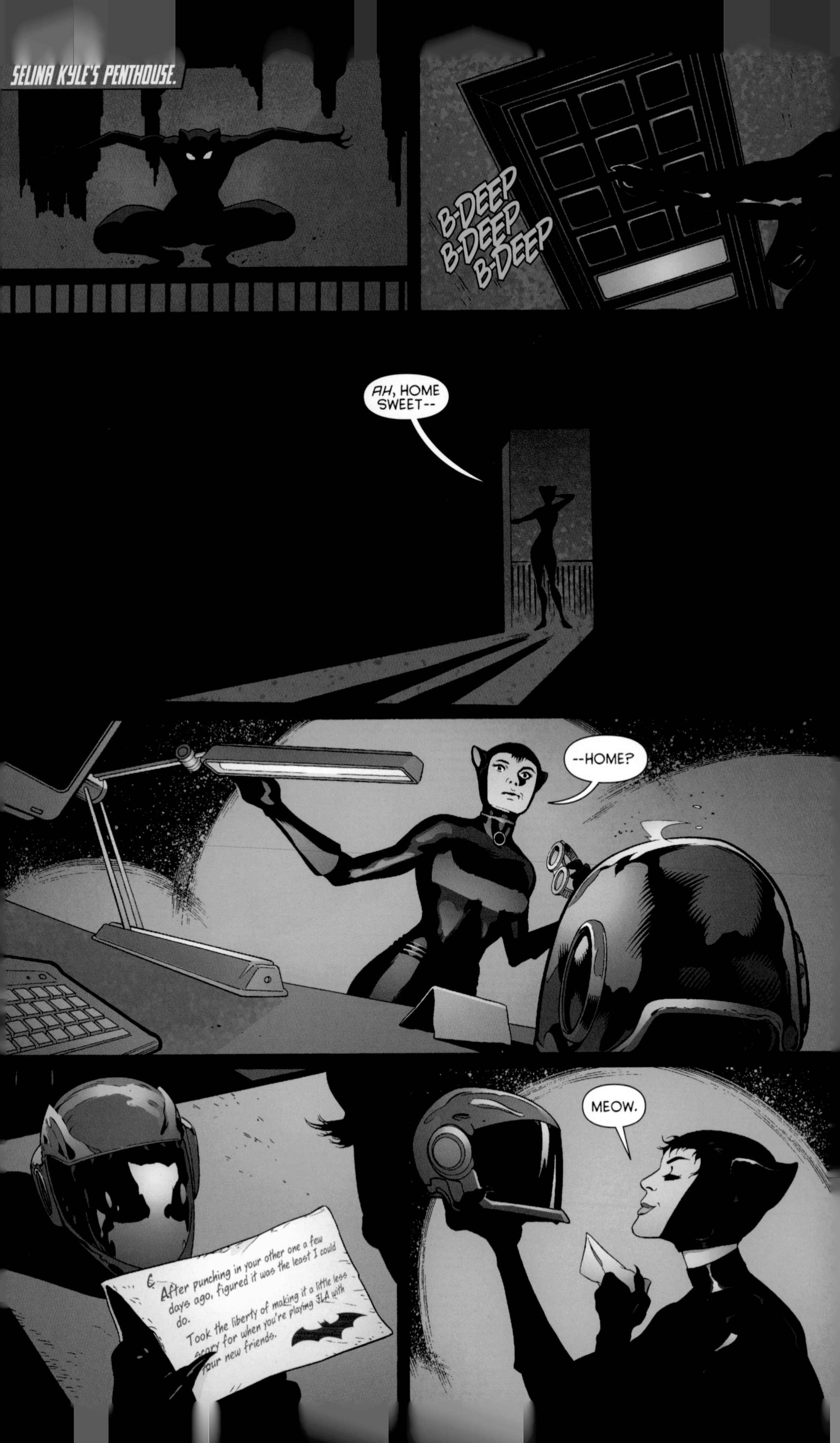
SELINA KYLE'S PENTHOUSE.
B-DEEP B-DEEP B-DEEP
AH, HOME SWEET--
--HOME?
E
After punching in your other one a few days ago, figured it was the least I could do.
Took the liberty of making it a little less scary for when you're playing JLA with your new friends.
MEOW.

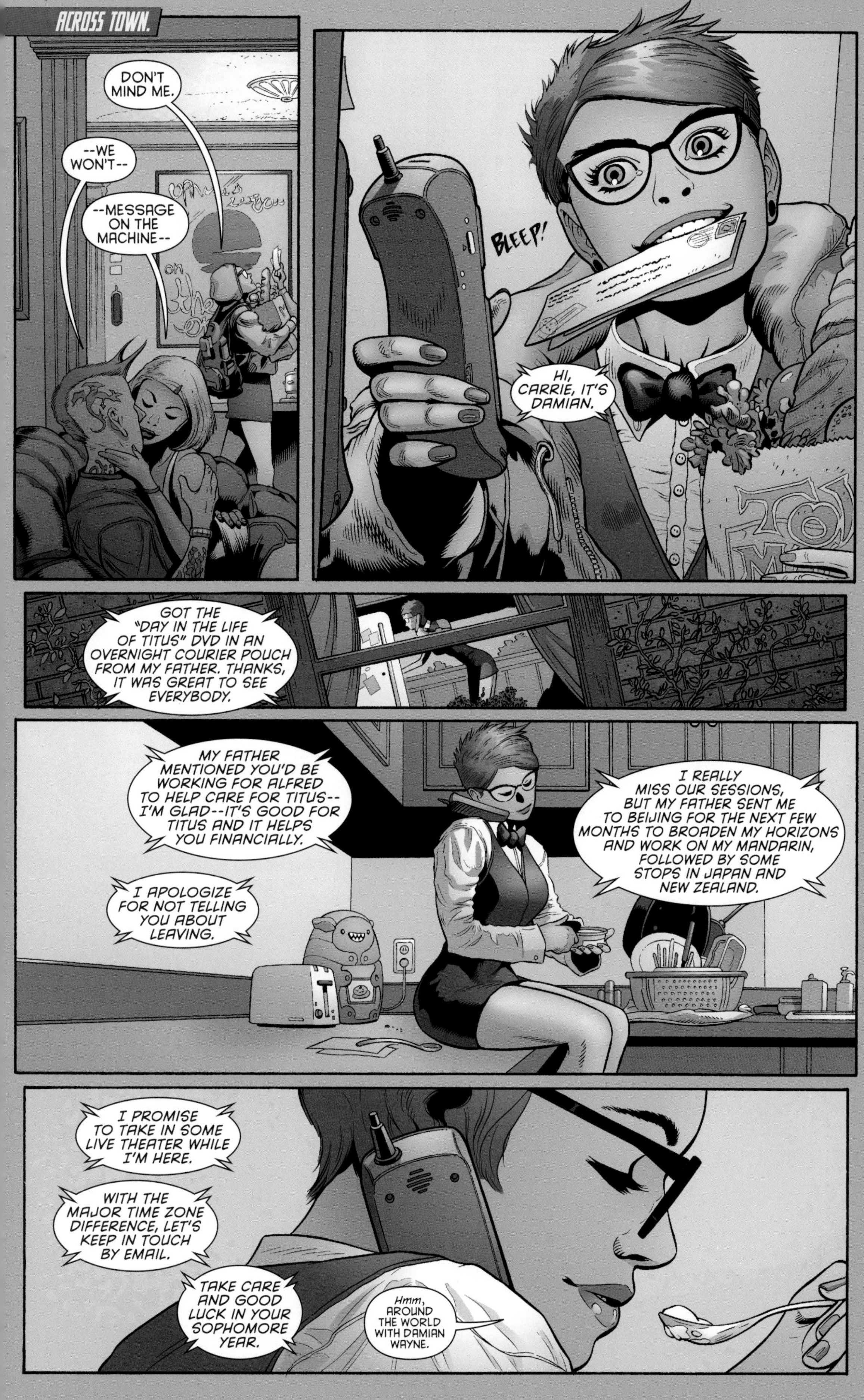
ACROSS TOWN.
DON'T MIND ME.
--WE WON'T--
--MESSAGE ON THE MACHINE--
BLEEP!
HI, CARRIE, IT'S DAMIAN.
GOT THE "DAY IN THE LIFE OF TITUS" DVD IN AN OVERNIGHT COURIER POUCH FROM MY FATHER. THANKS, IT WAS GREAT TO SEE EVERYBODY.
MY FATHER MENTIONED YOU'D BE WORKING FOR ALFRED TO HELP CARE FOR TITUS--I'M GLAD--IT'S GOOD FOR TITUS AND IT HELPS YOU FINANCIALLY.
I APOLOGIZE FOR NOT TELLING YOU ABOUT LEAVING.
I REALLY MISS OUR SESSIONS, BUT MY FATHER SENT ME TO BEIJING FOR THE NEXT FEW MONTHS TO BROADEN MY HORIZONS AND WORK ON MY MANDARIN, FOLLOWED BY SOME STOPS IN JAPAN AND NEW ZEALAND.
I PROMISE TO TAKE IN SOME LIVE THEATER WHILE I'M HERE.
WITH THE MAJOR TIME ZONE DIFFERENCE, LET'S KEEP IN TOUCH BY EMAIL.
TAKE CARE AND GOOD LUCK IN YOUR SOPHOMORE YEAR.
Hmm, AROUND THE WORLD WITH DAMIAN WAYNE.

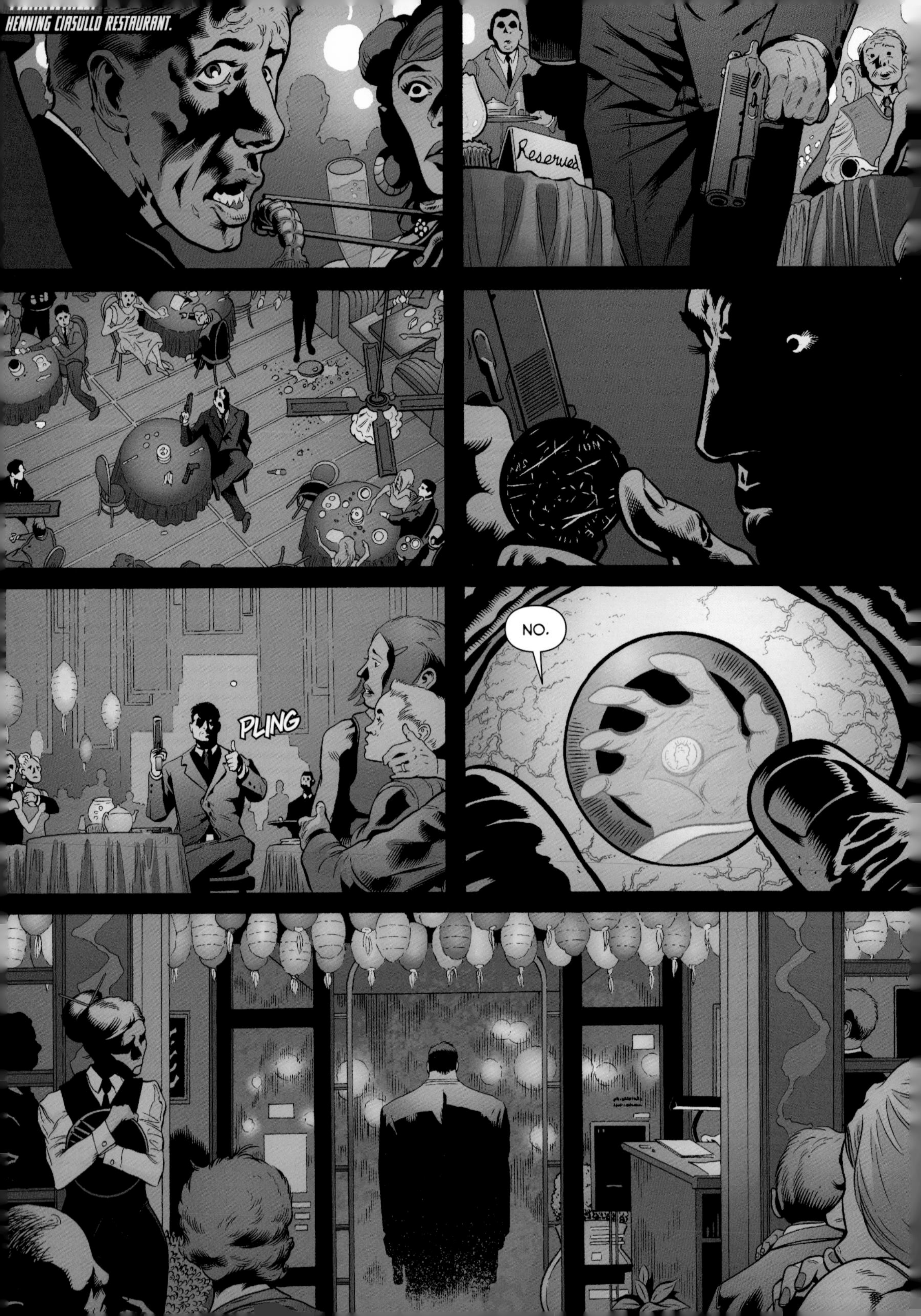
HENNING CIASULLO RESTAURANT.
Reserved
PLING
NO.

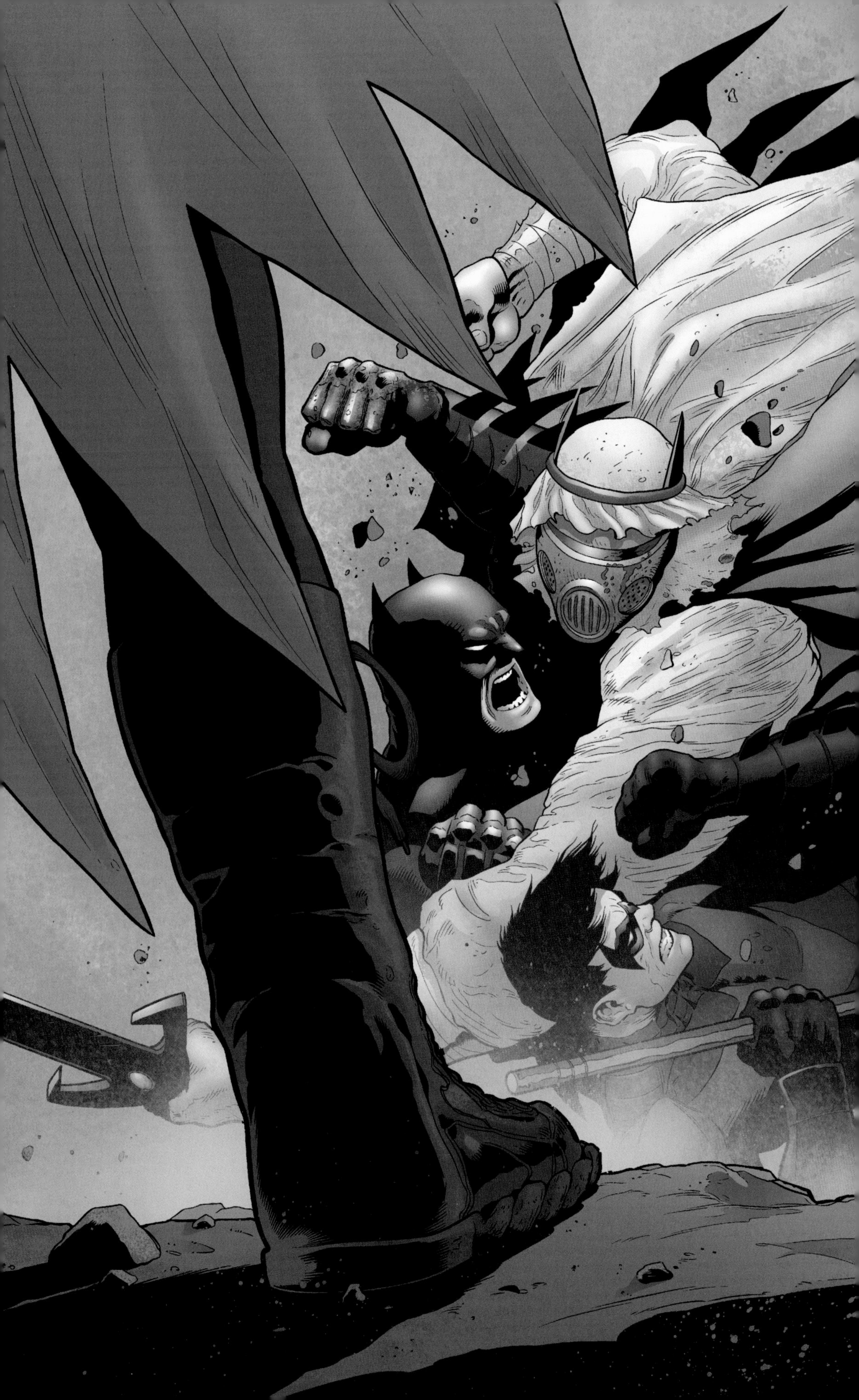

BATMAN AND NIGHTWING: ACCEPTANCE

PATRICK GLEASON penciller MICK GRAY & MARK JOHN IRWIN inkers

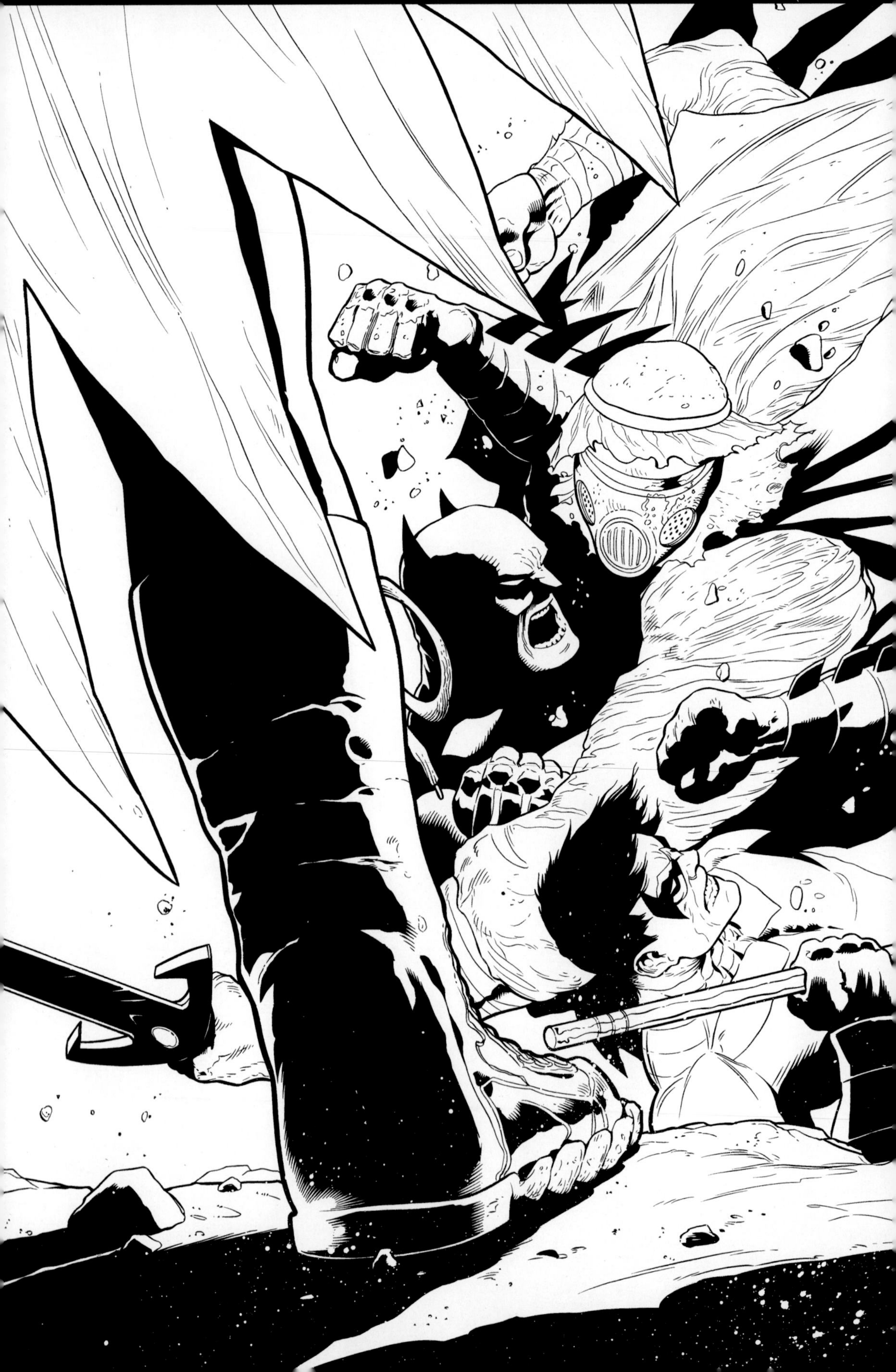

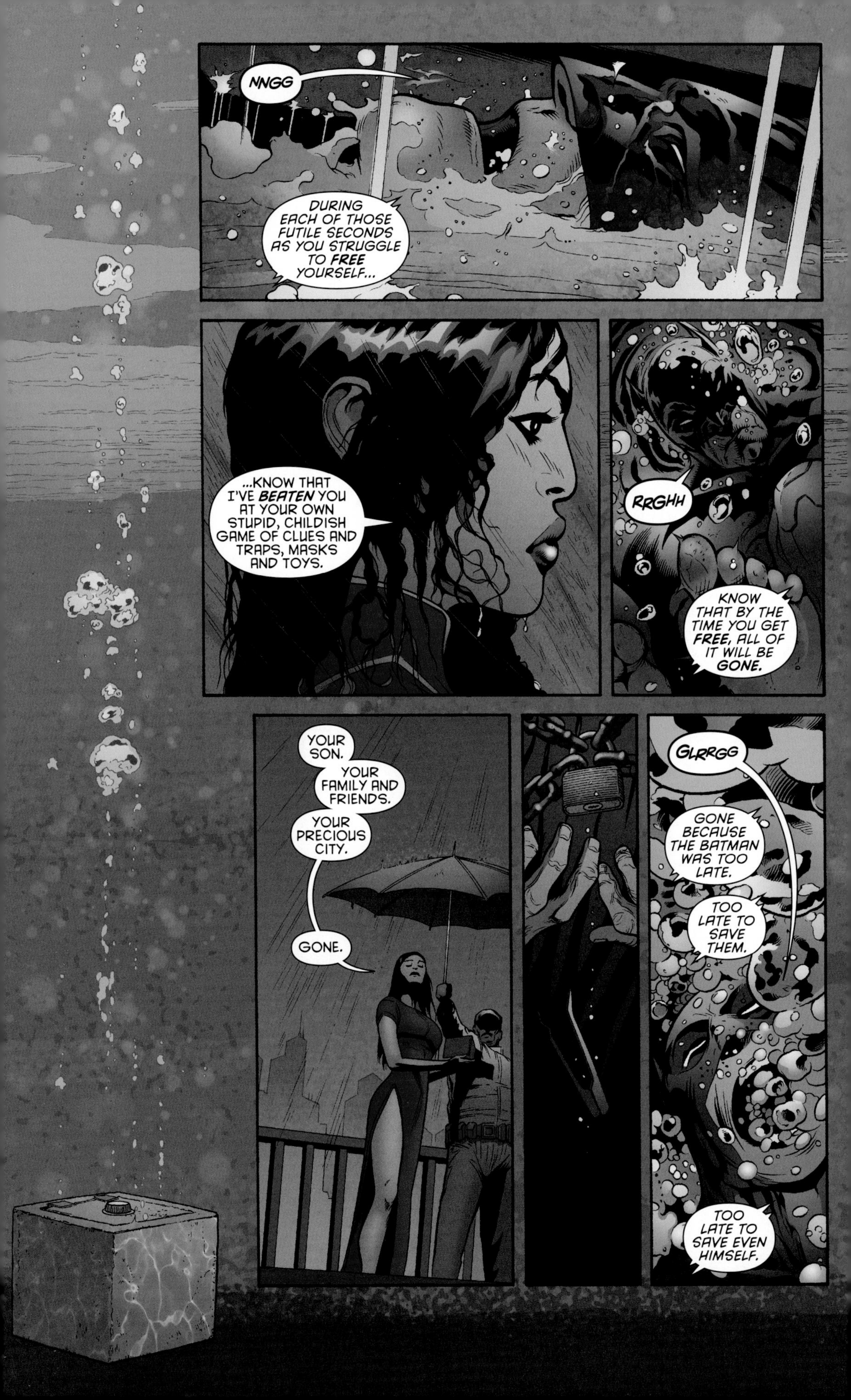
NNGG
DURING EACH OF THOSE FUTILE SECONDS AS YOU STRUGGLE TO **FREE** YOURSELF...
...KNOW THAT I'VE ***BEATEN*** YOU AT YOUR OWN STUPID, CHILDISH GAME OF CLUES AND TRAPS, MASKS AND TOYS.
RRGHH
KNOW THAT BY THE TIME YOU GET ***FREE***, ALL OF IT WILL BE ***GONE.***
YOUR SON.
YOUR FAMILY AND FRIENDS.
YOUR PRECIOUS CITY.
GONE.
GLRRGG
GONE BECAUSE THE BATMAN WAS TOO LATE.
TOO LATE TO SAVE THEM.
TOO LATE TO SAVE EVEN HIMSELF.

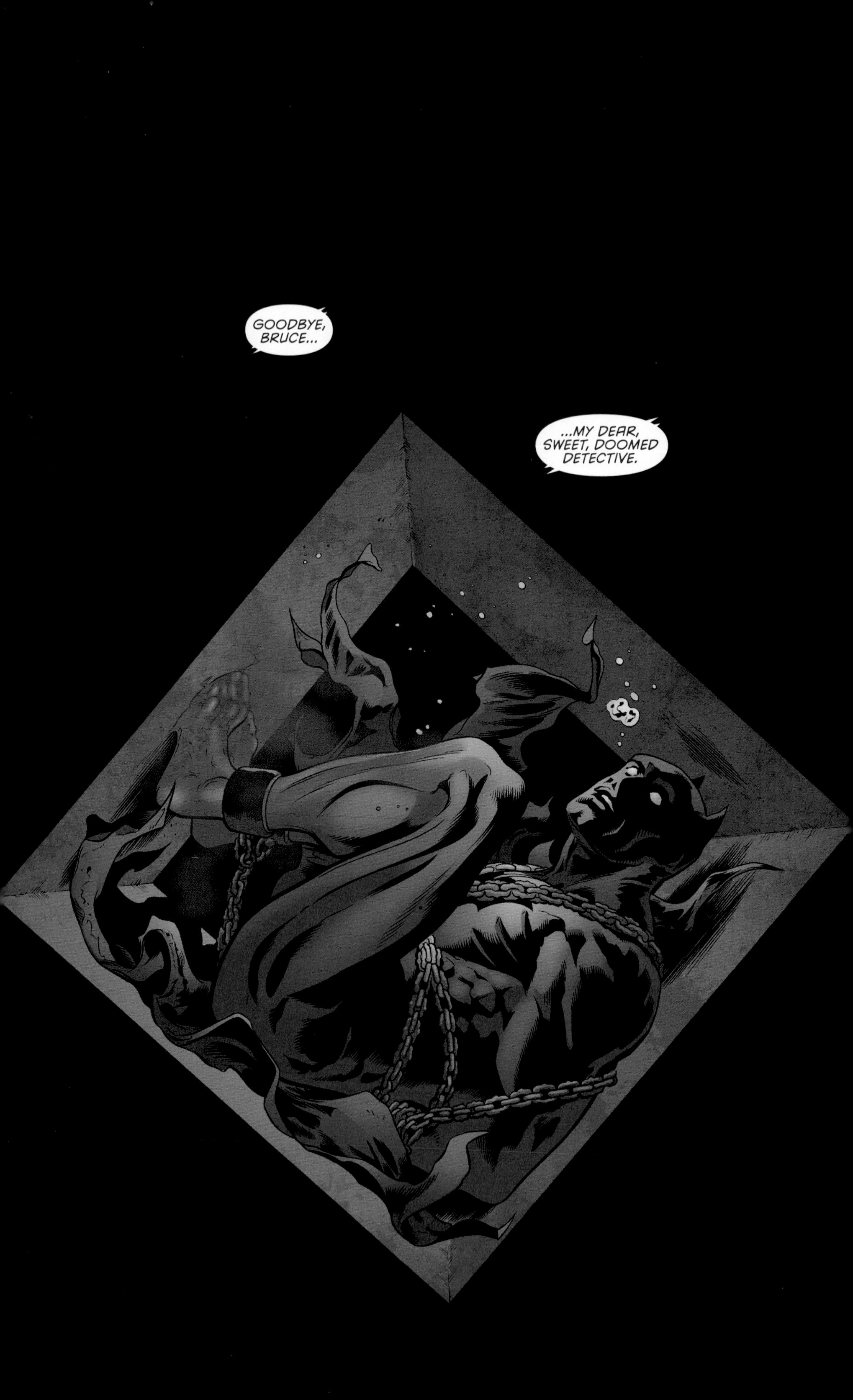
GOODBYE, BRUCE...
...MY DEAR, SWEET, DOOMED DETECTIVE.

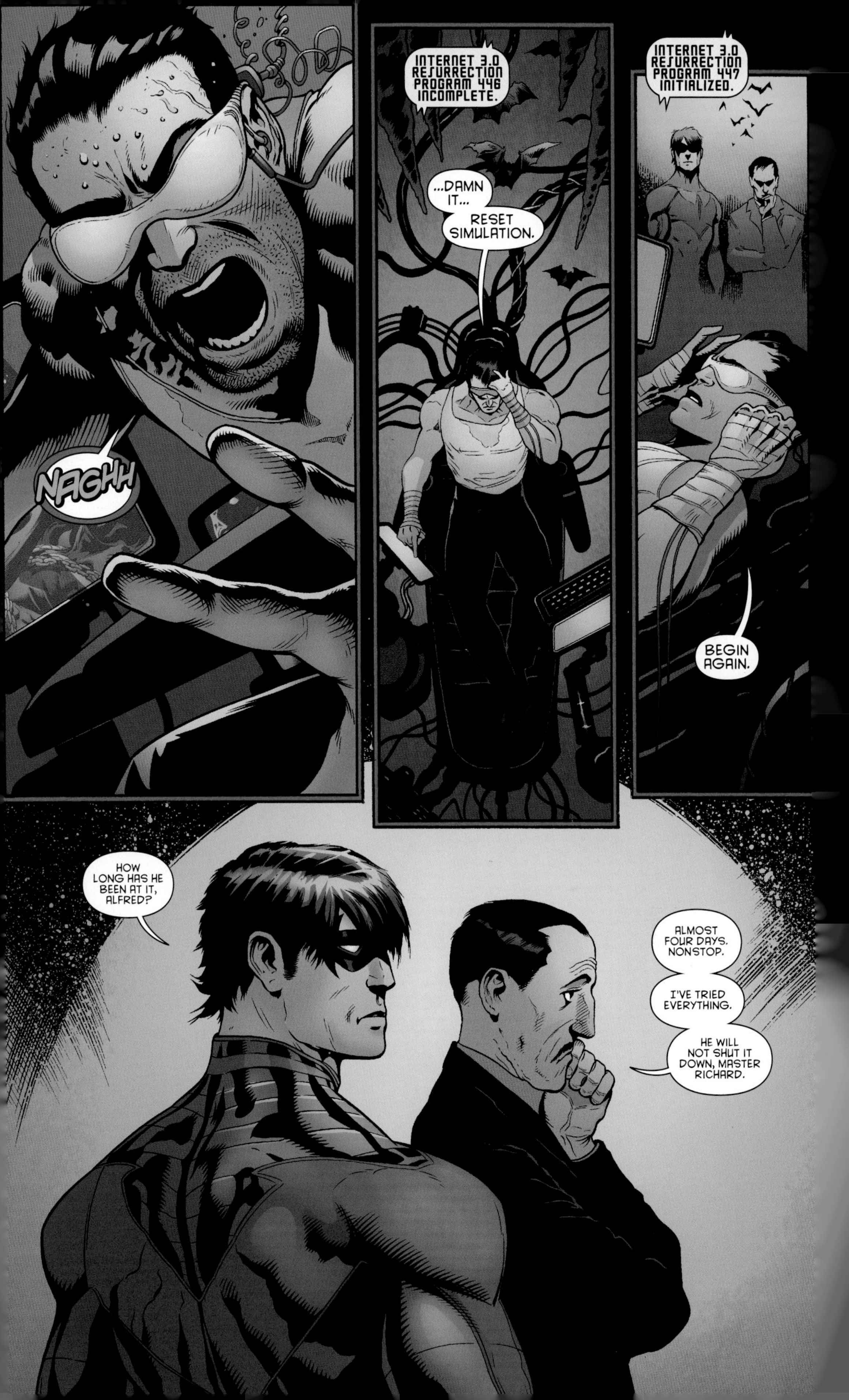
NAGHH
INTERNET 3.0 RESURRECTION PROGRAM 446 INCOMPLETE.
...DAMN IT...
RESET SIMULATION.
INTERNET 3.0 RESURRECTION PROGRAM 447 INITIALIZED.
BEGIN AGAIN.
HOW LONG HAS HE BEEN AT IT, ALFRED?
ALMOST FOUR DAYS. NONSTOP.
I'VE TRIED EVERYTHING.
HE WILL NOT SHUT IT DOWN, MASTER RICHARD.

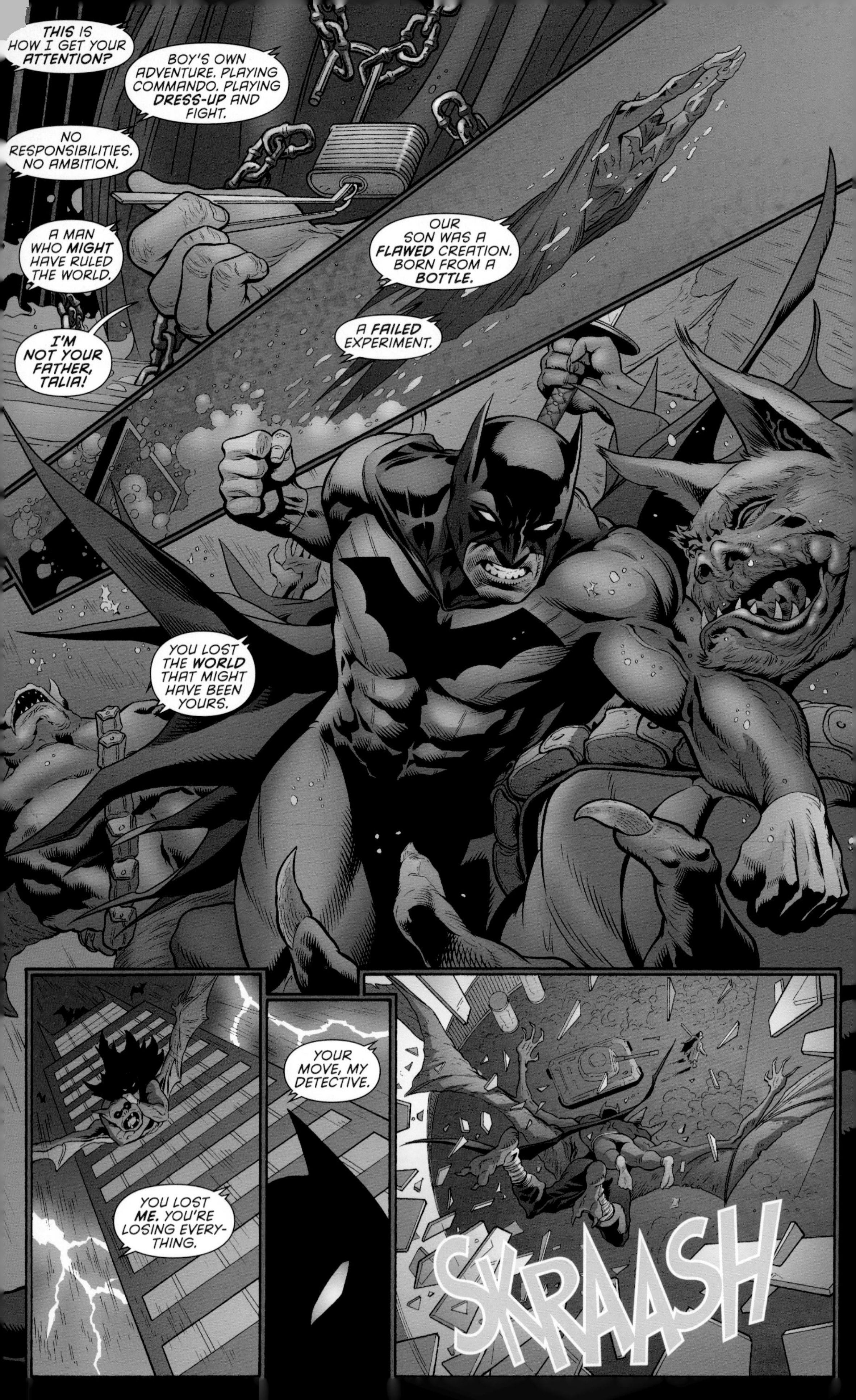
THIS IS HOW I GET YOUR ATTENTION?
BOY'S OWN ADVENTURE. PLAYING COMMANDO. PLAYING DRESS-UP AND FIGHT.
NO RESPONSIBILITIES. NO AMBITION.
A MAN WHO MIGHT HAVE RULED THE WORLD.
I'M NOT YOUR FATHER, TALIA!
OUR SON WAS A FLAWED CREATION. BORN FROM A BOTTLE.
A FAILED EXPERIMENT.
YOU LOST THE WORLD THAT MIGHT HAVE BEEN YOURS.
YOU LOST ME. YOU'RE LOSING EVERY-THING.
YOUR MOVE, MY DETECTIVE.
SKRAASH

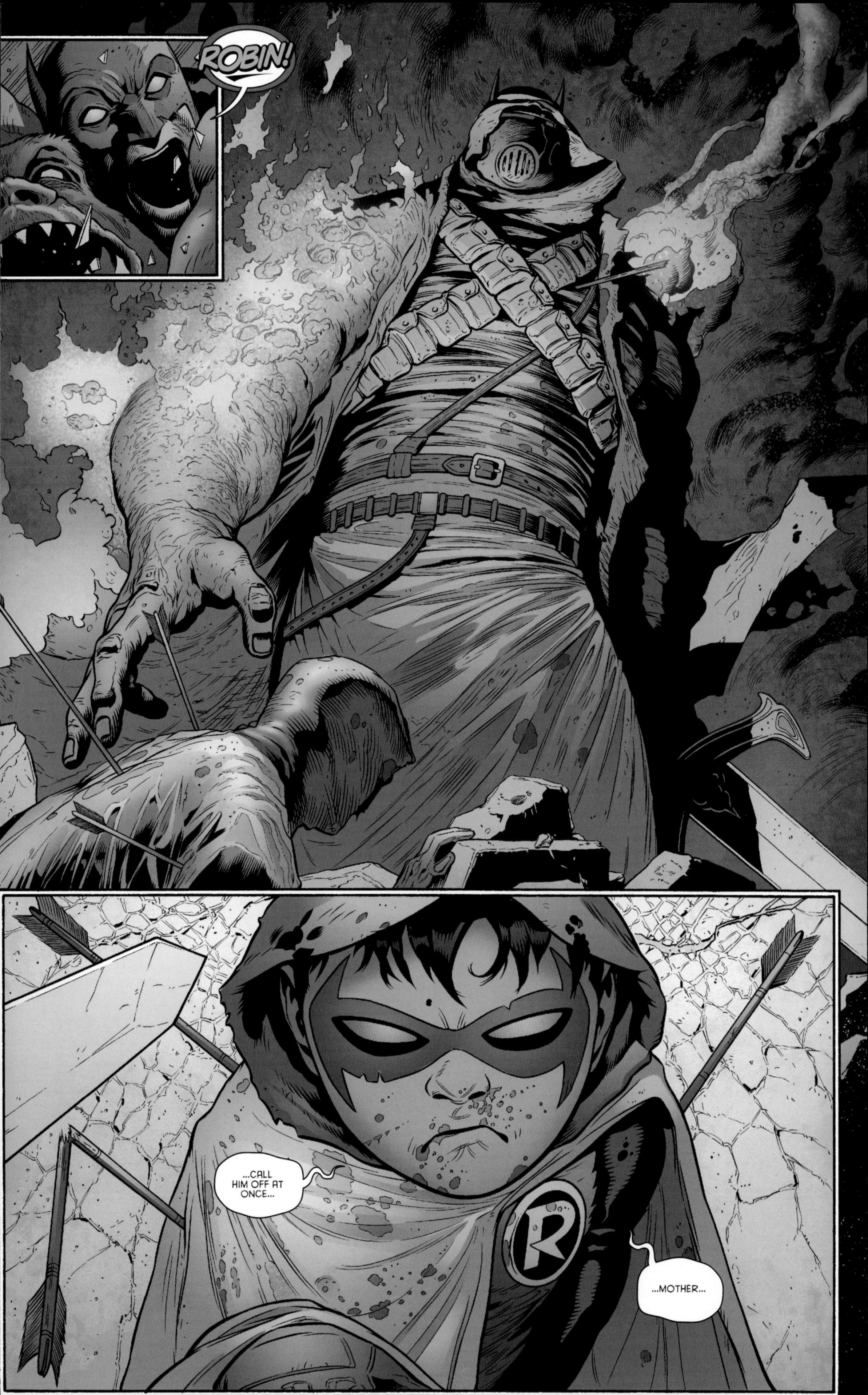
ROBIN!
...CALL HIM OFF AT ONCE...
...MOTHER...

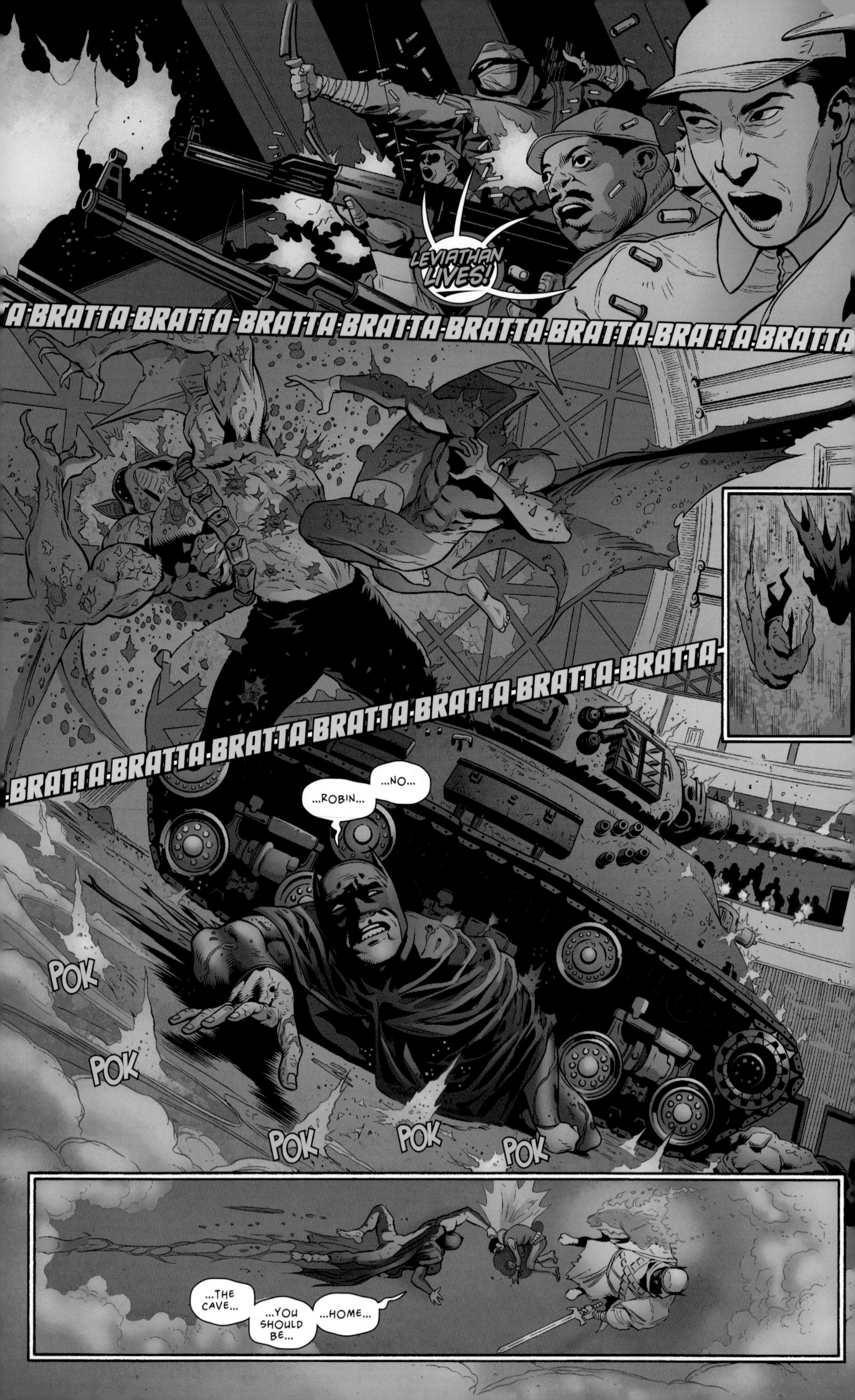
LEVIATHAN LIVES!
-TA-BRATTA-BRATTA-BRATTA-BRATTA-BRATTA-BRATTA-BRATTA-BRATTA-BRATTA-BRATT
BRATTA-BRATTA-BRATTA-BRATTA-BRATTA-BRATTA-BRATTA-BRATTA-
...ROBIN...
...NO...
POK
POK
POK
POK
POK
...THE CAVE...
...YOU SHOULD BE...
...HOME...

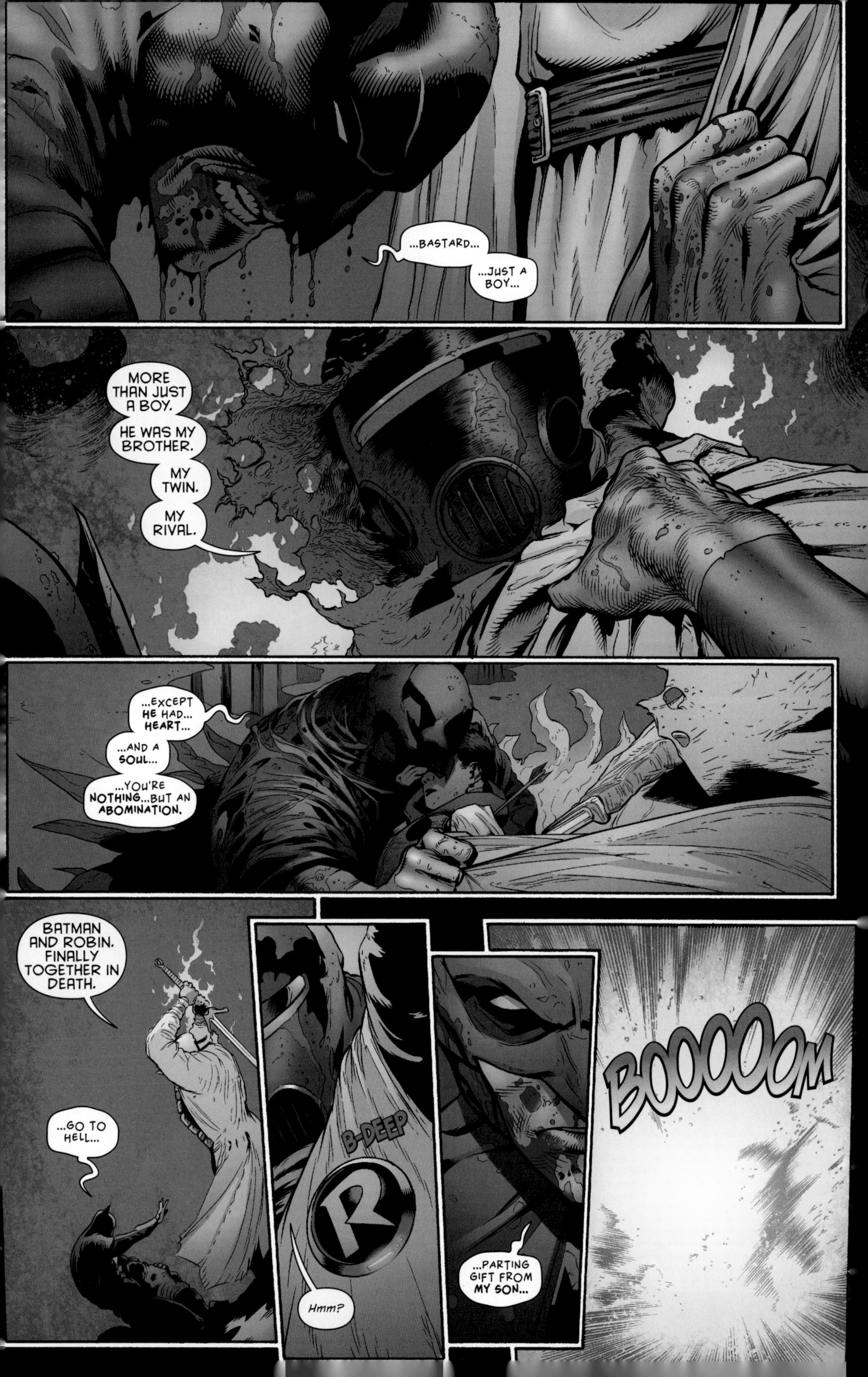
...BASTARD...
...JUST A BOY...
MORE THAN JUST A BOY.
HE WAS MY BROTHER.
MY TWIN.
MY RIVAL.
...EXCEPT HE HAD... HEART...
...AND A SOUL...
...YOU'RE NOTHING...BUT AN ABOMINATION.
BATMAN AND ROBIN. FINALLY TOGETHER IN DEATH.
...GO TO HELL...
B-DEEP
Hmm?
...PARTING GIFT FROM MY SON...
BOOOOOM

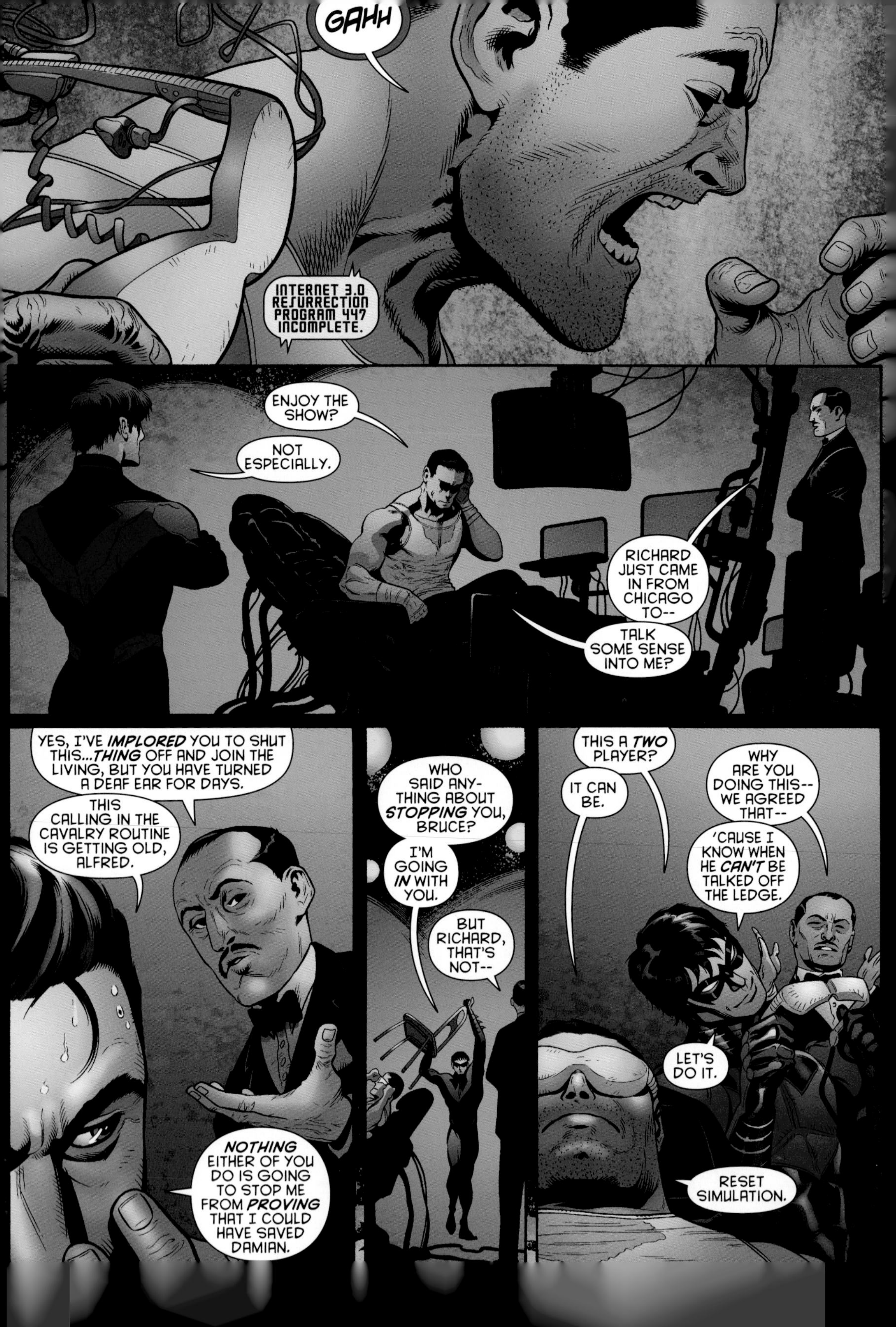
GAHH
INTERNET 3.0 RESURRECTION PROGRAM 447 INCOMPLETE.
ENJOY THE SHOW?
NOT ESPECIALLY.
RICHARD JUST CAME IN FROM CHICAGO TO--
TALK SOME SENSE INTO ME?
YES, I'VE IMPLORED YOU TO SHUT THIS...THING OFF AND JOIN THE LIVING, BUT YOU HAVE TURNED A DEAF EAR FOR DAYS.
THIS CALLING IN THE CAVALRY ROUTINE IS GETTING OLD, ALFRED.
NOTHING EITHER OF YOU DO IS GOING TO STOP ME FROM PROVING THAT I COULD HAVE SAVED DAMIAN.
WHO SAID ANY-THING ABOUT STOPPING YOU, BRUCE?
I'M GOING IN WITH YOU.
BUT RICHARD, THAT'S NOT--
THIS A TWO PLAYER?
IT CAN BE.
WHY ARE YOU DOING THIS-- WE AGREED THAT--
'CAUSE I KNOW WHEN HE CAN'T BE TALKED OFF THE LEDGE.
LET'S DO IT.
RESET SIMULATION.

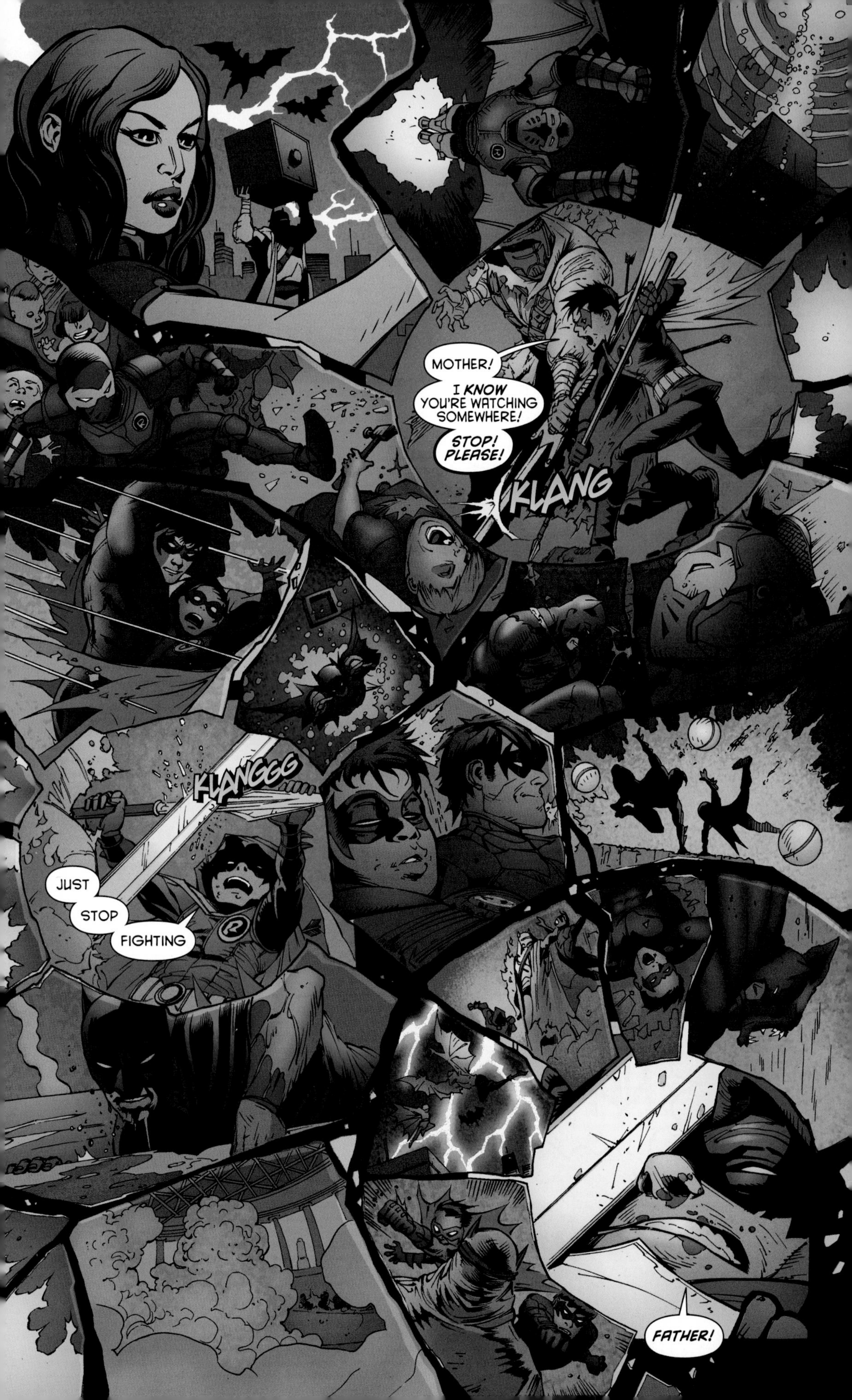
MOTHER!
I KNOW YOU'RE WATCHING SOMEWHERE!
STOP! PLEASE!
KLANG
KLANGGG
JUST
STOP
FIGHTING
FATHER!

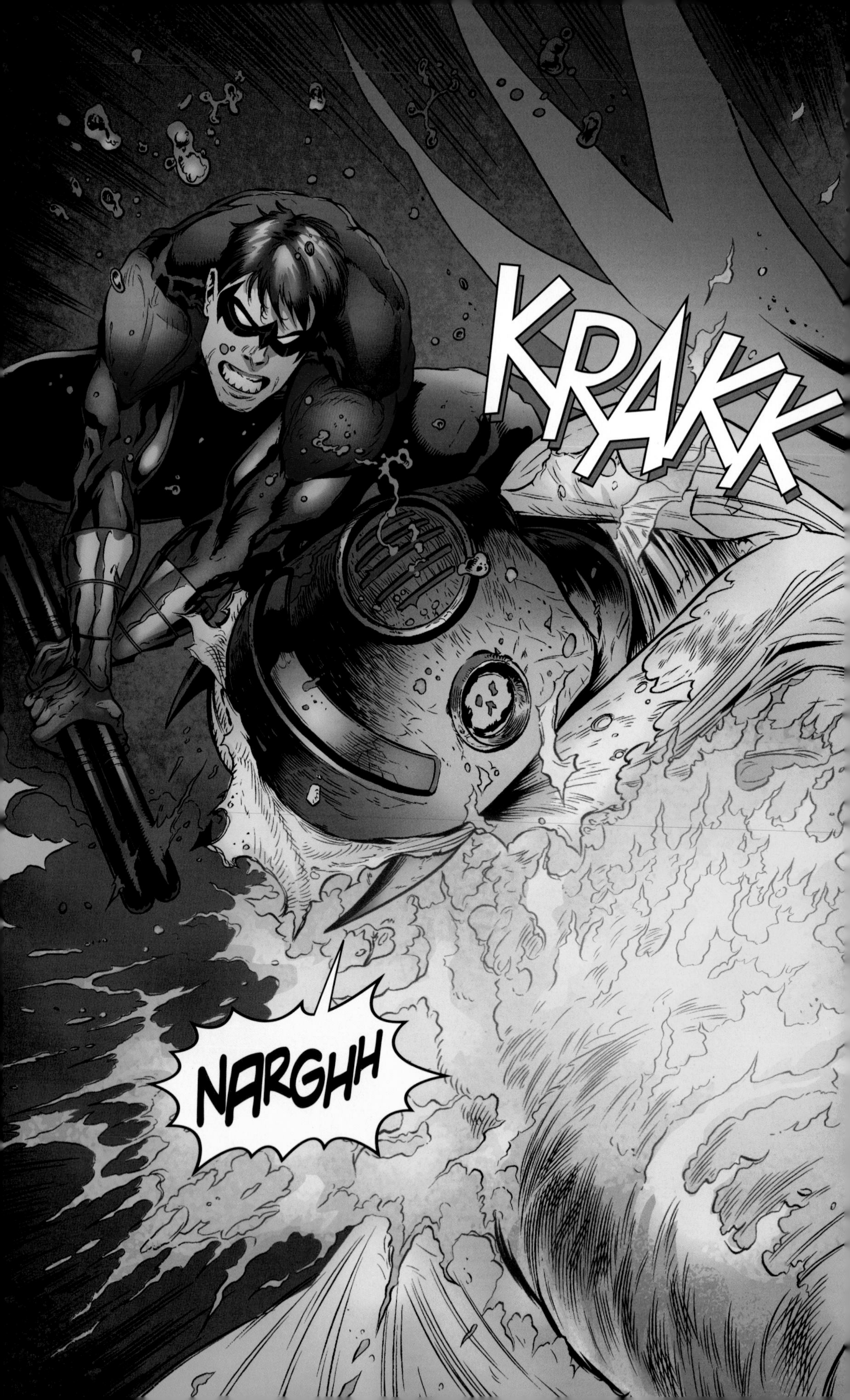
KRAKK
NARGHH

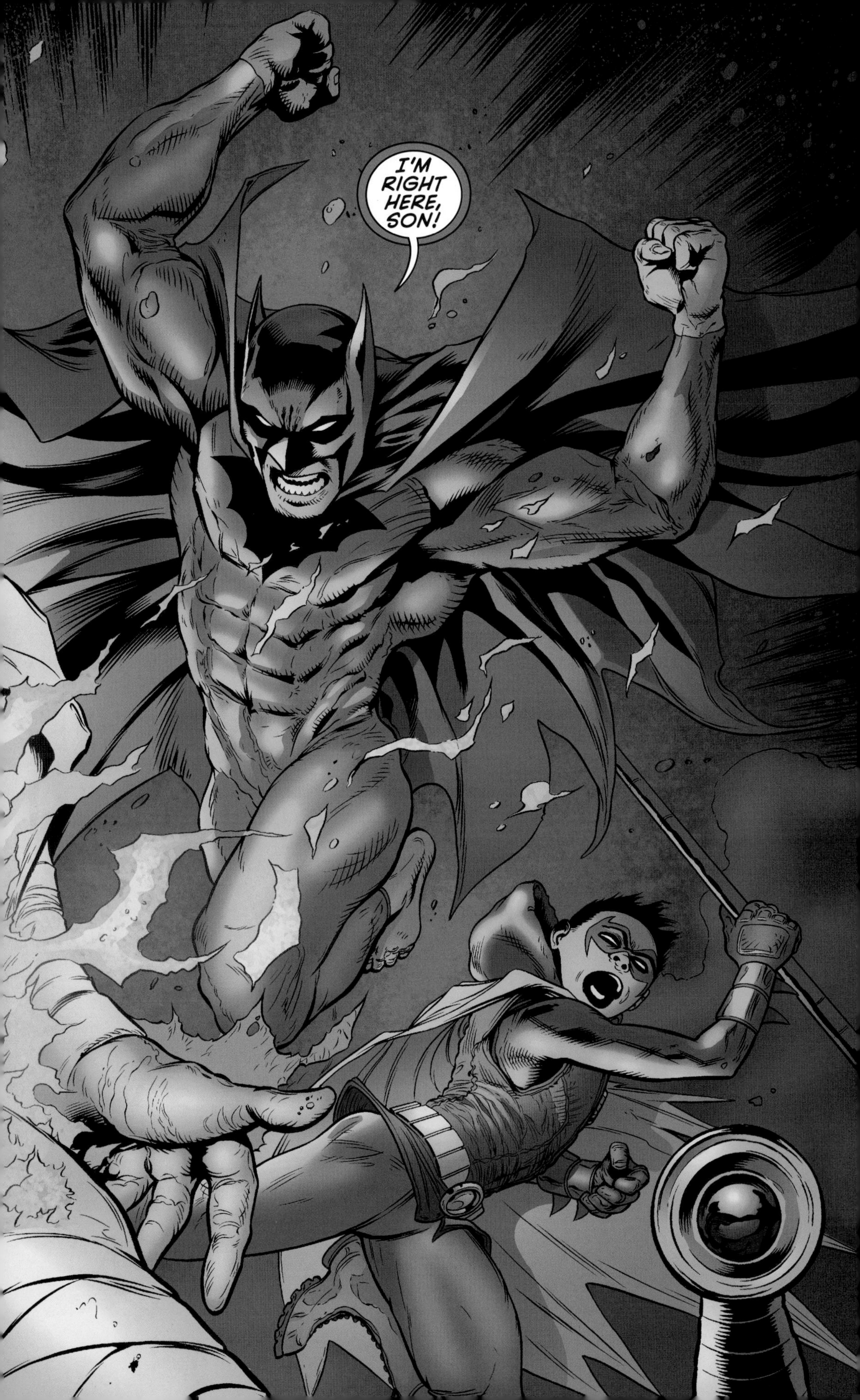
I'M RIGHT HERE, SON!

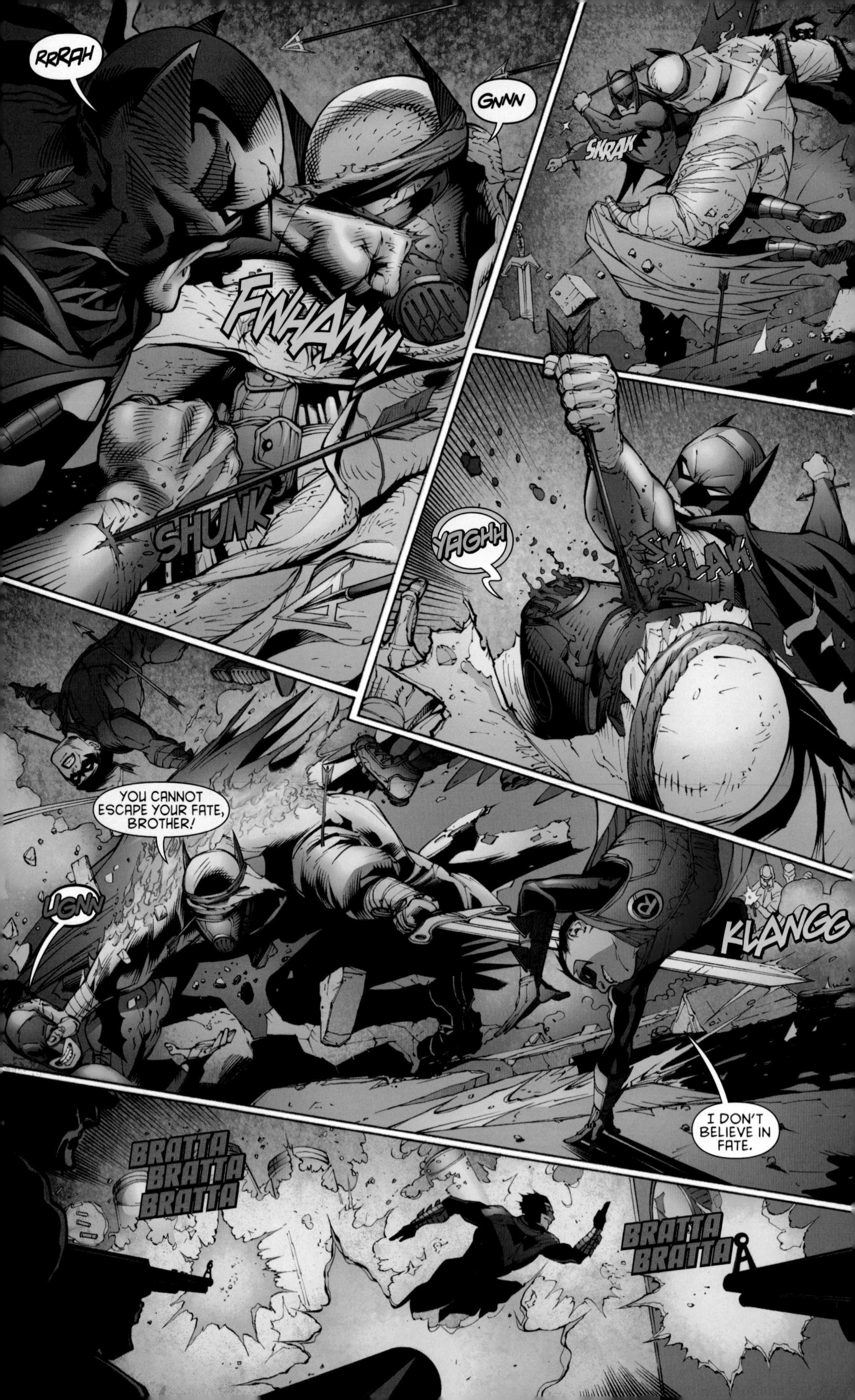
RRRAH
GNNN
FWHAMM
SHUNK
SKRAK
YAGHH
SKLAK
YOU CANNOT ESCAPE YOUR FATE, BROTHER!
UGNN
KLANGG
I DON'T BELIEVE IN FATE.
BRATTA BRATTA BRATTA
BRATTA BRATTA

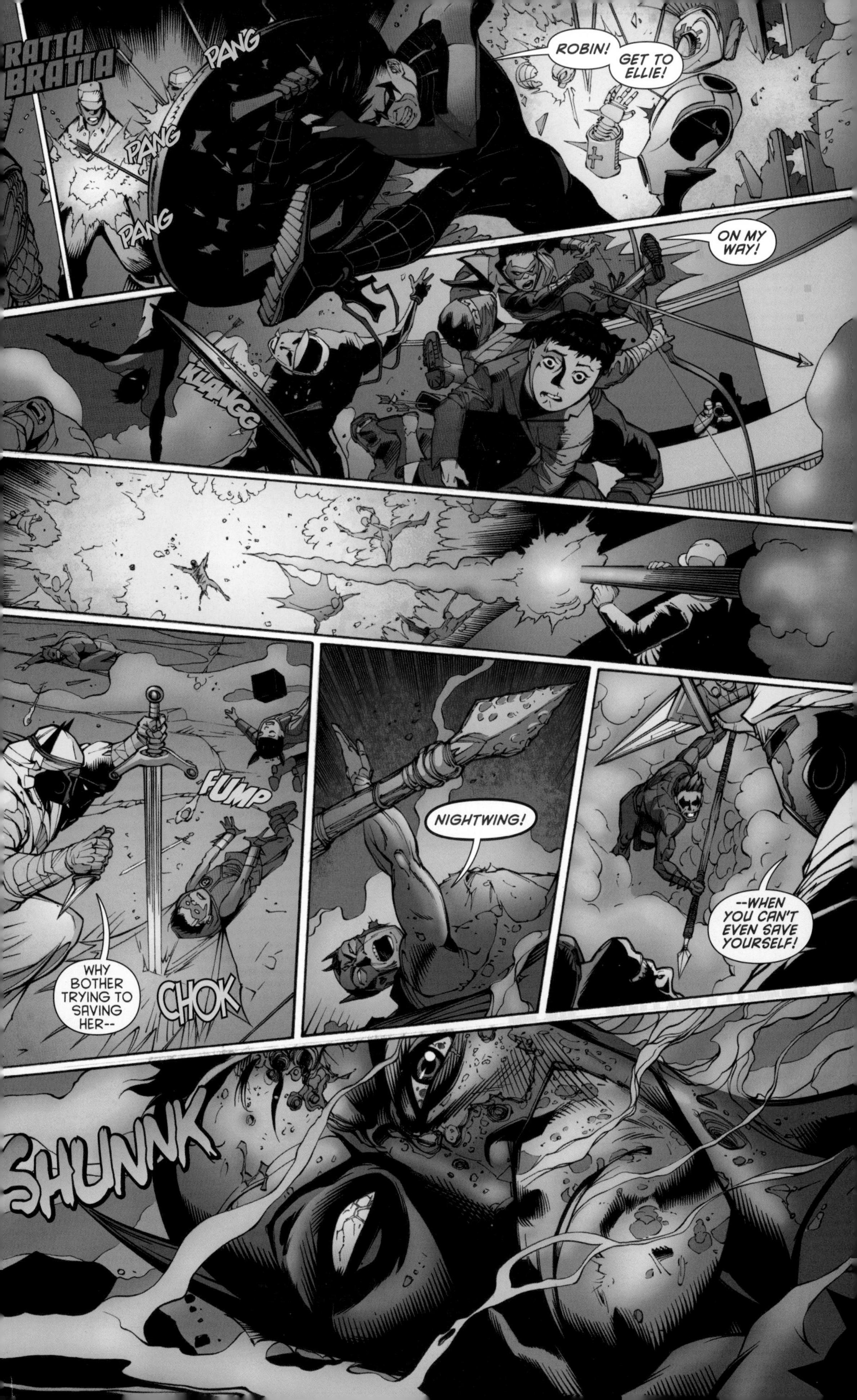
RATTA BRATTA
PANG
PANG
PANG
ROBIN!
GET TO ELLIE!
ON MY WAY!
KLANGG
FUMP
WHY BOTHER TRYING TO SAVING HER--
CHOK
NIGHTWING!
--WHEN YOU CAN'T EVEN SAVE YOURSELF!
SHUNNK

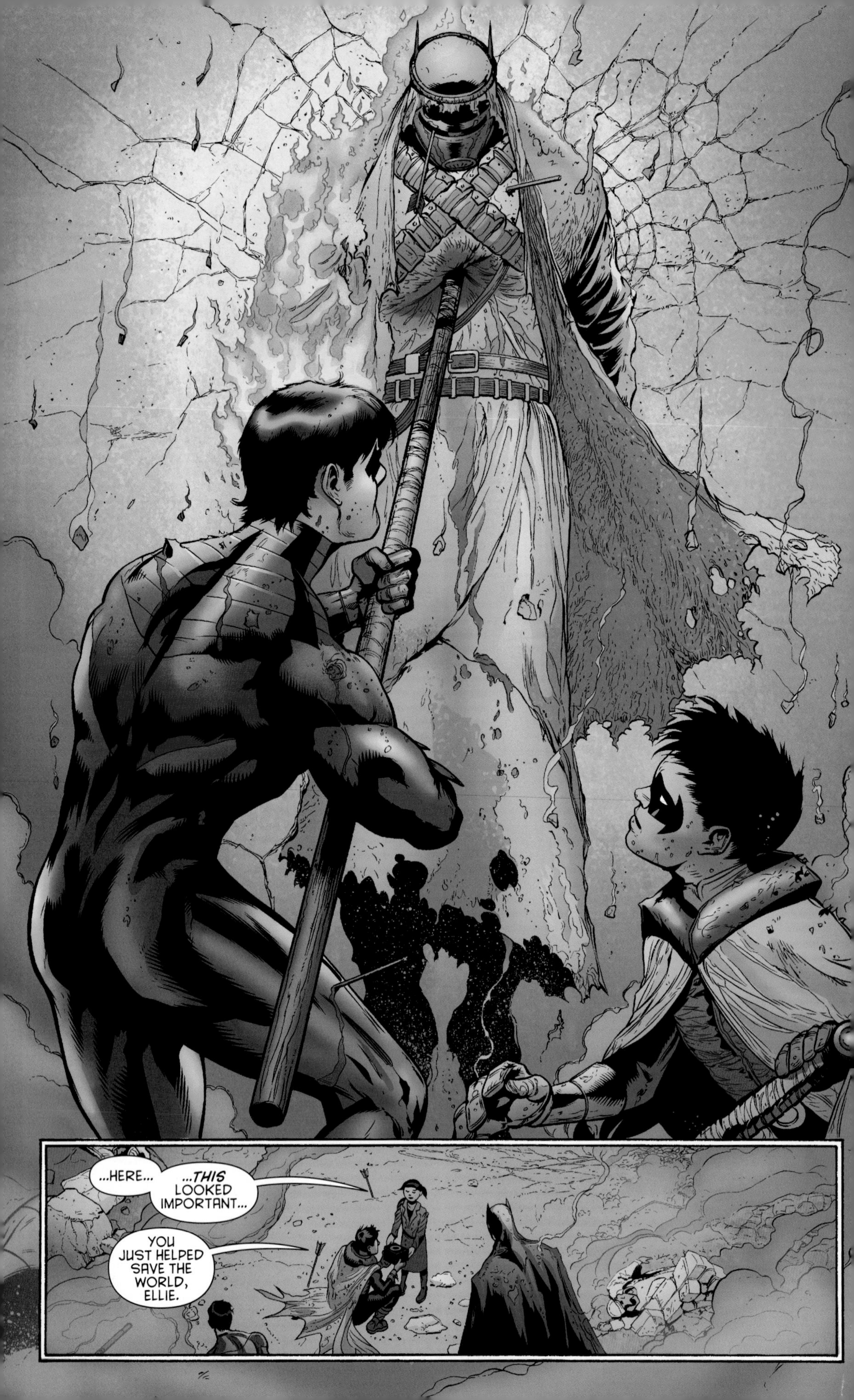
...HERE...
...THIS LOOKED IMPORTANT...
YOU JUST HELPED SAVE THE WORLD, ELLIE.

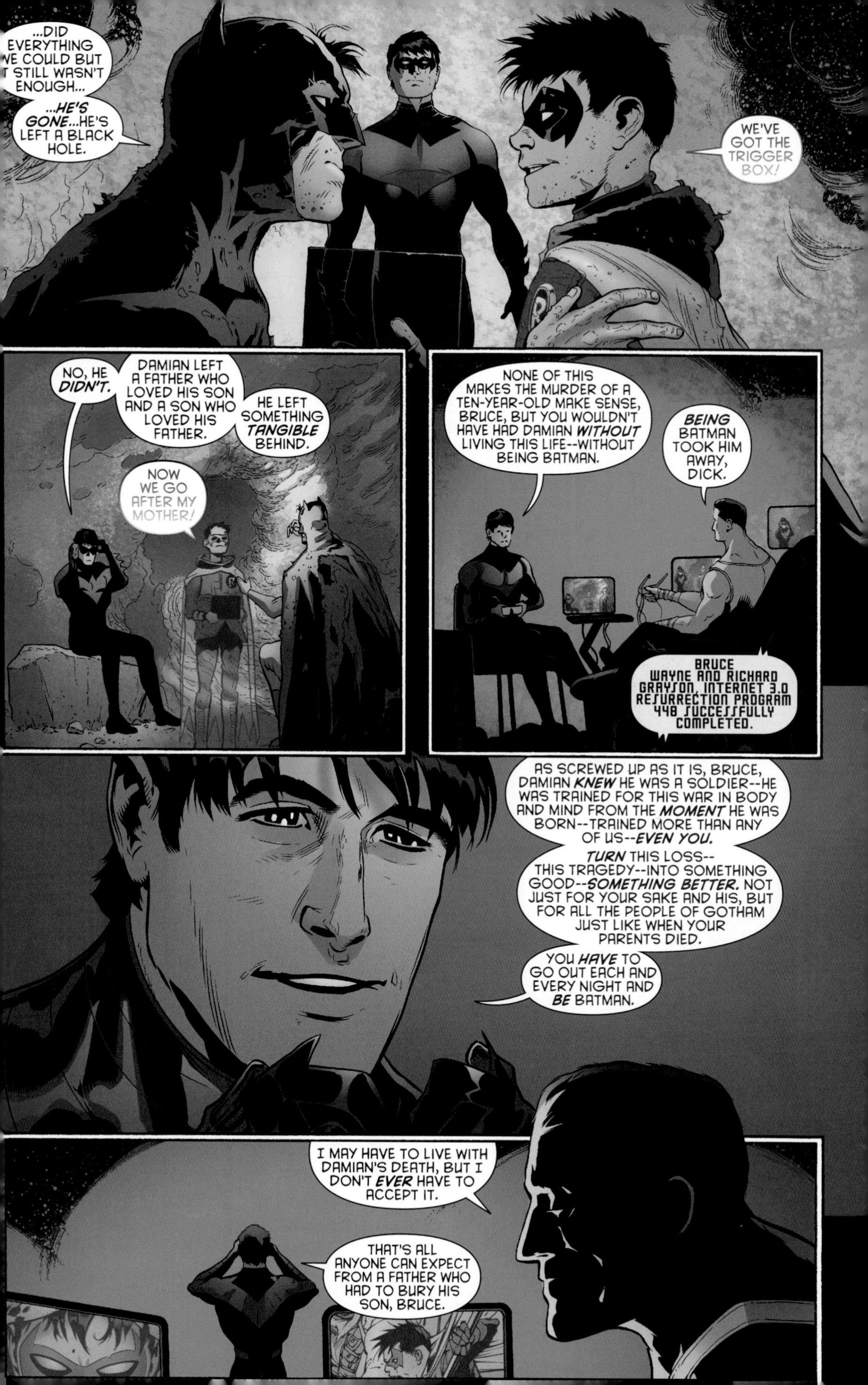
...DID EVERYTHING WE COULD BUT IT STILL WASN'T ENOUGH...
...HE'S GONE...HE'S LEFT A BLACK HOLE.
WE'VE GOT THE TRIGGER BOX!
NO, HE DIDN'T.
DAMIAN LEFT A FATHER WHO LOVED HIS SON AND A SON WHO LOVED HIS FATHER.
HE LEFT SOMETHING TANGIBLE BEHIND.
NOW WE GO AFTER MY MOTHER!
NONE OF THIS MAKES THE MURDER OF A TEN-YEAR-OLD MAKE SENSE, BRUCE, BUT YOU WOULDN'T HAVE HAD DAMIAN WITHOUT LIVING THIS LIFE--WITHOUT BEING BATMAN.
BEING BATMAN TOOK HIM AWAY, DICK.
BRUCE WAYNE AND RICHARD GRAYSON, INTERNET 3.0 RESURRECTION PROGRAM 448 SUCCESSFULLY COMPLETED.
AS SCREWED UP AS IT IS, BRUCE, DAMIAN KNEW HE WAS A SOLDIER--HE WAS TRAINED FOR THIS WAR IN BODY AND MIND FROM THE MOMENT HE WAS BORN--TRAINED MORE THAN ANY OF US--EVEN YOU.
TURN THIS LOSS-- THIS TRAGEDY--INTO SOMETHING GOOD--SOMETHING BETTER. NOT JUST FOR YOUR SAKE AND HIS, BUT FOR ALL THE PEOPLE OF GOTHAM JUST LIKE WHEN YOUR PARENTS DIED.
YOU HAVE TO GO OUT EACH AND EVERY NIGHT AND BE BATMAN.
I MAY HAVE TO LIVE WITH DAMIAN'S DEATH, BUT I DON'T EVER HAVE TO ACCEPT IT.
THAT'S ALL ANYONE CAN EXPECT FROM A FATHER WHO HAD TO BURY HIS SON, BRUCE.

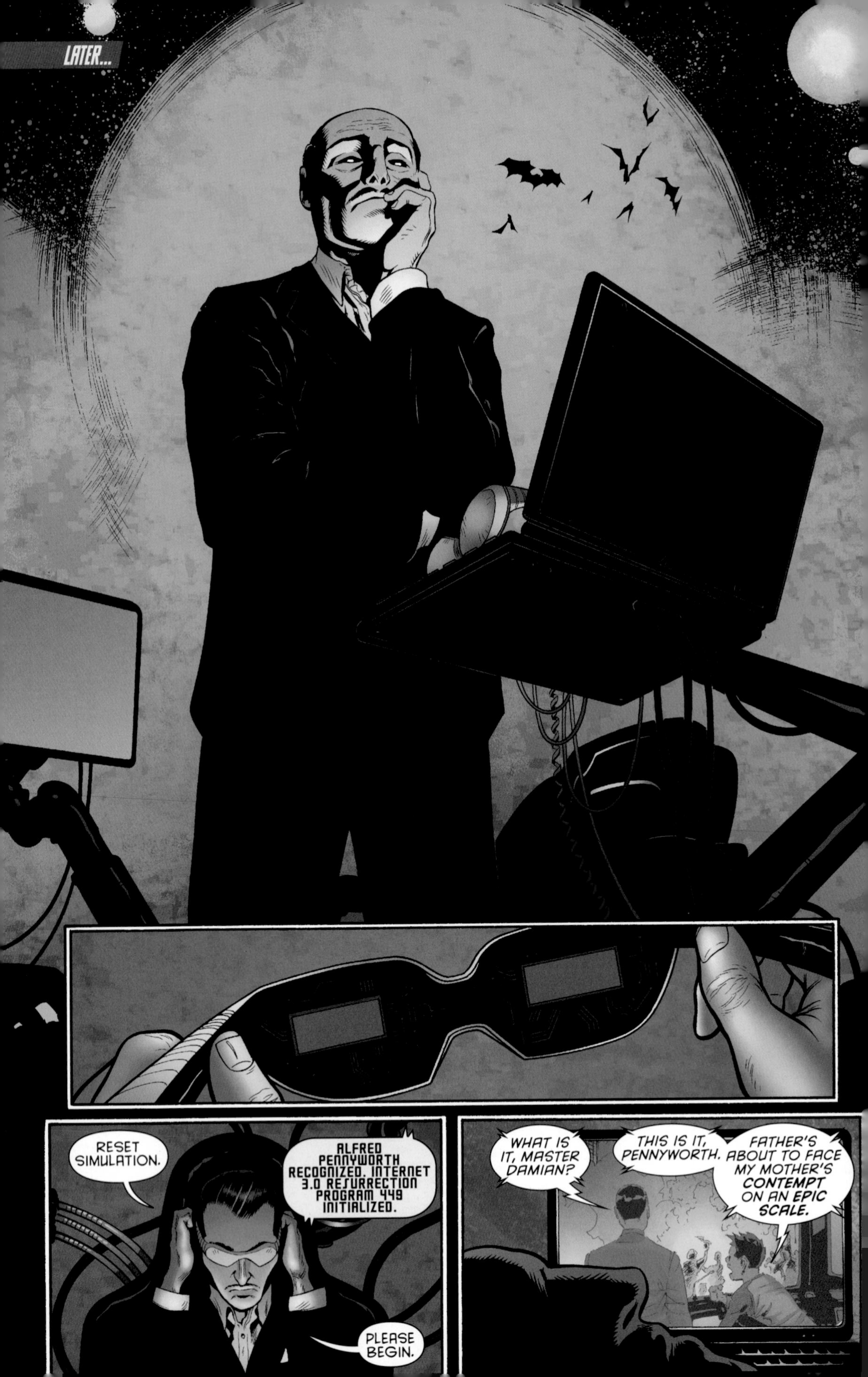
LATER...
RESET SIMULATION.
ALFRED PENNYWORTH RECOGNIZED. INTERNET 3.0 RESURRECTION PROGRAM 449 INITIALIZED.
PLEASE BEGIN.
WHAT IS IT, MASTER DAMIAN?
THIS IS IT, PENNYWORTH.
FATHER'S ABOUT TO FACE MY MOTHER'S CONTEMPT ON AN EPIC SCALE.

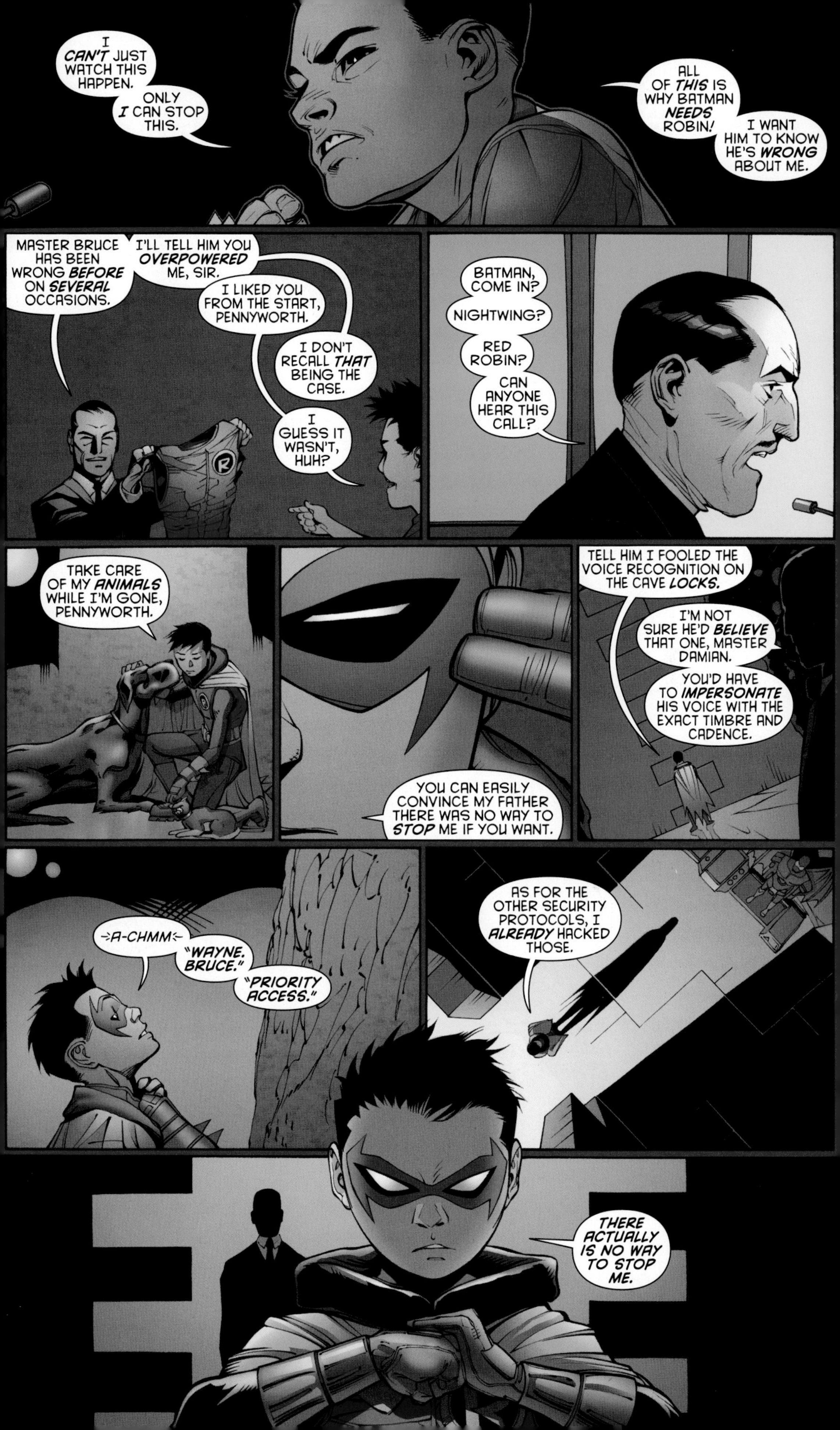
I CAN'T JUST WATCH THIS HAPPEN.
ONLY I CAN STOP THIS.
ALL OF THIS IS WHY BATMAN NEEDS ROBIN!
I WANT HIM TO KNOW HE'S WRONG ABOUT ME.
MASTER BRUCE HAS BEEN WRONG BEFORE ON SEVERAL OCCASIONS.
I'LL TELL HIM YOU OVERPOWERED ME, SIR.
I LIKED YOU FROM THE START, PENNYWORTH.
I DON'T RECALL THAT BEING THE CASE.
I GUESS IT WASN'T, HUH?
BATMAN, COME IN?
NIGHTWING?
RED ROBIN?
CAN ANYONE HEAR THIS CALL?
TAKE CARE OF MY ANIMALS WHILE I'M GONE, PENNYWORTH.
YOU CAN EASILY CONVINCE MY FATHER THERE WAS NO WAY TO STOP ME IF YOU WANT.
TELL HIM I FOOLED THE VOICE RECOGNITION ON THE CAVE LOCKS.
I'M NOT SURE HE'D BELIEVE THAT ONE, MASTER DAMIAN.
YOU'D HAVE TO IMPERSONATE HIS VOICE WITH THE EXACT TIMBRE AND CADENCE.
A-CHMM
"WAYNE. BRUCE."
"PRIORITY ACCESS."
AS FOR THE OTHER SECURITY PROTOCOLS, I ALREADY HACKED THOSE.
THERE ACTUALLY IS NO WAY TO STOP ME.

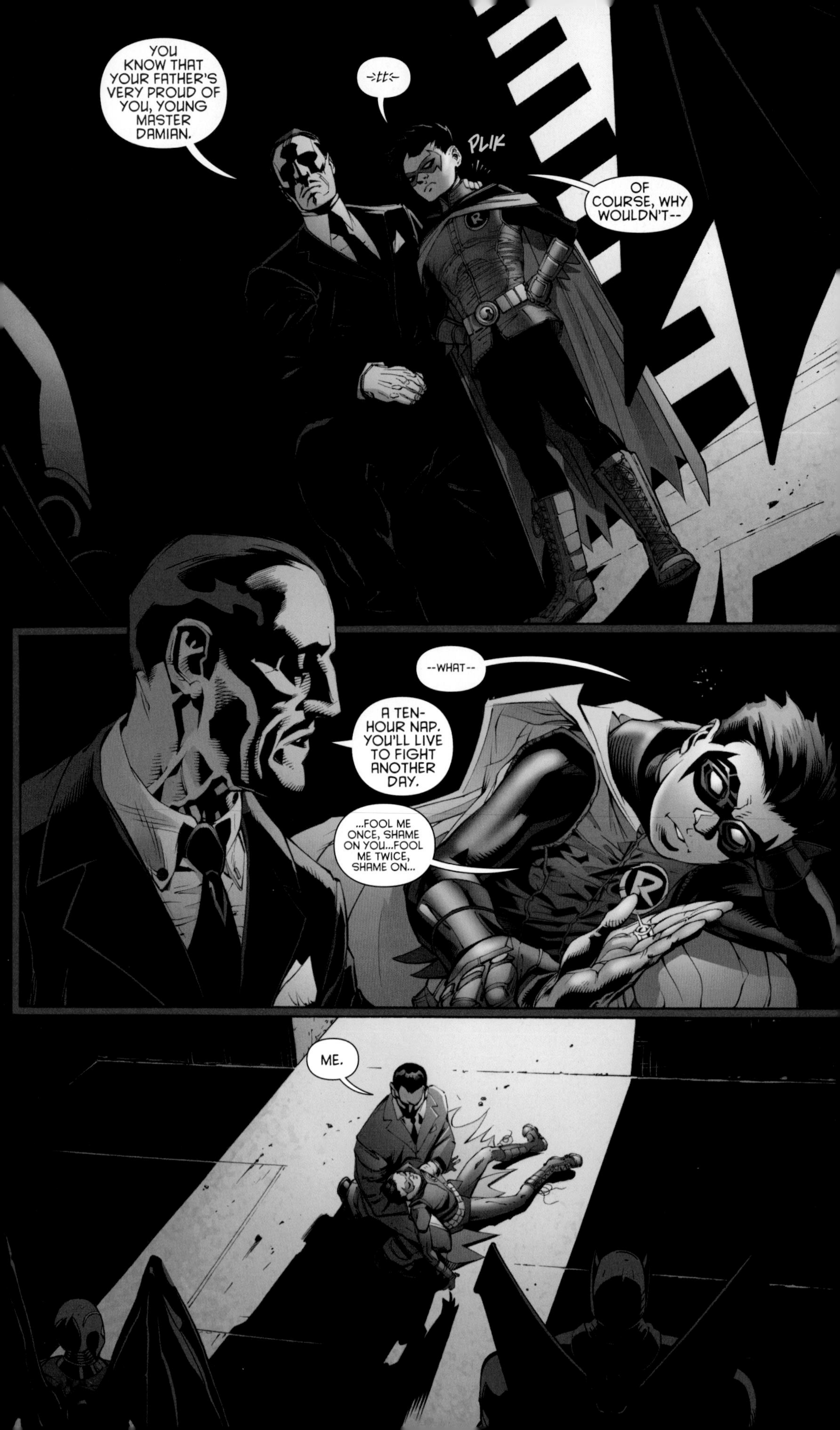
YOU KNOW THAT YOUR FATHER'S VERY PROUD OF YOU, YOUNG MASTER DAMIAN.
-tt-
PLIK
OF COURSE, WHY WOULDN'T--
--WHAT--
A TEN-HOUR NAP. YOU'LL LIVE TO FIGHT ANOTHER DAY.
...FOOL ME ONCE, SHAME ON YOU...FOOL ME TWICE, SHAME ON...
ME.

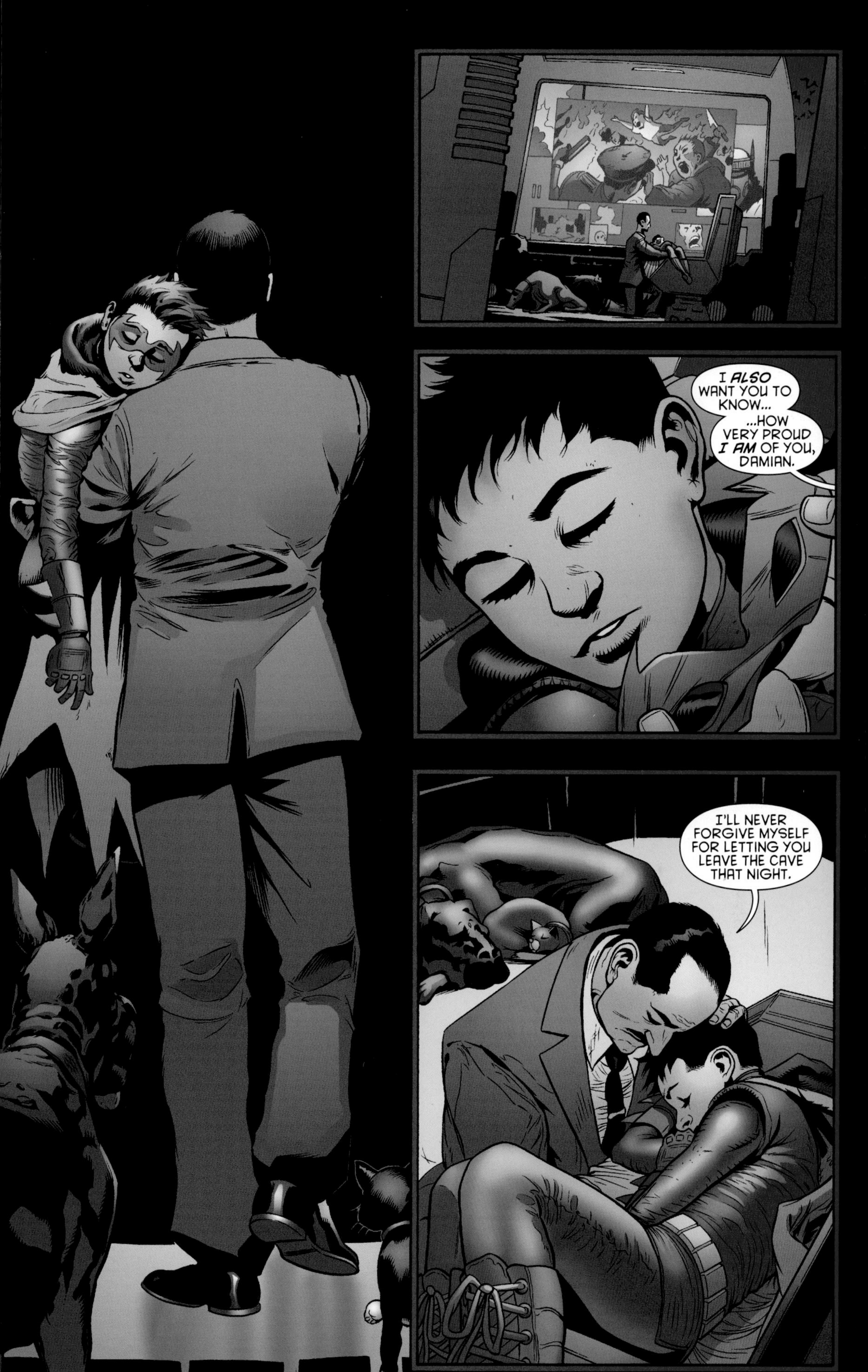
I ALSO WANT YOU TO KNOW...
...HOW VERY PROUD I AM OF YOU, DAMIAN.
I'LL NEVER FORGIVE MYSELF FOR LETTING YOU LEAVE THE CAVE THAT NIGHT.

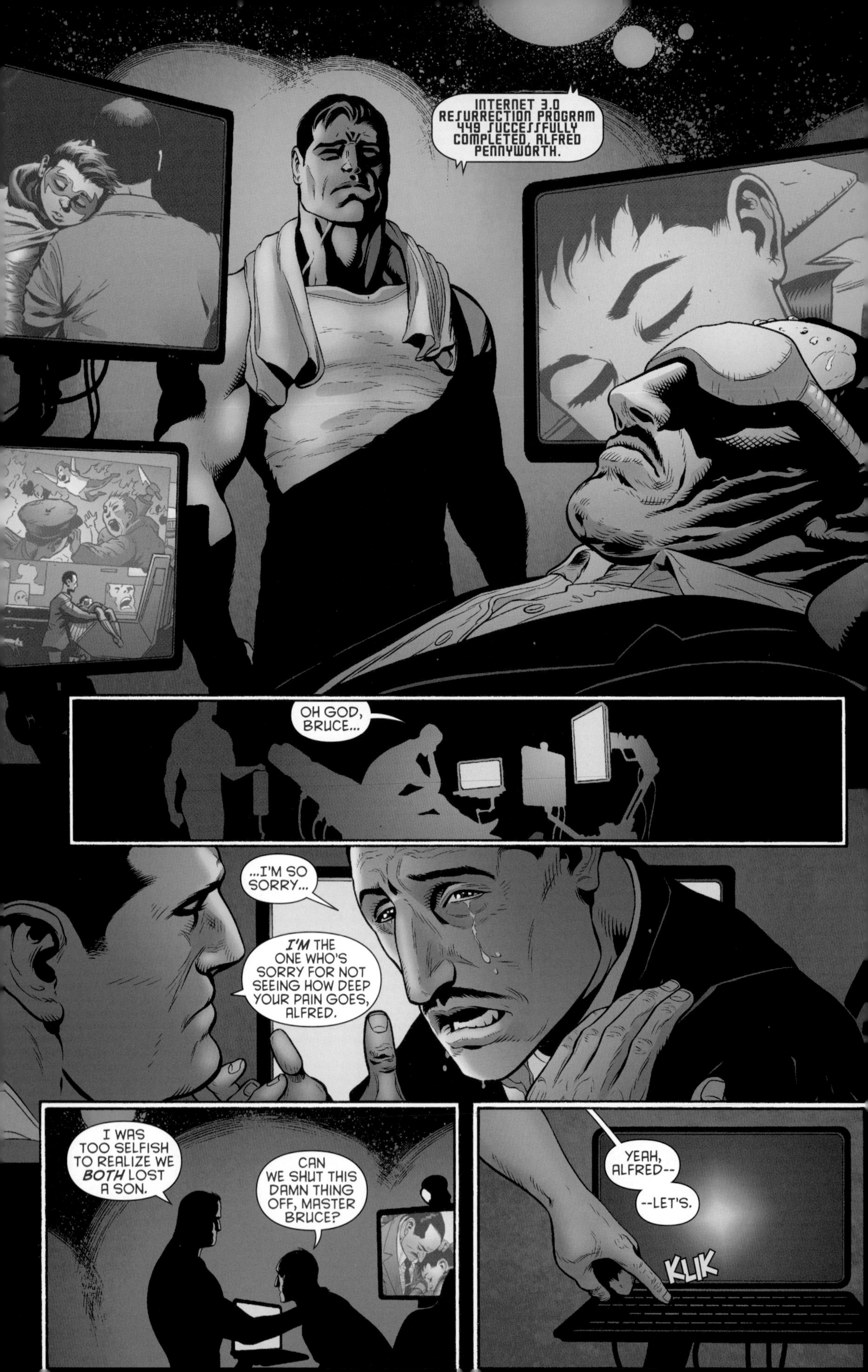
INTERNET 3.0 RESURRECTION PROGRAM 449 SUCCESSFULLY COMPLETED, ALFRED PENNYWORTH.
OH GOD, BRUCE...
...I'M SO SORRY...
I'M THE ONE WHO'S SORRY FOR NOT SEEING HOW DEEP YOUR PAIN GOES, ALFRED.
I WAS TOO SELFISH TO REALIZE WE *BOTH* LOST A SON.
CAN WE SHUT THIS DAMN THING OFF, MASTER BRUCE?
YEAH, ALFRED--
--LET'S.
KLIK

PAGE 1

And away we go for our full silent issue, Patrick. Aside from the splash image they subbed for the cover, Batman should appear even more sinister and foreboding during this issue in his body language and demeanor.

Also important is to give a sense of emptiness by the way you frame Batman/Bruce and Alfred during the course of the book. Negative space around their bodies/figures is key to get a sense of the isolation.

Pat, we're at Wayne Manor, specifically in Damian's room. This opening takes place at sunset as Bruce is sitting in a chair in front of the fireplace across from Damian's empty bed simply staring at it as the sun sinks outside, casting a shadow slowly across Bruce's features as the page progresses. This is a real character showcase, so go crazy on the facial details, which you draw so amazingly.

Panel 1
Angle close only on Bruce's eyes, as they look at us. There should be a sense of weariness and pain, yet a cold fury behind them too if you can pull it off.

Panel 2
Pull back a bit so we see more of Bruce's face and the shadow of the night moving across it.

Panel 3
Pull back some more so we see his head and shoulders, his gaze still fixed off panel.

PAGE 2

Splash.

We finally get to see a version of that cool foreboding shot of Bruce sitting in the high-back chair with Titus beside him in front of the smaller fireplace in Damian's room rather than the main one which you first envisioned. Anyway, there's no Damian, of course, and no painting above the mantle.

What Bruce is focused on is Damian's bed in the foreground. We can still see the indentation on his pillow.

TITLE AND CREDITS

BATMAN AND ROBIN #18

PENCILS BY PATRICK GLEASON INKS BY MICK GRAY

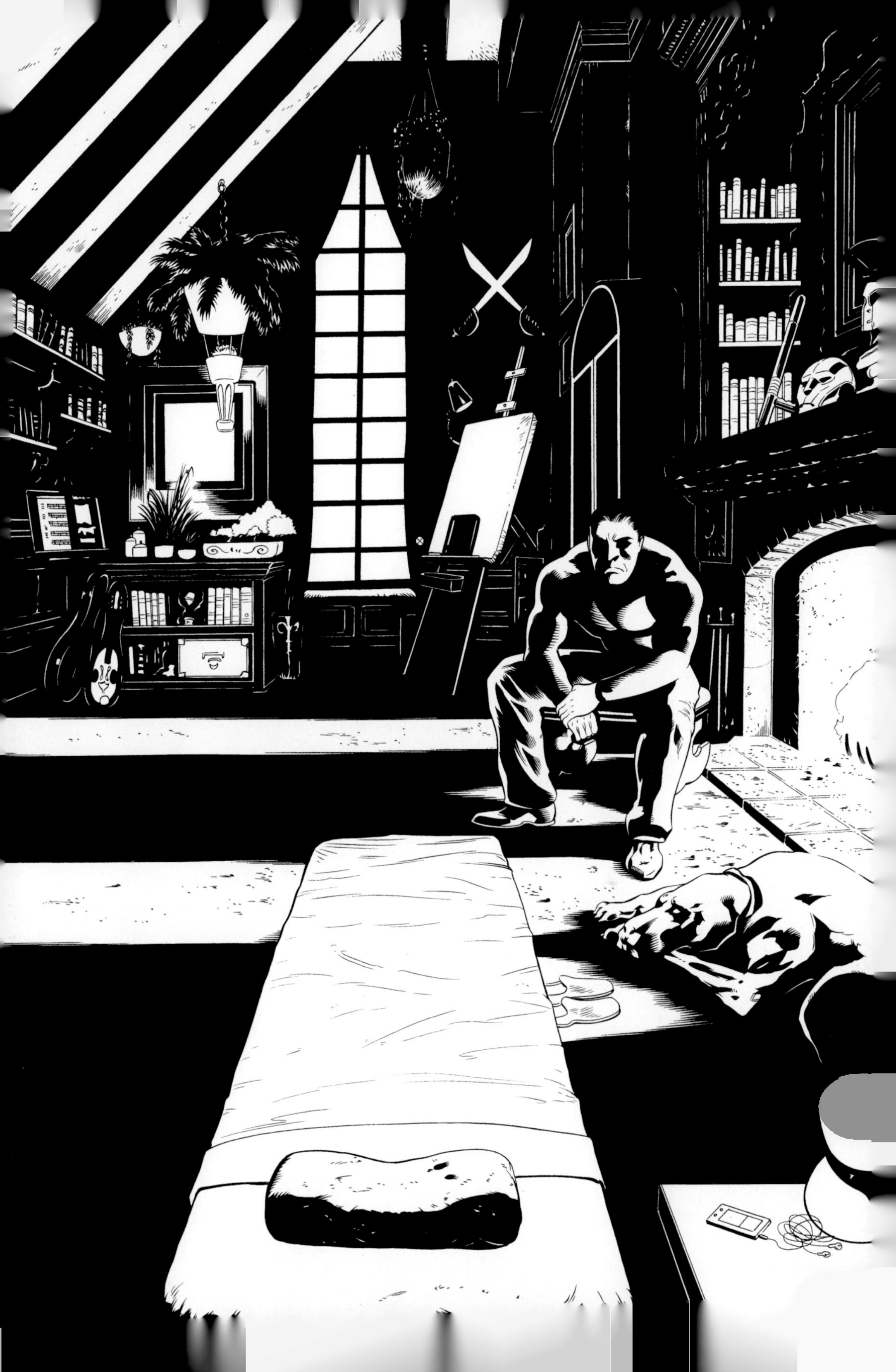

PAGE 3
Panel 1
Angle on Bruce as he's gotten up from the chair and walks towards Damian's desk.
Titus follows. And this could be a good spot to set the time of day and why the shadows were crossing his face by showing the window and the sun setting outside with the rays cutting lower through the room.

Panel 2
Angle over Bruce's shoulder as he's got a medium-sized sketchbook of Damian's opened on the desk in front of him. Also indicate a sheet of paper poking out from in-between some pages that he'll see in a moment. The pencil sketches should be of Titus, Alfred, and Damian's new cat too from BATMAN INC, and of course, Bruce, and maybe some other interesting sketches you feel would work, Pat. Maybe a sketch of some fireflies over the Wayne graves. This is obviously different from the violent images we saw earlier in the series to show some growth.

Panel 3
Angle looking up at Bruce looking through the sketchbook. Remember to keep the paper sheet poking out as he gets closer to it. Emotion is visible on his face.

Panel 4
Another shot of Bruce's perspective of the sketchbook. You choose what images, Pat. Ditto on the paper sheet.

Panel 5
Angle on Bruce as he's turned to see the PAPER SHEET, and written on it is a list of MOVIES AND PLAYS written in script. I'll give you a list when ya get to it. At the bottom of the list it also says: "I'm sure you'll enjoy them. CK" (*this stands for Carrie Kelley*)

MOVIE LIST:
on the waterfront
rebel without a cause
my left foot
cool hand luke
to kill a mockingbird
lawrence of arabia
the sand pebbles
grapes of wrath
the miracle worker
central station
gorillas in the mist
the lion in winter
china syndrome

Panel 6
Angle on Bruce as he closes the sketchbook while Titus watches.

Panel 7
Angle on Bruce standing beside the bed, his hand gently resting on the indentation on Damian's pillow.

PAGE 4

Panel 1
We're in the den, angle on Alfred's back, his hand holding up a thin canvas cover as he's looking at a PAINTING on an easel we can't see just yet.

Panel 2
Angle close on Alfred, trying to keep a stiff upper lip as he continues to hold the canvas cover up. Tears are streaming down his face as he stares at it.

Panel 3
Probably biggest on page. Angle only on the PAINTING Alfred's looking at. It matches the position all the Bat Family guys were in from issue #10 page 4. Make it more detailed, Pat, give the faces more weight and distinction than the original page. Anyway, the only difference is that DAMIAN IS UNFINISHED (a metaphor for his life). His body and face have been somewhat HALF COMPLETED, the rest of him is laid out/roughed in pencil. The other guys in the Bat Family are of course all finished.

Panel 4
Angle on Alfred with a hand over his eyes as he tries to control himself and hold back the tears.

Panel 5
Angle on Bruce in the shadows of the hallway watching Alfred and not wanting to step in and embarrass him. I'm guessing Alfred in foreground and Bruce in the background.

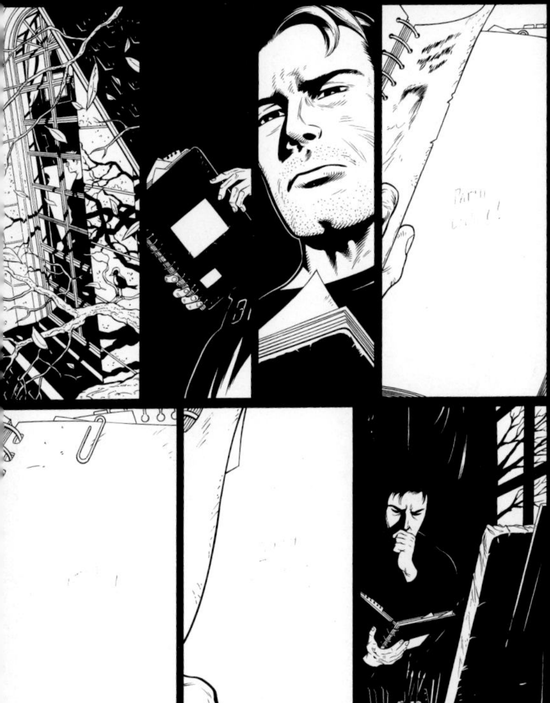
I'M SURE YOU'LL ENJOY THEM! -C
-C.K.-

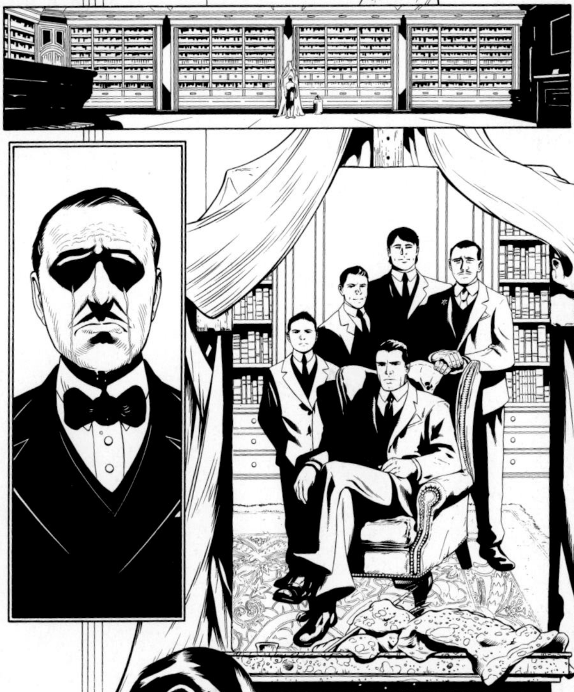

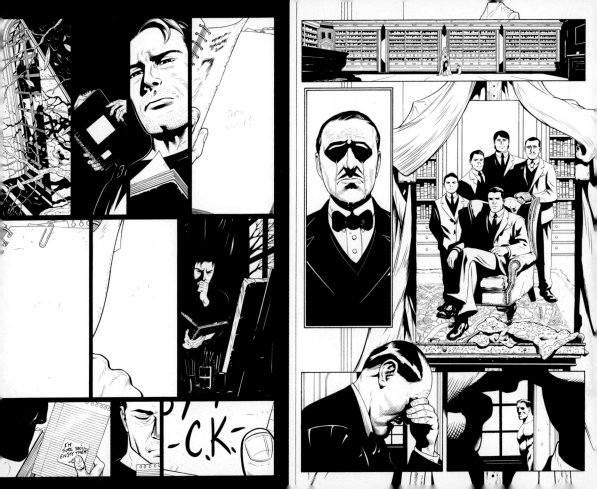

PAGE 5

Panel 1
Angle on Alfred knowing Bruce is approaching, as he pulls his jacket bottom straight with one hand and wipes his eyes with the back of his other hand without turning around. Think of that moment in Wrath of Khan when Spock is dying and he composes himself when he knows Kirk is there before turning around to face his old friend and captain.

Panel 2
Angle on Bruce as he joins Alfred at the painting staring at it together. Bruce has his hand on Alfred's shoulder.

Panel 3
Angle on Bruce as he starts to cover the painting, the last hint of Damian's unfinished figure staring back at us.

Panel 4
Angle on Alfred as he watches Bruce now slide the painting into a small inlaid wooden closet.

Panel 5
Angle on Alfred as he's turning the hands of a grandfather clock, which reveals the bat poles behind the bookcase that Bruce is stepping into. Look back at the way you showed the clock back in issue #1, page 6, panel 1. Alfred could be in the foreground and Bruce in the background.

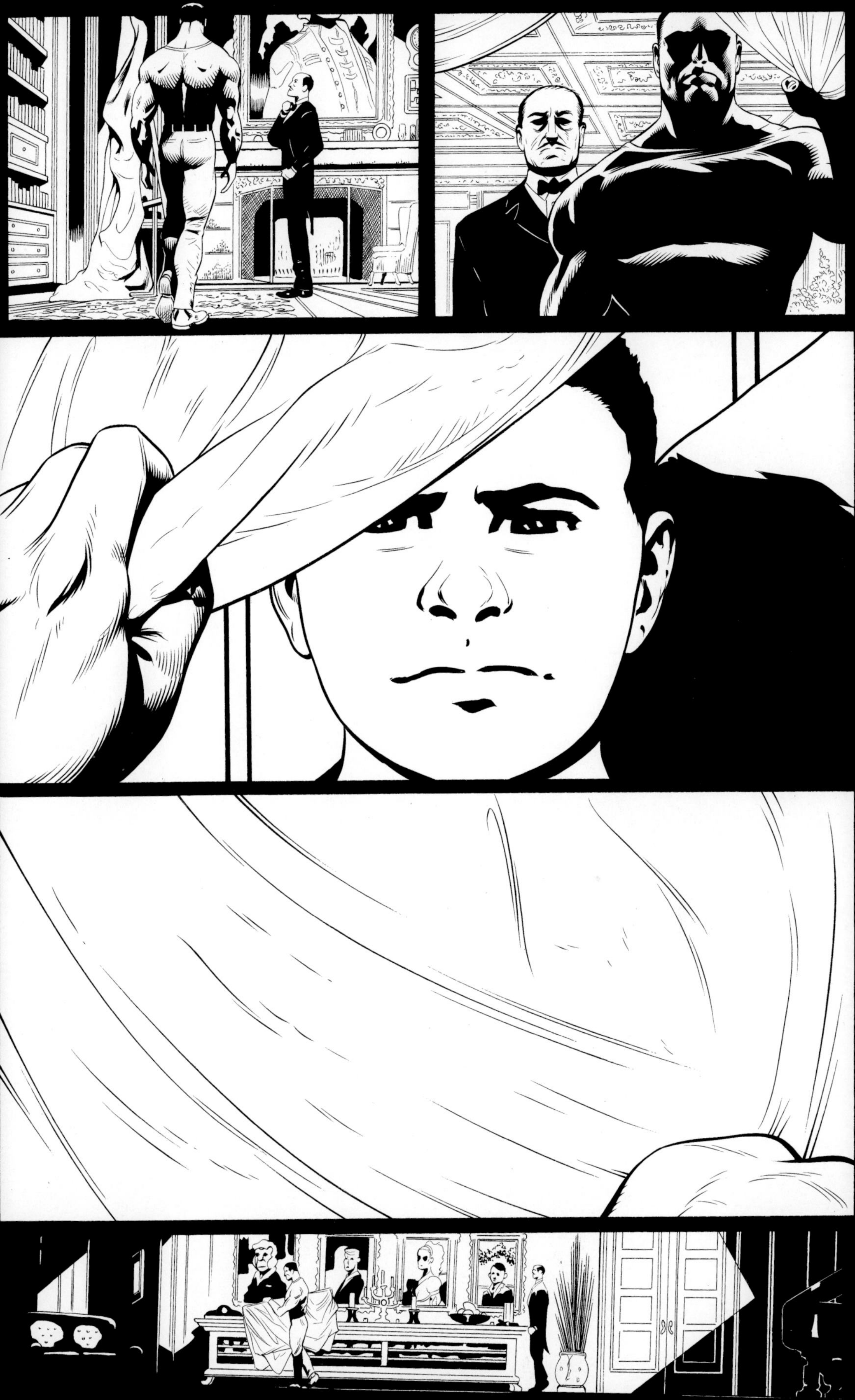

PAGE 6

All vertical panels from top to bottom of page.

Panel 1
Vertical panel of Bruce sliding down the pole tunnel in the dim light (there are tiny LED lights running down the wall).

Panel 2
Angle on Bruce as he sees Damian sliding down the other pole right across from him, a smile (not goofy) on his face like he can't wait to suit up and hit the streets.

Panel 3
Angle from above of Bruce and Damian sliding down the poles in the darkness towards the light coming from the cave below.

Panel 4
Angle on Bruce as he's reached the bottom with no sign of Damian. All he sees is the pole and a thin trail of blood running down it.

Panel 5
Angle on Bruce as he reaches towards the pole but there's no blood now.

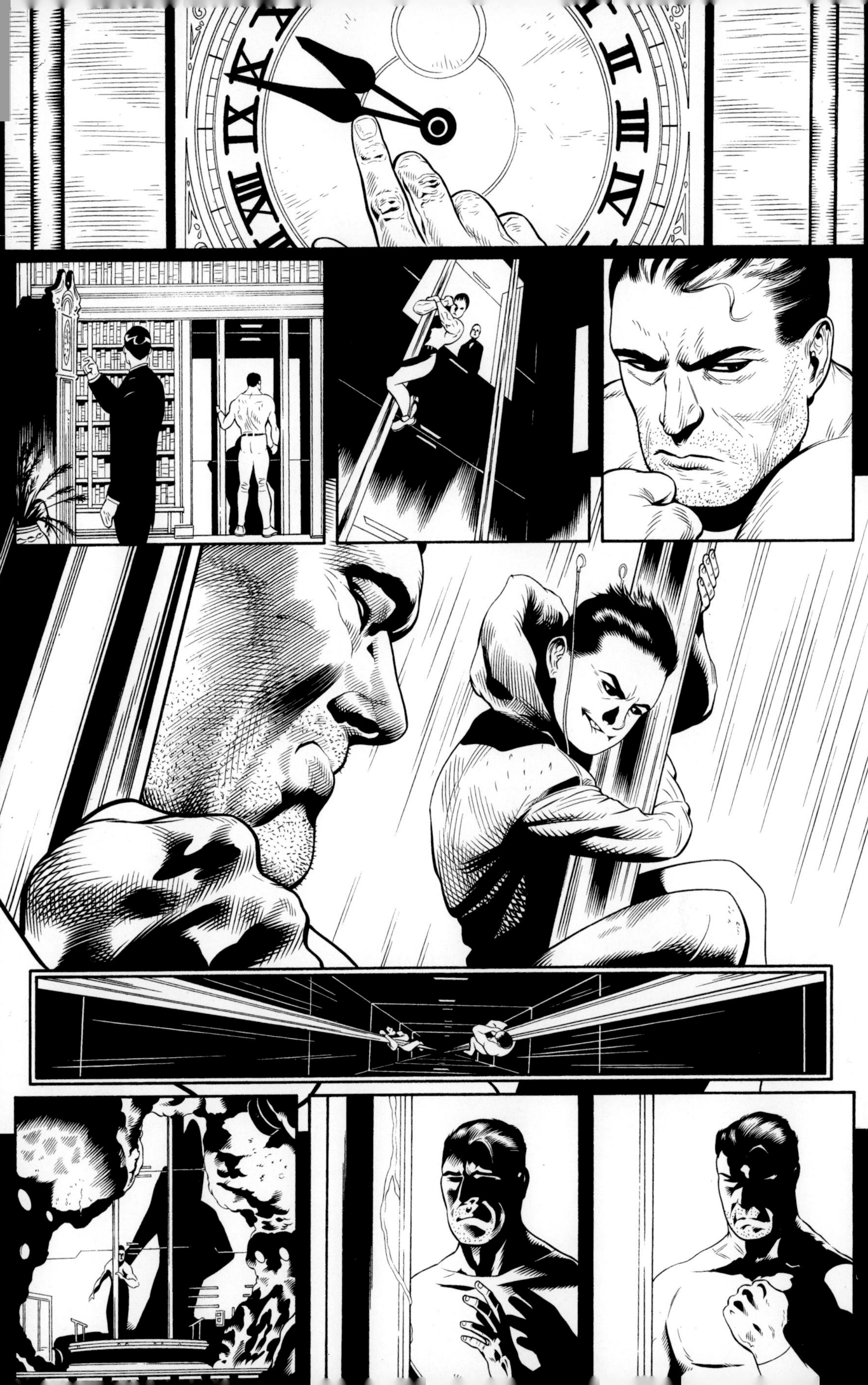

PAGE 7

Panel 1
Angle on Bruce at the lockers in his Bat suit without the cowl on. This is a bookend moment to the previous issue. Bruce is simply a warrior getting ready for his millionth battle as he puts on his gauntlets. He is standing there beside Damian's locker where we can see the Robin suit, gloves and boots ready to be worn.

Panel 2
Angle from behind Bruce as he stands in front of Damian's Robin uniform, simply staring at it.

Panel 3
Angle on Bruce as he places one of Damian's small Robin glove/gauntlets against the palm of his own large gloved hand. Think of it, Pat, like when your kid is born and you put that tiny little hand against yours and marvel at the difference in size.

Panel 4
Angle on Bruce as he's about to put his cowl on. His eyes have a lifelessness to them at this moment.

Panel 5
Angle on Batman walking past the case with Jason Todd's Robin suit. Angle this with the case in the foreground and Batman walking directly behind it without so much as giving it a glance. It's a profile shot so it appears in a way that Robin's uniform is superimposed over Batman.

Panel 6
Angle on Batman as he's now in the Batmobile, hitting a button on the console that starts to shut the canopy.

Panel 7
Thin horizontal, smallest on page as it barrels down the cave driveway.

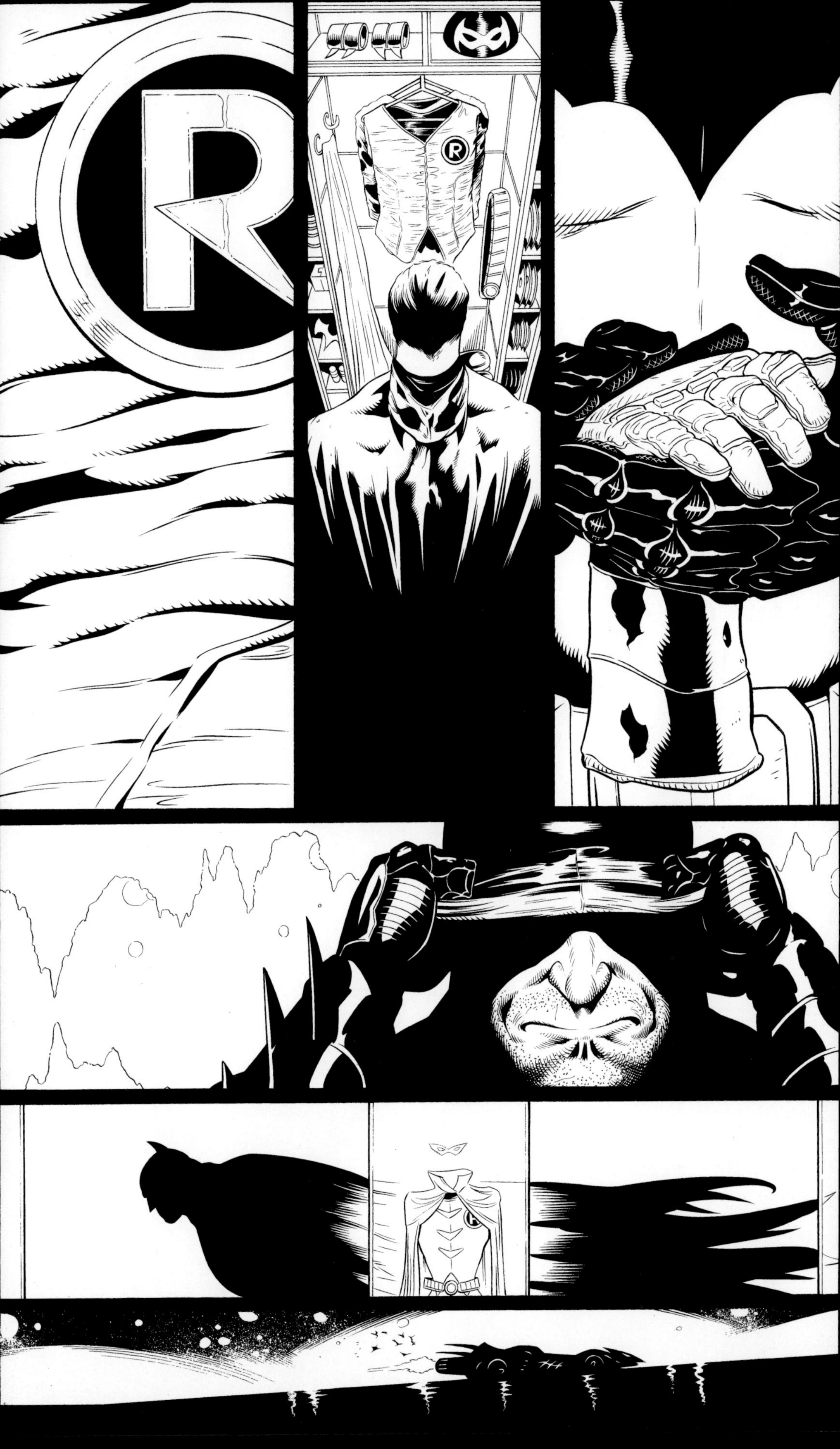

PAGE 8

Splash (the one you already did).

Batman and Robin swinging through the Gotham cityscape.

Father and son on their nightly patrol.

Just a note: this page will need to be recolored so it reads as night and not dawn or dusk.

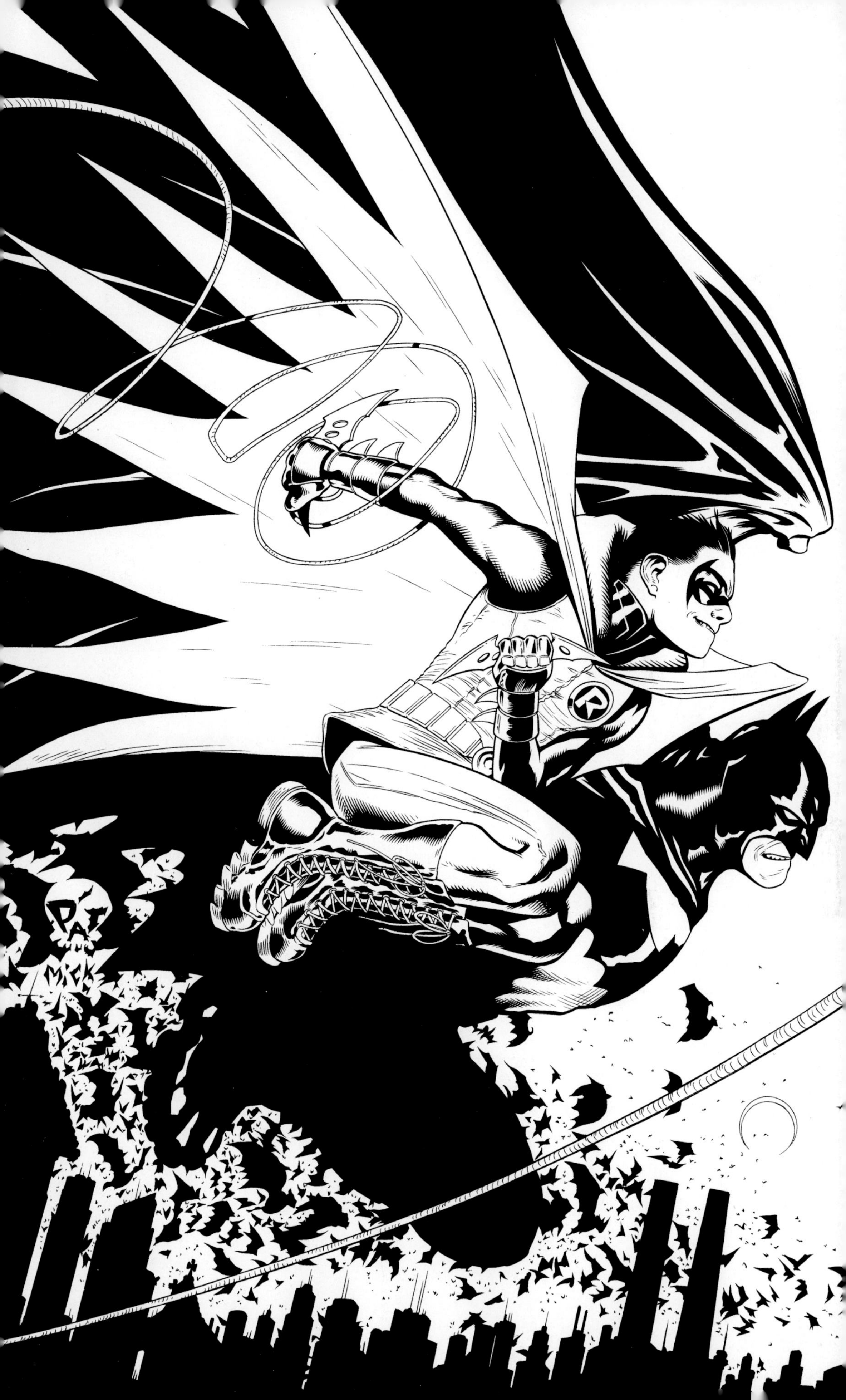

PAGE 9

Panel 1
Angle on Batman as he looks towards us over to Robin swinging beside him in the foreground, Robin's attention focused ahead, not aware his dad is looking at him. This is basically a closer shot of them in the splash except Bats is looking our way and he has a sense of subtle contentment across his face, proud to have his son with him, like all is right with the world.

Panel 2
Angle from Batman's perspective, behind his head, as we suddenly see that Robin is gone. There is no one swinging beside him all we see is an office building, lots of glass so we can see that only Batman is on patrol and also get a sense of the emptiness all around him in the reflection.

Panel 3
Angle closer on Batman's face as we now see that there's stubble on his face; his jaw tight as he realizes that Robin isn't there beside him.

Panel 4
Smallest on page. Close on a street sign that reads: PARK ROW. There are signs in NYC that are designed to have small squares on the sign that reveal some info about the street. This one should say: Gotham Historic District. Park Row. Would be great to have Batman's shadow seen moving across it.

Panel 5
Angle on Batman as he lands like a wraith on something we can't see just yet, his cape still up in the air behind him, the street sign we just saw visible in the background.

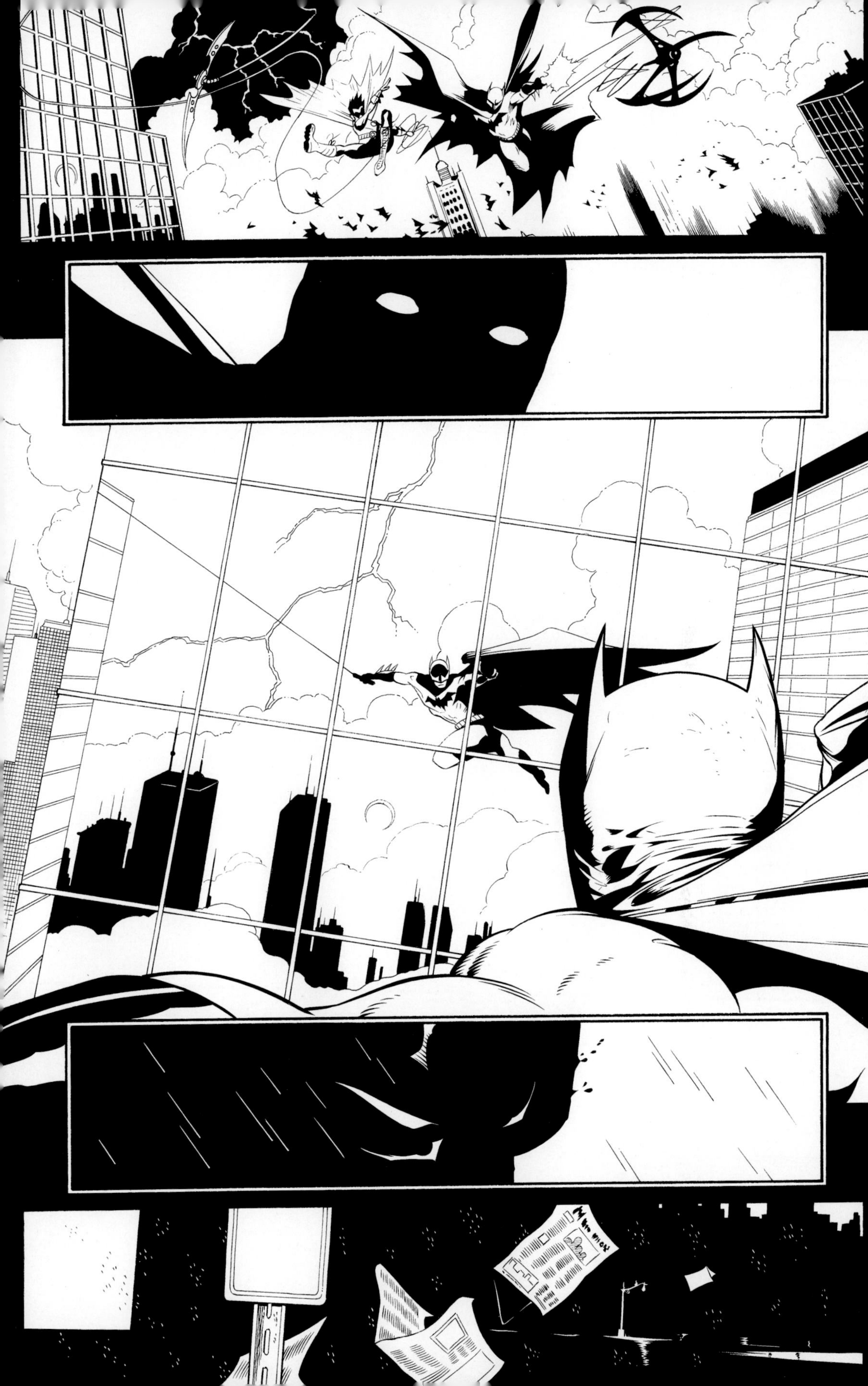

PAGE 10

Panel 1
Vertical panel. Half the page.

Batman crouching on top of the main pole of the old streetlight in Crime Alley that his parents were killed under. Angle this looking up at him so it feels more foreboding. PARK ROW/ CRIME ALLEY is still not a great neighborhood and I'm imagining that's it's taken somewhat of a beating in BATMAN INC. since I believe at the point that I'm writing this, Damian dies there. Now, whether that changes or not doesn't affect our scene except for the ref that will be needed on the current look of it. All that needs to be standing is the old streetlight where Bruce's parents and Damian died.

Think of this streetlight as the lone light in the darkness symbolically and figuratively.

Panel 2
Vertical panel. Half the page.

Reverse the camera angle so instead of looking up at Batman from the ground level, in this shot have the camera looking down at him atop the streetlight so we can see the halo of the light on the ground below.

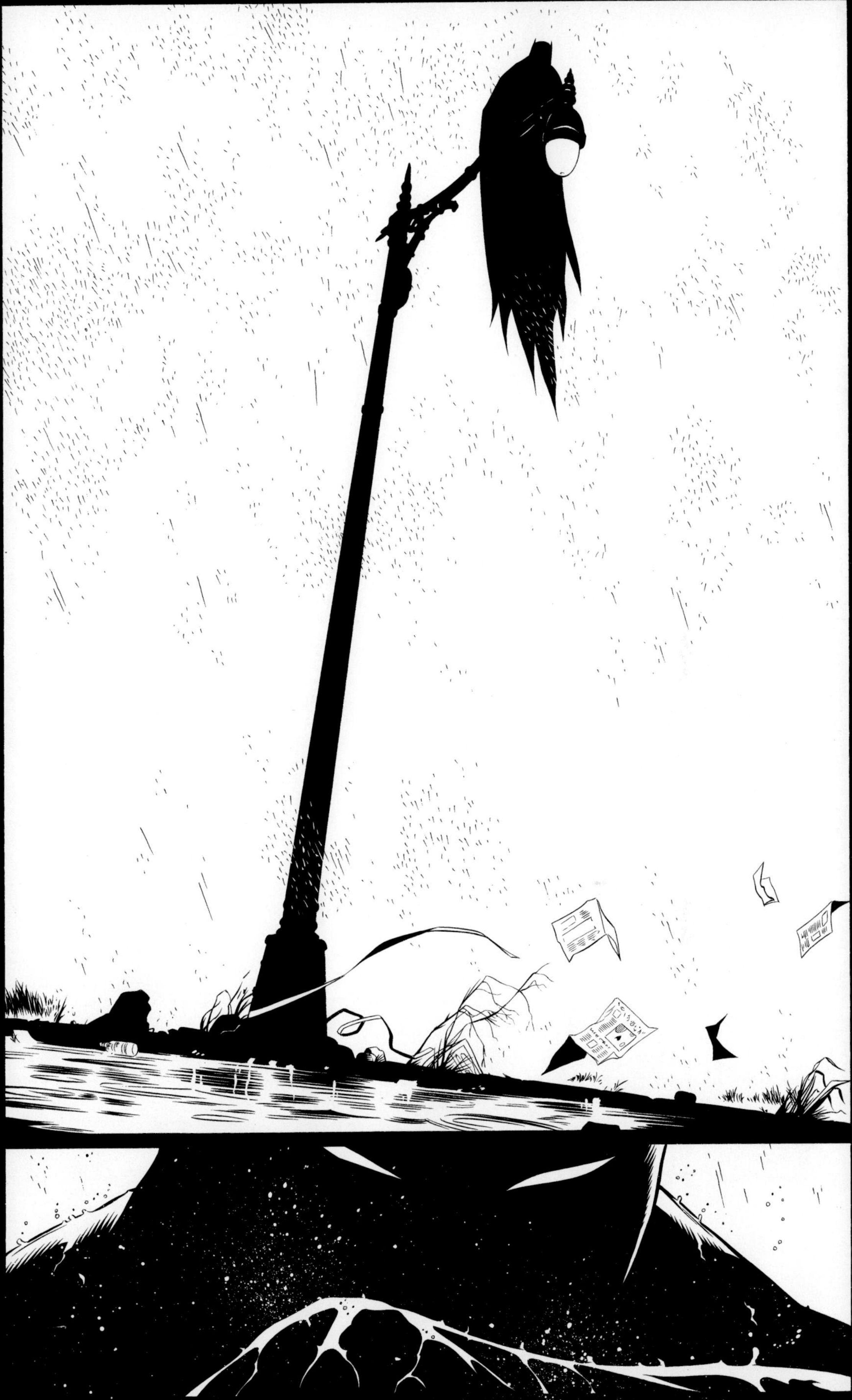

PAGE 11

Panel 1
Angle close on Batman, grim, chin to chest, as he surveys the surroundings. He is all angst, sporting the look of someone wishing there was evil he could smash in the face.

Panel 2
Angle on Batman as he traces his fingers over the ornate ironwork at the top of the light.

Panel 3
Angle close on Batman as he pushes some small button on his utility belt or on his gauntlet. Your call, Pat, as to where you want to draw it.

Panel 4
Angle from just above Batman looking straight down so we see him, the streetlight and the cast-light over the Batmobile as it pulls in directly below, its canopy drawn back as he now leaps towards it.

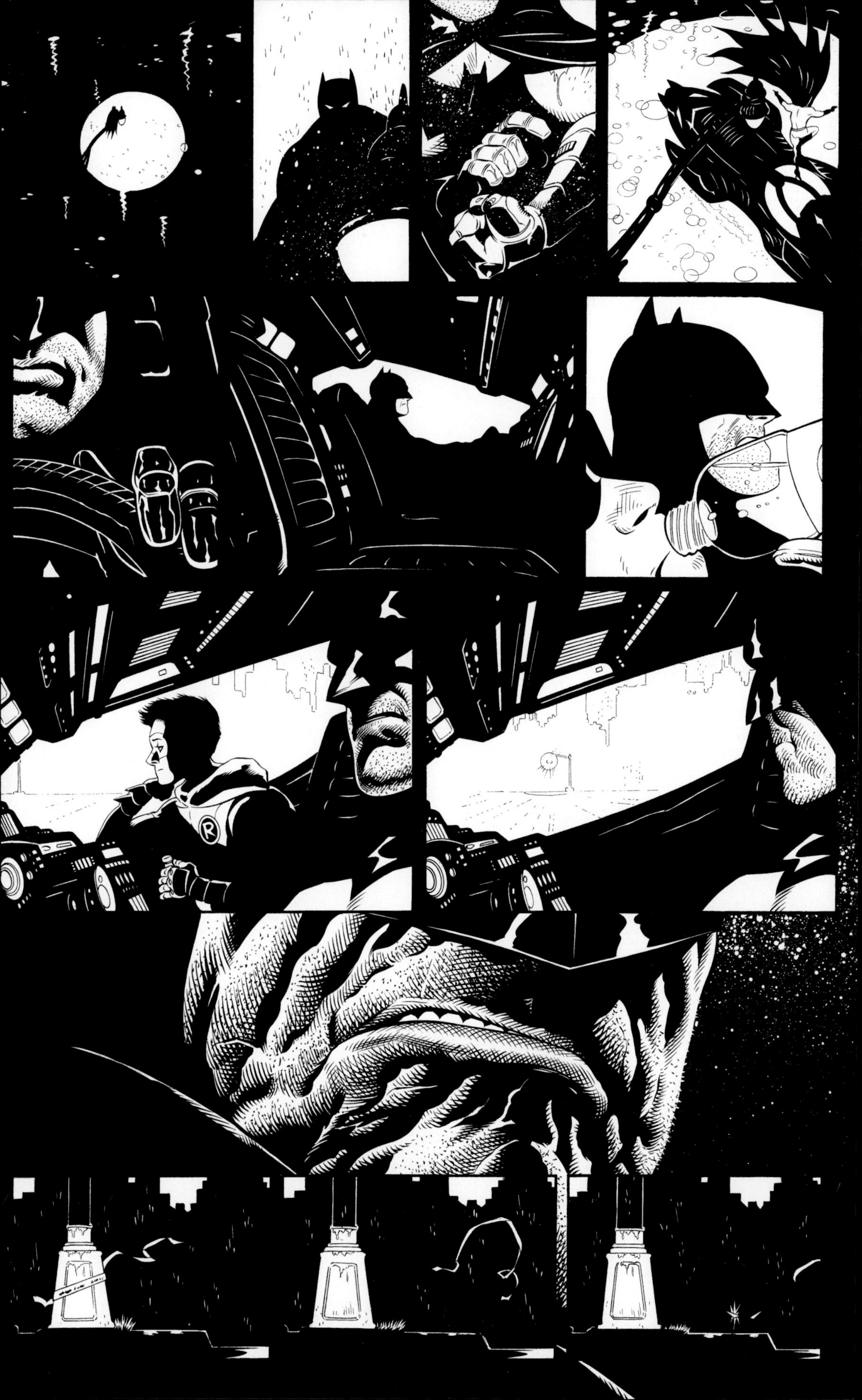

PAGE 12

I'm seeing horizontal panels across for this page, Patrick.

Panel 1
Angle on Batman, gripping the wheel with two hands, as he drives off.

Panel 2
Angle on Batman as he turns to see Robin sitting in the passenger seat, focused on some controls on the console.

Panel 3
Angle from Batman's perspective as Robin is gone again and we can see in the side mirror the streetlight reflected back at us, a lone sentry of light on the street as he drives away.

Panel 4
Angle on Batman as he suddenly turns the wheel hard.

Panel 5
Angle straight on Batman through the windshield of the car as he comes racing towards us like a rocket, both hands gripped tightly on the wheel, determined.

Panel 6
Angle close on Batman's face; he's got that look of a man who doesn't care about anything at the moment.

PAGE 13

Panel 1
Biggest on page as the Batmobile smashes directly into the base of the streetlight, ripping it away like a tree from its roots, the electrical cables that were tied into the main cables underneath the street flapping and sparking as the Batmobile speeds through it.

Panel 2
Angle on the streetlight as it crashes to the pavement just behind the Batmobile.

Panel 3

Angle from behind the Batmobile as it continues speeding down the street towards the darkness, no light now whatsoever left in its wake.

PAGES 14 and 15

Double-page spread.

It's spooky Batman time. You don't want to face Batman on a regular crime-fighting night, right? Well, tonight is a night when his punches, kicks, and batarang throws are harder than ever.

What I'm thinking for this page, Pat, is something along the lines we did back in our Corps days. Instead of Yat/Arisia we instead have a dark figure of Batman holding up his arms and leaping at us in the center of the spread, and in the folds or shadows of his cape are several visceral images of Batman on the edge, all darkness and dread, more like the various bad guys are being attacked by Dracula/Nosferatu and they are scared @$%#&. Batman in these assorted images should be just a figure of darkness, more of a living shadow actually, just the whites of his eyes seen on occasion as he brings the pain to the scum of Gotham.

If ya want you can toss in one or two of our Batfreaks (not Shmush though), but also make sure these bad guys are vicious-looking fellas and in the middle of doing some evil #!&* as Bats takes them out.

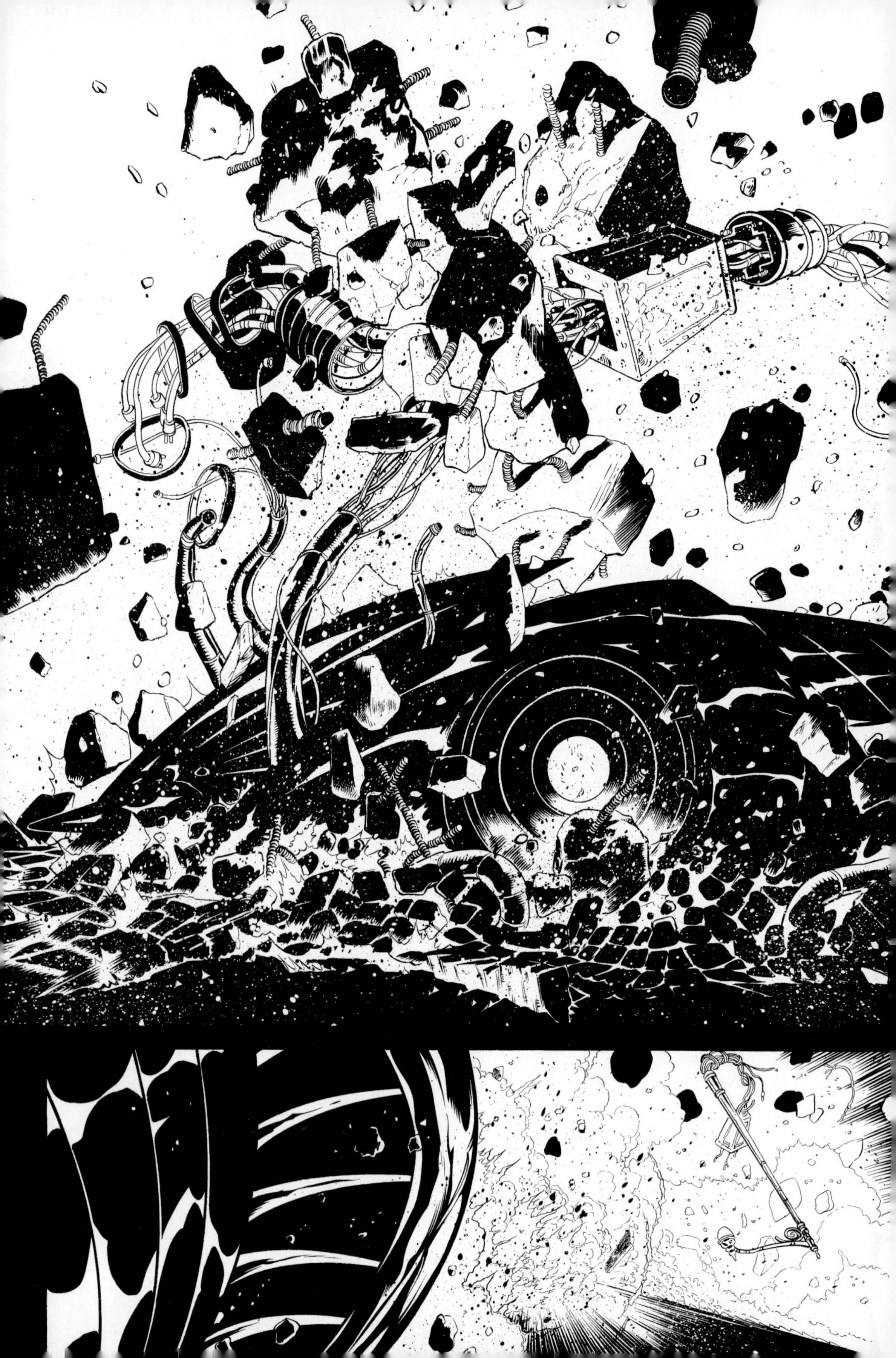

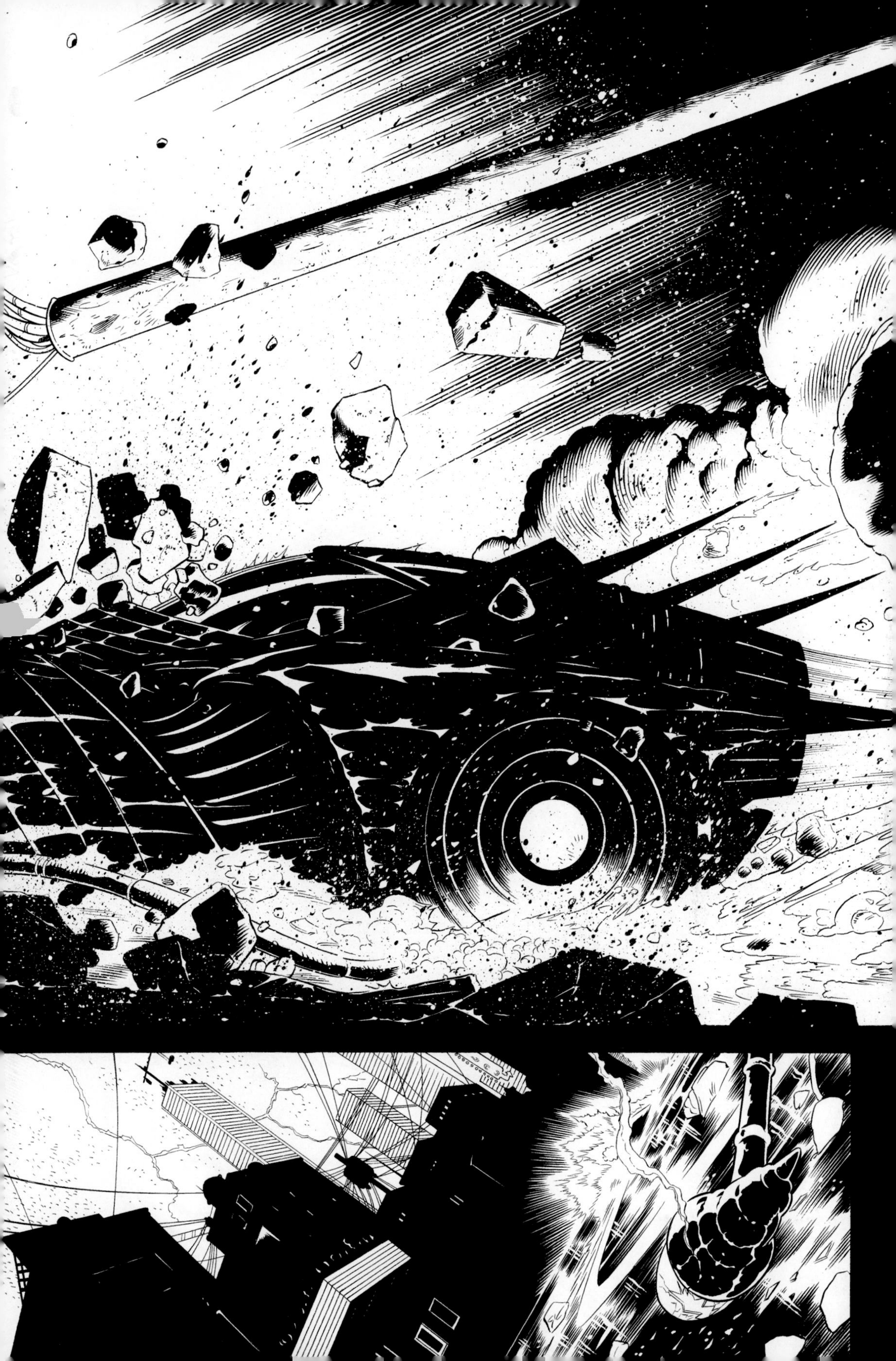

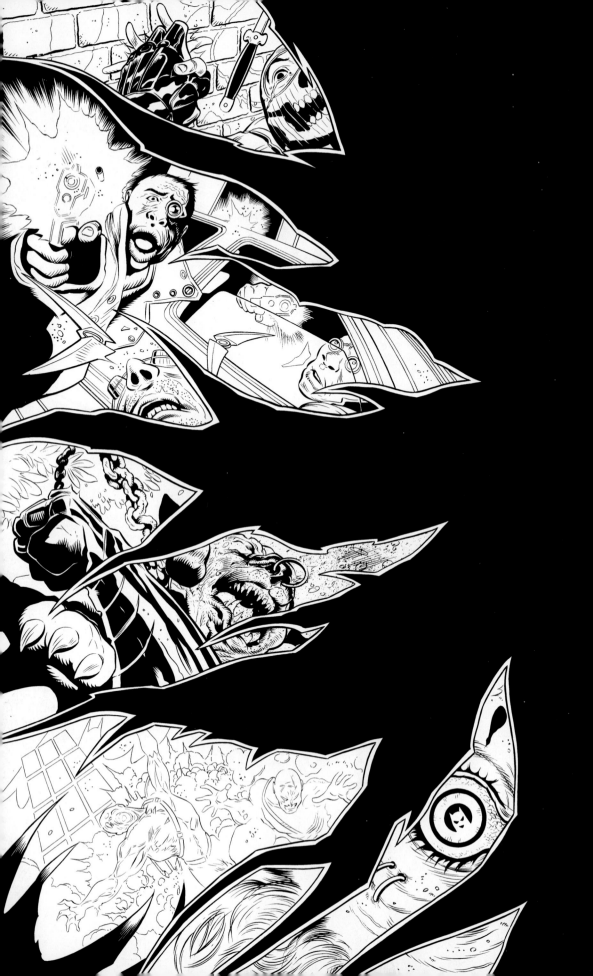

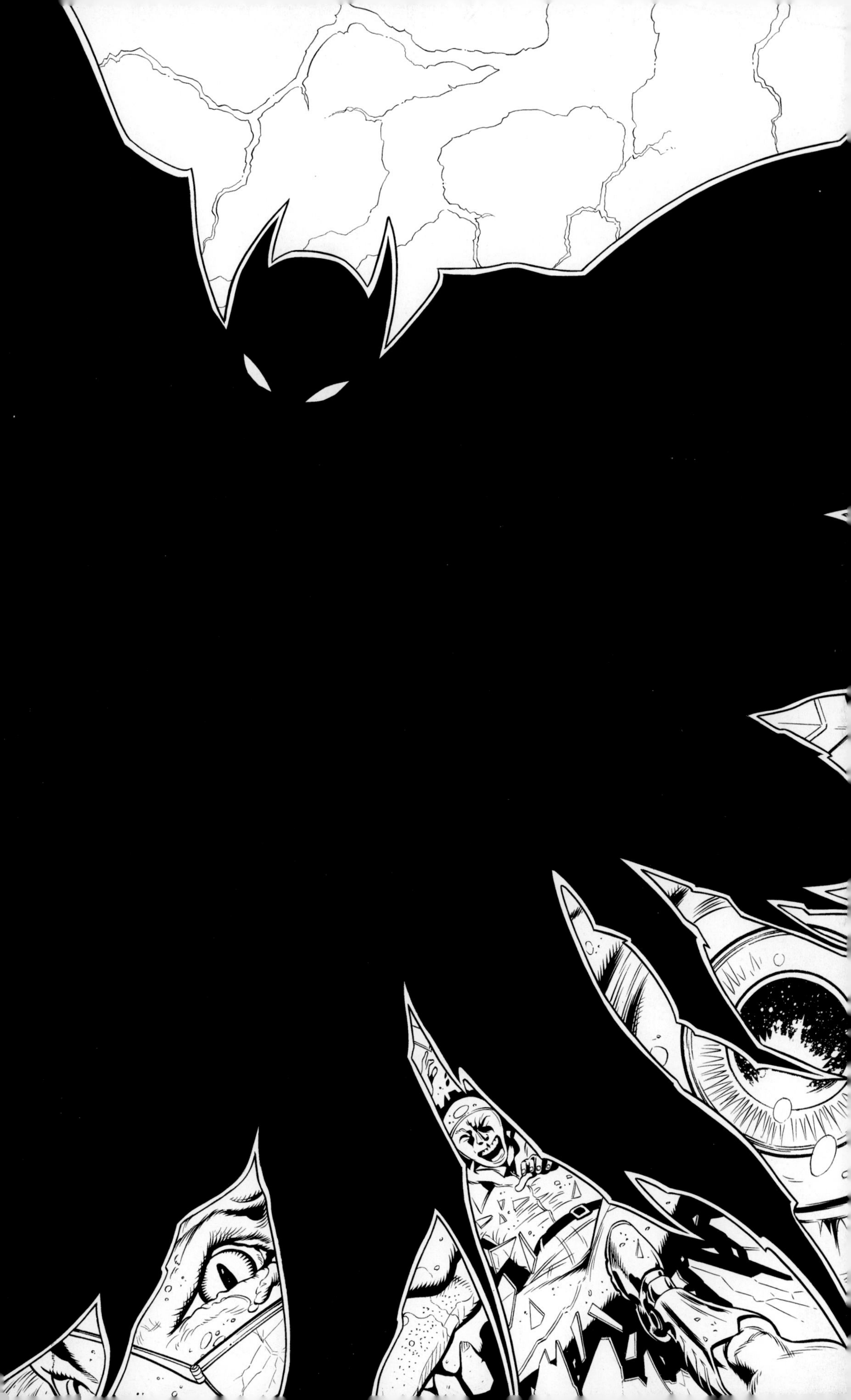

PAGE 16

Panel 1
Angle on GORDON asleep in his bed, no glasses, his cell phone ringing, the only light source.

Panel 2
Same angle on Gordon as he's still lying on his pillow only now he's got the cell pressed to his ear.

Panel 3
Angle from behind Gordon at his window, the curtain string in his hand, the curtain drawn up and the cell still pressed to his ear as we can see the BAT SIGNAL lit in the distance.

Panel 4
Angle close on Gordon's face, his glasses on, his hair slightly windswept as we're now atop police headquarters but we don't know it yet. Gordon's reaction is one of being taken aback by what he's seeing off panel.

Panel 5
Biggest on page. I'm thinking a high angle looking down at the Bat Signal shining bright in the darkness, Gordon is standing at the roof entrance beside BULLOCK and a UNIFORMED OFFICER as their gaze is fixed on the roof surface that is COVERED WITH BAD GUYS THAT BATMAN HAS "ARRESTED". The bad guys should be two or three deep stacked on top of each other, their hands and legs bound, with plastic tabs. Think of them like a deep-sea catch after the nets open up and flood the deck of a fishing boat.

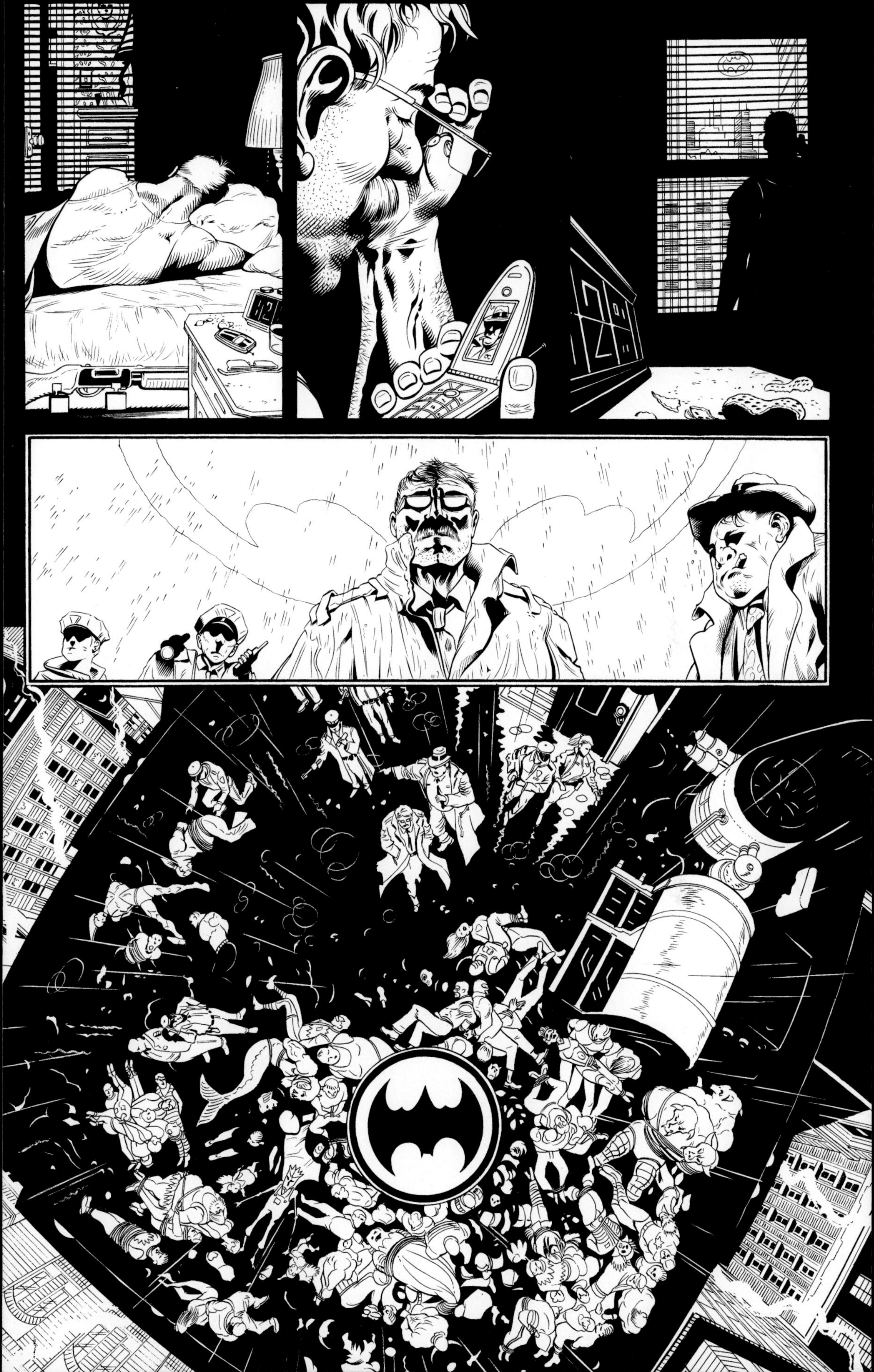

PAGE 17

Panel 1
Thin horizontal. Smallest on page. Angle on the Batmobile as it pulls into the cave, Titus is there waiting expectantly, thinking somehow Damian is going to appear and get out of the car.

Panel 2
Angle on Titus following Batman, in full uniform, spattered with an extreme night of hard work which in his world of crime-fighting is blood, dirt and grim along with scratches and dents walks . He's not drenched in blood, but make sure we can read that it is indeed blood. Bats simply walks without any emotion, not acknowledging Titus.

Panel 3
I'd like to introduce a bit here that I thought would make sense in the details of Bruce's world, and that is we follow Batman as he walks through basically a small decontamination unit that sprays over his uniform, washing away the night of pain he delivered to the scum of Gotham; a baptism of sorts, a ritual that allows him to become Bruce Wayne again. Titus follows on the other side of the unit.

Panel 4
Angle on Batman as he's in the process of pulling off his cowl, other uniform pieces already placed into a specific "used" rack for Alfred to address later. The only thing Bruce should be wearing is an under-armor type of jumpsuit. We want him to be completely without his accoutrements, to show him vulnerable and human (but let's talk, maybe we should have him with his chest plate still on so we see the bat, I'm not sure). Anyway, we can see his row of other uniforms and utility belts, wirepoons, etc., in a hi-tech unit beside Damian's uniform unit. Titus continues to watch him and wait for some attention.

Panel 5
As Bruce starts to turn away from the lockers he slightly trips against Titus who still looks for Bruce to show him some love, affection, anything. You know that kinda moment when you're not paying attention when a dog is around and you stumble a bit. Have Bruce catch himself by grabbing hard at his locker, tilting it a bit, some stuff falling out, but specifically a FOLDED PIECE OF PAPER tucked into a small Bat device.

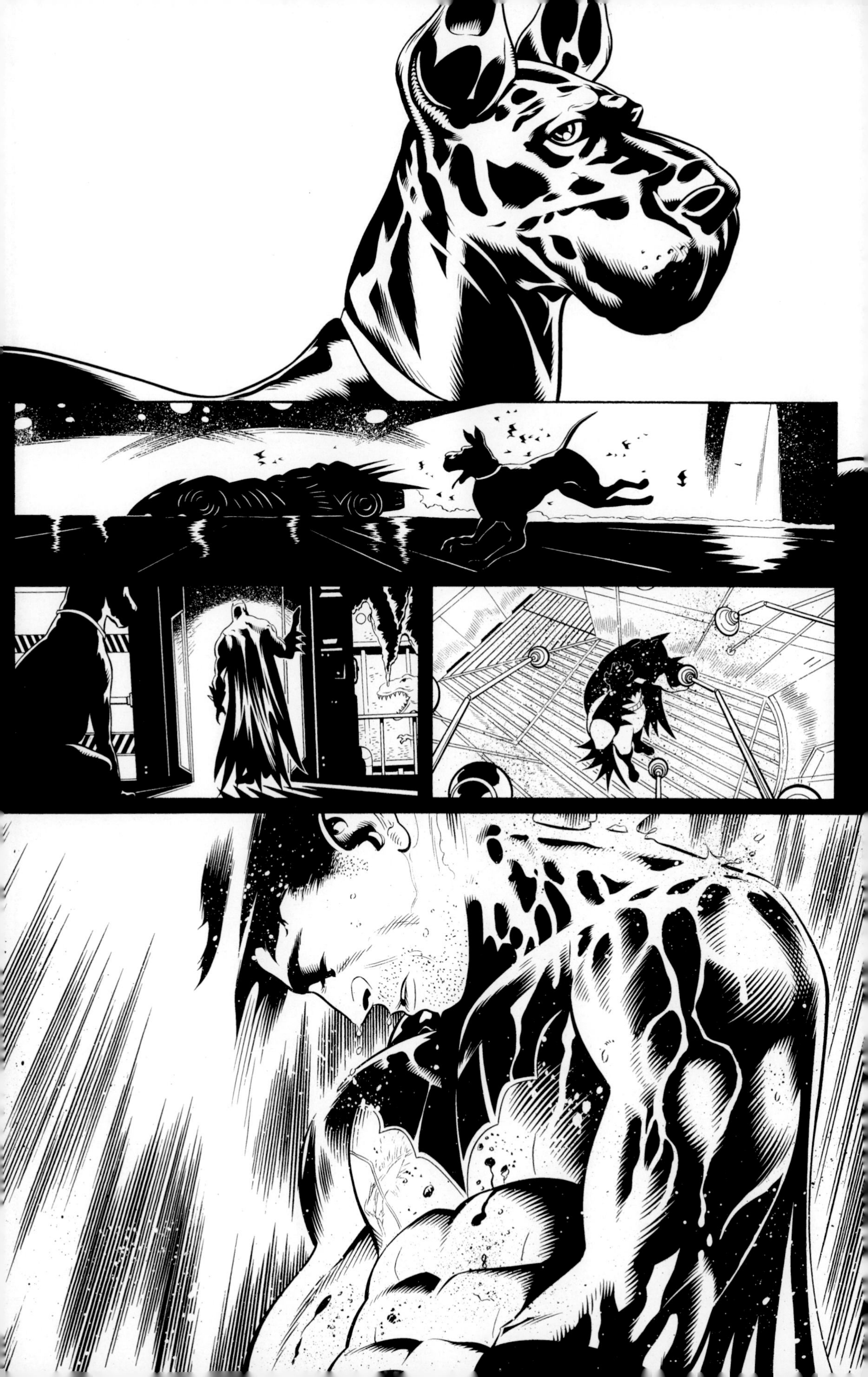

PAGE 18

Panel 1
Angle on Bruce as he still pays Titus no mind, as he picks up the fallen items from his locker.

Panel 2
Angle close on Bruce as he picks up the folded piece of paper.

Panel 3
Angle from behind Bruce as he reads the HANDWRITTEN NOTE.

NOTE: *I won't let you fight Leviathan alone. I need to help. But there's something I have to tell you that I know I'll never be able to tell you face to face, and that is my mother may have given me life, but you taught me how to live, father.*

Love and respect
your son,
Damian

Panel 4
Angle from below looking up at Bruce reading the note, tears stream down his face.

Panel 5
Angle on Bruce as he leans back against the locker, his hands gripping the note tight.

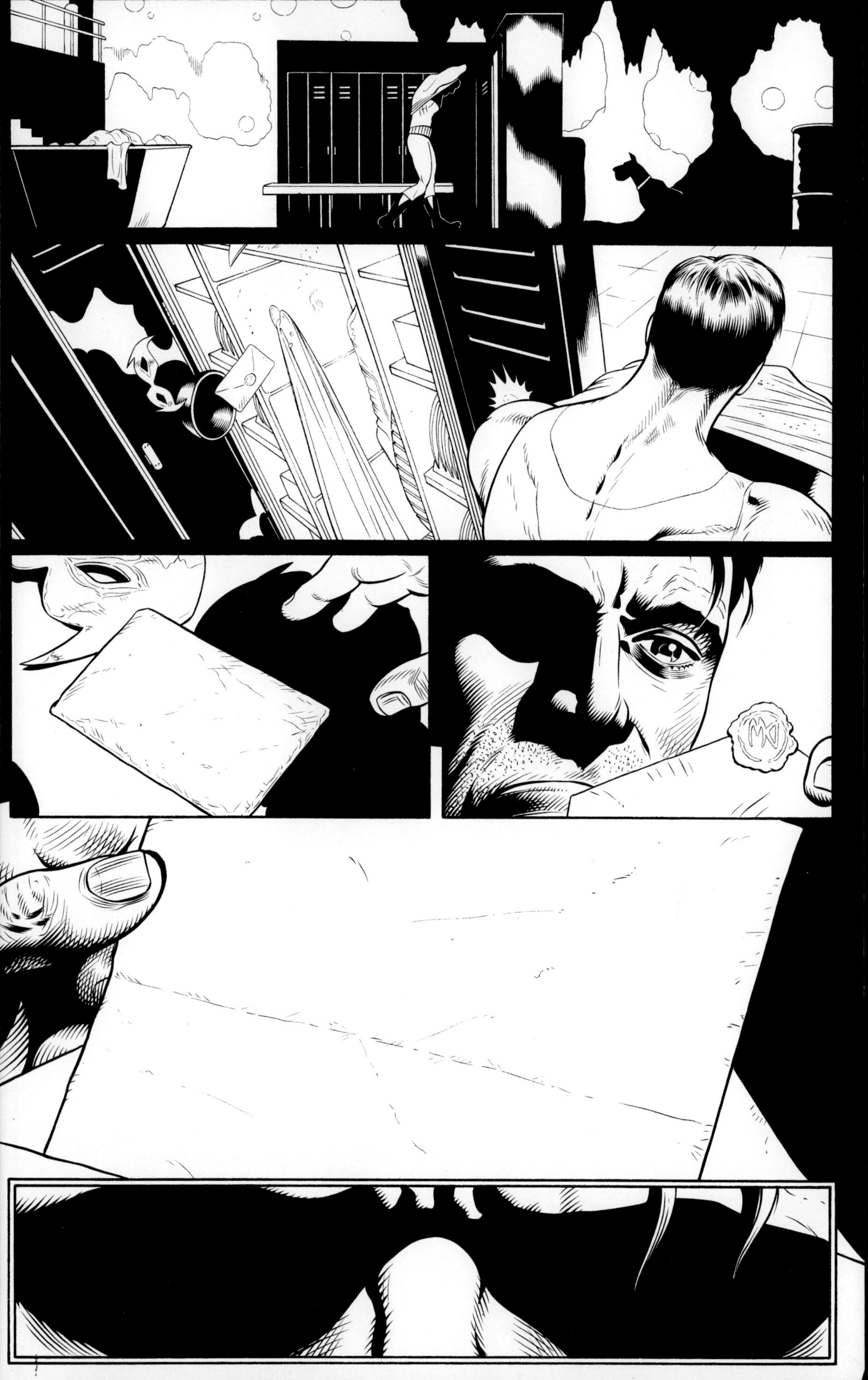

PAGE 19

Panel 1
Angle on Bruce as he lets out a primal scream that only a parent can understand. It's the kind of scream we've never seen before from him -- uncontrolled, a roar of pain and loss.

Panels 2 thru 5
In these panels have Bruce literally smash apart everything in the locker area, lifting and throwing, punching and screaming, his hands getting bloody, pieces of his uniforms and Damian's in midair, scattered all over the place. All the while poor Titus watches.

Remember, Bruce should be in full tilt mode here, no holding back, all his emotions unchecked.

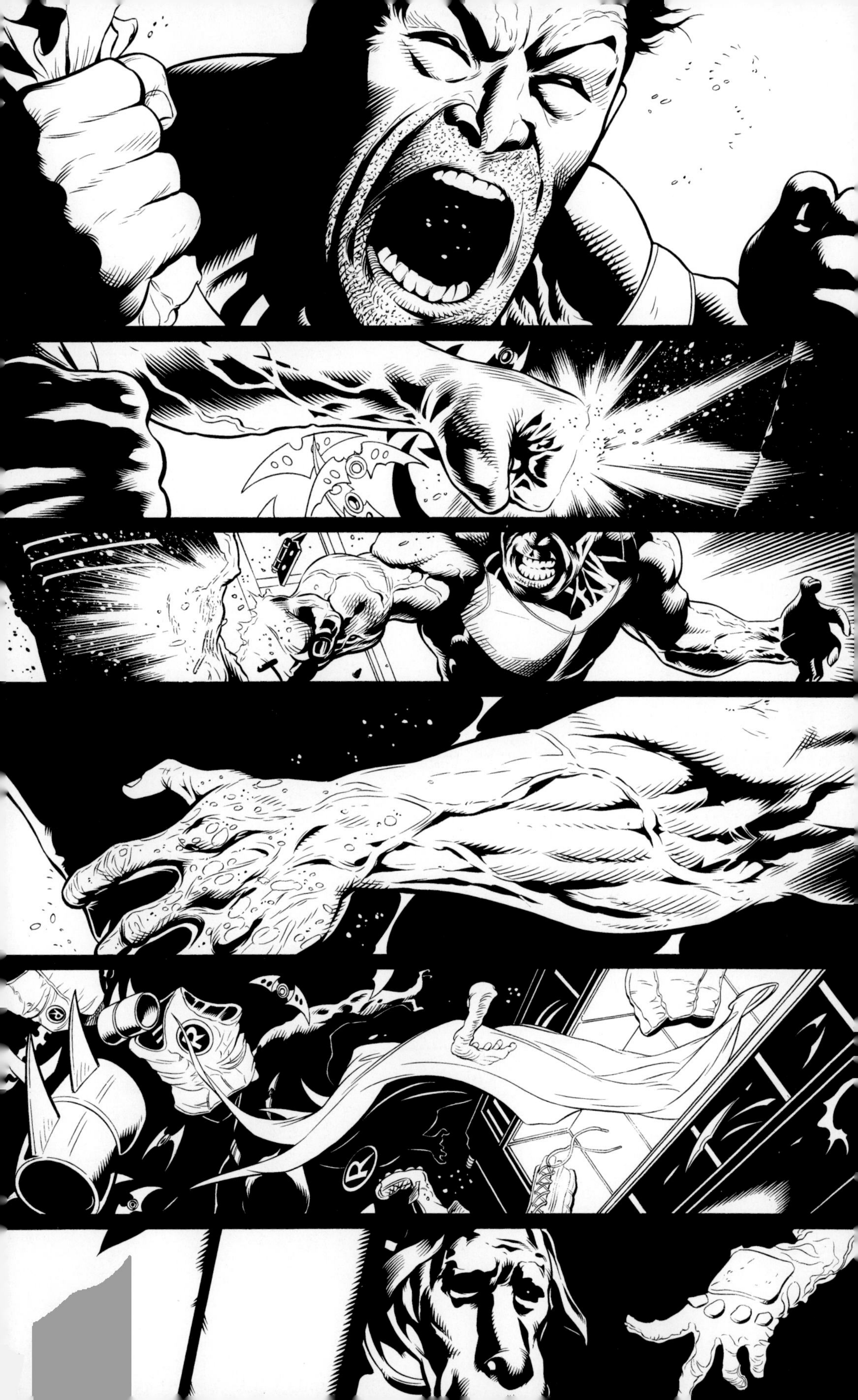

PAGE 20

Splash.

Looking down from above, but not too far up.

Bruce is on his knees, one hand clutching Damian's note, the other hand simply knuckles down, spent, chin to chest, shoulders and body slack, engulfed in the loss of his child.

Titus either stands there or is on his belly looking at Bruce, whatever you think looks best, Pat. A man and dog in pain.

Bat cowls and Robin cowls and uniforms, utility belts, gauntlets, boots, wirepoons, and other assorted stuff, etc, splayed and scattered around, visible.

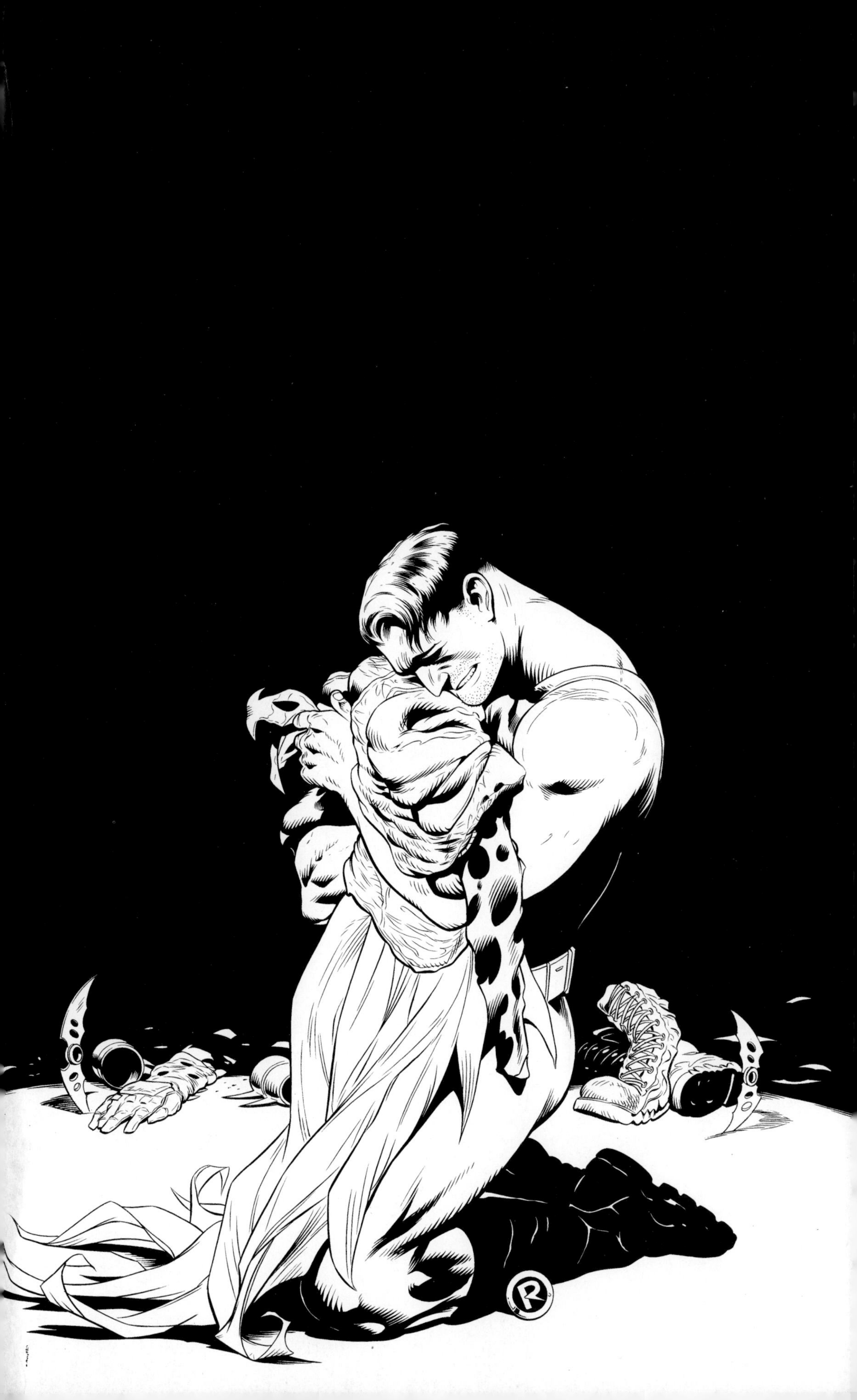

DC COMICS™

"Rock solid."—IGN

"This is the kind of Batman story I like to read: an actual mystery with an emotional hook."
—THE ONION/AV CLUB

START AT THE BEGINNING!

BATMAN & ROBIN
VOLUME 1: BORN TO KILL

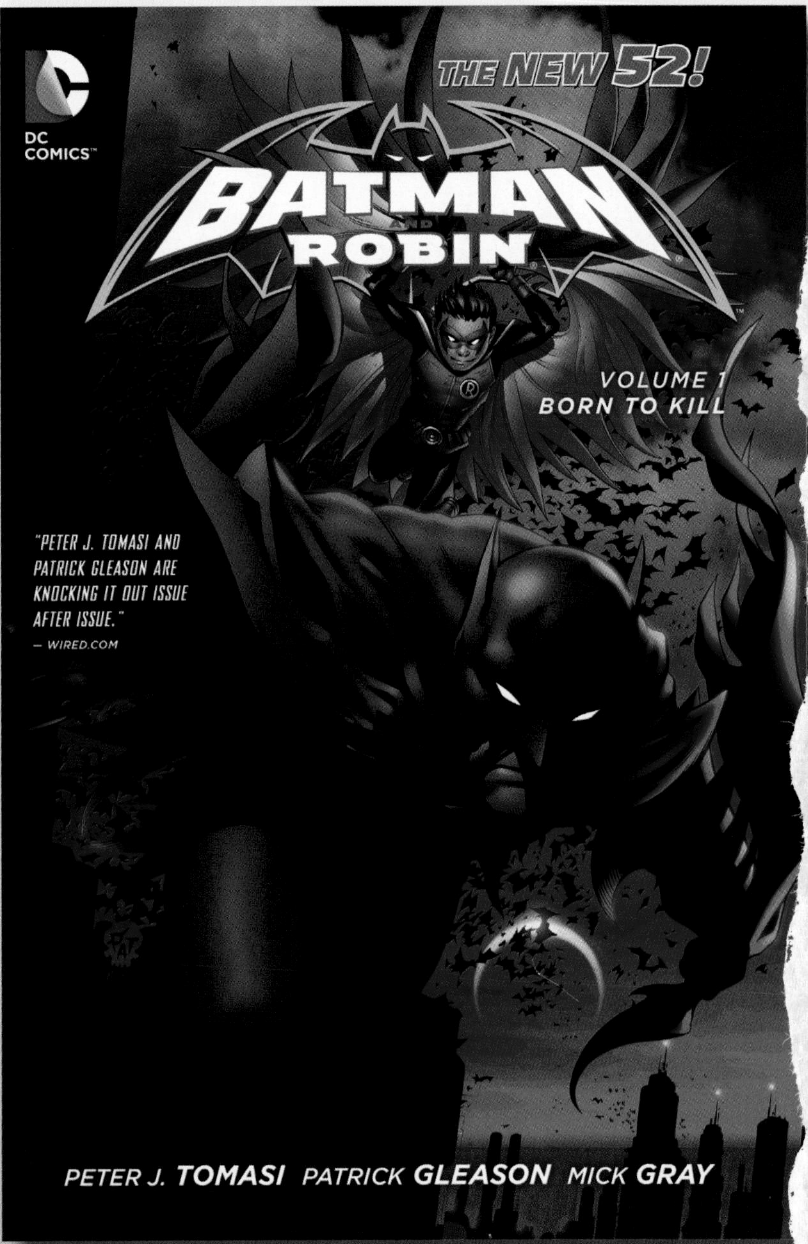

DC COMICS™
THE NEW 52!
BATMAN AND ROBIN
VOLUME 1
BORN TO KILL
"PETER J. TOMASI AND PATRICK GLEASON ARE KNOCKING IT OUT ISSUE AFTER ISSUE."
— WIRED.COM
PETER J. TOMASI PATRICK GLEASON MICK GRAY

BATMAN & ROBIN
VOL. 2: PEARL

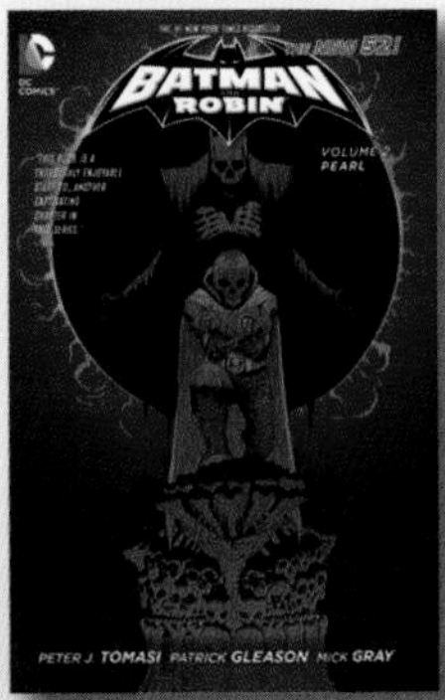

THE NEW 52!
BATMAN ROBIN
PETER J. TOMASI PATRICK GLEASON MICK GRAY

BATMAN & ROBIN
VOL. 3: DEATH OF THE FAMILY

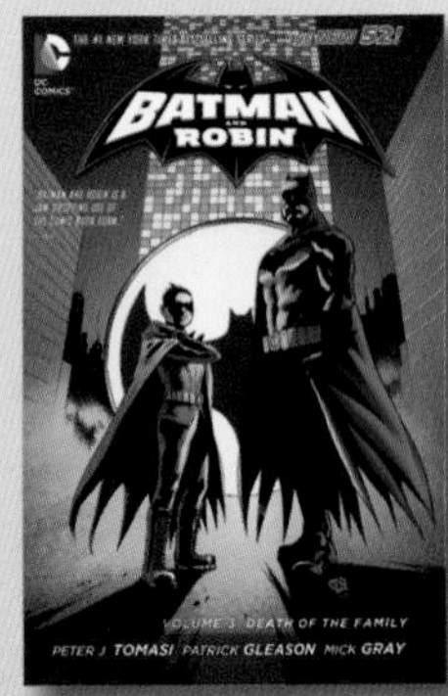

BATMAN ROBIN
VOLUME 3 DEATH OF THE FAMILY
PETER J. TOMASI PATRICK GLEASON MICK GRAY

BATMAN
INCORPORATED
VOL. 1: DEMON STAR

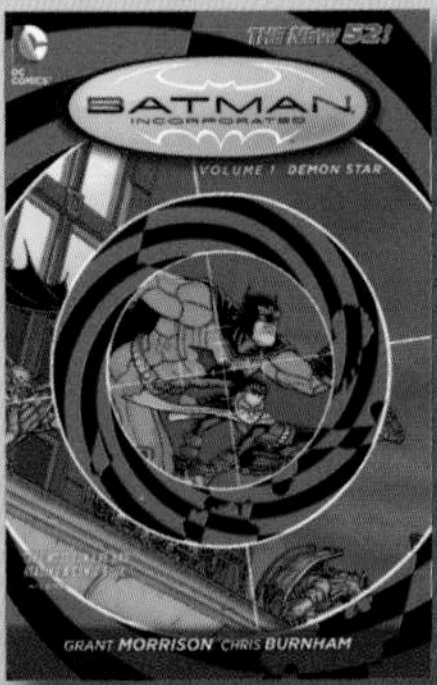

THE NEW 52!
BATMAN INCORPORATED
VOLUME 1 DEMON STAR
GRANT MORRISON CHRIS BURNHAM

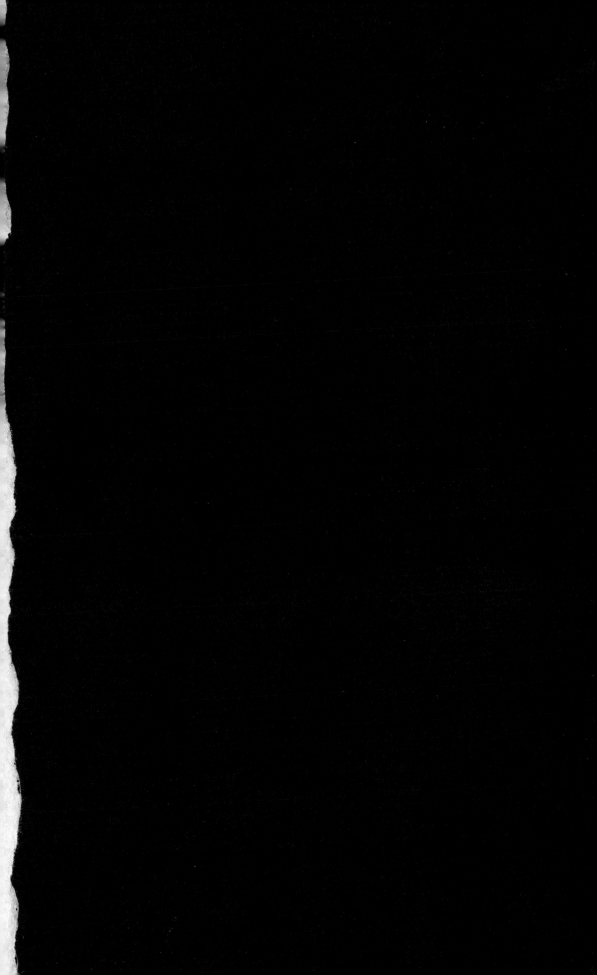